FROM THE OLD SOUTH TO THE NEW

Recent titles in
Contributions in American History

Series Editor: Jon L. Wakelyn

Sobering Up: From Temperance to Prohibition in Antebellum America, 1800-1860
Ian R. Tyrrell

Alcohol, Reform and Society: The Liquor Issue in Social Context
Jack S. Blocker, Jr.

War and Welfare: Social Engineering in America, 1890-1925
John F. McClymer

The Divided Metropolis: Social and Spatial Dimensions of Philadelphia, 1800-1975
William W. Cutler, III, and Howard Gillette, Jr.

The Southern Common People: Studies in Nineteenth-Century Social History
Edward Magdol and Jon L. Wakelyn

Northern Schools, Southern Blacks, and Reconstruction: Freedmen's Education, 1862-1875
Ronald E. Butchart

John Eliot's Indian Dialogues: A Study in Cultural Interaction
Henry W. Bowden and James P. Ronda

The XYZ Affair
William Stinchcombe

American Foreign Relations: A Historiographical Review
Gerald K. Haines and J. Samuel Walker

Communism, Anticommunism, and the CIO
Harvey A. Levenstein

Fellow Workers and Friends: I.W.W. Free-Speech Fights as Told by Participants
Philip S. Foner

FROM THE OLD SOUTH TO THE NEW

Essays on the Transitional South

Edited by Walter J. Fraser, Jr. and Winfred B. Moore, Jr.

Contributions in American History, Number 93

GREENWOOD PRESS
WESTPORT, CONNECTICUT • LONDON, ENGLAND

Library of Congress Cataloging in Publication Data
Main entry under title:

From the Old South to the new.

(Contributions in American history; no. 93 ISSN 0084-9219)
Selected papers from the Citadel Conferences on the
South held in 1978 and 1979.
Bibliography: p.
Includes index.
1. Southern States—History—1775-1865—Addresses,
essays, lectures. 2. Southern States—History—1865—
Addresses, essays, lectures. 3. Southern States—
Social conditions—Addresses, essays, lectures.
4. Southern States—Race relations—Addresses, essays,
lectures. I. Fraser, Walter J. II. Moore, Winfred B.
1949- III. Citadel Conference on the South.
F213.F8   975'.03   80-23315
ISBN 0-313-22534-6 (lib. bdg.)

Library of Congress Catalog Card Number: 80-23315
ISBN: 0-313-22534-6
ISSN: 0084-9219

First published in 1981

Greenwood Press
A division of Congressional Information Service, Inc.
88 Post Road West, Westport, Connecticut 06881

Printed in the United States of America

10 9 8 7 6 5 4 3 2 1

CONTENTS

Map and Tables   ix
Preface   xi

I. THE ORIGINS OF JIM CROW LAWS REVISED   1

  1. A Generation of Defeat   3
     David Herbert Donald

II. SOUTHERN LEADERSHIP: CHANGE OR CONTINUITY?   21

  2. From the Old South to the New: Another Look at the
     Theme of Change and Continuity   23
     Dan T. Carter

  3. The Ambivalence of Change: From Old South to New
     in the Alabama Black Belt, 1850–1870   33
     William L. Barney

  4. "Builders of a New State"—The Town Classes and Early
     Industrialization of South Carolina, 1880-1907   43
     David Carlton

III. THE CITY ELITE: THE CASE OF CHARLESTON,
     SOUTH CAROLINA   63

  5. Wealth and Class in Charleston in 1860   65
     Michael P. Johnson

vi   Contents

  ✓ 6. Social Structure and Urban Form: Charleston, 1860-1880   81
       John P. Radford

  ✓ 7. Leadership and Decline in Postwar Charleston, 1865-1910   93
       Don H. Doyle

  ✓ IV. LAW AND DISORDER: CASE STUDIES IN GEORGIA   107

      8. Law and Disorder in the Old South: The Situation in Georgia,
        1830-1860   109
        David J. Bodenhamer

      9. Whitecapping in Late Nineteenth-Century Georgia   121
        William F. Holmes

  ✓ V. SOUTHERN MYTHOLOGY: FICTION AND FILM   133

  ✓ 10. Southern Writers and the Image of Johnny Reb: Reflections
        of Regional Change Since Appomattox   135
        Stephen Davis

  — 11. Gone With the Wind: Film as Myth and Message   143
        Edward D. C. Campbell, Jr.

  ✓ VI. FOLLOWING THE COLOR LINE: QUESTIONS OF RACE
       RELATIONS   153

      12. Labor Dependency among Freedmen, 1865-1880   155
        Ronald L. F. Davis

      13. Urban Racial Violence in the South during World War II:
        A Comparative Overview   167
        James A. Burran

  ✓ VII. CASH'S BOOK: *THE MIND OF THE SOUTH* REVISITED   179

  ✓ 14. Race and Mastery: The Debate of 1903   181
        Mark K. Bauman

  ✓ 15. W. J. Cash and Southern Culture   195
        Bertram Wyatt-Brown

VIII. MIND OR MINDLESSNESS, PERSISTENCE OR PARADOX?:
CURRENTS OF SOUTHERN THOUGHT   215

16. Slavery and Confederate Nationalism   219
    Steven A. Channing

17. Hierarchy and Democracy: The Paradox of the Southern
    Experience   227
    Lawrence Goodwyn

18. Dorothy Tilly and the Fellowship of the Concerned   241
    Arnold Shankman

19. James McBride Dabbs: Spokesman for Racial Liberalism 253
    Robert M. Randolph

    Suggestions for Further Reading   265

    Index   281

    Notes on the Contributors   285

MAP AND TABLES

MAP

South Carolina Spindleage, 1907   46

TABLES

3.1   Socioeconomic Patterns in Dallas County, 1850-1860   34

3.2   Socioeconomic Patterns in Dallas County, 1860-1870   37

4.1   Seats on Original Boards of Directors, South Carolina
      Up-Country, 1880-1907: Residences   49

4.2   Mill Directors Residing in the South Carolina Up-Country,
      1880-1907, by Occupation   49

4.3   Mill Presidents Residing in the South Carolina Up-Country,
      1880-1907, by Occupation   53

5.1   Wealth Distribution in Charleston   67

5.2   Distribution of Nonslave Wealth in Charleston   68

5.3   Wealth Distribution in Three Antebellum Southern Cities
      and Charleston   69

5.4   Wealth Distribution in Ten Antebellum Northern Cities and
      Charleston   70

5.5   Wealth Distribution by Race   72

5.6   Wealth Distribution within Occupational Groups   73

PREFACE

This book is a collection of essays examining the South in transition from approximately 1850 to the present. The essays were selected from among the more than one hundred papers presented at The Citadel Conferences on the South in 1978 and 1979. A major question explored by these essays is whether the shift from the Old South to the New was characterized more by change or by continuity. The articles address this question through a variety of topics, including the reasons behind Jim Crow laws, the composition of Southern leadership, the causes of crime and violence, the changing pattern of race relations, the significance of mythology, and the currents of Southern thought. Whether attacking or defending existing interpretations, each article offers either fresh insights or new information on Southern history.

One of the most provocative essays is David Donald's reinterpretation of the Jim Crow laws, entitled "A Generation of Defeat." Using social science methodology, Donald suggests that Jim Crow laws were adopted in the 1890s primarily because old Confederate soldiers experienced a generational crisis. This crisis compelled them, as a final legacy, to codify their racial mores so that these mores would not be abandoned by succeeding generations of Southerners. Donald's thesis constitutes the first major challenge to earlier interpretations of Jim Crow by C. Vann Woodward and Joel Williamson.

The next six articles examine change and continuity in Southern leadership. Dan Carter's historiographical essay surveys the most recent literature on this subject. David Carlton's case study of the South Carolina piedmont supports C. Vann Woodward's theory that a new class of men assumed leadership after the Civil War. Challenging this view, however, are articles by William Barney, Michael Johnson, John Radford, and Don Doyle, whose studies of Alabama and Charleston, South Carolina, argue that the old planter class maintained its hegemony well into the New South.

The next four articles continue the change or continuity debate by focusing on aspects of Southern social history. In essays on two previously unexplored aspects of Southern crime and violence, David Bodenhamer and William Holmes offer different answers to the question of whether or not the causes of Southern criminal conduct were unique to the region. Articles by Stephen Davis on literary images of "Johnny Reb" and Edward Campbell on the public response to the movie version of *Gone With the Wind* demonstrate how mythology played an important role in shaping attitudes and easing the transition from one era to another.

Ronald Davis' article on black sharecroppers and James Burran's article on racial violence during World War II present new interpretations on two aspects of Southern race relations. Davis demonstrates that blacks were able to preserve their dignity and to maintain a higher degree of autonomy under the sharecropping system than has previously been recognized. By analyzing the urban race riots of the 1940s, Burran refutes the old idea that Southern black militancy of the Second Reconstruction originated during World War II.

The final six articles analyze currents of Southern thought. Three document cases of dissent from the dominant racial attitudes of the region. Mark Bauman shows that discussion of racial issues could be surprisingly open as long as Northerners did not participate. Arnold Shankman's article on Dorothy Tilly and Robert Randolph's essay on James McBride Dabbs are the first scholarly treatments of their subjects and document both the effectiveness and the limitations of white Southern racial reformers.

The remaining three articles on Southern thought explore this topic from broader perspectives. An essay of major importance is Bertram Wyatt-Brown's vigorous defense of W. J. Cash's classic, *The Mind of the South*. This article provides by far the best analysis yet written of Cash's impact on Southern historiography. Steven Channing's article addresses one of the many questions raised by Cash's book: Was Confederate nationalism prior to 1861 a myth or a reality? After surveying the manner in which others have responded to this question, Channing suggests a new answer. Finally, Lawrence Goodwyn's article presents a reflective analysis on Southern reformers and their legacies of paradox. He concludes, disturbingly, that the work of Southern reformers has usually resulted only in the strengthening of the very social, economic, and political hierarchies that they attacked.

Throughout the years, there have been many volumes of essays to appear on Southern history. This is one of them. As such, it is the offspring of those regional symposia that George Tindall has described as "one of the flourishing minor industries of the region." We believe, however, that periodic volumes of essays are a vital part of the constant reevaluation of Southern history. We believe also that the articles included in this volume are of high quality and shed new light on their respective topics. Therefore, it is our hope that this volume will promote the continuing dialogue, reexamination, and reevaluation of Southern history.

We are indebted to the president of The Citadel, Lieutenant General George M. Seignious II, who encouraged the undertaking of such projects in the humanities, and to The Citadel Development Foundation, whose generous financial support helped bring this project to fruition. We appreciate also the assistance and support of the past chairman of The Citadel History Department, Charles L. Anger, and the present chairman, John S. Coussons, and our colleagues on the history faculty. And we wish to thank Mrs. Annabella E. Dizon for patiently and efficiently handling tedious secretarial chores without complaint. Those individuals who participated in the conferences and offered suggestions on the papers to be included have contributed also to whatever merit this volume may have. Among these historians are: Howard N. Rabinowitz of the University of New Mexico; Daniel W. Hollis of the University of South Carolina; Walter B. Weare of the University of Wisconsin at Milwaukee; Melton A. McLaurin of the University of North Carolina at Wilmington; Robert J. Brugger of Harvard University; Patrick G. Gerster of Lakewood Community College; James M. Russell of the University of Tennessee at Chattanooga; Ernest M. Lander of Clemson University; Jack J. Cardoso of the State University of New York at Buffalo; James T. Moore of Virginia Commonwealth University; Carl G. Ryant of the University of Louisville; Jon L. Wakelyn of the Catholic University of America; and Jane and William Pease of the University of Maine at Orono.

Walter J. Fraser, Jr.
Winfred B. Moore, Jr.
Department of History
The Citadel

THE ORIGINS OF JIM CROW LAWS REVISED

This volume begins with an article that offers a provocative, new interpretation of one of the most important issues in Southern history—the origins of Jim Crow. In "A Generation of Defeat," Professor David Herbert Donald surveys existing interpretations that seek to explain the rising racism, disfranchisement, and segregation that swept the South during the 1890s. He believes that all of these interpretations, from Populism to Social Darwinism, are inadequate and fail to explain convincingly the origins of Jim Crow. He suggests that this phenomenon may be understood better by the application of "generational theory."

Donald argues that the battlefield experiences of the Civil War created a "generational consciousness" among the young soldiers of the Confederacy, coarsening them and shaping their values. Reinforcing the war experiences were the twin traumas of defeat and "betrayal" by freedmen, who refused to "stay in their places." In the soldiers' minds, this betrayal caused paternalistic attitudes toward blacks to give way to "absolute hatred." For a generation whose "psychological mainspring snapped at the end of the war," adjustments to these postwar realities were difficult. Reaching "middle adulthood" in the 1890s, the war generation feared that their successors might forget their achievements and abandon the values that had sustained them. To prevent this, and to perpetuate their values, the old soldiers founded Confederate veterans' organizations, built monuments, and even resorted to terrorism. The ultimate step in preserving their legacy for future generations, Donald concludes, was the passage of segregation and disfranchisement laws that "should be viewed as the final acts, the last bequests" of the "generation of defeat."

1

A GENERATION OF DEFEAT
David Herbert Donald

One of the most puzzling problems in Southern history is the sharp deterioration in race relations that occurred during the final decade of the nineteenth century. The 1890's, as Rayford W. Logan has written, marked the nadir in black-white relations throughout the United States.[1] Nowhere was racism more virulent than in the South during this era. The occurrence of 2,500 lynchings—mostly of blacks, and mostly in the South—during the last sixteen years of the century tells the whole story in one way. As C. Vann Woodward has shown, this period also saw enactment of Jim Crow laws, beginning with the requirement that railroad passenger cars be racially segregated and finally extending to provision for Jim Crow Bibles in Georgia courts and Jim Crow elevators in Atlanta offices. Even if one accepts the views of Mr. Woodward's critics, who argue that de facto segregation had long prevailed in the South, there can be no disputing his conclusion that it was in the 1890's that racial discrimination began to be codified into law.[2]

Accompanying the institutionalization of segregation was the almost total disfranchisement of blacks throughout the Southern states. Mississippi led the way in 1890 with a requirement that voters be able to read and interpret the Constitution to the satisfaction of registration officials, who were white. Louisiana improved upon the Mississippi example by requiring a literacy test of all voters except the sons and grandsons of persons who had voted in state elections before 1867. Since no Louisiana Negroes had voted before that date, the provision permitted white illiterates to vote but required the literacy test of all black voters. South Carolina held its disfranchising convention in 1895; North Carolina amended its constitution to limit suffrage in 1900; Alabama and Virginia acted in 1901-1902, and Georgia adopted a restrictive constitutional amendment in 1908. By the beginning of the twentieth century, in other words, virtually all blacks in the South were denied the vote.[3]

The explanations historians have given for this rise of Southern racism beginning in the 1890's have not been completely convincing. Early writers on the subject, themselves products of a racially segregated society, saw discrimination and disfranchisement as the natural order of things and consequently felt no need to explain why these developments occurred when they did. More recent historians, brought up to hate and oppose racial discrimination, have more often written to condemn, rather than to explain, the developments of the 1890's. It is notable that, with the exception of William J. Cooper's fine book on *The Conservative Regime* in South Carolina,[4] we still do not have studies that attempt to understand the mind of Southern whites during this era.

Of the several theories adduced to account for the rise of segregation, the disfranchisement of blacks, and the increase in racial violence in the South during the 1890's, the least persuasive attributes these developments to the influence of Social Darwinism, with its stress on the alleged racial superiority of whites as a result of natural selection and the survival of the fittest. Few Southern whites doubted the innate superiority of their race; but fewer justified their views in Darwinian terms. Neither biological nor Social Darwinism was in vogue below the Mason-Dixon line. The typical Southern view was that of a Kentucky lawyer who wrote: "When I can snatch the time from my professional duties, I try to keep up with the superficial scientific discoveries and theories of the day but I confess that Darwin and his grandfather the monkey puzzle me."[5] In a region dominated by Baptists and Methodists, constantly agitated by fundamentalist revivals, only the audacious or the suicidal advocated natural selection. Southerners found it more convincing to justify the inferior place they assigned the Negro by citing the curse on the seed of Ham than by quoting Darwin or Thomas Huxley.

Another insufficient explanation connects Southern racial violence, segregation, and disfranchisement to fears, or anticipations, of what Northerners might think and of what Northern congressmen in Washington might do. Some historians argue that during the 1870's and 1880's Southern whites hesitated formally to segregate and disfranchise blacks lest they encourage Rebublican wavers of the bloody shirt and provoke renewed intervention in Southern affairs from a national government still controlled by Northern Republicans. But the introduction of Henry Cabot Lodge's bill for federal supervision of elections[6] alerted Southern whites to the danger that, with backing from a national Republican administration, blacks might resume the active political role they had played during Reconstruction. Consequently they moved as expeditiously as possible to institute constitutional provisions eliminating black voting.

But this is an explanation that explains too much—or too little. If Southern whites were fearful of Northern reaction to disfranchisement of blacks during the 1880's—even when Cleveland from their own party was in the White House—the near-passage of the Lodge bill should have made them even more cautious. Alternatively, they must have known that their success in defeating the Lodge bill meant that unquestionably they could kill any other foreseeable federal "interference" in Southern elections, so that the constitutional amendments of the 1890's were unnecessary. Of course Southern congressmen in Washington were constantly on the alert to possible moves that would rejuvenate the Republican party in the South, but ever since 1876 most recognized the decreasing Northern commitment to Negro suffrage.

Nor is it plausible to argue that the racial violence of the 1890's, accompanied by segregation and disfranchisement, resulted from restiveness or self-assertiveness on the part of Southern blacks. It was in the 1860's that blacks were politically active and an aggressive black leadership began to emerge in Southern Republican parties; but the restoration of "home rule" effectively terminated this development. It was in the 1870's when, partly as a result of the prolonged depression, partly as a consequence of white oppression, an exodus of blacks from the South, notably to Kansas, began;[7] but by the 1890's this had dwindled to a trickle. By the mid-1880's Southern blacks, in defeat and despair, seemed to have acquiesced in the subordinate role which whites had assigned them. Booker T. Washington's "Atlanta Compromise" speech of 1895 marked the public acceptance of that second-class citizenship by the recognized spokesman of the black population.

The most widely accepted explanation of the movement to disfranchise blacks in the 1890's is that first advanced by Paul Lewinson in his once influential, though now nearly forgotten, book, *Race, Class, and Party*.[8] Anticipating the findings of J. Morgan Kousser in *The Shaping of Southern Politics*, Lewinson argued that the restoration of "home rule" did not mean the elimination of black voting. A surprising proportion of Southern blacks continued to vote—or were voted by their landlords—and so long as there were no sharp divisions among Southern whites, there were no loud protests against the practice. But, as a black editor in Little Rock observed: "The greatest danger that threatens democratic supremacy in the South is that the 'out faction' always gravitates toward the Negro and secures his aid to route [sic] the 'ins.' "[9] That tendency was exhibited in the candidacy of several Independents during the 1880's, and by the 1890's it became a regular practice. Bourbon planters of the black belt marched their field hands to the polls to support the regular Democratic nominees for office, while Populists, capitalizing on the loose linkage between the Southern Farmers' Alliance and the Colored Alliance, sought black support for their candidates. With disorganization and demoralization rampant, white leaders felt obliged to eliminate the Negro from politics once and for all. "Sometimes," Lewinson writes, "the demand came from the white counties, seeking protection against the use of the Negro by Black Belt politicians, sometimes, where 'the more responsible of the democrats' took alarm, from the Bourbon party."[10]

Though plausible, Lewinson's explanation, which has been followed by Professor Woodward and most other historians of the postwar South, presents difficulties. Nowhere is there a record of a "summit conference" among white leaders of opposing factions, which agreed to a kind of "SALT" restriction on the deployment of that most dangerous explosive, the black vote. Such an agreement would be unique in all the history of the suffrage in America, since from the earliest days of the Republic rival factions and parties have sought to win new voters through expanding, not restricting, the franchise.[11] Moreover, the timing of any such disfranchising agreement is wrong; most of the Southern states moved to eliminate Negro voters after the Populist party had peaked, after Populist leaders had trailed back into the Democratic party, and after the threat of white schism had disappeared.

A further difficulty with Lewinson's scenario is that, in addition to being improbable, it was unnecessary. During the 1880's Southern whites had already devised such ingenious and effective methods of controlling or negating the black vote that Henry W. Grady could write in 1890: "The Negro as a political force has dropped out of serious consideration."[12] The poll tax, as Professor Kousser has shown, was one very effective way of disfranchising blacks, especially when it was accompanied by residency requirements and by stipulations that a voter prove he had paid the tax for several consecutive years. A more reputable device was the secret ballot, which seemed to be a reform measure but which practically worked to disqualify the numerous black illiterates.[13] South Carolina devised a fiendishly clever system with its "eight-box" law, which required a voter to fill out a separate ballot for each office and to deposit each one in its own individual receptacle—the arrangement of which could be changed at random by white election officials.[14] Since as late as 1900 a majority of the black adult males in seven Southern states were illiterate, the technique resulted in black disfranchisement.

So effective were these measures—to say nothing of social and economic pressure, or of latent and overt violence—that even in a state like Mississippi some whites saw no need to take further steps to eliminate black voting. A good many Mississippi editors agreed with Senator Walthall that the calling of a constitutional convention to disfranchise blacks was "an unnecessary, expensive, and dangerous experiment." In vetoing the call for a convention in 1888, Governor Lowry stated: "Quiet reigns throughout our borders . . . the colored people are content and happy. . . . Why disturb society . . . ? Why agitate and convulse the country?"[15] Nevertheless, in state after state, conventions assembled to do what had already been done, to write into constitutions what had already been accomplished by long practice.

Perhaps a better way to understand the developments of the 1890's is to think of that decade as a phase in the life-cycle of the Southern white disfranchisers. For this purpose it is helpful to draw on the growing body of sociological and psychological literature dealing with generational theory.[16] I suggest that segregation and disfranchisement should be viewed as the final public acts, the last bequests, of the Southern Civil War generation.

When one speaks of a "generation," he has to begin with qualifications and disclaimers. Unfortunately for the social scientists—but fortunately for the human race—babies are born in pretty much the same numbers every year—not in bunches every seventeen or thirty years. A child grows up among those who are both older and younger than himself, and there are no sharp breaks between age-groups. When a historian talks of a generation, then, he has to look for something more than mere chronological boundaries; he must find the subjective ties of shared experience that give to members of an age-cohort a sense of self-identity, a feeling that they are sharers of a peculiar destiny. As Robert Wohl has written in his fascinating account of *The Generation of 1914*: "A historical generation is not defined by its chronological limits or its borders. It is not a zone of dates; nor is it an army of contemporaries making its way across a territory of time. It is more like a magnetic field at the center of which lies an experience or a series of experiences. It is a system of references and identifications that gives priority to some kinds of experience and devalues others—hence it is relatively independent of age. . . . What is essential to the formation of a generational consciousness is some common frame of reference that provides a sense of rupture with the past and that will later distinguish the members of the generation from those who follow them in time."[17]

For the Southern whites who were in early manhood or who reached maturity in the 1860's, the Civil War was just such an experience, and it provided just such a common frame of reference. Of course I am here talking not so much about the high officials of the Confederate government or the general officers of the Confederate army, most of whom had reached maturity long before 1861, but about the young men who comprised the bulk of the Southern fighting forces. Any sampling of soldiers' diaries or journals or letters reveals that this war—perhaps more than most wars—produced a distinct break in consciousness. The Confederate soldier was just as aware as his Union counterpart that his generation had a unique fate, since it was "touched by fire." As the war progressed, both soldiers and civilians found that their interests and preoccupations of the pre-war years were fading in their memories; it was as though history prior to 1861 had been erased. At the same time the future after the war seemed incredibly remote. It is this sense of altered consciousness, far more than any experimentation in state socialism or in stronger governmental centralism, that most nearly justifies Professor Emory Thomas' view that the Confederacy was a revolutionary experience.[18]

Members of the Civil War generation—the young men and women between the ages of, say, seventeen and thirty in 1861— correctly thought of themselves as living in an age of heroes, as performing acts of gallantry and chivalry beyond the imagination of the stay-at-home generation of their elders. Most were perhaps less aware that the war also produced a coarsening of moral fiber, an insensitivity to human suffering unknown to the older generation. The best account that I know of this transformation of values is in Thomas Wolfe's semi-fictional "Chickamauga," based on recollections of North Carolina Civil War veterans:

Lord, when I think of hit! [His narrator begins.] When I try to tell about hit thar jest ain't words enough to tell what hit was like. And when I think of the way I was when I joined up—and the way I was when I came back four years later! When I went away I was an ignorant country boy, so tenderhearted I wouldn't harm a rabbit. And when I came back after the war was over I could a-stood by and seed a man murdered right before my eyes with no more feelin' than I'd have had for a stuck hog. I had no more feelin' about human life than I had for the life of a sparrer. I'd seed a ten-acre field so thick with dead men that you could have walked all over hit without steppin' on the ground a single time. . . . I'd seed so much fightin' and killin' that I didn't care for nothin'. I just felt dead and numb like all the brains had been shot out of me.[19]

In the best of circumstances survivors of such wartime experiences have difficulty in readjusting to the placid mores of civilian life. In the case of white Southerners at the end of the Civil War the problem was greater because they suffered two sharp and almost simultaneous traumas, which served to reinforce wartime indifference to death and insensitivity to suffering.

The first of these was the experience of defeat. It is hard for us today to realize how startling, how earth-shaking to most Southerners was the collapse of the Confederacy. Knowing the vast superiority in numbers and equipment of the Northern armies, aware that the Confederacy suffered shortages of men, of supplies, of horses, and of food, we tend to see the defeat of the South as inevitable—or, at least, to believe that ultimate Northern victory was predictable after Vicksburg and Gettysburg. But the Confederates themselves were unaware of any such historical inevitability. To the very end most thought that, even though they might have lost a battle, a state, or an army, the South ultimately would be victorious.

One of the most revealing passages in the diary of General Josiah Gorgas, the unemotional, well informed ordnance chief of the Confederacy, is his account of the emergency council that President Jefferson Davis called in April 1865, at Danville, Virginia, where the Confederate government had retreated after the fall of Richmond. Arriving before the cabinet secretaries and other chiefs of bureaus, Gorgas was greeted by the President: "We have just received, Gorgas, the worst news that we could have—Gen. Lee has surrendered his army." Never before, noted Gorgas, had the President "addressed me without the prefix of my rank. He was standing when he spoke and then sat down and bowed his head upon his hands for a moment." "I never saw the President moved but by that shock," Gorgas recalled. "It unnerved him completely." It is significant that Gorgas was as surprised by the news of Lee's surrender as was Davis. Indeed, two years after Appomattox Gorgas still did not think Lee's action had been necessary; and as late as July 1867, as the political horizons darkened, he asked in his diary: "Would it not be better to take up arms and defend ourselves to the last. . . . "[20]

If the leaders of the Confederacy greeted defeat with incredulity, private citizens and common soldiers were equally unbelieving. The unpublished diary of Samuel A. Agnew, a preacher and planter at Brice's Cross Roads in Mississippi, suggests how slowly the bad news traveled and with what skepticism it was accepted. An initial report on April 11 of Lee's surrender was recorded as "preposterous," and three days later Agnew gave some credence to a story that the Confederacy would be saved because of the impending war between the United States and France. Agnew refused to believe a newspaper that announced Joseph E. Johnston's surrender to Sherman but accepted a rumor that Mosby had captured President Lincoln. As late as April 20, Agnew recorded that people were "generally incredulous" about Lee's surrender, even though the newspapers carried repeated stories confirming the details. "No one is willing to believe it," Agnew noted, though most were willing to admit that "if it is so 'we're gone up.' "[21]

Nearly every Southern manuscript collection for the period echoes the note of unbelief that defeat had really happened. For instance, one Floridian at the end of April 1865 speculated that the assassination of Lincoln would produce "anarchy in Yankeedom" and that the French would "save us by armed intervention from the last act in the drama"; but if neither eventuality occurred, he vowed—weeks after Appomattox—"We will still fight the battle of freedom alone."[22] As late as 1870 there were Southerners who refused to accept defeat. One Louisiana planter and lawyer in that year urged that the surrender of Lee and Johnston be regarded as the beginning of an armistice, not of a peace, since the Confederacy would rise again. "I see no hope—for us—but in war . . . " he alerted his friends, "whenever—be it now or in fifty or a hundred & fifty years hence—a favorable opportunity shall present itself."[23]

I am not suggesting, of course, that most Confederates wanted to continue the fighting or that they were unwilling to return to the Union. But these reactions, which could be endlessly multiplied, do indicate that the end of the Confederacy was so unexpected, so cataclysmic, as to leave most Southerners dazed and unbelieving. General Gorgas' diary entry written four weeks after Lee's surrender accurately recaptured the Southern mood: "The calamity which has fallen upon us in the total destruction of our government is of a character so overwhelming that I am as yet unable to comprehend it. I am as one walking in a dream, and expecting to awake. . . . It is marvelous that a people that a month ago had money, armies, and the attributes of a nation should to-day be no more, and that we live, breathe, move, talk as before—will it be so when the soul leaves the body behind it?"[24]

While still reeling from the recognition that they were the first generation of Americans ever to endure defeat, Southern whites suffered a second severe trauma over the ending of slavery. Despite insistent Confederate propaganda warning that the war aim of the Union was to free the slaves, despite widespread knowledge of Lincoln's proclamations, many Southern whites at the end of the war simply did not believe in emancipation. "What will be done with the negroes is still unknown," the Reverend Samuel Agnew of Mississippi recorded in his diary as late as May 1865. "The negroes themselves evidently think they are free, but they may be too hasty in their conclusions."[25] A well informed planter in Tuscaloosa, Alabama, agreed: "Most persons consider the Negro as now a free man, that emancipation is accomplished. I do not. I believe it will be left to the states, to decide whether it shall be immediate or gradual & every thing I see or hear from Washington confirms me in this belief."[26]

Finally forced to recognize that emancipation was a reality, Southern whites apparently expected the freedmen to continue to behave as they had when slaves. They believed that Negroes themselves accepted inferiority as their natural and normal condition. This is not to suggest that all Southern whites credited the prewar arguments justifying slavery as a positive good; indeed, the insistently repetitive note of the proslavery argument suggests that there were still many Southerners who needed convincing. Southern whites, whether in the army or at home, knew that during the war slaves were often restive, negligent in their labor, and disobedient. But such conduct did not suggest the approaching end of slavery; rather, it reinforced their stereotypes about Negro behavior and the need to keep blacks under constant supervision and discipline. Not even the exodus of blacks who followed the Union armies challenged Southern whites' perceptions that subordination was the natural condition of blacks; in their view, such defections were caused by ignorance on the part of the slaves and by willful meddling on the part of the Yankee soldiers.

It was, then, a shock beyond credence for whites to discover that blacks after emancipation were not going to stay in their place and work on the plantations. Everywhere there was a sense of betrayal—a word that frequently recurs in the correspondence of the times—a sense made more acute because it often seemed that the very slaves who had been most trusted and esteemed were the earliest to leave the plantations. "Those we loved best, and who loved us best—as we thought—were the first to leave us," a Virginian lamented. The actions of the freedmen forced Southern whites to recognize that they did not know—that they never had known—how blacks thought and felt. They were compelled to abandon their cherished belief in slavery as a patriarchal system, which mutually linked whites and blacks in ties of friendship and loyalty. In many Southern hearts the old feeling of condescending benevolence toward blacks was replaced, as the Memphis *Argus* noted, with "absolute hatred."[27]

Set apart from their elders by the coarsening experience of war, deeply traumatized by a sense of defeat and betrayal, Southerners of the Civil War generation had to struggle during the twenty-five years after the conflict simply to survive. Part of their task was that of rebuilding and physically restoring their war-torn region. Southern cities had been looted or burned; Southern railroads were on the verge of collapse; levees along the Mississippi had gone untended, or had been dynamited by Union soldiers; large tracts of fertile land had been given over to broomsedge and pine seedlings. Everywhere there were shortages—shortages of capital, shortages of cash, shortages of food, shortages of seed, shortages of clothing and medicine. Yet as Roger L. Ransom and Richard Sutch persuasively argue, one can exaggerate the destruction, if not the distress, wrought by the war in the South.[28] The land, which had made the section enormously wealthy before the war, was still as rich as ever. To individual owners the loss of capital invested in slaves might seem calamitous; but for the section as a whole emancipation simply meant the transfer of "capitalized labor" from the slaveowners to the former slaves themselves. Certainly the slowness of Southern recovery, as compared to the rapid rehabilitation of West Germany, Italy, and Japan after far greater losses in the Second World War, suggests that devastation alone is not enough to account for the economic problems of the region during the twenty-five years after the war.

Most white Southerners blamed their problems on the inefficiency and unreliability of free black labor. No refrain is more constantly repeated in the correspondence of the postwar period. "There is no dependence in a negro," wrote the overseer of an Alabama plantation to its owner in 1866; "freedom has struck in and it is hard to get out."[29] "The negros [sic] work so little and steal so much," lamented another Alabama planter; "it is impossible to make anything with them upon any plan of employing of them you can adopt."[30] There can be no question that there were enormous difficulties, both economic and psychological, in evolving a new relationship between labor and management, and it was inevitable that there should be a certain amount of milling about until that new pattern emerged. Yet there is striking agreement among the careful scholars who have recently reexamined the economic history of the postwar South that the productivity of black labor under freedom was almost exactly what it had been under slavery—with the significant exception that, wherever possible, black women were spared work in the fields.

It is tempting to explain the slowness of Southern recovery after the war in demographic terms. Certainly the loss of more than a quarter of a million able-bodied Southern men—perhaps one out of every five who served in the Confederate armies—and the wounding and maiming of hundreds of thousands more must have deprived the section of leadership and energy that it desperately needed. The 1870 census tabulation of the number of male citizens over twenty-one—a category that excludes postwar immigrants, who settled mostly in the North—shows that all the Southern states had significantly fewer—3 to 6 percent fewer—members of the adult labor force than did the states of the North and West.

Some scholars have argued that the disproportionately small number of able-bodied males created a new role for white women in the South, who had become accustomed to managing plantations and operating businesses during the war. To the death of over 20,000 Alabama soldiers Robert Gilmour attributes the sharp shift in the sex ratio in the white population of that state between the ages of twenty and thirty; in 1860, 51 percent of this age cohort was male, but in 1870, 54 percent was female. Young widows with sizable estates were numerous, and it is easy to understand the decision of one returning Alabama soldier, casting about for a mate, to "let youth sing the praises of beauty," while he himself preferred "the eye with a soul in its glances—Oh! a gentle widow for me."[31] Anne F. Scott suggests that many Southern women who had managed farms and stores during the war continued to do so during the postwar era, when, as Myrta L. Avary noted, "The great mass of Southern women had to drop books for broomsticks, to turn from pianos and guitars and make music with kettles and pans."[32] Joan Cashin has discovered that in northwestern Georgia after the war significant numbers of widows, along with their children, worked in textile mills.[33]

But our knowledge of the demographic changes that resulted from the war remains sketchy, and for every scholar who has found significantly altered patterns there is another who discerns no meaningful shifts. Jonathan M. Wiener's fascinating study of the Alabama Black Belt shows no increase in the proportion of female planters during the Civil War and Reconstruction years, and Wiener suggests that most women who were planters in 1870 were the widows of elderly men who died of natural causes, not the relicts of young war heroes.[34] Similarly Frank Huffman's close statistical study of Clarke County, Georgia, finds only a very slight change in the proportion of white females who owned or operated farms.[35]

If then the slow recovery of the South after the Civil War cannot be closely linked to the physical devastation of the conflict, to changes in the productivity of the labor force, or to demographic shifts, perhaps it can be better understood in terms of the psychological difficulties that members of the Civil War generation had in dealing with postwar realities. A case study—one that does not even pretend to be typical or representative—can best make the point. Let us recount the story of George and Anne Collins, of North Carolina and Mississippi. Just before the outbreak of the war, George P. Collins, scion of a middling North Carolina planter family, married Anne Cameron, daughter of Paul Cameron, reputed to be the wealthiest man in the state with huge landholdings in North Carolina, Tennessee, Alabama, and Mississippi, which he managed with extraordinary Scottish shrewdness.[36] So canny was Cameron that, while most of his fellow planters were subscribing their produce for Confederate loans, he stored his unginned cotton in cabins on his several plantations, and right after the war he sold it for an inflated price. After Appomattox Cameron was wealthier than he had been before the war.

Very different was the fate of his son-in-law, Collins, who enlisted in the Southern army at the outbreak of hostilities and served until the end of the war. Waiting to be paroled after Joseph E. Johnston's surrender, Collins recognized that he, like other members of the generation of defeat, was going to find it hard to adjust to the postwar era. As if anticipating failure, he wrote to his wife on April 30, 1865: " . . . I feel more down cast with the prospect of attempting to start anew than I had thought possible, but I must trust the hand that feeds the sparrow. . . . " Once discharged, he returned to his father's plantation, where he found conditions "truely [sic] appalling." "No one," he lamented to his wife, "can comprehend the difficulties against which I am contending [—] the want of tools, mechanics and everything else that is requisite to carry on the business successfully." It soon became apparent that the family farm could not support him and his siblings.[37]

Cameron then permitted Collins to choose any one of the several plantations he owned and agreed to finance him until he could get underway. Collins chose the Cameron plantation in Tunica County, Mississippi, to which he, his wife, his children, and some seventeen North Carolina black field hands moved in December 1865. Though Collins found "everything out of repair [—] fences down . . . ditches filled up, logs to roll & so many other things to do that I scarcely know where to begin," he started off with high hopes and even reported optimistically: "My Negroes are cheerful & obedient & work well so far. . . . "[38] But after that his frequent letters to his father-in-law were a chronicle of disasters. Bad weather and flooding from the Mississippi River caused his 1866 crop to be small, and what cotton he did make was not picked because his field hands had cholera. He made a better crop the next year, but a drop in the price of cotton, together with the high commissions Memphis merchants charged on necessary supplies, left him broke. After balancing the books for 1867, Collins ruefully wrote Cameron: "I do not feel hopeful at all. I can not see any profit in cotton at the present rates nor do I see any prospect of its improvement in the future."[39] The Collinses fared a little better in 1868, but it took all they made that year to make up for the losses of the two previous years. On and on the struggle went. By 1872, complaining of discriminatory taxation, of county courts dominated by carpetbaggers and blacks, who would not allow him to collect debts or enforce labor contracts, and of the constant idleness and debauchery of his field hands at political rallies, Collins was ready to accept defeat: "My own bitter experience here shows me that nothing is to be expected here except a dog's life & a bare pittance. . . . Every year my capital gets less & less & I see my all slipping away through my fingers. It is hard to give up after all I have gone through here but I see no other hope [;] there is nothing to live for."[40] But Cameron bailed his son-in-law out again and again until 1880, when Collins, "in perfect despair," concluded that "there was no hope at all."[41] After one more Mississippi flood, Collins gave up for good, returned to North Carolina, and managed one of the gins that Cameron owned.

On first reading, the letters of George and Anne Collins seem to be a record of heroic exertions in the face of insurmountable odds. No one, a reader is inclined to believe, could have dealt better than they with the natural disasters, with the disease and plague, with the unruly labor and the unsympathetic government officials, with the plummeting cotton prices. But a closer study of the Collins correspondence suggests that this may not be the whole story. One clue is an early letter a Memphis friend wrote to Cameron; at just the time the Collinses were reporting their deprivations and hardships, the Tennessee correspondent quite innocently expressed his great pleasure in seeing George and Anne so often in Memphis and recounted the adventures that his wife and Anne had in purchasing for the latter a supply of crinoline, laces, and ribbons, together with a very stylish French corset.

As one looks at the letters again, it becomes increasingly clear that the Collinses, who were not idle, nor dissolute, nor, in their own view, wasteful, could not adjust their scale and style of living to postwar circumstances. They simply could not recognize, or cope with, the fact that, with the withdrawal of many black women from field work after emancipation, the size, and hence the total productivity, of the work force was diminished; Ransom and Sutch estimate this reduction at about 30 percent. At the same time they did not understand that free black laborers, whether wage hands, renters, or share croppers, were in a position to demand a far larger proportion of the total output of a plantation than slaves had been. Labor's share of the output, according to Ransom and Sutch, amounted to only 22 percent of the total before the war and rose to 56 percent after freedom.[42]

Shrewd old Paul Cameron, who had amassed his fortune during bad times as well as good times before the war, understood the problem better than did his children, brought up in the plentiful 1850's. When he set Collins up on the Mississippi plantation in 1865 he gave a strong warning: "You must make up your mind to get along with just what will do. We are to have a great revolution in society & social life—and those who do not now go to work & make a manly effort to sustain themselves & families will go down. . . . You will have to provide for yourself—you will have to *labour* to live either by your *head* or your *hands*."[43] After supporting the Collinses—along with other children who had similar difficulties in making their own way in the postwar era—Cameron by the 1880's was in despair. "I have neither mental or physicall [sic] capacity for my position as the head of a large and exacting household [he wrote his daughter]. It calls up an expression of an old friend & neighbor . . . 'Paul it does very well,' speaking of his expensive family, 'when the children all suck the mammy but I tell you when they suck the daddy it is the devil!' This used to make me laugh . . . ; but now it comes back upon [me] with painful thought & anxiety."[44]

Of course I am not suggesting that the Collins' experience was typical. Not every returning Confederate veteran was wiped out financially, year after year; and not every business failure in the New South had a wealthy father-in-law to bail him out. Nor am I implying that the whole quarter of a century after Appomattox was a period of depression, since after the severe shocks of the 1870's the 1880's were relatively prosperous in much of the South. Yet the Collins' story does serve as a trope for that of the whole Southern Civil War generation, a generation cut off from its roots by the war experience and doubly traumatized by a sense of defeat and betrayal. With their whining tone of self-defense and self-pity, George Collins' letters speak for a generation whose psychological mainspring snapped at the end of the war.

Yet with limited energy, limited emotional range, and limited imagination they had to try to create a new social and economic order in the South.

A number of indices suggest how limited were their horizons. The slow economic recovery of the South can, as I have tried to suggest, best be attributed not to wartime devastation or lessened productivity of labor but to decline in entrepreneurial leadership, from the men of Paul Cameron's generation to those of George Collins'. The figures that Jay Mandle has recently published, showing the dearth of technological innovation in cotton production, as compared to the proliferation of patents for machines to thresh and harvest grain,[45] underscore the impoverishment of the Southern imagination, to a decline in initiative and innovation. Also suggestive is the drop in both quantity and quality of Southern family correspondence by the 1880's. The rich Southern epistolary tradition was perfectly embodied in the voluminous and beautifully written letters of the Charles C. Jones family, which Robert Manson Myers had admirably edited in *The Children of Pride*.[46] There are scores of valuable and informative collections of family papers for the war years and the early days of Reconstruction. But for the late 1870's and 1880's there is a dearth; even intimate family letters for this period tend to be short, businesslike, perfunctory, and non-literary. Indeed, one might almost say that they are non-literate, for there seems to have been marked decline in Southern grammar, spelling, and handwriting by the 1880's.

Necessarily, then, the new order that rose in the South after the Civil War was limited. Economically it rested upon sharecropping. Politically it insured the supremacy of the Democratic party. Socially it insisted on the subordination of the black race. These three goals had to be maintained at all costs, including fraud and force. Members of the generation who, like Thomas Wolfe's veteran, had walked through fields covered with dead men were not likely to be squeamish about bloodshed. Members of the generation who felt their slaves had betrayed them were not likely to be paternalistic toward blacks.

By the 1890's members of the Civil War generation began to reach what Daniel J. Levinson calls the phase of "middle adulthood" in their life cycle. If he survived the war, the Confederate soldier who had been twenty in 1860 would, of course, have entered his fifties by 1890. He had reached that psychological stage that Erik Erikson designates as "generativity," which is primarily marked by its "concern in establishing and guiding the next generation." At this stage in the human life-cycle, says Ortega y Gasset, a generation attempts to make "its ideas and aims the governing ones in every sector of society (such as politics, business, religion, art and science)" and "devotes itself to implementing those aims."[47]

Entering their fifties, Southerners of the Civil War generation were deeply concerned that their successors, soon to take leadership in the society, would fail to understand their achievements, brought about with such difficulty, and might violate their precedents, established with such risk. The most familiar effort of the Civil War generation to shape the life and thought of its successors was the establishment of numerous Confederate veterans' organizations during the late 1880's and 1890's. In promoting these groups General John B. Gordon repeatedly stressed that the organizations must not be limited to surviving Confederate soldiers and sailors but should also include "that large contingent of sons of veterans, who, too young to have received the baptism of fire, have nevertheless received with you the baptism of suffering and sacrifice." In addition to urging the erection of monuments to "our great leaders and heroic soldiers" and the compilation of data "for an impartial history of the Confederate side," the constitution of the United Confederate Veterans called for a deliberate effort "to instill into our descendants a proper veneration for the spirit and glory of their fathers, and to bring them into association with our organization, that they may . . . finally succeed us and take up our work where we may leave it."[48]

Racial segregation and disfranchisement represented a parallel attempt on the part of the Civil War generation to shape the future. Cherishing a bitter sense of defeat and betrayal, the members of the War generation did not themselves need rules or laws to keep the Negro "in his place." Inured to suffering and bloodshed, they had no qualms about using terrorism, as well as economic pressure and political chicanery, to suppress the Negro vote. But they could not be sure that the next generation of white Southerners, who had not themselves had a baptism of fire, who had not experienced the traumas of defeat and betrayal, would share their sense of urgency. In all the voluminous literature concerning the disfranchisement of blacks in the 1890's there is no more revealing document than a letter published in the Jackson *Clarion-Ledger* from a former Confederate colonel: "The old men of the present generation can't afford to die and leave their children with shot guns in their hands, a lie in their mouths and perjury on their souls, in order to defeat the negroes. The constitution can be made so this will not be necessary."[49]

Through the debates on disfranchisement this concern with warning, protecting, preserving the next generation—even against its own will—is a recurrent theme. The now elderly Southerners of the Civil War generation knew how illusory is communication across generational boundaries. They could have anticipated the maxim of the Spanish philosopher Unamuno that the young man can no more comprehend his elders than the sick man can understand what his robust neighbor means by health. Anticipating that the young men of the South would not understand the tribulations of the past or the dangers of the future, the generation of defeat moved in the 1890's to confine its successors in a prison with four walls: racial separation; disfranchisement of blacks; allegiance to the Democratic party; and reverence for the Lost Cause. The extent of their success is attested by the infrequency with which white southerners escaped from these narrow confines in the half-century after 1890.

Notes

1. Rayford W. Logan, *The Negro in American Life and Thought: The Nadir, 1877-1901* (New York: Dial Press, 1954).

2. Woodward's views are presented in his *Origins of the New South, 1877-1913*, vol. X of *A History of the South*, ed. Wendell Holmes Stephenson and E. Merton Coulter (Baton Rouge: Louisiana State University Press, 1951), and in *The Strange Career of Jim Crow*, rev. ed. (New York: Oxford University Press, 1957). For a sampling of criticisms of Woodward's work, see Joel Williamson, ed., *The Origins of Segregation* (Lexington, Mass.: D. C. Heath and Company, 1968).

3. For a concise summary of state actions on disfranchisement, see Woodward, *Origins*, pp. 321-49.

4. William J. Cooper, Jr., *The Conservative Regime: South Carolina, 1877-1890* (Baltimore: Johns Hopkins University Press, 1968).

5. George B. Hodge to William Preston Johnston, Oct. 20, 1871, Johnston MSS., Tulane University, New Orleans.

6. The best account of this legislation is Richard E. Welch, Jr., "The Federal Elections Bill of 1890: Postscripts and Prelude," *Journal of American History*, LII (December 1965), 511-26.

7. Nell I. Painter, *The Exodusters: Black Migration to Kansas after Reconstruction* (New York: Alfred A. Knopf, 1977); Robert G. Athearn, *In Search of Canaan: Black Migration to Kansas, 1879-80* (Lawrence: The Regents Press of Kansas, 1978).

8. Paul Lewinson, *Race, Class, and Party: A History of Negro Suffrage and White Politics in the South* (New York: Grosset & Dunlap, 1965; originally published in 1932).

9. J. Morgan Kousser, *The Shaping of Southern Politics: Suffrage Restriction and the Establishment of the One-Party South, 1880-1910* (New Haven: Yale University Press, 1974), p. 18.

10. Lewinson, *Race, Class, and Party*, p. 79.

11. Chilton Williamson, *American Suffrage from Property to Democracy* (Princeton: Princeton University Press, 1960).

12. Lewinson, *Race, Class, and Party*, p. 67.

13. Kousser, *The Shaping of Southern Politics*, pp. 52-60.

14. Cooper, *The Conservative Regime*, pp. 100-103.

15. Albert D. Kirwan, *Revolt of the Rednecks: Mississippi Politics, 1876-1925* (New York: Harper Torchbooks, 1965), pp. 61, 63.

16. Three perceptive studies that will serve as an introduction to this literature are: Karl Mannheim, *Essays on the Sociology of Knowledge* (London: Routledge & Kegan Paul, Ltd., 1952), pp. 276-322; Alan B. Spitzer, "The Historical Problem of Generations," *American Historical Review*, LXXVIII (December 1973), 1353-85; and Morton Keller, "Reflections on Politics and Generations in America," *Daedalus*, CVII (Fall 1978), 123-35.

17. Robert Wohl, *The Generation of 1914* (Cambridge: Harvard University Press, 1979), p. 210.

18. Emory M. Thomas, *The Confederacy as a Revolutionary Experience* (Englewood Cliffs: Prentice-Hall, 1971).

19. Thomas Wolfe, *The Hills Beyond* (New York: Harper & Row, 1941), pp. 84-85.

20. Josiah Gorgas, Diary, April 9 and July 9, 1867, typescript in Gorgas MSS., University of Alabama.

21. Samuel A. Agnew, Diary, April 11, 14, and 20, 1865, Agnew MSS., Southern Historical Collection, University of North Carolina at Chapel Hill.

22. F. F. L'Engle to Edward L'Engle, April 29, 1865, L'Engle MSS., ibid.

23. Randall Lee Gibson to William Preston Johnston, July 19, 1870, Johnston MSS.

24. Gorgas, Diary, May 4, 1865, typescript, Gorgas MSS.

25. Agnew, Diary, May 8, 1865, Agnew MSS.

26. H. C. Taylor to R. Jemison, Jr., June 28, 1865, Jemison MSS., University of Alabama.

27. For full discussions of Southern white responses to emancipation, see Eugene D. Genovese, *Roll, Jordan, Roll* (New York: Pantheon Books, 1974), pp. 97-112; Leon F. Litwack, *Been in the Storm So Long* (New York: Alfred A. Knopf, 1979), pp. 104-66; and James L. Roark, *Masters Without Slaves* (New York: W. W. Norton & Company, 1977), pp. 111-15.

28. Roger L. Ransom and Richard Sutch, *One Kind of Freedom: The Economic Consequences of Emancipation* (Cambridge: Cambridge University Press, 1977), Chapter III.

29. William O'Berry to Paul C. Cameron, Feb. 6, 1866, Cameron MSS., Southern Historical Collection, University of North Carolina at Chapel Hill.

30. Samuel Arrington to A. H. Arrington, Oct. 25, 1868, and Jan. 1, 1871, Arrington MSS., ibid.

31. Robert Gilmour, "The Other Emancipation: Studies in the Society and Economy of Alabama Whites during Reconstruction" (unpublished Ph.D. dissertation, Johns Hopkins University, 1972), pp. 187-88.

32. Anne Firor Scott, *The Southern Lady: From Pedestal to Politics, 1830-1930* (Chicago: University of Chicago Press, 1970), pp. 96-98.

33. Joan E. Cashin, "The Civil War and the Southern White Family: Chattooga County, Georgia, 1860-1871" (unpublished seminar paper, Harvard University, 1979).

34. Jonathan M. Wiener, *Social Origins of the New South: Alabama, 1860-1885* (Baton Rouge: Louisiana State University Press, 1978), pp. 16-18.

35. Frank Jackson Huffman, Jr., "Old South, New South: Continuity and Change in a Georgia County, 1850-1880" (unpublished Ph. D. dissertation, Yale University, 1974), pp. 221-23.

36. On Cameron and his North Carolina holdings, see Charles Richard Sanders, *The Cameron Plantation in Central North Carolina (1776-1973)* (Durham: Duke University Press, 1974).

37. George P. Collins to Anne Collins, April 30, May [26], and June 5, 1865, Cameron MSS.

38. George P. Collins to Paul C. Cameron, Jan. 15, 1866, ibid.

39. Ibid., Jan. 26, 1868.

40. Ibid., Jan. 6, 1872.

41. George P. Collins to Anne Cameron, Dec. 9, 1880, ibid.

42. Ransom and Sutch, *One Kind of Freedom*, pp. 44-46, 4.

43. Paul C. Cameron to George P. Collins, Sept. 27, 1865, ibid.

44. Paul C. Cameron to Anne Collins, Jan. 22, 1883.

45. Jay R. Mandle, *The Roots of Black Poverty: The Southern Plantation Economy after the Civil War* (Durham: Duke University Press, 1978), Chapter V.

46. Robert Manson Myers, ed., *The Children of Pride: A True Story of Georgia and the Civil War* (New Haven: Yale University Press, 1972).

47. Daniel J. Levinson et al., *The Seasons of a Man's Life* (New York: Ballantine Books, 1978), pp. 29, 278-304; Erik H. Erikson, *Childhood and Society*, 2nd ed. (New York: W. W. Norton & Company, Inc., 1963), pp. 266-68.

48. General John B. Gordon to the former soldiers and sailors of the Confederate States of America, Sept. 3, 1889, printed in *Address of the United Confederate Veterans, March 26, 1896; Constitution and By-Laws of the United Confederate Veterans . . . Adopted at Houston, Texas, May 23, 1895*—both found in the Confederate Veterans Collection, Tulane University.

49. Vernon Lane Wharton, *The Negro in Mississippi, 1865-1890* (Chapel Hill: University of North Carolina Press, 1947), p. 207.

II

SOUTHERN LEADERSHIP:
CHANGE OR CONTINUITY?

One of the continuing debates among Southern historians is the degree to which the Civil War and Reconstruction brought a genuine change in the nature of Southern leadership. In "From the Old South to the New: Another Look at the Theme of Change and Continuity," Dan T. Carter observes that only recently have scholars challenged C. Vann Woodward's thesis that the post-Civil War years marked a "watershed" in Southern history, when "new men with new ideals" gained power over the planter elite. Among the most "intriguing challengers," Carter believes, are the new generation of radical historians whose spiritual godfather is Karl Marx. The works of these scholars—Jonathan Wiener, Dwight Billings, and Jay Mandle—share the common theme of a "continuing planter hegemony" controlling and repressing its class enemies up to the present day. But other than warning historians against the too frequent discovery of "watersheds," Carter remains skeptical that such sophisticated Marxist analysis offers any better answer to the question of change or continuity in Southern leadership than the traditional, eclectic approaches.

The next two articles demonstrate the historiographical disagreement over the continuity-discontinuity question. Although the Civil War was an epochal event, William L. Barney argues in "The Ambivalence of Change: From Old South to New in the Alabama Black Belt, 1850-1870," that there was an essential continuity between the antebellum and the postbellum periods. In the face of inevitable economic and demographic changes during this twenty-year period, Barney shows that first Southern Whigs and later the "New Departure" Democrats tried to cope with these changes by applying Northern business practices to the Southern economy. In both the prewar and the postwar periods, however, agrarian Democrats of the planter class thwarted such efforts by appealing to regional pride and fears that the South might be transformed into the "Yankee" image. Although the planter class did continue in power in Alabama, Barney concludes that "the origins of the post-Redemption New South were rooted in the contradictions of an Old South civilization that struggled to contain, if not deny, the very changes it was generating."

Although continuity may have been the case in Alabama, David Carlton's article, " 'Builders of a New State'—The Town Classes and Early Industrialization of South Carolina, 1880-1907," argues that such was not the case in the Palmetto State. Carlton argues that the interpretations of Wiener, Billings, and Mandle have lent support "to a serious misinterpretation of post-bellum Southern history." Specifically, Carlton challenges their theses that a "continuing planter hegemony" either "economically inhibited and ideologically cowed" the modernizing commercial and industrial elite or was itself the "modernizing elite." Neither was the case, Carlton maintains, in the up-country of South Carolina. He shows that the textile corporations founded there were organized and led by locals, usually engaged in commerce or the practice of law. The traditional "planter elite" played no significant role in this process. As the mill towns of the up-country multiplied, the emerging, local commercial and industrial elite realized that its economic future was tied directly to the "up building" of these rising "urban" centers. These new "town people" were the "modernizing elite" who altered forever the rural South Carolina up-country. Refuting the recent theme of "continuity" in the postwar South, Carlton has reemphasized the older thesis of change or discontinuity.

2

FROM THE OLD SOUTH TO THE NEW: ANOTHER LOOK AT THE THEME OF CHANGE AND CONTINUITY

Dan T. Carter

In a South of change, it is always comforting to return to Charleston—to step south of Broad Street on a warm spring evening and mentally exorcise every McDonald hamburger stand and Brake-O shop from here to El Paso. But it can only be a brief vacation. The bulldozers of C. Vann Woodward's vivid metaphor are smashing headlong through the physical and intellectual landmarks of the region. Of course, this is nothing new in my current home in Atlanta, which has been in a state of constant reconstruction since William Tecumseh Sherman sponsored the city's first urban redevelopment project during the late unpleasantness.

But even the little town of Florence, South Carolina, where I shopped with my family on a Saturday afternoon in the 1940s and went to the movies for nine cents, has been physically transformed. As a child, I saw much the same community my father had observed in the 1920s. During the last two decades, however, Florence has become a paradigm of a changing small-town America with a decaying downtown ringed by factories, fast-food strips, and a sterile string of shopping centers along its perimeter. As a transplanted Georgian, it is enough to make me want to move to Savannah and open an antique store. But I've checked the real estate prices and discovered that they are almost as bad as Atlanta's, bid upward by refugees from the Big Apple fed up with high taxes and unconvinced that Mayor Koch can clear New York's streets of muggers and incontinent and unleashed dogs.

To talk about the good old days of the disappearing South (and the not so good old days) hardly qualifies one for the Insight of the Year Award, but a review of recent historical writings on the post-Civil War South has led me to examine, in the context of this session, the question of proper burial dates. Let me reassure you that I am not going to deal with the hoary question of whether or not the "South" has disappeared. As one historian recently remarked, symposia on the disappearing South must rank high among the major growth industries of the region, certainly in a sector of the economy as depressed as academia. Thus, while I am not quite ready for the region itself to vanish, like most of you I suspect, I am more than willing to stop talking about it. Instead, I'm going to raise an innovative approach to Southern history since the 1850s.

I am going to explore the question of change and continuity in the modern South.

As in all things postbellum, the alpha, if not the omega, is C. Vann Woodward and his *Origins of the New South*. It is only a slight exaggeration to say that Professor Woodward's study of the late nineteenth-century South has, for the study of Southern history, a role similar to that of Martin Luther's ninety-five theses on the cathedral door at Wittenberg. Unlike the harassed founder of the Protestant Reformation, however, Professor Woodward's provocative arguments remained essentially unchallenged for a decade and a half.[1] When one considers that this was the period when thousands of graduate students were earning their spurs by cannibalizing their academic overlords, the feat becomes all the more remarkable. As James Tice Moore recently summarized Woodward's thesis, the triumph of the "redeemers" in the 1870s and the 1880s represented "fundamental irreversible change." Although Woodward saw, and often emphasized, the links between the postwar and the antebellum South, in his view a new class gained power over traditional ones: "Whigs over Jacksonians, capitalists over agrarians. New men with new ideals clearly held sway in the revisionist South." Thus, the Civil War, emancipation, and the First Reconstruction amounted to an irreversible watershed in Southern history.[2] As recently as 1972, Sheldon Hackney could conclude in an article in the *Journal of Southern History* that Woodward's thesis was basically unchallenged.[3]

If Hackney's essay were written today, it would have a different conclusion. A few titles hint at the shift in emphasis among historians: *Place Over Time: The Continuity of Southern Distinctiveness; The Persistent Tradition in New South Politics*; and *The Roots of Black Poverty*. These titles only suggest the shift in historical analysis that seems to have increasingly minimized change and instead emphasized the strong links between the past and the present.

Three years after Hackney published his essay on the *Origins of the New South*, for example, George Brown Tindall sought to reemphasize the "thread of continuity" that ran from "bourbonism through populism to progressivism in the New South." The Bourbons had reconciled tradition with innovation, inventing a New South even as they retained the vision of a traditional organic community. While the Populists *appeared* to challenge this vision, in reality they shared its major essentials. Finally, the Progressives succeeded in bending Populist measures to traditional Bourbon goals. And built into this political synthesis of the Progressives was the "persistent tradition of community in the South."[4]

While Tindall's lectures amounted to a slight shift in focus, Moore has recently insisted that Woodward overemphasized the war as a dividing line in Southern history. In a historiographical survey of the historical literature dealing with the South from 1870 to 1900, Moore insists that New South innovators played a distinctly secondary role to traditionalists in formulating government policy. While "parvenus, urbanites and persistent Whigs" may have made their way into the leadership of the Democratic party during the postwar years, established antebellum policies continued, policies that acknowledged the primacy of agriculture and moved only halfheartedly to promote industrial and urban growth. There was, concludes Moore, a basic "continuity between the Old and New South. All things had not changed with Appomattox, much less with the Compromise of 1877."[5]

Casting his net even wider, Carl Degler reached the same conclusion in his Fleming Lectures in 1976. Reaching beyond politics and toward an analysis of the distinctive culture of the South, Degler reviewed the oft-described factors that have shaped a distinctive South: the relative absence of non-Anglo-Saxon white ethnics, fundamentalist Protestantism, and a propensity for violence. But the root source of Southern distinctiveness, he argued, was the peculiar racial and economic institution of the slave plantation. And even though slavery as a legal institution ended in 1865, the overarching structure of the plantation and its offshoots retained their vitality in important ways. Racial subordination, sharecropping, and the lien system were rickety replacements for the peculiar institution, but they were serviceable substitutes well into the twentieth century. Despite the rhetorical flourishes of the New South, rhetoric that had its origins in the commercial stirrings of the Old South, the region remained essentially agricultural and unchanged in important essentials long after the war. And that continued distinctiveness, said Degler as he appropriated one of Wilbur J. Cash's metaphors, had its "tap root in the Old South" of plantation slavery.[6]

Other works in social and economic history often reflect a similar perspective. In his study *The Political Economy of the Cotton South*, Gavin Wright is intent on measuring the effects of the Civil War and emancipation on the region's economy, but he emphasizes the basic coherence and continuity of Southern economic history over the nineteenth century as a whole. While Roger L. Ransom and Richard Sutch develop a somewhat different analysis in their discussion of the economic consequences of emancipation, they also return again and again to the antebellum roots of the postwar Southern economy.[7]

The most intriguing challenge to Woodward's emphasis on the discontinuity between the Old and the New South, however, has come from a generation of radical historians, unscathed by the bruising polemics of the Cold War and unembarrassed by Karl Marx. Three of these works seem particularly intriguing to me: Jonathan Wiener's *Social Origins of the New South: Alabama, 1860-1885*, Jay R. Mandle's *The Roots of Black Poverty: The Southern Plantation Economy after the Civil War*, and Dwight Billings' *Planters and the Making of a "New South": Class, Politics and Development in North Carolina, 1865-1900*.[8]

These works bear little relationship to the crudely polemical studies of a James L. Allen or a Herbert Aptheker.[9] They are Marxist in the sense that Karl Marx is a spiritual godfather. Thus, there is likely to be an obligatory reference to him, or even a perfunctory quotation, but in terms of methodology and approach, they are more directly influenced by recent Marxist scholars: A. G. Frank, Maurice Dobb, Immanuel Wallerstein, Barrington Moore, Robert Rhodes, Paul Baran, and—via Eugene Genovese—that Sardinian theoretician and revolutionary, Antonio Gramsci.[10] Moreover, they vary considerably in their emphases and in approaches to analyzing Southern history. Nevertheless, I would argue that they are essentially bound together by a common set of intellectual assumptions about the critical role of class conflict, upper-class hegemony in Southern society, and the continuity of Southern economic and social history through the nineteenth and into the twentieth century.[11]

Wiener, a former student of Barrington Moore, argues that the planter class in Alabama—Eugene Genovese and C. Vann Woodward notwithstanding—survived intact after the war and "persisted" at approximately the same rate as before 1860.[12] His account of Alabama from 1860 to 1885 (and by implication to 1900) is the story of the ideological and economic triumph of the planters over their class enemies; yeoman farmers, tenants, merchants, and industrialists. The planters were essentially antibourgeois, and they sought, in Wiener's summary, to "keep black labor tied to the plantations [through coercion], and to preserve the state's fundamentally agrarian society. . . . " They did so by exerting political, economic, and ideological pressure within the state and by achieving an alliance with Northeastern finance and industry, which sought to thwart the rise of Southern competition in iron and steel production.[13] In Wiener's vivid metaphor, borrowed from Moore, the Alabama planters, like the Junkers of the nineteenth century, had strengthened a labor-intensive "Prussian Road" to economic development, economic development that "preserves and intensifies the authoritarian and repressive elements of traditional social relations."[14]

In a last chapter that owes as much to Gramsci as the earlier ones to Moore, Wiener concludes that the planter class maintained ideological and economic hegemony from the 1840s through the 1890s although the "openly violent racism and oppression of the 1890's . . . [indicated] the beginning of the deterioration of planter hegemony."[15] It was a class that had been subtly modified by the war and Reconstruction. Wiener rejects the notion that the war brought no fundamental changes. But it was a class that maintained its hegemony over other rival classes in Alabama society at least for twenty-five years after the Civil War, possibly longer.[16] There was no break at 1865.

With some modifications, Billings reaches similar conclusions in his account of North Carolina from 1865 to 1900, finding the same planter-class hegemony through the late nineteenth century and well into the twentieth. And while Billings only occasionally uses the forceful image of the "Prussian Road" to economic development, he offers the same kind of interpretation. North Carolina planters supported (and controlled) modernization efforts that were more bourgeois (superficially) only because of objective demographic conditions: notably, the presence of a large yeoman farmer class and the absence of a strong cotton plantation economy after the 1870s.

The pattern was strikingly similar to that described by Wiener. In the case of North Carolina, however, the planter class turned to the textile industry as a means of maintaining its power and influence. In the agricultural sector, this planter class continued to rely on "nonwage" black labor (tenancy) and in the emerging textile industry, cheap white labor. In both cases, these patterns of economic development were justified by a continuation of the antebellum intellectual upper-class ideology. "The slaveholders' hegemony, far from dying out, persisted as the paternalism of the plantation was translated into mill villages."[17] Such a pattern of economic development was an unusually "brutal process" for the lower classes, argues Billings, and it was carried out only by using the ruthlessly repressive force of the state. But it did succeed in stifling important changes in the state's economy and social structure.[18] In fact, argues Billings, the planters retained control of postwar developments, politically and economically, in North Carolina and throughout the South well into the twentieth century. Like Wiener, Billings believes that the "emerging" middle class that appears in *Origins of the New South* is simply a figment of Woodward's imagination, at best a shadow of a genuine middle class, hopelessly in the shadow of the hegemonic planter class. It is a point driven home by his superficial analysis of recent developments in North Carolina that, Billings argues, reflect the continuing conservative nature of modernization in the South. As he argues in the last paragraph of his study, the New South is "hardly new at all."[19]

Mandle's study of the Southern plantation economy since the Civil War is at once far more ambitious in scope and yet more limited in its research methodology. Mandle is a Marxist economist who is primarily interested in exploring the causes of persistent black poverty in America, a persistence he finds rooted in the continuation of the plantation long after slavery had disappeared. He says less about class relationships in Southern society than Billings and Wiener. But his findings supplement their argument that, although shaken by the trauma of emancipation, the basic economic, political, and ideological hegemony of the planter class remained intact after 1865. Over the next eighty-five years, despite the pamphleteering of the New South boosters, they maintained their stronghold on the Southern economy by resisting typically bourgeois forms of agricultural development—particularly those pioneered in the Midwest—concentrating instead on maintaining nonmarket mechanisms for mobilizing and forcing an exploited laboring class to perform agricultural work at unnaturally low wages. In this regard, such socially coercive mechanisms as peonage, paternalism, and institutionalized violence were of critical importance.[20]

Faced with this planter-class hegemony, the black Southern tenant-proletariat could respond only by fleeing. But the planter class had cleverly blocked large-scale industrial development in the South and had exploited white workers' racism to black employment so that there was no industrial alternative. At the same time, Northern racism and the continuation of European migration to the North meant that no market existed for black labor outside the South. Thus, Southern blacks became a nomadic peasantry, wandering from plantation to plantation, caught in the iron grasp of a coercive labor system that rewarded them barely enough to survive. Only during World War II, argues Mandle, did Northern demand for labor finally overwhelm the mechanism for maintaining a coercive plantation labor system. At that point, and that point alone, the planter class turned to modern, more capital-intensive forms of agricultural development (a move neatly symbolized by the development and utilization of the cotton picker), abandoning the Prussian Road to economic development.[21]

I have neglected many aspects of the works of Wiener, Billings, and Mandle, notably, their attempt to view the South in a comparative context with other Third World "dependent" agricultural economies. But the essential point for our discussion is that they have argued for a history of the nineteenth-century South—political, economic, intellectual, and cultural—of one piece. And while they might disagree about precisely when the planter class began to surrender its hegemony (Billings would deny that it had ever surrendered it), their theme is the same in important essentials. Through the noise and smoke of apparent political conflict in the post-Civil War South, little has changed. For the ruling classes, whether in the figure of Paul Cameron of North Carolina and his hundreds of black peasant workers or in that of Robert Woodruff of Atlanta and his thousands of Coca Cola employees, traditional ruling classes remain in the driver's seat of Southern society. This is continuity with a vengeance.

If such an interpretation is valid, it considerably simplifies the task of studying Southern history and culture. We have only to understand the hegemonic culture of the ruling class and trace its almost uninterrupted triumph over the past two hundred years. If one wished to be perverse in analyzing this approach to Southern history, one could argue that, despite all the emphasis on "class conflict" and the "struggle of conflicting classes for hegemony," it all bears some similarity to the old consensus history of the 1950s. To be sure, there was some conflict, and the "consensus" was maintained through coercion and deceit, but the political and economic maneuverings described by traditional historians become little more than a disagreement between different wings of the ruling class over tactics and strategy.

I might add that it is a particularly bleak scenario for Southern liberals who have plundered through their region's history in search of a usable past, for there is nothing here except an unending litany of the truckling of Southern liberals and reformers to the dictates of the ruling class. I do not think that there would be any of us particularly anxious to root for the Birmingham bourgeois industrialists as opposed to the prebourgeois planter class because the former will promote "modern" as opposed to "Prussian" economic development.

I think it is fair to say that "bourgeois" historians have sometimes avoided hard judgments about the role of class distinctions and class conflict by excessively emphasizing irony, paradox, and ambiguity. But without arguing for an Aristotelian mean in developing historical interpretations, I would suggest that it is equally misleading to write history as though such factors did not exist. Billings, for example, has included numerous biographical profiles in his study of North Carolina, but these figures emerge as bloodless archetypes of the planter class or of the rising industrial bourgeoisie, marching to the drumbeat of a master ideology rather than contrary human beings caught up in a complex web of relationships and ideas that defy easy generalizations. Mandle's discussion of the interrelationship of technological change and social factors in the cotton South is at times persuasive and insightful. But in his zeal to argue that the plantation-owning class preferred the coercion of a large laboring class (mainly black sharecroppers) to the more capital-intensive and sophisticated technological means of production, he comes perilously close to arguing that the untidy processes of technological innovation can be summoned at the will of the ruling class.[22] Dr. Faust may have been able to summon the creative forces of the universe at will; mere mortals cannot, even a hegemonic ruling class. Wiener's book, with its critical questions about class roles in Alabama society, is more firmly rooted in the quantitative data, in the secondary literature, and in extensive research in the planter newspapers of Alabama. But Wiener at critical points reaches too quickly for the explanation that securely fits his thesis even when there are plausible alternative explanations for the motivation and behavior of the individuals (and the "classes") he describes.[23]

In making these critical observations, I am certain that I reflect my own instinctive biases. At its most superficial level, my uneasiness stems from the occasionally grating tone and argumentative style of radical historians. I often suspect that, quite apart from his intellectual merits, Genovese has been warmly regarded by traditional Southern historians because of the "Southern" courtesy with which he has treated his conservative ideological opponents, even if the Sicilian *embrazia* is sometimes followed by a sliver of steel between the ribs. Fortunately, most of the works I have discussed do not reach the petulant standard set by Moore when he gracelessly dismissed the lifetime work of a scholarly "opponent" as "rubbish."[24]

But I would like to believe that my skepticism is based on more substantive grounds. I remain unconvinced that a Marxist analysis—even a subtle and sophisticated one—is any more useful in explaining essential developments in Southern history than are traditionally eclectic approaches. I am particularly skeptical after having read David Carlton's recently completed study of cotton mill workers and the middle class in South Carolina from 1880 to 1920. Carlton, a former student of C. Vann Woodward, does not always agree with his mentor in describing economic and social developments in the late nineteenth and early twentieth centuries. But his conclusions form a striking refutation of the notion of the "hegemony" of the planter or any other ruling class. The middle class that emerges from his study was often reactionary, selfish, and bigoted, but it was hardly the hapless tool of the ruling classes that seems to have captured the imagination of many newer historians of the post-Civil War South. At the very least, his study is a timely reminder of the warning of Carl Degler that any analysis that begins with fixed assumptions about clear-cut class conflict and ruling-class hegemony runs the danger of becoming a tautology.[25]

Still, it is a healthy situation when we no longer have to lower our voices and look over our shoulders when we discuss the nature of class and even class conflict in Southern society. And if Gramsci and A. G. Frank are not always reliable guides to the intricacies of Southern history, they offer— along with the works of more traditional historians—a timely reinforcement of Marcus Cunliffe's warning that American historians have an excessive propensity for discovering watersheds. As George Tindall noted, "Continuities in history are seldom, if ever, completely broken. Tradition has a stubborn way of asserting itself."[26] It might even be better to forget the whole dichotomy of change and continuity except as a mental filing system for temporarily arranging historical data in our minds.

But then what would we have to talk about at the next symposium?

cf Gilded Age ?

Notes

1. C. Vann Woodward, *Origins of the New South, 1877-1913* (Baton Rouge: Louisiana State University Press, 1951).

2. James Tice Moore, "Redeemers Reconsidered: Change and Continuity in the Democratic South, 1870-1900," *Journal of Southern History*, XLIV (August 1978), 357-78.

3. Sheldon Hackney, "*Origins of the New South* in Retrospect," *Journal of Southern History*, XXXVIII (May 1972), 214-16.

4. George Brown Tindall, *The Persistent Tradition in New South Politics* (Baton Rouge: Louisiana State University Press, 1975), p. xii.

5. Moore, "Redeemers Reconsidered," p. 378.

6. Carl Degler, *Place Over Time: The Continuity of Southern Distinctiveness* (Baton Rouge: Louisiana State University Press, 1977), p. 132.

7. Gavin Wright, *The Political Economy of the Cotton South: Households, Markets, and Wealth in the Nineteenth Century* (New York: Norton, 1978); Roger L. Ransom and Richard Sutch, *One Kind of Freedom: The Economic Consequences of Emancipation* (Cambridge, England: Cambridge University Press, 1977). For a review of the issues involved in the works of Wright, Ransom and Sutch, and other economic historians, see Harold Woodman's "Sequel to Slavery: The New History Views the Postbellum South," *Journal of Southern History*, XLIII (November 1977), 523-54.

8. Jonathan Wiener, *Social Origins of the New South: Alabama, 1860-1885* (Baton Rouge: Louisiana State University Press, 1978); Jay R. Mandle, *The Roots of Black Poverty: The Southern Plantation Economy after the Civil War* (Durham, N. C.: Duke University Press, 1979); Dwight Billings, *Planters and the Making of a "New South": Class, Politics and Development in North Carolina, 1865-1900* (Chapel Hill: University of North Carolina Press, 1979).

9. All readers with pronounced masochistic tendencies are referred to James L. Allen's *Reconstruction: The Battle for Democracy, 1865-1876* (New York: International Publishers, 1937). See also Herbert Aptheker, *American Negro Slave Revolts* (New York: Columbia University Press, 1943).

10. Mandle, *The Roots of Black Poverty*, pp. 3-15; Billings, *Planters and the Making of a "New South,"* pp. 3-24; Wiener, *Social Origins of the New South*, pp. 186-87.

11. My discussion of these works focuses on these common themes, but I should emphasize that they are quite different in a number of important ways.

12. Wiener, *Social Origins of the New South*, pp. 3-34. Wiener's conclusions concerning planter-class persistence are based on many sources, but he has concentrated on Marengo County, Alabama, for his most intensive analysis of census and tax data. In my mind, Wiener's provocative study raises many questions even as it answers others. For example, it may be, as Wiener argues, that the rate of "planter persistence" within the economic and social elite continued at approximately the same rate after the war as before. But this begs the question of just how "persistent" one may describe any elite when it disappears at the rate of 50 percent or more each decade.

13. Wiener, *Social Origins of the New South*, p. 71.

14. Ibid., pp. 71-72.

15. Ibid., p. 221.

16. Ibid., pp. 186-221.

17. Billings, *Planters and the Making of a "New South,"* p. 130.

18. Ibid., pp. 70-95.

19. Ibid., p. 232.

20. Mandle, *The Roots of Black Poverty*, pp. 14-15, passim. For a discussion of some of the problems involved in measuring the level of coercion, see Pete Daniel, "The Metamorphosis of Slavery, 1865-1900," *The Journal of American History*, LXVI (June 1979), 88-89.

21. Mandle, *The Roots of Black Poverty*, pp. 84-97.

22. Ibid., pp. 52-70. I do not wish to misrepresent Mandle's argument. He does *not* argue that the planter class decided not to invent the cotton picker. He argues instead that the basic technology was available well before the cotton picker was perfected and developed; instead, the absence of a substantial demand by Southern cotton planters discouraged inventors and developers from solving the final technological hurdles. While there is clearly a relationship between the demand for a product or a process and the efforts of inventors and developers to create this product or process, it is far more problematical than Mandle's manipulation of patent data and abstract theories would have us believe. The inability of agricultural engineers to solve the basic problems of flue-cured tobacco harvesting—despite millions of dollars of investment and years of experimentation by the best agricultural engineers in the nation—should make one skeptical of at least some of the assumptions that underlie his discussion of technology and Southern agriculture.

23. Thus, Wiener cites an instance in the 1880s when the Supreme Court of Alabama refused to hold landlords responsible for their tenants' debts to merchants. This was evidence, argues Wiener, that the court "supported the planters in their attempts to weaken merchants' ability to do business with black belt tenants." This may be true. But the court seems to have been on unassailable constitutional grounds in reaching its decision. Moreover, its decision reflects an ideology that is far more in keeping with classical bourgeois economics rather than with the ideology (such as it was) of the planter class. Wiener, *Social Origins of the New South*, p. 105. See *Bell v. Hurst*, 75 Alabama 44. I should add that I basically agree with Wiener on the importance of merchant-planter conflict on this point.

24. Barrington Moore, Jr., *Social Origins of Dictatorship and Democracy: Lord and Peasant in the Making of the Modern World* (Boston: Beacon Press, 1966), p. 117.

25. Degler, *Place Over Time*, pp. 80-81.

26. Tindall, *The Persistent Tradition*, p. 2.

3

THE AMBIVALENCE OF CHANGE: FROM OLD SOUTH TO NEW IN THE ALABAMA BLACK BELT, 1850–1870

William L. Barney

For all the complexities inherent in any analysis of the transition of "Old South to New," the problem has commanded at least the persuasive simplicity of lending itself to a neat chronological division demarcated by the year 1865, which witnessed both the finality of Confederate defeat and the end of slavery. To be sure, Emory Thomas has recently reminded us again of the erosion of the ideals of the Old South under the pressures of the industrial and bureaucratic demands of the Confederate mobilization effort, and Jonathan Wiener has argued cogently that reports of the demise of the antebellum planter elite in the Alabama Black Belt have been greatly exaggerated.[1] However, the extent to which our entire conceptualization of the nineteenth-century South has been distorted by forcing its history into an antebellum and postbellum mold has not been centrally addressed.

This paper, based on newspaper and manuscript census research in Dallas County, Alabama, will argue that the process of change in this plantation county after the Civil War represented a continuation of the same dynamics of material and ideological response that had developed by the late antebellum period.

By the 1850s, if not earlier, Dallas County had all the attributes traditionally associated with a plantation district of the Old South—a wealthy planter class, expanding cotton production, a large and growing slave population, and a fervid commitment to the preservation of slavery. In the midst of the fertile prairie soil of central Alabama, known as the Black Belt, and with access to international cotton markets via direct river transport to Mobile, the plantation regime had consolidated its power in Dallas County in the generation since the establishment of the county in 1818.[2] Dallas County shared fully in the general Southern prosperity of the 1850s, during which the per capita wealth of its adult white males rose from $6,870 to $19,070.[3] By the eve of the Civil War, the only apparent threat to its prosperity and value structure was the external challenge mounted by the rise of political abolitionism in the North under the leadership of the Republican party. Yet by an inescapable logic, the very process of expanding and consolidating the socioeconomic base of plantation agriculture[4] had produced in prewar Dallas County a dialectic of change in which the threat to order and stability came also from within.

Southern whites in Dallas County were no more able to escape the social and ideological consequences of an intensifying involvement in a market economy than were their hard-driving Yankee counterparts in the North.[5] Indices that reflect the nature and pace of social change within Dallas County in the 1850s are summarized in table 3.1. Three conclusions from the table stand out. First, and perhaps most striking, was the geographic mobility of the county's white population.[6] Two-thirds of the adult white males left during the decade. Second, and related to the patterns of inward and outward migration, was the sharp drop in the percentages of farmers and slaveowners. As the ownership of land and slaves became increasingly concentrated in the hands of a planter elite, young men left the countryside in search of cheap land and farming opportunities. The net white population, however, remained virtually constant over the decade because of an

Table 3.1
SOCIOECONOMIC PATTERNS IN DALLAS COUNTY, 1850-1860

WHITE MALES AGE 20 AND OVER	*1850*	*1860*
Household heads	63.2%	58.0%
Boarders[a]	20.5%	29.0%
Married	55.3%	53.2%
Kin ties within beat[b]	31.7%	27.5%
Southern born	90.1%	82.5%
Left during decade	66.1%	-
Own real property	43.4%	40.9%
Own slaves	48.0%	40.5%
Farmers[c]	30.7%	20.5%
Artisans/Clerks	14.3%	25.6%
N	1,869	2,144

Source: Federal manuscript census schedules of 1850 and 1860 for Dallas County.

[a]Men living in a household not headed by kin (i.e., not the same surname).
[b]Approximated by deriving the percentage of all adult white males with the same surname as other male household heads in the same beat.
[c]Includes those who meet the two conditions of owning land and of listing their occupations as farmers.

influx of young men possessing the craft and merchandising skills demanded by the burgeoning economy of Selma, the county's largest town, or else willing to accept jobs as economic servicing agents for the planters, most notably as overseers.[7] Third, and suggestive of a broad range of social transformations engendered by the very maturity of the plantation economy, was the decline in a number of indices—kinship ties, rates of marriage, ethnic homogeneity—that were critical to the agragarian South's vision of the proper social order. Central to this vision was an agrarian network of social dependencies bound together by ties of kinship and patriarchal authority.[8] Undermined by high rates of geographic mobility, declining opportunities in the countryside, and the arrival of ethnic outsiders— Northerners, Irish, and Germans anxious to meet Selma's economic needs by filling nonagrarian occupations that most Southern whites tried to avoid[9]—this social vision increasingly failed to describe the reality of the volatile, complex, and heterogeneous order evolving in Dallas County.

In a debate rendered excruciatingly difficult by the imperative need to preserve and protect slavery, the ideological response to this internal process of change could be nothing less than ambivalent. Although both political parties within the county, the Democrats and the Whigs, were solidly united behind slavery, they embraced conflicting programs and emphasized different value orientations with which to confront the problem of change. Order and vindication—these were the goals of both the Democrats and Whigs. For the Democrats, a party whose power in Dallas County rested on strong rural majorities, especially in plantation districts,[10] order was to be achieved by expanding the marketplace of slavery into the federal territories, an expansion that was to be guaranteed, at least in its initial stages, by congressional protection for the rights of slaveholders. This solution promised not only additional land for the sons of planters but also, and paradoxically, economic relief for Southern whites unable to compete with the spread and intensification of plantation agriculture. Of equal importance was the insistence by the Breckinridge Democrats that their territorial policies alone could vindicate the rights and liberties of all Southern whites against the moral onslaughts of the antislavery North.[11]

Rather than attempting to recreate in the territories traditional slaveholding communities, the Whigs in Dallas County approached the goals of order and vindication from the perspective of men more prone to welcome and control change for their own benefit. Whereas the good society for Dallas Democrats was always rooted in the countryside and the plantation, and the proper use of political power involved protecting individual liberties and local communities from the corrupting tendencies of centralizing outside agencies, the Whigs saw in economic and political modernization a means of strengthening internal order and of refurbishing the self-respect of Southern whites beset by hostile external criticism.[12] Speaking largely for

commercial interests in Selma anxious to expand the mercantile and manufacturing base of Selma's economy,[13] the Whigs offered a program that
called for more, not less, change in the South's traditional social order. Railroads to market slave-produced cotton and to tap new sources of wealth,
factories to provide jobs for the nonslaveholders, foundries to refine Alabama's minerals and to burn its coal, public schools to educate and uplift
the children of the poor, and temperance to indoctrinate the work force in
self-control and moral sobriety—here was a Whig program for economic
and social progress under the aegis of an interventionist and supportive
state.[14] For all its stress on prosperity and order, this Whiggish call for a
New South was intended to vindicate the Old South. As one Selma editor
put it: "Then shall we be rich and prosperous—independent and happy as a
people. Then shall we be proud of our exhibitions and challenge comparison with any other people—void of any morbid feeling or sensitiveness of
inferiority in any particular."[15]

Smacking too much of entrepreneurial, pietistic Yankeeism, and too
closely linked with the programs of the hated Republicans, the Whigs' vision of a New South was stillborn in the 1850s. Although the efforts of
Selma to attract rail lines in the 1850s were matched by sporadic programs
of state aid for internal improvements by the legislature in Montgomery, a
majority of Southern whites in Dallas County, as elsewhere, clung to the
agrarian and aggressively proslavery values of the Democratic party. In a
slave society where the "subject condition of the slave made every man
struggle as by intuitive repugnance to that feeling of servility which characterized them,"[16] the Southern Democracy could always successfully invoke
the ethos of an agrarian republicanism with its promise of economic and
moral independence. That ethos, first imbedded in the crusade to protect
Southern rights within the Union and then in the effort to institutionalize
those rights outside the Union, was so persuasive precisely because it could
be set against frightening symbols of servility, whether in the form of
Northern abolitionism or Southern industrialization.[17]

The prewar attempt of Dallas County Whigs to remake the Old South
with slavery intact into a modernizing version of the free labor North was
revived in the context of emancipation soon after the Civil War. In alliance
with former Douglas Democrats, particularly those who had been active cooperationists during the secession crisis,[18] Whiggery in the guise of the pro-
Johnson National Union coalition proclaimed in the summer of 1866 a
"New Era" for Selma and its agricultural hinterland.[19] As before the war,
the impetus for the movement came from commercial, banking, and manufacturing interests in Selma seeking economic hegemony over the plantation
districts of central Alabama and the cementing of their ties with Northern
sources of capital and finished goods. Citing the destruction of slavery, the
disruption of rural labor patterns, the desperate condition of many whites,

and the overwhelming need for outside capital and state aid, proponents of the New Era were confident that the economic rationale for their program was now compelling.[20] When tied to the political need to reestablish Northern respect for Southern rights,[21] the call for economic development was seemingly clinched.

Events, of course, would soon reveal that the proclamation in 1866 of a New Era in Selma, or virtually anywhere in the South, was quite premature. The data included in table 3.2 encapsulate some key social and eco-

Table 3.2

SOCIOECONOMIC PATTERNS IN DALLAS COUNTY, 1860-1870
WHITE MALES AGE 20 AND OVER
URBAN DALLAS

	1860	*1870*
Household heads	58.0%	58.7%
Boarders	29.0%	28.1%
Married	53.2%	54.7%
Own real property	40.9%	31.8%
Own no property	35.0%	50.1%
Per capita wealth	$19,068	$3,525
N	2,144	2,087

RURAL DALLAS[a]

	1860	*1870*
Farmers	27.2%	27.6%
Tenants/Farm laborers	6.9%	31.3%
Kin ties within beat	28.5%	29.2%
Persisted since last decade	51.4%	60.2%
N	1,540	1,215

Source: Federal manuscript census schedules of 1860 and 1870 for Dallas County.

[a]Exclusive of the Selma beats.

nomic shifts within Dallas County during the war decade, shifts that precluded any commitment by a majority of whites to a program of action or internalization of values associated with the conquering North. The staggering drop in the per capita wealth of adult white males and the massive spread of farm tenancy registered blighted expectations and a burden of poverty in which relief was thrown back on traditional sources of authority, family and kin. As contrasted with the prosperous 1850s, the 1860s were a decade of social restabilization. Confederate mobilization, combined with the economic decline in the Black Belt, resulted in a 35 percent drop in the number of newcomers who entered rural Dallas County in the 1860s compared with the 1850s.[22] Moreover, men who returned home after the war, faced with the economic necessity of rebuilding and with responding to the psychological yearning to put down roots after the trauma of the war, were less mobile than their counterparts in the 1850s.[23]

It was these men, the Confederate veterans and the majority of the white rural populace, who by 1870 had been resident in Dallas County for at least a decade, who defined the county's attitudes toward postwar conditions. That response, although it did not assume definite political shape until the call for the formation of a white man's Democratic party in January 1868,[24] was predicated on the same values and fears that had galvanized rural Dallas County in favor of the Breckinridge Democracy, immediate secessionism, and Southern nationalism. The core fear behind the refusal to submit to Yankeeism—be it before, during, or after the war—was that loss of personal honor and autonomy so brilliantly played on in a wartime editorial in the Selma press. Confederate defeat would mean that:

Our children are to be learned obedience to their Yankee masters, and their spirits broken while they are young. They are to be taught the doctrine that they are *inferior* to the dominant race, and that the negro is their equal. The Yankees are to take possession of the South, and after paying the expenses of the war by the confiscation of our land and negroes, they will institute free labor in the place of slave labor. . . . Our wives and daughters will be put in factories, and others will be made acquainted, experimentally, with the song of the shirt.[25]

From the perspective of most rural Democrats in Dallas County after the war, there was little in this editorial of 1862 that had not or was not about to happen. Conspicuous by their absence in the political affairs of Dallas County between 1865 and 1867,[26] these Breckinridge Democrats nonetheless were unmoved by the rhetoric of the New Era. As planters, they rejected a course of social and economic action that would further disrupt the countryside by raising taxes and by feeding scarce capital and labor into towns and factories; as impoverished farmers, tenants, and day laborers, they recoiled from the New Era's offer to abandon the dream of economic independence for industrial labor or by its open sponsoring of competition between white and black labor so as to determine which was best fit to meet the changed conditions of plantation agriculture.[27]

In the last analysis, despite the almost insurmountable obstacles of

capitalization and agrarian opposition, any call for a new departure for the
South just after the Civil War was doomed by the overwhelming need to
vindicate the Confederate war dead. In that vindication would come the
emotional solace to purge by myth the shame and degradation of defeat and
poverty. Mythical homage to the Confederate soldier cut across class lines
and, eventually, party lines by enshrining those ideals of the past that were
all the more appealing given the uncertainties of the present. As a fusion of
the planter's sense of duty and honor, the yeomanry's virile manliness and
physical courage and, most arrestingly, the idealized Southern woman's
ennobling mission of self-sacrifice, the Confederate dead symbolized the
three dominant value constructs of the old order.[28] As for the surviving soldiers, they were, to quote a letter written to the Selma *Daily Messenger* in
1866, "the life and soul of the South. Without them she would become a pu-
trid carcass, exciting the contempt even of those miserable vultures who
would gloat over her rottenness."[29]

To honor these men was to worship an idealized past that would be cor-
rupted and despoiled if the present generation submitted to Yankee domination. Thus, to a majority in Dallas County, the calls of the business leaders
of Selma for a New Era under Johnsonian Reconstruction amounted to a
sophistical campaign to accomplish just that degraded end. However, as
long as the campaign for change was associated with local leaders known to
the community and was not part of a drive to secure political and civil
rights for the former slaves, it received a respectful hearing. With the passage of the Military Reconstruction Act of 1867 and the organization in
Dallas County in the same year of a Republican party, composed primarily
of men not active in politics before the war,[30] conditions had fundamentally
altered. The Yankees, the wealthiest group in Dallas County as measured
by birth cohorts in 1870,[31] were now seen as making a bid, in a cynical alliance with blacks, for both political control and economic superiority. In-
exorably, the cycle of Radical Reconstruction fell into place.

By 1870, any notions of a New South had given way to the efforts of the
white majority not to blaspheme the memory of the Confederate dead. Indeed,
the Cult of the Lost Cause became so compelling that it has been all too easy to
forget that the origins of the post-Redemption New South were rooted in the
contradictions of an Old South civilization that struggled ambivalently to contain, if not to deny, the very changes that it was generating.

Notes

1. Emory M. Thomas, *The Confederate Nation: 1861-1865* (New York: Harper
& Row, 1978); Jonathan M. Wiener, *Social Origins of the New South: Alabama,
1860-1885* (Baton Rouge: Louisiana State University Press, 1978).

2. John Hardy, *Selma: Her Institutions and Her Men* (Selma: Times Book and Job

Office, 1879), and Walter M. Jackson, *The Story of Selma* (Birmingham, Ala.: Birmingham Printing Company, 1954); both contain much useful information on the antebellum history of Dallas County.

3. Figures compiled from the 1850 and 1860 U. S. manuscript census schedules for Dallas County, microfilmed copies of which were used at the University of North Carolina at Chapel Hill. By 1860, Dallas County was the leading cotton-producing county in Alabama and 76.8 percent of its population were slaves.

4. The classic treatment of this process remains Ulrich Bonnell Phillips, "The Origin and Growth of the Southern Blacks," reprinted in Eugene D. Genovese, ed., *The Slave Economy of the Old South* (Baton Rouge: Louisiana State University Press, 1968), pp. 95-116.

5. Richard D. Brown, *Modernization: The Transformation of American Life, 1600-1865* (New York: Hill and Wang, 1976), passim.

6. Overseers and tenant farmers were the most mobile of all the major occupational categories. Only 21.7 percent of the former and 25.4 percent of the latter residents in Dallas County in 1850 persisted during the decade.

7. Whereas the net white population in rural Dallas County dropped by 8 percent during the 1850s, whites in Selma nearly doubled from 973 to 1,809; W. Brewer, *Alabama: Her History, Resources, War Record, and Public Men. From 1540 to 1872* (Montgomery: Barrett and Brown, 1872), p. 208. The leading occupation among newcomers in rural Dallas County was that of overseers, who represented 22.6 percent of rural newcomers in the 1850s.

8. Bertram Wyatt-Brown, "The Ideal Typology and Ante-Bellum Southern History: A Testing of a New Approach," *Societas,* V (Winter 1975), 1-29.

9. For example, Northerners and the foreign born represented 3.5 percent of the farmers and planters in 1850 but 45.9 percent of the shopkeepers, 37.9 percent of the merchants, and 23.4 percent of the artisans.

10. Rural beats were over 60 percent Democratic in the 1850s, a figure that rose to over 80 percent in plantation beats, such as Pleasant Hill, Carlowville, and Portland; Election Returns, Secretary of State Files, Alabama Department of Archives and History, Montgomery, Alabama.

11. William L. Barney, *The Secessionist Impulse: Alabama and Mississippi in 1860* (Princeton: Princeton University Press, 1974), pp. 101-52.

12. J. Mills Thornton, *Politics and Power in a Slave Society: Alabama, 1800-1860* (Baton Rouge: Louisiana State University Press, 1978), especially pp. 321-42.

13. The normal Whiggish majority in Selma can be traced in the Election Returns, Secretary of State Files. Over half of all the politically active businessmen and artisans in the presidential campaign of 1860 in Dallas County were Bell Whigs.

14. Selma *Alabama State Sentinel*, February 1; April 5, 7; May 12, 1855.

15. Ibid., September 29, 1855.

16. From the editorial, "A Higher Civilization," Selma *Daily Messenger*, July 22, 1866.

17. Thornton, *Politics and Power in a Slave Society*, passim, is superb on the political implications on this agrarian ethos.

18. In July 1866, a county convention in Selma appointed twenty delegates to a state convention of the National Union party. From the fifteen delegates whose party affiliations could be traced back to 1860, seven were Bell Whigs and six were

Douglas Democrats. All but one of the Douglas men had been active cooperationists in 1860. For the list of delegates, see the Selma *Daily Messenger*, July 15, 1866.

19. "Come along, neighbor, and begin a new era here," Selma *Daily Messenger*, July 6, 1866. For the rationale behind the much more popular term, the New South, which caught on in the 1880s, see Paul M. Gaston, *The New South Creed: A Study in Southern Mythmaking* (New York: Alfred A. Knopf, 1970).

20. Selma *Daily Messenger*, June 21; July 4, 6, 31; August 4, 1866.

21. Letter of John Forsyth, quoted in ibid., September 25, 1866.

22. Rural newcomers in the 1850s totaled 747 men; in the 1860s, 484, of whom 42 percent were tenants or farm laborers in 1870.

23. This tendency to stay put after the war, in combination with the drop in rural newcomers, explains the marked rise in the percentage of rural persisters noted in table 3.2.

24. Jackson, *The Story of Selma*, pp. 225-58; Selma *Daily Messenger*, January 7, 1868.

25. Selma *Morning Reporter*, March 5, 1862.

26. For example, all but two of Dallas County's twenty delegates to the state convention of the National Union party in August 1866 had been active Breckinridge Democrats in 1860.

27. Rural opponents of change, labeled "pigheads" by Selma *Daily Messenger*, also were quick to condemn the Selma press for "obsequiousness" to Northern interests and opinion; see the *Daily Messenger*, August 26, 1866.

28. This fusion was explicit in an editorial that appeared in the Selma *Daily Messenger*, June 30, 1866.

29. Ibid.

30. Of the thirty organizers of the Dallas County Republican party, identified from the Selma *Daily Messenger*, March 29, 1867, only six had been active in the presidential campaign of 1860. Three of these men had been Douglas Democrats, two Bell Whigs, and one, Benjamin F. Saffold, had been a Breckinridge Democrat who switched to a cooperationist position in 1860.

31. The $9,013 per capita wealth of the thirty-two adult male New Englanders resident in Dallas County in 1870 easily made them the wealthiest birth cohort in the county. Although the number of Northern newcomers from the previous decade was less in 1870 (123) as opposed to 1860 (125), the wealth of the ethnic Yankees, which had actually increased during the 1860s, was concentrated in Selma businesses, highly visible, and politically inflammatory.

4

"BUILDERS OF A NEW STATE"—THE TOWN CLASSES AND EARLY INDUSTRIALIZATION OF SOUTH CAROLINA, 1880–1907

David Carlton

In keeping with the intuitive notion that the Civil War was the great watershed of Southern history, a long-accepted historical interpretation has held that the catastrophe of the 1860s separated two vastly different social orders. On the one hand, it did away with the legendary world of the planters, flowery, courtly, and vaguely preposterous; on the other, it raised up a poor, wounded, but recognizably American society run by storekeepers, bankers, and emerging industrialists, seeking to reconcile its ruined past with the national future. As C. Vann Woodward expresses it in his classic survey of the region in the late nineteenth century, "the 'victory of the middle classes' and 'the passing of power from the hands of landowners to manufacturers and merchants,' which required two generations in England, were substantially achieved in a much shorter period in the South"; the results included "changes of a profound and subtle character in the Southern ethos—in outlook, institutions, and particularly in leadership."[1] Succeeding explorations in Southern social and economic history offer similar analyses. Harold D. Woodman in his study of the Southern cotton-marketing system de-emphasizes the Civil War as a causative factor in favor of longer term structural changes in the Southern economy, but his delineation of the emerging social order is similar to that of Woodward. More recently, Roger Ransom and Richard Sutch have modified Woodman's argument by restoring the war, or more properly emancipation, to center stage, thus placing new emphasis on the disjuncture between the Old South and the New.[2]

In the past several years, however, a challenge has been issued to this interpretation, mounted by younger historians influenced by Eugene Genovese and, especially, Barrington Moore. Beginning with the same assumptions about antebellum society made by those who posit major social change in the postwar South, these scholars argue that the most striking characteristic of the New South was its strong structural continuity with the

Old, particularly the continued dominance of a small landholding elite that caused the development of the region to proceed in variously defined "reactionary" directions. While some members of this group, such as Jay R. Mandle, frame their arguments in modest, limited forms, others ascribe wide-ranging social consequences to the proposition of continued planter hegemony. Beginning with evidence that the antebellum planter elite in Alabama maintained its landholdings in the years immediately following the Civil War, Jonathan Wiener elaborates a thesis that planters remained in political and ideological control of the South long after the destruction of slavery; their rule, he argues, inhibited the formation of modernizing groups, such as commercial and manufacturing interests, obstructed economic development, and generally maintained the region as a backward-looking, premodern society. A completely different tack is taken by Dwight B. Billings, Jr., in a study of North Carolina. Finding that a majority of the cotton mills operating in the Tar Heel state in the aftermath of the Civil War were headed by "planters and prominent agrarians," he argues that the landed elite actively sponsored industrialization and a conservative form of modernization, a Southern version of Moore's "Prussian Road" to the modern world.[3]

I propose here to present some evidence bearing on the emerging debate over the nature of post-bellum Southern society,[4] having chiefly to do with patterns of industrial development and industrial leadership in the South Carolina up-country during the period 1880-1907.[5] I take this approach principally because my interest in the topic is an outgrowth of my larger work on the industrialization of South Carolina.[6] However, the question of industrial leadership is of some intrinsic importance in assessing two of the arguments made by advocates of the "continuing planter hegemony" hypothesis: the contention of Wiener that the modernizing elites of commerce and industry were economically inhibited and ideologically cowed by the dominant planters, and the assertion of Billings that the planters themselves constituted the modernizing elite. The available evidence on industrial development in South Carolina, I believe, suggests that these positions fail to explain the historical events in question and lend support to a serious misinterpretation of postbellum Southern history.

The modern textile industry in South Carolina became a major economic and social force in the years between 1880 and 1910. At the beginning of this period, the industry in the state consisted of thirty-four firms employing a mere 2,000 operatives; by the end, it consisted of 147 firms with over 45,000 operatives. In the latter year, it was estimated that 115,000 people, nearly all of them white, lived in South Carolina's mill villages, accounting for around 17 percent of the white population of the state.[7] While several spurts of growth occurred in the first fifteen years of the period, the bulk of the mills came into existence in the middle 1890s and after. I have compiled a list of one hundred corporations organized to build mills in the up-country between 1880 and 1907;[8] of these, seventy-four received their charters after 1894, while 90.7 percent of all net increases in capital stock reported to the secretary of state between 1887, when charter records were first kept, and 1907 were made after 1894. Nineteen of the corporations were organized in the banner year of 1900, accounting for $3,265,000 in initial authorized capitalization. As the industry as a whole burgeoned, individual firms increased enormously in size and sophistication. The average number of spindles per firm, a mere 5,887 in 1880, reached 25,899 by 1907, a three-and-a-half-fold increase over a period of just over a quarter century.[9]

As striking as the sharp expansion of the industry around the turn of the century is its pattern of concentration. The accompanying map shows the geographic distribution of spindleage in the state in 1907. Of the 3,695,920 spindles reported in place by August Kohn's survey of that year, 2,955,804, or 80 percent, were located in the up-country; 93.5 percent of those up-country spindles belonged to mills first built after 1880.[10] Furthermore, the pattern of concentration within the up-country belies the frequent assumption that the growth of the South Carolina textile industry stemmed from a movement of cotton mills to cotton fields. Of the one hundred firms on the list cited above, seventy-six built their plants either in or immediately adjacent to incorporated towns with populations in 1910 of over 1,000. Another nine were located in or adjacent to towns of less than 1,000 in 1910 that nonetheless had been incorporated prior to the organization of the mill corporation. Only fifteen of these firms built truly isolated mill villages, generally to take advantage of a water-power site. These isolated mills, to be sure, tended to be much larger than the town mills, running an average of 42,740 spindles as compared with 24,983 in mills with urban or suburban locations; the Pelzer Manufacturing Company, operating four mills clustered around a shoal in the Saluda River, controlled 130,000, the largest single concentration of spindleage in the state. Despite the large size of the isolated firms, though, over three quarters of both spindleage and mill employment was clustered around the towns, over one quarter around the three leading mill centers, Anderson, Greenville, and Spartanburg.[11]

It appears, then, that, at least in the area under study, the picture of the South Carolina mill village as an isolated, rural "industrial plantation" is somewhat overdrawn. What, though, were the reasons for the tendency of mills to cluster around towns? Purely economic considerations, of course, played a major role, especially those associated with transportation, as virtually all the towns with mills were located on rail lines. The increasing efficiency of steam power relative to water power, along with the development in the early 1890s of hydroelectric power and its long-range transmission, freed factories from the need to locate along rivers and cope with floods and droughts, while steam power required reliable supplies of coal

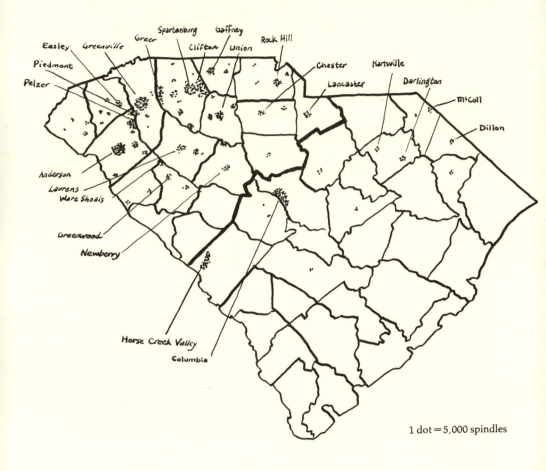

Easley
Greenville
Spartanburg
Gaffney
Greer
Rock Hill
Clifton
Union
Piedmont
Chester
Hartsville
Darlington
Pelzer
Lancaster
McColl
Dillon
Anderson
Laurens
Ware Shoals
Greenwood
Newberry
Horse Creek Valley
Columbia

1 dot = 5,000 spindles

SOUTH CAROLINA SPINDLEAGE, 1907

Source: August Kohn, *The Cotton Mill of South Carolina* (Columbia: S.C. Department of Agriculture, Commerce and Immigration, 1907), pp. 95-98.

shipped in by rail.[12] In addition, as industrialization proceeded, mills became increasingly dependent on distant sources for reliable supplies of their raw material. The image of the cotton mill in the cotton field, purchasing its fiber from local farmers as they brought it to the rear platform, progressively lost whatever validity it had had as the mills began to crowd each other on up-country water courses and at rail points. By 1900, Spartanburg manufacturer John H. Montgomery was advising his New York agent that existing mills had completely soaked up the local cotton, forcing his firms to obtain much of their raw material from areas farther South.[13] Kohn reported in 1907 that in seven leading textile counties mill consumption of cotton exceeded local production by 138 percent.[14] The quality of cotton also was a constraining factor, for mills frequently found the neighborhood product unsuitable due to insufficient length or lack of uniformity of staple, and so ended up buying from the richer areas of the Black Belt and the Delta.[15] The same rail lines used to ship materials in could, of course, be used to ship products out, and the use of rail lines as rights-of-way for telegraph lines helped assure that transportation hubs also became centers of communication with the far-flung marketing networks for cotton and textiles.[16] It was no accident that one-third of the firms organized during the period 1880-1907 located their mills along what is now the main line of the Southern Railway, with its connections to the Alabama and Mississippi cotton regions, the Birmingham coal fields, and the Northeastern marketing centers.

There were, then, good economic reasons for mills to be located in and around "urban" centers in the South Carolina up-country. However, they do not completely explain the appearance of the mills, for that requires not only the opportunity but also the willingness and wherewithal to take advantage of it. In order to understand the onset of industrialization, then, it is necessary to study the men who led the movement and their motivations. To this end, I have collected the names of 476 individuals, members of the original boards of directors of ninety-eight of the one hundred firms building mills in the up-country between 1880 and 1907.[17] The original board was the one elected by the subscribers to the stock of a new corporation at its organizational meeting; after the general incorporation law of 1886, the names of the board members were reported to the South Carolina secretary of state prior to issuing a charter.[18] The original boards cannot be taken as representative of all the capital and entrepreneurial resources combining to create the mills, for it was standard practice to raise a sizable proportion of the capital stock of an enterprise after it was chartered.[19] However, they are representative of the groups initiating the organization of cotton manufacturing firms; thus, a study of certain of their basic characteristics can illuminate the industrial impulse.

Of the 476 board members on my list, I have been able to identify 384 persons, accounting for 80.7 percent of the total number of individuals and

85.3 percent of the total number of seats they held.[20] Who were these men? To begin with, the overwhelming majority of them were local residents. The data on residence of mill directors, summarized in table 4.1, indicate that a large majority of those identified used the same post office as did the mill itself. Over three quarters lived in the same county as the mills they directed, and nearly 90 percent lived within the South Carolina up-country. Of those few seats held by individuals outside the region, over two-thirds were held by persons from Charleston or from the Northeast, with a handful held in two sizable commercial centers on the periphery of the region, Columbia and Charlotte.

If the mill directors were chiefly local in their residence, analysis of their principal occupations indicates that they were heavily oriented toward commerce.[21] As table 4.2 shows, nearly half the directors residing in the up-country were merchants at the time they acquired their manufacturing interests.[22] As a rule, they dealt in general merchandise or supplies, reflecting the lack of commercial differentiation in the up-country at this time; however, more specialized shopkeepers, such as dry goods merchants, grocers, and even druggists, jewelers, and booksellers, appeared on the lists, suggesting an increasingly "urbane" commercial economy. The increasing complexity of commerce also is indicated by the presence among the directors of forty-nine bankers, in a region that had boasted few banking institutions prior to the Civil War, and by the representation of drummers and corporate managers, such as packing-house agents, harbingers of the nationalization of the American economy.[23] If all the commercial categories were combined into a single group, it would account for 60 percent of the intraregional directors and over 60 percent of the total number of seats they held.

The second largest occupational group comprised agriculturists of various kinds and sizes; however, men whose principal calling was that of "farmer" or "planter" played comparatively minor roles in the industrial movement. Thirty-six of the ninety-eight mills had "agrarians" sitting on their boards, but their role was significant in only a handful of cases, chiefly in lower Pickens County and among the early York County mills. Only two of the firms could be described as dominated by agrarian interests. The Norris Manufacturing Company, constructed on Twelve Mile Creek in Pickens County in 1895, was headed by D. K. Norris, a prominent Anderson County planter, Allianceman, and Tillmanite from an Orangeburg County family; low-country planting interests contributed heavily to the enterprise.[24] More striking was the Goldville Manufacturing Company, organized in 1900 to build a mill in lower Laurens County. One of the few firms surveyed with virtual closed ownership, it was controlled by James Blalock, a large landowner who decided to spin into yarn some of the 1,000 bales of cotton produced annually on his plantation. The Goldville mill was

Table 4.1

SEATS ON ORIGINAL BOARDS OF DIRECTORS, 98 MILL CORPORATIONS, SOUTH CAROLINA UP-COUNTRY, 1880-1907: RESIDENCES OF IDENTIFIED DIRECTORS

	NO. SEATS		%	
Persons Outside Up-Country	68		11.8	
Northeast		24		4.2
Charleston		22		3.8
Charlotte		8		1.4
Columbia		9		1.5
Other		5		0.9
Up-Country Residents	508		88.2	
Same locality as mill		356		61.8
Same county as mill		96		16.7
Adjacent county		43		7.5
Other		13		2.2
Total	576		100.0	

Table 4.2

MILL DIRECTORS RESIDING IN THE SOUTH CAROLINA UP-COUNTRY, 1880-1907, BY OCCUPATION

	NO. SEATS		%	NO. INDIVS.		%
Commerce	315		62.0	204		59.9
Merchants		250	49.2		158	46.5
Bankers		49	9.6		30	8.8
Other commercial		8	1.6		8	2.3
White collar		8	1.6		8	2.3
Manufacturing	38		7.5	24		7.1
Cotton		29	5.7		17	5.0
Other		9	1.8		7	2.1
Professional	91		17.9	63		18.6
Lawyers		61	12.0		39	11.5
Other		30	5.9		24	7.1
Agriculture	59		11.6	44		12.9
Other	5		1.0	5		1.5
Total	508		100.0	340		100.0

by far the best example in South Carolina of the "vertical integration of the cotton industry under the control of the planters"; that being the case, it is significant that it underwent two reorganizations before 1907, ending the period surveyed with a different name, considerably shrunken capitalization, and a board composed of Columbia capitalists and purged of Blalocks.[25] The declining influence of the Blalocks in their mill paralleled that of agriculturists in the industry; while farmers and planters held 14.9 percent of the seats in mills organized up to 1894, they held only 10.1 percent of those seats opened by the great boom of the turn of the century.

Professional men made up a third major occupational grouping. The most important profession was the one with the closest ties to commerce, the law; lawyers, in fact, held more directorates than farmers, although they were fewer in number. Of the group of "other professionals," eighteen of thirty were physicians; the rest included a mill engineer, several newspaper editors, a college professor, a schoolteacher, and two ministers. These men have received a great deal of attention from such scholars as Broadus Mitchell, who especially loved to dwell on the spectacle of clergymen leading an industrial crusade.[26] However, except for a Methodist minister who was briefly president of the mill at Fountain Inn before being shifted to another charge by his conference; the schoolteacher, who somehow amassed the wherewithal to buy $10,000 worth of Abbeville mill stock; and the mill engineer, Joseph E. Sirrine of Greenville, these miscellaneous professionals played peripheral roles in industrial development.[27]

The smallest of the four major occupational groupings was composed of the manufacturers; of these, the bulk were in cotton textiles. Three of them, D. E. Converse and A. H. Twitchell of Glendale and A. J. Sitton of Pendleton, were veteran cotton mill men whose association with the industry predated 1880 and who were lending their experience and accumulated capital to the newer enterprises. The vast majority of this group, however, consisted of young men who assumed their seats at a median age of thirty-four. Nearly half of these were sons of older manufacturers, such as Campbell Courtenay, James D. Hammett, John A. Smyth, and C. M. Bailey; the rest were rising "practical mill men," such as E. R. Cash of Gaffney, uncle of W. J. Cash, and Robert E. Ligon of Anderson, who entered the industry as a bookkeeper for the Anderson Cotton Mill and became a career manager. Assuming their seats mainly after 1895, the Cashes and Ligons were the advance guard of a developing corps of modern corporate executives.[28]

Of those directors living outside the region, the fourteen men residing in the Northeast were the most important. Twelve of these men, holding twenty-two of the twenty-four Northeastern seats, were connected with the textile industry, but only one was principally a manufacturer; on the other hand, six were commission merchants (four from one firm, Woodward,

Baldwin and Company of Baltimore and New York), three were textile machinery manufacturers, and two were mill engineers. These were men generally uninhibited by any need to protect existing investments in Northern mills; on the other hand, as suppliers of capital goods and services to the textile industry, they were anxious to expand their Southern trade.

Aside from one case, when in 1889 a group of Northern investors moved a complete mill from Newburyport, Massachusetts, to the Spartan Mills plant in Spartanburg, Northern investment rarely took the form of a physical or corporate move South. As a rule, Northern investors preferred a low profile, investing in Southern enterprises led by local entrepreneurs familiar with conditions and respected in the community.[29] They entered the region chiefly by setting up alliances with indigenous groups of capitalists. Woodward, Baldwin and Company established close relations with the Saluda Valley mills at Piedmont and Pelzer, aided in the latter case by a marriage tie between Pelzer's president, Ellison A. Smyth, and the Baldwins. By the early twentieth century, the Baltimore firm represented twenty-one South Carolina mills, sixteen of them in counties lying along the Saluda River, where the influence of Smyth and the pioneer Greenville industrialists was most strongly felt.[30] A similar connection with a group of Spartanburg capitalists helped introduce the closely related interests of Deering, Milliken and Company, a New York commission house, and Lockwood, Greene and Company, a Boston engineering firm, to the opportunities available in Southern textiles.[31] Other investors entered the field through Southern agents, such as J. E. Sirrine, who headed Lockwood, Greene's Greenville office before striking out on his own; the mill engineer W. B. Smith Whaley of Columbia; and two Charlotte-based "packagers" of mills, D. A. Tompkins and H. S. Chadwick. All four engaged in aggressive promotion of new textile firms in connection with their engineering and machinery businesses.[32]

The caution of Northern investors venturing South appeared not only in their insistence on developing local contacts but also in their tendency to enter a firm only in the later stages of its development, usually responding to an appeal from the firm for funds to make up a capital shortfall. The board of the Pacolet Manufacturing Company, for example, consisted at the time of its organization in 1882 entirely of South Carolinians, but by 1883 had Amos Lockwood of Lockwood, Greene and J. D. Murchison of Baltimore as members. By 1895, one-third of its stock was held in the Northeast.[33]

For the reasons given above, Northern interests had only scanty representation on the original boards of directors of up-country mills. That fact, however, obscures the vital contribution made by Northerners to the industry's success. Of special importance were the commission merchants, who in many respects organized the industry. They brought prospective manufacturers together with engineers and machinery men, who supplied important technical services unavailable in a region only on the threshold of development. By virtue of their connections with the great Northeastern textile markets, they were able to supply a constant and indispensable stream of advice on salable constructions of cloth and levels of production, in effect making major production decisions for the client firm. Their contacts among capitalists and major financial institutions enabled the more important houses to serve as investment bankers for the mills, floating stock and bond issues and loans, guaranteeing credit extended by suppliers, and, most importantly, serving as sources of short-term capital for the financing of operations, which in a chronically capital-short region would otherwise have been difficult.[34] The commission merchants and other Northern investors have frequently been accused of helping perpetuate the "colonial economy" of the South;[35] however, their role was on balance conducive both to economic development and to social modernization in the South. Above all, their alliance with the developing local commercial and industrial elites provided those elites with an important source of strength independent of the traditional Southern power structure.

The other major outside source of capital and entrepreneurial talent was Charleston, the long-time mercantile capital of the state. With the decline of the old factorage system and the failure of the newer phosphate industry to supply an adequate outlet for their excess funds, Charleston capitalists were looking to the up-country. Practically all Charleston capital invested in up-state mills came from the closely intertwined mercantile and phosphate interests. Leading the movement were Francis J. Pelzer, the leading cotton factor and a leading phosphate manufacturer, and Ellison A. Smyth, a former cotton factor and banker who became the single most important up-country industrialist. However, thirteen of Charleston's twenty-two seats were on the boards of three firms—Pelzer, Enoree in Spartanburg County, and Courtenay in Oconee County—all large water-power developments controlled by Charleston interests. The other nine seats were scattered among nine different corporations. Thus, while Charleston investments in such firms as Pelzer could be enormous, they exaggerate the influence exercised by Charleston interests over the development of the industry.

Despite important contributions of capital and expertise from outside the region, then, the data on mill directors indicate that the organization of mill corporations in the South Carolina up-country was largely accomplished by local people, chiefly engaged in the occupations of commerce and law. These tendencies among the early industrial leadership appear even more strongly among the most important mill officials, the presidents. All but four of the seventy-two identified presidents lived within the region; of the four, one was a Charlestonian who moved to Oconee County, two were Charlotteans, and one was from Gastonia, North Carolina. As to occupation, table 4.3 indicates an overwhelming preponderance of commercial

Table 4.3
MILL PRESIDENTS RESIDING IN THE SOUTH CAROLINA UP-COUNTRY,
1880-1907, BY OCCUPATION

	NO. SEATS		%		NO. INDIVS.		%	
Commerce	58		68.2		49		68.1	
Merchants		50		58.8		42		58.3
Bankers		5		5.9		4		5.6
Other		3		3.5		3		4.2
Manufacturers	10		11.8		7		9.7	
Cotton		5		5.9		4		5.5
Other		5		5.9		3		4.2
Lawyers	6		7.1		6		8.3	
Other professional	1		1.2		1		1.4	
Agricultural	9		10.6		8		11.1	
Other	1		1.2		1		1.4	
Total	85		100.1		72		100.0	

Note: Percentages were subject to rounding.

men at the head of operations. On the other hand, not only did few farmers or planters serve as mill presidents, but the firms over which they presided averaged only $92,000 in initial capitalization; by comparison, the average initial capitalization for new firms during the period 1887-1907, for which complete data are available, was $171,000. Commercial dominance of the presidential ranks, of course, made perfect sense in a region that was only beginning to develop a pool of industrial managers. The principal duties of a mill president were financial and commercial, not technical, as can be seen in the fact that nearly 60 percent of the mill presidents combined the offices of president and treasurer. Pioneer manufacturer D. E. Converse assured the promoters of the Pacolet Manufacturing Company that "any good business man that could control men and money could manage a cotton mill." H. P. Hammett, in a letter to the Newberry banker R. L. McCaughrin endorsing the latter's proposed mill project, argued that:

Your experience and reputation as a financier in this country, and your knowledge of and familiarity with the commercial part of the operations, is a guarantee to me that those departments will be well and wisely managed.

As for technical expertise, "Your judgement of the fitness of men will always enable you to keep a good manufacturer in the mill."[36]

While the localism and commercial orientation of the up-country industrial leadership are important factors, they achieve full significance only on the community level. For that reason, a brief examination of a single sizable group of local directors is in order. Within a four-year period stretching from 1899 to 1904, six major cotton mill corporations constructed factories on the outskirts of the town of Anderson.[37] The forty-three directors' seats on the boards of these mills were held by twenty-nine individuals, all of whom have been identified. Of these, two commission merchants and a machinery manufacturer represented out-of-state interests; every other director but one lived in Anderson County, and that one director, veteran cotton manufacturer James L. Orr of Greenville, belonged to a prominent Anderson family. Twenty-one of the twenty-nine resided in or near the town of Anderson. Of these, eleven were merchants, three bankers, three lawyers, one a physician and druggist, one a cotton oil manufacturer, and one the rising young textile executive Robert E. Ligon. Only two farmers sat on the boards, one a resident of Anderson, the other from the nearby rural community of Varennes. If only those directors holding more than one seat are considered, an even tighter picture emerges; ten men (seven merchants, two bankers, and Ligon) held twenty-four directorates, or over half the to- tal. The influence of Anderson capital was not confined to its own neigh- borhood. Three of the twenty-one Anderson directors combined with other Andersonians to establish the Calhoun Mills at Calhoun Falls, a site on the Charleston and Western Carolina Railroad some thirty miles toward Au- gusta. Three members of the group also joined with several residents of the town of Iva, eighteen miles toward Augusta, to build a mill there.

Such extension of interests by a local group of capitalists to outlying areas was typical only of the three largest up-country manufacturing centers, but the dominance among the industrial leadership of commercial interests based in the towns was typical of the entire up-country. In that general ob- servation, in fact, lies the key to understanding the stimulus to industrialize that appears so strongly in the region in the late nineteenth and early twen- tieth centuries. The crucial feature was less the rise of the commercial classes, important as that was, than it was the rise of the town, not as a mere aggregation of competing businessmen, but as a social organism im- parting distinctive ideas about social organization and the pursuit of progress.

The development of the up-country town as a major social force dated from the aftermath of the Civil War.[38] At that time, the antebellum eco- nomic structure of South Carolina, as of the South in general, lay in utter disarray. The cords binding the interior to the great factorage centers of the coast were largely destroyed by physical destruction, neglect, and the Union blockade. Worse, the fundamental productive unit, the plantation, lay shattered by emancipation. As the economy was recreated, a striking new pattern emerged. The new credit system, using as its basic security a lien on the prospective cotton crop, came to be administered, not by factors working through planters, but by small local merchants dealing directly with the tenant farmers and sharecroppers who replaced the plantation gangs as the basic agricultural labor force of the cotton South. At the same time, the rail system, which in antebellum times had functioned largely as an adjunct to commercial Charleston, was being rearranged to permit direct overland communication with the Northeast. This important change in Southern economic life had many consequences, but among the most socially far-reaching was its creation of numerous small interior market towns situated on the rail lines. A single line, the Atlanta and Charlotte Air Line, stimulated the creation of eleven new towns along its route in its first ten years of operation and made Greenville and Spartanburg the major commercial centers of the up-country. By 1880, thirteen up-country towns were of sufficient importance to be classified as "rural cotton centers" by Ransom and Sutch.

As the towns grew, they developed new economic and social institutions under the sponsorship of more or less cohesive groups of leaders from the business and professional communities. Often, the central role was performed by the owners of the large general mercantile and cotton firms. The four most important establishments—Heath, Springs and Company in Lancaster; W. L. Roddey and Son in Rock Hill; S. Bleckley and Company in Anderson; and Walker, Fleming and Company in Spartanburg—each boasted an estimated worth in 1889 of between $100,000 and $200,000.[39] The role of the members of the firm of Walker, Fleming and Company in the economic and civic life of Spartanburg is illustrative of the relationship of the rising commercial elite to the towns. The firm was founded in 1866 by Joseph Walker; in 1872, he took as a partner Dr. C. E. Fleming, a physician who had just returned from a postwar sojourn in the West. In 1876, they were joined by John H. Montgomery, a farmer who had moved to town and become a fertilizer merchant. When Montgomery left the firm in 1884, the remaining partners took in J. H. Sloan, a young merchant, and became Walker, Fleming and Sloan. The Walker, Fleming partners could easily have rested content with running one of the largest up-country mercantile firms; however, since they identified their own interests closely with those of the town, their energies spilled over into a variety of activities having as their common object the "upbuilding" of Spartanburg. Joseph Walker was a director of one Spartanburg bank and president of another, and served as head of a building and loan association. In addition, he was a director of three railroads (two of them feeding into Spartanburg), a fire insurance company, a cotton oil mill, and the local daily newspaper. His civic activities included six terms as mayor of Spartanburg; his administration was marked by major street improvements, the expansion of police and fire protection, and the completion of the Opera House. "There has scarcely been any important enterprise undertaken in the history of Spartanburg," asserted a biographer, "in which he has not been an efficient actor." C. E.

Fleming was involved in many of the same economic enterprises; his civic activities included the secretaryship of the board of trustees of the town library, the vice-presidency of the board of trade, and the presidency of the board of trustees of the graded school system, all of which he helped organize. All three of the partners served on the original board of trustees of Converse College. Most important of all, however, at least for present purposes, the partners were intensely involved in the industrialization of the Spartanburg area. In 1881, the firm bought the Trough Shoals water power site on the Pacolet River southeast of town, and the next year organized the Pacolet Manufacturing Company, of which Montgomery became president. In later years, Montgomery became president of Spartan Mills, Fleming of the Whitney Manufacturing Company, and Sloan of the Beaumont Manufacturing Company, all located in or adjacent to the town of Spartanburg. The firm was well represented on the boards of directors of local mills, Walker, Fleming, and Sloan serving on three apiece, and Montgomery on four.[40]

The varied interests and energy of the Walker, Fleming partners were characteristic of numerous groups of merchants and professionals, large and small, in the various up-country towns. Common to them all was a view of the town as a sort of informal corporate enterprise whose identity was embodied in a complex of interlocking institutions and whose advancement, civic and economic, was the sine qua non both of their economic welfare and of their enjoyment of its fruits. Their devotion to material progress was coupled with a faith in cooperative effort as the key to achieving community goals. "If we want our town to grow," argued a Newberry editor, "we must go to work all together to inaugurate such enterprises as will make it grow." Newspapers extolled "the pooling of interests and combination of resources" as "more than anything else conducive to the upbuilding of a city"; young merchants choosing locations picked their hometowns on the basis of "the spirit of unity manifest in most of its leading citizens."[41] The combination of such attitudes with the accumulation of disposable wealth spurred the creation of a distinctive town culture, characterized by the aggressive development of an economic and institutional life whose complexity and sophistication had never before been seen in the up-country.

It was this "town spirit," borne chiefly by ambitious young business leaders, that led to an industrial surge at the turn of the century.[42] In this sense, Mitchell was correct in arguing that the "rise of the mills" was a community enterprise. The cotton mill was ranked only behind the railroad as an efficacious means of building up local fortunes. The profitability of cotton manufacturing, lucrative as it seemed, was only one of its lures to prospective town investors. Mills were expected to raise local real estate values and to attract an increased population to the town, with a resultant expansion of trade. As large purchasers of cotton, they were to bid up local cotton prices and attract outlying farmers to sell (and buy) in the town. Industrial demand for capital goods, it was hoped, would stimulate auxiliary industries. The result of establishing a cotton mill, then, was to be a significant increase in the wealth of the entire community, wealth not simply to be used for private enjoyment but also to help finance the new civic improvements, the schools and colleges, and all the other amenities with which the ambitious townsmen sought to surround themselves. Finally, the massive buildings and towering smokestacks were to serve as advertisements of the town's vigor and energy and, ultimately, as emblems of civic pride. At this level, expressions of devotion to the dream of local glory sometimes approached awkward poetry, as when a Spartanburg editor called for a mill as "something about which the business men of the city can talk—boast of—'the best in the South,' &c, something to please the ladies and something for the children to wonder at."[43]

For these reasons, then, the "townspeople" banded together in corporations to build cotton mills, at a pace that by the turn of the century became breathtaking. In so doing, they forever altered the landscape and the social order of the South Carolina up-country, introducing new forms of society, creating new social classes and class conflicts, and, above all, leading the traditional South one step closer to the modern American mainstream. To be sure, while the "townspeople" were a modernizing elite, they were not "modern" in any ideal-typical sense. Evangelical piety and old republican virtue were fully as important to them as competitive individualism and the free market. Even while they proceeded with their industrial schemes, they worried about the social consequences and adopted measures ranging from "cotton mill paternalism" to modern social legislation to deal with them.[44] Their conservatism, though, does not make them in any way extensions of the planter class or analogues to Prussian Junkers.[45] They were, by and large, small-town businessmen, endowed like all their kind with a combination of faith in the material future and fears for the moral future, both faith and fear ironically stemming from their perception of the way in which their own activities were altering the world. Like all men in history, they were bound both to their past and to their future. As deeply attached as they were to a vision of the Southern past, however, they chose to strive toward an urban and industrial future. Ultimately, their choice was that of the South.

Notes

1. C. Vann Woodward, *Origins of the New South, 1877-1913.* A History of the South, vol. 9 (Baton Rouge: Louisiana State University Press, 1951), pp. 140-41.

2. Harold D. Woodman, *King Cotton and His Retainers: Financing and Marketing the Cotton Crop of the South, 1800-1925* (Lexington: University of Kentucky Press, 1968), esp. Chap. 25; Roger Ransom and Richard Sutch, *One Kind of Freedom: The Economic Consequences of Emancipation* (New York: Cambridge University Press, 1977). Woodman argues that crucial changes in the Southern economic structure began to occur in the 1850s with the expansion of railroads and interior commerce. For a provocative interpretation of the implications of these changes for late antebellum society, see J. Mills Thornton III, *Politics and Power in a Slave Society: Alabama 1800-1860* (Baton Rouge: Louisiana State University Press, 1978).

3. Jay R. Mandle, *The Roots of Black Poverty: The Southern Plantation Economy after the Civil War* (Durham, N.C.: Duke University Press, 1978); Jonathan M. Wiener, *Social Origins of the New South: Alabama, 1860-1885* (Baton Rouge: Louisiana State University Press, 1978); Dwight B. Billings, Jr., *Planters and the Making of a "New South": Class, Politics, and Development in North Carolina, 1865-1900* (Chapel Hill: University of North Carolina Press, 1979). Studies along similar lines for Mississippi by Lester Salamon and for Atlanta by Floyd Hunter exist in unpublished form.

4. While it is beyond the scope of the present paper to delve into the nature of antebellum Southern society, it should be noted that the assumptions about the antebellum South commonly made by most writers on the postwar period are open to question. On this point, see Thornton, *Politics and Power*, which, by stressing Alabama planters' close links to the world market, Whiggish politics, and widening commercial and industrial interests in the 1850s, suggests that the distinction between planters and such other "classes" as merchants and industrialists may be overdrawn. See esp. pp. 40-42, Chap. 5.

5. I am defining the "up-country" as that part of the state lying north and west of Aiken, Lexington, Richland, Kershaw, and Chesterfield counties, comprising eighteen modern counties (see map, p. 46).

6. David L. Carlton, "Mill and Town: The Cotton Mill Workers and the Middle Class in South Carolina, 1880-1920" (Ph. D. diss., Yale University, 1977).

7. U.S. Census Office, *Eleventh Census, 1890*, vol. 6: *Manufactures*, p. 584; U.S. Department of Commerce and Labor, Bureau of the Census, Bulletin No. 74, *Census of Manufactures, 1905: Textiles*, Tables 16 and 18; South Carolina Department of Agriculture, Commerce and Industries, Labor Division, *Report, 1910*, p. 33.

8. Much of the following analysis is based on information compiled on this group of mill corporations, comprising those organized to build up-country mills named in August Kohn's 1907 directory; see August Kohn, *The Cotton Mills of South Carolina* (Columbia: South Carolina Department of Agriculture, Commerce and Immigration, 1907), pp. 214-17. I have subtracted those early mills listed by J. K. Blackman as having been in operation in 1880; ibid., p. 20. In all cases in which two or more corporations operated the same mill, I have used the original firm alone. The basic formation on the various firms (capitalization, date of organization, and names of officials) was collected from the South Carolina Secretary of State Charter Books for Private Corporations, 1887 through 1907, in South Carolina Department of Archives and History, Columbia; and Gustave G. Williamson, Jr., "Cotton Manufacturing in South Carolina, 1865-1892" (unpub. Ph. D. diss., Johns Hopkins University, 1954), Tables 2 and 3.

9. South Carolina Secretary of State, *Annual Reports, 1887-1907*; Kohn, *Cotton Mills*, p. 91. Billings' study of cotton mill "ownership" (see *Planters*, pp. 62-69) ends in 1884, on the assumption that no important change in the pattern of development takes place after that date. Most of Billings' mills, however, were extremely small (with a median spindleage of 1,800), water-powered rural mills, many of which were survivals of antebellum times and most of which bore little resemblance to the much larger factories built around the turn of the century. See Richard W. Griffin, "Reconstruction of the North Carolina Textile Industry, 1865-1885," *North Carolina Historical Review* 41 (1964), 51-53, for the list of mills used by Billings. Both Wiener and Billings tend to assume that the patterns they discern in the immediate postwar period persist for decades, if not generations, afterward.

10. Compiled from Kohn, *Cotton Mills*, pp. 91-98.

11. Compiled from ibid., pp. 86-98.

12. Williamson, "Cotton Manufacturing," pp. 148-49.

13. John H. Montgomery to Seth M. Milliken, January 17, 1900. John H. Montgomery Letterbook (on microfilm), South Caroliniana Library, University of South Carolina, Columbia.

14. Kohn, *Cotton Mills*, p. 178.

15. David R. Coker, "Papers Read Before the Manufacturers' Association of South Carolina at Their Annual Meetings, June 1908 and 1911" (Hartsville, S.C.: Hartsville Publishing Co., n.d.).

16. Alfred D. Chandler, Jr., *The Visible Hand: The Managerial Revolution in American Business* (Cambridge: Harvard University Press, 1977), pp. 89, 188, 195; Woodman, *King Cotton*, p. 273.

17. Gathered from South Carolina Secretary of State Charter Books and, for boards missing from the official records: Charleston *News and Courier*, January 22, 1880, for Clifton Manufacturing Co.; ibid., May 26, 1880, for Fishing Creek Manufacturing Co.; ibid., February 4, 1881, for Pelzer Manufacturing Co.; ibid., February 13, 1882, for Huguenot Mills; Douglas Summers Brown, *A City Without Cobwebs: A History of Rock Hill, S.C.* (Columbia: University of South Carolina Press, 1953), p. 186, for the Rock Hill Cotton Factory; Spartanburg *Carolina Spartan*, April 19, 1882, for the Pacolet Manufacturing Co.; Newberry *Herald and News*, May 10, 1883, for the Newberry Cotton Mills; Rock Hill *Herald*, May 5, 1887, for Fort Mill Manufacturing Co.; Elliott White Springs, *Clothes Make the Man* (New York: J. J. Little and Ives, 1948), p. 27, for Chester Manufacturing Co.; *Carolina Spartan*, March 14, 1888, for Whitney Manufacturing Company; and Anderson *Intelligencer*, June 7, 1888, for Anderson Cotton Mills. Original boards for the Cherokee Falls Manufacturing Co. (1882) and the Mills Manufacturing Company (1895) could not be determined. The original board of directors of Spartan Mills (1890) changed drastically soon after its organization; in this one case, I have used the second board. On the nature and background of the change, see Allen Heath Stokes, Jr., "John H. Montgomery: A Pioneer Southern Industrialist" (unpub. M.A. thesis, University of South Carolina, 1967), pp. 54-61.

18. *South Carolina Statutes at Large* 19 (1886), 540-50.

19. According to state law at the time, a charter could be granted to a private corporation when 50 percent of its capital stock had been subscribed and 20 percent had been paid in. *Code of Laws in South Carolina*, 1902 (Columbia: The State Com-

pany, 1902), Chap. 48, sections 1883-84.

20. I made use of a number of sources in identifying directors; they are (in order of use): (A) biographical directories, from which were drawn around 60 percent of the identifications. The principal directories used were: *Cyclopedia of Eminent and Representative Men of the Carolinas of the Nineteenth Century*, vol. 1: *South Carolina* (Madison, Wis.: Brant and Fuller, 1892); J. C. Garlington, *Men of the Time* (Spartanburg, S.C.: Garlington Publishing Co., 1902); J. C. Hemphill, ed., *Men of Mark in South Carolina*, 4 vols. (Washington: Men of Mark Publishing Co., 1908); Geddings Hardy Crawford, ed., *Who's Who in South Carolina* (Columbia: McCaw of Columbia, 1921); Walker Scott Utsey, ed., *Who's Who in South Carolina, 1934-1935* (Columbia: Current Historical Assoc., 1935); Yates Snowden, ed., *History of South Carolina*, vols. 3-5 (Chicago and New York: Lewis Publishing Co., 1920); and David Duncan Wallace, *The History of South Carolina*, vol. 4 (New York: American Historical Society, 1934); (B) various descriptive accounts of South Carolina towns and counties, too numerous to list; (C) city directories, chiefly for Charleston, although a 1905 directory for Anderson also was consulted; and (D) the manuscript census returns for 1880 and 1900, on microfilm at the South Carolina Department of Archives and History, Columbia.

21. Billings, *Planters*, pp. 62-69, used lists of prominent local landowners to establish his point that a majority of early North Carolina mill owners were "planters and prominent agrarians." Wiener, commenting on an earlier draft of this paper, has argued that my use of principal occupations to characterize the directors understates the degree to which large planters appear among the local elite since many doctors, lawyers, and merchants also held large tracts of land. There was, to be sure, considerable interpenetration among the various occupational groups, and any man apt to be influential in a cotton-manufacturing corporation was apt to own sizable amounts of land, the most important kind of capital in what was still a largely agrarian society. However, there are technical problems involved in the use of landownership as a variable. Wiener's 1870 census data on value of real estate are unavailable for succeeding censuses, and the bulk of the directors have been identified by other means than the census. Billings' method is too rough to be of much value. More importantly, the use of landholding begs the question by assuming that large-scale landownership made an individual ipso facto a member of the "planter class." Whatever the social meaning of landownership in the antebellum South, it became decidedly more complex and ambiguous in the postwar years, and many large landowners by then were men whose outlook on life partook little of the old planter or agrarian ideal. In addition, if one proceeds on the assumption that control of the means of production is the crucial factor to be determined, it can be argued that control of credit is at least as important as control of land; yet this, the principal source of the power of the commercial classes in the postbellum South, is ignored by both Wiener and Billings. While the use of principal occupation as a measure presents some problems, especially in deciding on the classification of borderline cases (a necessarily subjective process), it is the best method I know of making use of the available data to present the basic orientation of the elite population presently under consideration.

22. For purposes of convenience, I have used the occupation of a director in 1880

or at the time he took his first seat, whichever came later. Thus, pioneer cotton manufacturers, such as John H. Montgomery and Ellison Smyth, are identified as merchants, although they assumed the bulk of their seats as manufacturers.

23. On antebellum banks, see the list in Alfred Glaze Smith, Jr., *Economic Readjustment of an Old Cotton State: South Carolina, 1820-1860* (Columbia: University of South Carolina Press, 1958), p. 194; on the "drummer" as a late nineteenth-century phenomenon, see Chandler, *Visible Hand*, p. 219.

24. *Cyclopedia of Eminent and Representative Men*, vol. 1, 430-31.

25. *Our Monthly* (Clinton, S.C.) 37 (August 1900), 453. The quote is from Wiener, *Social Origins*, p. 203.

26. Broadus Mitchell, *The Rise of Cotton Mills in the South*, Johns Hopkins University Studies in Historical and Political Science, series 39, no. 2 (Baltimore: Johns Hopkins University Press, 1921), pp. 134-36.

27. Rev. Watson B. Duncan, *Twentieth Century Sketches of the South Carolina Conference, M.E. Church, South* (Columbia, S.C.: The State Co., 1901), pp. 274-75; Abbeville *Press and Banner*, May 13, 1896; Samuel B. Lincoln, *Lockwood Greene: The History of an Engineering Business, 1832-1958* (Brattleboro, Vt.: Stephen Greene Press, 1960), pp. 155-56, 191-92, on J. E. Sirrine.

28. Stokes, "Montgomery," pp. 56-61.

29. Mary Baldwin Baer and John Wilbur Baer, *A History of Woodward, Baldwin and Company* (Annapolis, Md.: private, 1977), p. 21; John H. Montgomery to John A. Fant, November 15, 1899. Montgomery letterbook, South Caroliniana Library.

30. Baer and Baer, *Woodward, Baldwin*, pp. 22, 71.

31. Stokes, "Montgomery," passim.

32. On Tompkins, see Howard B. Clay, "Daniel Augustus Tompkins: An American Bourbon" (unpub. Ph.D. diss., University of North Carolina, 1950); on Chadwick, see George Sweet Gibb, *The Saco-Lowell Shops: Textile Machinery Building in New England, 1813-1949*, Harvard Studies in Business History, vol. 16 (Cambridge: Harvard University Press, 1950), p. 312; on Whaley, Fenelon Devere Smith, "The Economic Development of the Textile Industry in the Columbia, S.C., Area from 1790 Through 1916" (unpub. Ph.D. diss., University of Kentucky, 1952). Billings attempts to use Tompkins as an illustration of continued planter rule in the postwar South by stressing his background as "the college-educated son of a South Carolina planter who had financed his earliest business enterprises" (*Planters*, pp. 64, 123-25). He neglects to note, however, that Tompkins worked his way through college and served an extended apprenticeship as an engineer and machinist, and that the "investment" was a $400 loan to help Tompkins open his machinery business. Even assuming that Tompkins' "planter" background controlled his behavior, Billings supplies no evidence that Tompkins' outlook was any different from that of other "bourgeois" of his time. See Clay, "Tompkins," pp. 7-25.

33. *Carolina Spartan*, May 2, 1883; list of stockholders of Pacolet Manufacturing Co., December 31, 1895, in F. E. Taylor Papers, South Caroliniana Library.

34. For a discussion of the role played by the leading commission merchant handling South Carolina accounts, see Baer and Baer, *Woodward, Baldwin*; see also Williamson, "Cotton Manufacturing," pp. 66-67, 220-22; Mitchell, *Rise*, pp. 241-55.

35. E.g., Woodward, *Origins*, p. 308.

36. *Carolina Spartan,* May 17, 1883; H. P. Hammett to R. L. McCaughrin, February 17, 1886, in H. P. Hammett Letterbooks (on microfilm), South Caroliniana Library.

37. The six were (1) The Orr Cotton Mills (1899); (2) The Riverside Manufacturing Co. (1900); (3) The Cox Manufacturing Co. (1900): (4) The Brogon Mills (1902); (5) The Gluck Mills (1903); and (6) The Toxaway Mills (1903). A seventh, The H. C. Townsend Cotton Mill, was very small and was in effect wholly owned by a local lumber dealer.

38. The succeeding paragraph is based on Ransom and Sutch, *One Kind of Freedom,* esp. pp. 116-19, 300-305; Woodman, *King Cotton,* chaps. 23-25; and Carlton, "Mill and Town," pp. 14-23.

39. The Mercantile Association of the Carolinas, *Reference Book, July 1889* (Wilmington, N.C.: Jackson and Bell, 1889).

40. The discussion of Walker, Fleming and Co. is based on sketches in *Cyclopedia of Eminent and Representative Men,* vol. 1, 344-45, 462-65, 482-83; Fronde Kennedy et al., *A History of Spartanburg County* (Spartanburg, S.C.: Band and White, 1940), pp. 205, 213, 221, 222; *Historical and Descriptive Review of the State of South Carolina* (Charleston: Empire Publishing Co., 1884), vol. 3, 155-56; and Charleston *News and Courier,* July 28, 1890.

41. Newberry *Herald and News,* February 6, 1890; Columbia *State,* January 3, 1894; W. C. Hamrick, *Life Values in the New South* (Gaffney, S.C.: by the author, 1931), p. 107.

42. Of the directors of mills organized between 1895 and 1907, over 80 percent were born in 1848 or later; the median year of birth for the group was 1857. The vast majority of those organizing mills in the boom years, then, came of age in the years following the Civil War, and were in effect the first generation to "make it" in the "New South."

43. Carlton, "Mill and Town," pp. 48-62; the quote is from *Carolina Spartan,* May 30, 1883.

44. Carlton, "Mill and Town," passim.

45. Billings' thesis that the industrialization of North Carolina was a Prussian- or Japanese-style "revolution from above" rests in part on an implicit comparison of Southern industrialists to an abstract model of a "bourgeois" man that he suggests existed in the North (see *Planters,* p. 105) but that I submit has never existed anywhere. See esp. Stuart Brandes, *American Welfare Capitalism* (Chicago: University of Chicago Press, 1976), which demonstrates that "paternalism" was by no means unique to the South in this period. See also Anthony F. C. Wallace's remarkable book *Rockdale: The Growth of an American Village in the Early Industrial Revolution* (New York: Knopf, 1978); not only does the "paternalism" he finds in the antebellum cotton mills of Delaware County, Pennsylvania, sound strikingly familiar to a student of the Southern industry, but his "Northern" entrepreneurs appear as far less "modern" in their outlook than Billings assumes them to be.

III

THE CITY ELITE: THE CASE OF
CHARLESTON, SOUTH CAROLINA

Few cities offer more fertile ground for exploring the topic of elite leadership than Charleston, the most self-conscious of Southern cities. The authors of the three following articles examine aspects of class leadership in Charleston from 1860 to 1910. They answer some questions while raising others about the role of the city elite in the South during the late nineteenth century.

Professor Michael P. Johnson in "Wealth and Class in Charleston in 1860" uses census data to determine the "material basis of the class structure of the city" on the eve of the Civil War. He finds that 20 percent of the population owned almost all of the wealth, while most free, white Charlestonians were propertyless. Thus, the economic status of most white Charlestonians was much closer to that of slaves than to that of the elite, wealthy, slaveholding population. Therefore, Johnson believes that "from the perspective of most white Charlestonians, class divisions were as obvious as racial divisions." Violations of the caste system and the competition of slaves with the white working class exacerbated class divisions and bred class tension and potential class conflict. Charleston's elite was well aware of this, Johnson concludes, but they did nothing. Any change may have threatened the social structure and their own vested interests.

Urban geographer Professor John P. Radford in "Social Structure and Urban Form: Charleston, 1860-1880" supports Johnson's view as to the influence and values of the city's elite. In his examination of the "social geography" and the "morphology" (or physical form) of the city, Radford finds little change during the twenty-year period of Civil War and Reconstruction. By comparison to the western urban experience, this was unique. Despite the personal tragedy and physical destruction, neither Charleston society, its "social geography," nor its "morphology" was turned "bottom side up." This was due to the influence of an entrenched, conservative elite whose "tastes . . . motives [and] perceptions . . . retarded the process of modernization." Like Johnson's elite, Radford's "aristocrats" were interested less in change than in continuity.

The conclusions reached about the values and influences of Charleston's elite by both Johnson and Radford bear a striking resemblance to those of Professor Don H. Doyle in "Leadership and Decline in Postwar Charleston, 1865-1910." While admitting that there were external forces that caused economic stagnation in the city following the Civil War and that there were efforts to stimulate growth, Doyle argues that a major obstacle to expansion came from an internal source: the city's conservative elite. Its social and business organizations reflected its "cult of leisure" and a "tradition-bound cast of mind." Status was awarded on the basis of family ties and social graces, while innovative, entrepreneurial talent that challenged these mores was thwarted. The elite refused to "surrender their ideals and the whole system of social organization that was integrally connected to their ideology." Unlike some other cities of the New South, Doyle concludes, the pervasive influences of Charleston's backward-looking elite managed to preserve the values of the Old South well into the "New."

5

WEALTH AND CLASS IN CHARLESTON IN 1860

Michael P. Johnson

During June and July 1860, census marshals went door-to-door through the city of Charleston collecting information for the federal census.[1] By "personal inquiry of each head of family," the marshals were instructed to obtain the value of the real and personal property owned by each individual, along with a variety of other information. The value of all real estate was supposed to be reported, no matter where it was located. Marshals were instructed "not to consider any question of lien or encumbrance," but "simply . . . to enter the value as given by the respondent." Personal property was supposed to include such items as "bonds, mortgages, notes, slaves, live stock, plate, jewels, or furniture; in fine, the value of whatever constitutes the personal wealth of individuals." The census marshals' instructions cautioned that "Exact accuracy may not be arrived at, but all persons should be encouraged to give a near and prompt estimate for your information."[2]

Charlestonians' answers to the questions of the census marshals were preserved in the manuscript census schedules. Those answers are the basis of this study of the distribution of wealth among the city's free population on the eve of the Civil War.[3] The wealth reports, along with other information reported to the census marshals, allow us to estimate the accuracy of the census data, to describe how wealth was distributed in the city, and to focus on features of the relationship between wealth and class.

Charlestonians reported owning wealth of a little over $38 million, about equally divided between real and personal property.[4] Other data indicate that Charlestonians significantly underestimated their wealth when they reported it to the census marshals. In a separate schedule of the census, marshal William H. Gibbes noted that the city assessor's book valued wealth in the city at well over $54 million.[5] Since the assessor's book has not survived, as far as I know, I have not been able to confirm the accuracy of

Gibbes's report. But if that was the value of the wealth owned by the city's residents in 1860, then the federal census marshals were told about only 70 percent of it.[6] Most likely, individuals with considerable wealth gave the census marshals a very conservative estimate of its value.[7] If so, then the data analyzed in this paper understate the proportion of wealth owned by wealthier individuals.

In spite of this bias toward the low side, the wealth data from the census merit careful study. Although Charleston was not on the best of terms with the federal government in the summer of 1860, there was no evidence that Charlestonians refused to cooperate with the census marshals, who were themselves Charleston residents. Seven of the eight were listed in the current city directory; four were listed eight years earlier in the 1852 directory.[8] Although other Charlestonians may not have known the census marshals personally, it is unlikely that they perceived the marshals as total strangers or as meddlesome outsiders representing the federal government. None of the marshals reported any resistance to their inquiries. The census schedules themselves give every indication of having been completed systematically, fully, and conscientiously. The wealth data in the census are far from perfect, but they are certainly the best information available.[9] Like an old photograph in which the image is blurred and faded, the census reports are flawed but nonetheless quite revealing.

At first glance, it might appear that the best way to study the distribution of wealth would be to consider the wealth of each free adult in the city.[10] But if that were done, it would mistakenly portray dependent members of wealthy households—such as spouses, children, and other relatives—as having little or no wealth. For example, wives in the wealthiest households in Charleston owned less than 1 percent of the total household wealth.[11] In fact, of course, the lives of these women and of other dependent household members were deeply affected by the wealth of the head of the household. Therefore, the best first approximation to the social significance of wealth ownership is to consider the household as the basic unit of wealth holding and the wealth of the head of the household as the best index of the wealth of all household members.[12] In Charleston, only 18 percent of the free population were heads of household—some 4,644 in all. But they owned 86 percent of all the wealth reported to the census marshals. Analysis of the distribution of this wealth reveals the material basis of the class structure of the city.

The one word that best describes the distribution of wealth in Charleston is "unequal." The richest 1 percent of the population[13] owned wealth ranging from $104,000 to $538,000. In all, as table 5.1 shows, these forty-eight individuals owned 27 percent of the city's wealth.[14] Just over 3 percent of the population—some 160 people—owned half of the wealth.[15] More than three quarters of the city's wealth was owned by the top 10 percent of the

Table 5.1
WEALTH DISTRIBUTION IN CHARLESTON

LOWER LIMIT PERCENTILE OF WEALTH GROUP	MINIMUM WEALTH IN GROUP	TOTAL WEALTH SHARE IN GROUP (%)	CUMULATIVE SHARE OF TOTAL WEALTH (%)
1%	$104,200	26.9	26.9
2%	$ 70,000	12.2	39.1
3%	$ 51,200	8.1	47.2
4%	$ 42,000	7.3	54.5
5%	$ 35,000	5.6	60.1
10%	$ 18,000	16.8	76.9
15%	$ 10,600	9.7	86.6
20%	$ 6,000	6.5	93.1
25%	$ 4,000	3.0	96.1
30%	$ 2,000	2.3	98.4
100%	$ 0	1.6	100.0

Gini coefficient = 0.887
N = 4,644 heads of household

population; the top 20 percent owned 93 percent of the wealth. The bottom 70 percent owned less than 2 percent of the wealth. The bottom 56 percent owned no wealth whatever. In short, a handful of Charlestonians owned most of the wealth, a fifth of the free population owned almost all of the wealth, and most Charlestonians were propertyless.[16]

Compared with the nation as a whole, Charleston had much more than its share of the very rich and the very poor. In the entire country, only one man in 1,000 owned $111,000 or more; in Charleston, nine times as many men owned wealth of that magnitude.[17] Only 1 percent of all Americans owned as much as $40,000, but four and a half times as many Charlestonians owned that much.[18] At the other extreme, the 56 percent of Charlestonians who owned no property was half again as many as in the nation as a whole.[19] Given these extremes of wealth in the city, it makes a great deal of difference what one considers the average wealth in Charleston. The mean wealth in the city was just over $7,000, three and a half times larger than the mean wealth in the North and almost twice as large as the mean wealth in the South.[20] Yet 81 percent of the people of Charleston owned less than the mean wealth. Indeed, the median wealth holding in the city—namely, the minimum wealth owned by the top half of the population—was zero.

These measures actually understate the inequality of wealth ownership in the city since they consider slaves as property rather than as people. If the value of the slaves owned by individual slaveowners is deducted from their total wealth and the slaves are included as propertyless members of the population, the result will be a more accurate portrait of the wealth distribution among the entire population of the city. When these adjustments are made, as table 5.2 demonstrates, the degree of inequality is increased significantly.[21] Over one-third of the nonslave wealth in the city was owned by less than 1 percent of the population. Ninety percent of the nonslave wealth was owned by 10 percent of the people. Almost three quarters of the population was propertyless.

Such extreme inequality was not unique to Charleston. It was characteristic of other antebellum Southern cities. Compared with rural areas, cities had more very rich people and many more poor people. In the rural Cotton South, for example, the top 10 percent of the population owned 57 percent of the wealth, compared with 77 percent owned by Charleston's top 10 percent.[22] But in Baltimore, New Orleans, and St. Louis, the top 1 percent of the population owned 40 percent of the wealth, compared with only 27 per-

Table 5.2
DISTRIBUTION OF NONSLAVE WEALTH IN CHARLESTON

LOWER LIMIT OF WEALTH GROUP	PROPORTION IN EACH WEALTH GROUP		CUMULATIVE PROPORTION IN AND ABOVE WEALTH GROUPS	
	% OF WEALTH	*% OF POPULATION*	*% OF WEALTH*	*% OF POPULATION*
$100,000	33.8	0.8	33.8	0.8
$ 50,000	23.1	1.5	56.9	2.3
$ 10,000	34.6	8.5	91.5	10.8
$ 5,000	4.3	4.1	95.8	14.9
$ 1,000	3.8	9.4	99.6	24.3
$ 100	0.4	4.3	100.0	28.6
$ 0	0.0	71.4	100.0	100.0

Gini coefficient = 0.918
N = 7,190

Notes: Wealth attributable to slave property was deducted from the total reported wealth of each wealth group; each slave was assumed to be worth $900. Of course, many wealthy Charlestonians owned slaves outside the city, and these were not reported on the slave schedules for the city. It is impossible to estimate the extent of this practice. But since the attempt here is to measure the distribution of nonslave wealth in Charleston, it should not greatly affect this distribution. Slaves were included in the population as propertyless potential wealth holders. Their household size was assumed to be 5.28, the same as that of the lowest wealth group. Thus, the 13,441 slaves in Charleston (excluding the Neck) were estimated to comprise 2,546 slave households.

cent in Charleston, as table 5.3 shows.[23] The top 10 percent in Charleston owned slightly less than the same group in the other Southern cities, but the second decile of Charleston wealth holders owned almost twice as much as those in the other Southern cities. Thus, the wealth owned by the top fifth of the population in Baltimore, New Orleans, and St. Louis was virtually identical to that in Charleston, 92 percent versus 93 percent. But Charleston contained a much larger share of propertyless individuals compared with the other Southern cities, 56 percent versus about 30 percent. Overall, the distribution of wealth in the four cities was similar but not identical.

Compared with ten Northern cities in 1860, Charleston was quite different.[24] There were more rich people in Charleston, and they owned a larger share of the wealth, as table 5.4 illustrates. For example, 17 percent of Charlestonians owned $10,000 or more, compared with only 5 percent of men in northern cities. These wealthy Charlestonians owned 89 percent of the total wealth, compared with the wealthy Northerners' 76 percent. If only the free population of Charleston is considered, then Charleston had about the

Table 5.3
WEALTH DISTRIBUTION IN THREE ANTEBELLUM SOUTHERN CITIES AND CHARLESTON

LOWER LIMIT PERCENTILE OF WEALTH GROUP	PROPORTION OF WEALTH IN PERCENTILE GROUP	
	BALTIMORE, NEW ORLEANS, ST. LOUIS	*CHARLESTON*
1%	39.6 ⎤	26.9 ⎤
2%	13.1 ⎥	12.2 ⎥
3%	6.9 ⎥ 83.2	8.1 ⎥ 76.9
4%	6.8 ⎥	7.3 ⎥
5%	4.1 ⎥	5.6 ⎥
10%	12.7 ⎦	16.8 ⎦
20%	8.7	16.2
30%	4.9	5.3
40%	2.0	1.6
50%	0.7	0.0
60%	0.3	0.0
70%	0.1	0.0
80%	0.0	0.0
90%	0.0	0.0
100%	0.0	0.0

Source: The Baltimore, New Orleans, and St. Louis data were taken from Gallman, "Trends in the Size Distribution of Wealth," Appendix, Table A-1, p. 22.

Note: Percentages were subject to rounding.

Table 5.4
WEALTH DISTRIBUTION IN TEN ANTEBELLUM NORTHERN CITIES AND
CHARLESTON

PROPORTION AT OR ABOVE WEALTH GROUP LIMITS

LOWER LIMIT OF WEALTH GROUP	PROPORTION OF POPULATION		PROPORTION OF WEALTH	
	NORTHERN CITIES	CHARLESTON	NORTHERN CITIES	CHARLESTON
$100,000	0.3	1.2	27.5	28.7
$50,000	0.9	3.4	42.8	49.7
$10,000	4.8	16.6	76.2	88.8
$5,000	8.3	23.0	85.9	94.9
$1,000	20.4	37.5	97.0	99.6
$100	42.0	44.2	99.9	100.0
$0	100.0	100.0	100.0	100.0

Source: The data for Northern cities were taken from Soltow, "The Wealth, Income, and Social Class of Men in Large Northern Cities," pp. 238-39. The ten cities were Boston, Philadelphia, Newark, Washington, D.C., Pittsburgh, Cleveland, Cincinnati, Chicago, Milwaukee, and San Francisco.

same proportion of propertyless individuals as the Northern cities. But if Charleston's slaves are considered, then Charleston had considerably more propertyless individuals, 72 percent versus 58 percent, and the distribution of wealth in Charleston was correspondingly much more sharply skewed. If only the free populations are compared, another important difference between Charleston and Northern cities was in the proportion of small property holders. In Charleston, only 7 percent of the free population owned wealth worth less than $1,000; yet 28 percent of men in the Northern cities owned this much. Although only one-third or one-fourth as many men in Northern cities attained the wealth levels of rich Charlestonians, Charleston contained only one-fourth as many small wealth holders as Northern cities. In short, a much larger fraction of the Charleston free population was rich by Northern standards; a much larger fraction of the free population of Northern cities was poor by Southern standards, but not propertyless.[25]

In the North, a free labor ideology emphasizing thrift, hard work, and equality of opportunity encouraged poor men to consider disparities of wealth a temporary condition that could be overcome by individual effort.[26] Elements of free labor ideology were not completely absent in the South.[27] But as a rule, poor white men in the South were less frequently encouraged to strive upward than to look downward and to be thankful they were not black. Even if poor white men never benefited economically from slavery, they always benefited socially, they were told. The fundamental division in Southern society was supposed to be not along class lines within white society but along racial lines dividing whites from blacks.[28] In Southern cities, there were two important problems with this argument. First, the wealth of most whites was more comparable to that of blacks than to that of rich whites. Second, in the course of the antebellum years, slaveholders increasingly came to see themselves as a class with distinct economic, social, and political interests. By 1860, this development had created a society in which class divisions among whites were more significant than they had been since the late eighteenth century.[29]

In this brief paper, it is impossible to build a conclusive case for these arguments. But it is possible to consider whether or not the arguments are consistent with the evidence of the distribution of wealth in Charleston along lines of race and slave ownership.

In Charleston in 1860, racial divisions had many forms, and were glaringly obvious. For example, as table 5.5 shows, 99 percent of the wealth was owned by whites, although 15 percent of the free population was composed of free people of color.[30] Compared with all whites, the free people of color were much worse off. Over three quarters of them owned no property whatever.[31] Free mulattoes, who accounted for two-thirds of the free people of color, were better off than free blacks.[32] More free mulattoes than free blacks were propertyholders (24 percent versus 19 percent) and five of the six free people of color who owned $10,000 or more were mulattoes. Mulattoes' mean wealth was $712, compared with $379 for free blacks. But the most important racial division was not within the free black community but between blacks and whites. A convenient summary of the division is the mean wealth of whites: $8,251, 11 times greater than the mean wealth of mulattoes and 22 times greater than that of free blacks.

However, the racial difference in wealth holding was in fact between the rich people of Charleston, all of whom were white, and the slaves and free people of color. Three quarters of Charleston's whites owned less than $5,000. Among these whites, the distribution of wealth was very similar to that among the free people of color. For example, the mean wealth of whites who owned less than $5,000 was $506, midway between the wealth of mulattoes and blacks and less than the $607 mean wealth of all the free people of color. Clearly, whatever the other differences between whites and blacks in Charleston, most whites had in common with blacks a very low level of wealth. The distance separating propertyless slaves from most whites and free people of color was large enough legally and socially. But these groups were much closer to the wealth of slaves than they were to the wealth of rich Charlestonians. Among the quarter of Charleston's whites who owned more than $5,000, the mean wealth was over $29,000, fifty-eight times larger than the mean wealth of all the rest of Charleston's

Table 5.5
WEALTH DISTRIBUTION BY RACE

PROPORTION OF POPULATION

LOWER LIMIT OF WEALTH GROUP	WHITES	MULATTOES	BLACKS	ALL FPC*
$100,000	1.4	—	—	—
$50,000	2.7	—	—	—
$10,000	15.4	1.2	0.4	1.0
$5,000	7.3	1.6	1.3	1.5
$1,000	15.6	15.6	11.1	14.2
$100	6.9	5.1	6.2	5.5
$0	51.8	76.4	80.9	77.8
(N)	(3,923)	(488)	(225)	(713)
Mean Wealth	$8,251	$712	$379	$607

PROPORTION OF WEALTH

LOWER LIMIT OF WEALTH GROUP	WHITES	MULATTOES	BLACKS	ALL FPC*
$100,000	28.7	—	—	—
$50,000	21.0	—	—	—
$10,000	38.7	0.33	0.03	0.36
$5,000	5.8	0.19	0.07	0.26
$1,000	4.1	0.49	0.14	0.63
$100	0.4	0.05	0.02	0.07
$0	0.0	0.00	0.00	0.00
TOTAL	98.7	1.06	0.26	1.32

Note: This table excludes eight Indians.
Free People of Color.

whites. From the perspective of most white Charlestonians, class divisions were as obvious as racial divisions.[33]

After 1830, the political and ideological mobilization in defense of slavery made slaveowners more and more aware that whatever their differences on other issues, they shared a common interest in slaveownership and faced a common enemy in the North.[34] Yet the very process by which slaveholders developed a sense of themselves as a class sharpened class divisions in

Southern society among whites. Emphasis on the social significance of slaveholding tended to call attention to the differences between rich and poor at the very moment when poor whites were asked to consider themselves aristocrats because they were not black.

In Charleston in 1860, most rich Charlestonians were slaveholders, and almost all nonslaveholders were poor.[35] Nearly three out of every four Charlestonians did not own slaves.[36] Nine out of ten people who had less than $5,000 were slaveless.[37] Of those who owned $5,000 or more, over three quarters were slaveholders.[38] The mean wealth of slaveholders was $21,264, twelve times greater than that of nonslaveholders.[39] Altogether, slaveholders owned 82 percent of all the wealth in the city.

The contrast between slaveholders and nonslaveholders focused and reinforced the differences between Charleston's working class and the planters, merchants, and professionals who composed the city's economic elite. For example, 80 percent of the planters in Charleston and 53 percent of the lawyers reported owning $5,000 or more, as table 5.6 shows.[40] But only 3 percent of the carpenters, 2 percent of the clerks, and 0.2 percent of the laborers owned that much. Indeed, 79 percent of the carpenters, 93 percent of the clerks, and 95 percent of the laborers reported no wealth of any sort. The mean wealth of planters was almost $54,000; that of lawyers was over

Table 5.6
WEALTH DISTRIBUTION WITHIN OCCUPATIONAL GROUPS

PROPORTION OF INDIVIDUALS AT OR ABOVE WEALTH GROUP LIMIT

LOWER LIMIT OF WEALTH GROUP	PLANTERS	LAWYERS	CARPENTERS	CLERKS	LABORERS
$100,000	13.3	2.0	0	0	0
$50,000	29.5	6.0	0	0	0
$10,000	77.1	39.2	1.5	1.1	0.2
$5,000	80.0	53.1	3.3	2.4	0.2
$1,000	80.0	57.1	16.6	5.8	2.9
$100	80.0	57.1	20.5	6.6	5.4
$0	100.0	100.0	100.0	100.0	100.0
(N)	(105)	(51)	(391)	(618)	(647)
MEAN WEALTH	$53,996	$14,340	$674	$318	$80
% SLAVE-OWNERS	79.0	75.0	4.4	4.9	0.2

$14,000. Carpenters' mean wealth was $674, clerks' was $318, and laborers' was $80. Predictably, 95 percent of the carpenters and clerks and 99.8 percent of the laborers did not own slaves, while more than three quarters of the planters and lawyers were slaveholders.

Charlestonians were well aware of the class divisions in their society. The dominance of wealthy slaveholders meant, as Judge J. T. Withers explained, that "There is a peculiar duty on the part of a Government which holds slaves to protect that description of property."[41] Yet protecting slave property could endanger the interests of working-class whites.[42] White stevedores, for example, protested the competition of slaves who hired themselves out. They asked, "are [white stevedores] not as good citizens as any other class in the city?" to which they replied emphatically, "and they ask the same protection."[43] But how could a society dominated by wealthy slaveholders provide equal protection for slave property and working-class whites?

The problem was intensified by the working of the labor market, which subverted the caste system and strengthened class resentments. The Charleston grand jury noted in January 1860 that "it is proper that the line of demarcation between the castes should be clear and distinct, more particularly at this time, for reasons which need not be mentioned here." Regardless of what was proper, some Charlestonians created, in the words of the grand jury, "a nuisance, which calls loudly for a remedy, [namely] the riding in public carriages and other vehicles of free negroes and slaves, and in many cases driven by white men."[44] Just as the violations of racial propriety undermined the caste system, competition with slave labor deepened class divisions among whites. In December 1860, shortly before South Carolina resolved to secede, a "master mechanic" warned that, "In placing the negro in competition with white mechanics—a superior intellectual power—you drag the latter down to a level with the former, and the consequence is, the latter is, to some extent, and I am sorry to say it, regarded by some as being no better than the former. This is well calculated to breed discontent and hatred on the part of the white mechanic, and make him an enemy of our institution. . . ."[45] Given the structure of wealth and class in Charleston in 1860, such warnings could be heard, but they could not be heeded—at least not without endangering the social structure they were designed to protect.

Notes

1. Only in the fourth ward, the largest in the city, did the enumeration continue into August. August 2 was the last day information was collected. In the third and seventh wards, the marshals worked through nearly all of July. In the fifth and eighth wards, they were finished in the first week of July. In the first, second, and sixth wards, the census was completed during June.

2. The instructions to the census marshals are conveniently quoted in Lee Sol-tow, *Men and Wealth in the United States, 1850-1870* (New Haven: Yale University Press, 1975), p. 1.

3. The entire free population of the city is included in this study. Of course, er-rors are inevitable in a study of this magnitude. Although I have tried to eliminate them, I am under no illusion that I have been completely successful. However, I am confident that the errors are small enough in number and limited enough in scope to have negligible influence on the conclusions of this study. For example, my figure for the free population of Charleston—based on several passes through the entire set of free population schedules—is 123 less than that recorded in the 1860 published cen-sus. My study includes 26,306 people; the published census reported 26,429. (Both figures exclude the 284 free people who lived in the Neck, outside the city limits.) The difference between the two figures is only 0.47 percent. In other words, this study includes 99.53 percent of the population reported in the published census. A combination of errors by the census office and by me probably accounts for the dif-ference. The most likely source of census office error is the counting of empty dwell-ings as people. Census marshals assigned numbers to dwellings, some 4,924 in all. Only 4,644 dwellings were occupied, according to my count. Since the 280 unoccu-pied dwellings took up a line on the census manuscript page, it is likely that when census office clerks summarized the number of people listed on a page they occasion-ally made a mistake and counted an unoccupied dwelling as a person. That could easily account for most of the 123 people "extra" (or "missing," depending on whom you believe).

The city census of 1861 is of little help in correcting this problem. First, the population of the city would be expected to be somewhat different since it was taken a year after the federal census. Second, the city census counted 6,692 dwel-lings in the city. Unlike the federal census, this count included houses occupied by slaves and assigned more than one number to what was in fact the same building —for example, when a family lived above a shop, the family quarters were counted as one house, the shop as another, although they were parts of the same building. See Frederick A. Ford, *Census of the City of Charleston, South Carolina for the Year 1861* (Charleston: Evans and Cogswell, 1861), pp. 4, 7.

4. The total reported wealth was $38,226,150. The value of real estate accounted for 52 percent of the total.

5. Gibbes's report is at the beginning of the section for the city of Charleston in Schedule 6, Social Statistics, of the manuscript 1860 census schedules. He reported $54,597,879 as the total value of real and personal property. Real property ac-counted for 46 percent of the total.

6. If the total real and personal property values reported in the free schedules of the census are compared with these figures, 78.6 percent of the real property value in the assessor's book was reported in the free schedules, while only 62.4 percent of the personal property appearing in the assessor's book was reported in the census.

7. Of course, without access to the assessor's book, I have no way to confirm this assumption. Gibbes also reported that the residents paid $379,611 in real estate taxes. Since real estate was taxed at the rate of 1.4 percent, the taxable real estate was valued at $27,115,071, almost $2 million more than the real estate value reported from the assessor's book, $25,307,414. The census reports should have been higher,

of course, since they were supposed to include the value of all real estate owned, not just the real estate in the city. For the rate of taxation, see *List of Taxpayers of the City of Charleston for 1860* (Charleston: Evans and Cogswell, 1861), p. 335. For the best analysis of wealth based on tax assessments, see Edward Pessen, *Riches, Class and Power Before the Civil War* (Lexington, Mass.: D. C. Heath, 1973).

8. The one unlisted census marshal also was probably a city resident since his surname, DeVeaux, was shared by many other long-term residents.

9. Among the most important recent studies that have used census data to analyze wealth distribution are Jonathan M. Wiener, *Social Origins of the New South: Alabama, 1860-1885* (Baton Rouge: Louisiana State University Press, 1978), pp. 3-34; Gavin Wright, *The Political Economy of the Cotton South: Households, Markets, and Wealth in the Nineteenth Century* (New York: Norton, 1978), pp. 15-42; Randolph B. Campbell and Richard G. Lowe, *Wealth and Power in Antebellum Texas* (College Station: Texas A & M Press, 1977); Peter H. Lindert and Jeffrey G. Williamson, "Three Centuries of American Inequality," in Paul Uselding, ed., *Research in Economic History, An Annual Compilation of Research, Volume 1, 1976* (Greenwich, Conn.: J A I Press, 1976), pp. 69-123; Soltow, *Men and Wealth*; Lee Soltow, "The Wealth, Income, and Social Class of Men in Large Northern Cities of the United States in 1860," in James D. Smith, ed., *The Personal Distribution of Income and Wealth* (New York: National Bureau of Economic Research, 1975), pp. 233-76; Lee Soltow, "Economic Inequality in the United States in the Period from 1790 to 1860," *Journal of Economic History*, 31 (1971), 822-39; Robert E. Gallman, "Trends in the Size Distribution of Wealth in the Nineteenth Century: Some Speculations," in Lee Soltow, ed., *Six Papers on the Size Distribution of Wealth and Income* (New York: National Bureau of Economic Research, 1969), pp. 1-30. For an important analysis of wealth distribution in the eighteenth century based on studies of inventories of estates, see William George Bentley, "Wealth Distribution in Colonial South Carolina" (Ph.D. diss., Georgia State University School of Business Administration, 1977).

10. Most studies ignore the wealth of women, but see Gallman, "Trends in the Size Distribution of Wealth," pp. 19-20. Soltow's *Men and Wealth* examines the wealth of males twenty years old or over. Campbell and Lowe's *Wealth and Power in Antebellum Texas* analyzes the wealth of household heads.

11. In the fifty-nine households in which the wealth of all household members totaled $100,000 or more, the wealth of the wives accounted for only 0.6 percent of the total. In households lower down the wealth spectrum, wives owned a larger share of the household wealth, ranging from 3 to 5 percent. This is of considerable significance for an analysis of the distribution of wealth within households. That topic is beyond the scope of this brief paper.

12. Of course, a more complete study also would examine the distribution of wealth within households. A glimpse of the overall pattern can be obtained by examining the proportion of the free population accounted for by household members and their respective shares of total household wealth. Spouses made up 10.9 percent of the city's free population and owned 2.4 percent of the total wealth reported in the census. Coresiding children of the household head composed 35.0 percent of the population and owned 1.9 percent of the wealth. Coresiding relatives of the household head (defined as persons with the same surname as the household head but

whose age, sex, or order of listing in the manuscript census indicated that the persons were neither the spouse nor the children of the household head) accounted for 5.6 percent of the population and 3.7 percent of the wealth. Lodgers (defined as persons whose surname was different from that of the household head—many of them were not kin of the household head, but many others were presumably in-laws, although the relationship cannot be proved with the census data) were 30.7 percent of the population and owned 6.1 percent of the total wealth. In all, dependent members of households made up 82.2 percent of the population but owned only 14.1 percent of the wealth. The vast majority of these people owned no property whatever. But that fact had drastically different meanings, depending on the wealth of the head of the household.

13. The term "population" here and subsequently (unless stated otherwise) refers to the free heads of household, numbering 4,644.

14. By the term "city's wealth," I mean the total wealth owned by the city's 4,644 heads of household, which totaled $32,795,790. In the remainder of this paper, this sum is the basis for all references to total wealth.

15. Fifty percent of the total wealth was owned by 3.3 percent of the population.

16. This remains true even when the wealth of all household members is considered. The major impact of adding the wealth of other household members is to reduce the proportion of propertyless from 55.8 percent to 51.6 percent and to decrease slightly the proportion of wealth owned by the top groups. Considering the wealth of all household members has minimal impact on the wealth distribution because the share of household wealth owned by heads of household was remarkably consistent across wealth groups; it ranged from a low of 85.2 percent for households with total wealth between $1,000 and $4,999 to 87.6 percent for the richest households. The only exceptions were households in the lowest wealth category ($100 to $999), in which the heads of household owned 90.4 percent of the wealth. This group had negligible impact since it contained only 0.3 percent of the wealth reported to the census marshals.

17. The figures for the nation are for adult males rather than for heads of household. They are nonetheless roughly comparable with the Charleston data. See Soltow, *Men and Wealth*, p. 101.

18. Ibid.

19. The national comparison is with men whose total estate was less than $100; they represented 38.2 percent of adult men in 1860. Among the Charleston group, only one person reported wealth of less than $100; hence, this selection of a comparison group. See Soltow, *Men and Wealth*, p. 23.

20. According to Soltow (*Men and Wealth*, p. 65), the mean wealth of adult men in the North was $2,040; that in the South was $3,978; the national mean was $2,580. The Charleston mean was $7,062.

21. For similar calculations for other Southern regions, see Soltow, *Men and Wealth*, pp. 66-67, 134; Campbell and Lowe, *Wealth and Power in Antebellum Texas*, pp. 146-53; and Gallman, "Trends in the Size Distribution of Wealth," pp. 7-9.

22. The data on the Cotton South are from Wright, *The Political Economy of the Cotton South*, p. 26. The Gini coefficient for the Cotton South was 0.728. Wealth distribution in the Cotton South was not atypical of that in other regions of the

South, according to Albert W. Niemi, Jr., "Inequality in the Distribution of Slave Wealth: The Cotton South and Other Southern Agricultural Regions," *Journal of Economic History*, 37 (1977), 747-54. But even in the South Carolina low country, wealth was distributed more equally than in Charleston, according to the valuable study of Charles Winston Joyner, "Slave Folklife on the Waccamaw Neck: Antebellum Black Culture in the South Carolina Low Country" (Ph.D. diss., University of Pennsylvania, 1977), pp. 31-32.

23. The data on Baltimore, New Orleans, and St. Louis are from Gallman, "Trends in the Size Distribution of Wealth," pp. 22-23. Gini coefficients based on these data are 0.898 for Baltimore and 0.897 for New Orleans.

24. The Northern cities that form the basis of this comparison are Boston, Philadelphia, Newark, Washington, D.C., Pittsburgh, Cleveland, Cincinnati, Chicago, Milwaukee, and San Francisco. The data are from Soltow, "The Wealth, Income, and Social Class of Men in Large Northern Cities," pp. 236-42. It is worth noting once again that Soltow's valuable data are based on adult men while the Charleston data deal with heads of household.

25. The mean wealth of men in Northern cities was $2,346, only one-third the mean wealth in Charleston. Although wealthy individuals made up a much smaller fraction of the population in these Northern cities, they still owned by far the largest share of the wealth. Thus, the Gini coefficients for Northern cities are higher than the Charleston coefficient. For the Northern cities as a group, the coefficient was 0.924. Soltow, "The Wealth, Income, and Social Class of Men in Large Northern Cities," pp. 236-39.

26. See Eric Foner, *Free Soil, Free Labor, Free Men: The Ideology of the Republican Party Before the Civil War* (New York: Oxford University Press, 1970), esp. pp. 11-39.

27. See, for example, C. Vann Woodward, "The Southern Ethic in a Puritan World," in his *American Counterpoint: Slavery and Racism in the North-South Dialogue* (Boston: Little, Brown, 1971), pp. 13-46.

28. See George M. Fredrickson, *The Black Image in the White Mind: The Debate on Afro-American Character and Destiny, 1817-1914* (New York: Harper and Row, 1971), pp. 43-70.

29. On the Revolution and its aftermath, see Richard Walsh, *Charleston's Sons of Liberty: A Study of the Artisans, 1763-1789* (Columbia: University of South Carolina Press, 1959), and Peter H. Wood, " 'Taking Care of Business' in Revolutionary South Carolina: Republicanism and the Slave Society," in Jeffrey J. Crow and Larry E. Tise, eds., *The Southern Experience in the American Revolution* (Chapel Hill: University of North Carolina Press, 1978), pp. 268-93. On the critical years between 1790 and 1815, see the superb dissertation by Mark D. Kaplanoff of Cambridge University.

30. For an excellent study of free blacks in the entire state, see Marina Wikramanayake, *A World in Shadow: The Free Black in Antebellum South Carolina* (Columbia: University of South Carolina Press, 1973). On Charleston, see E. Horace Fitchett, "Traditions of the Free Negroes in Charleston, South Carolina," *Journal of Negro History*, 25 (1940), 140-42; and E. Horace Fitchett, "The Origin and Growth of the Free Negro Population of Charleston, South Carolina," *Journal of Negro History*, 26 (1941), 421-37. For the postwar period, see the important

study by Thomas Holt, *Black Over White: Negro Political Leadership in South Carolina During Reconstruction* (Urbana: University of Illinois Press, 1977).

31. In 1870, according to Soltow, about 80 percent of nonwhites were property-less. See Soltow, *Men and Wealth*, pp. 144-45.

32. Individuals were listed by the census marshals as mulattoes or blacks. I have simply used those designations, understanding full well that their usage was imprecise and unpredictable.

33. Sexual divisions in the society were equally obvious. Female-headed households were consistently less well off than male-headed households of the same race. A full exploration of these issues is beyond the scope of this paper. For an analysis of the significance of race in the decision to secede, see Steven A. Channing, *Crisis of Fear: Secession in South Carolina* (New York: Simon and Schuster, 1970).

34. This position is presented very forcefully by Gavin Wright in *The Political Economy of the Cotton South*. See also Eugene D. Genovese, *The Political Economy of Slavery: Studies in the Economy and Society of the Slave South* (New York: Random House, 1965), and Eugene D. Genovese, *The World the Slaveholders Made: Two Essays in Interpretation* (New York: Random House, 1969).

35. For data on the Cotton South, see Wright, *The Political Economy of the Cotton South*, pp. 10-42.

36. The exact figure is 72.9 percent. Once again, it is worth noting that by "Charlestonians" is meant the 4,644 heads of household in the city.

37. The exact figure is 87.6 percent.

38. The exact figure is 76 percent. The relationship between wealth and slaveholding is summarized in the table below.

Lower Limit of Wealth Group	Nonslaveholders as Percentage of Wealth Group
$100,000	10.9
$50,000	17.3
$10,000	20.3
$5,000	35.8
$1,000	69.6
$100	85.3
$0	92.6

Aside from the obvious correlation, three things deserve special comment. First, when wealth is plotted against the proportion of slaveholders at each wealth level, $5,000 is the point at which about half of the wealth holders were slaveholders. Second, a sizable minority of the wealthier individuals did not report owning slaves in Charleston. In fact, they may have owned slaves who lived outside the city and therefore did not appear on the Charleston slave schedules. Finally, 193 individuals who reported owning no property appeared in the slave schedules as slave owners. These people either drastically understated their wealth or they did not actually own the slaves but were hiring them. So far, I have not been able to determine which of these was the case. Therefore I have simply taken both (contradictory) reports—wealth and slaveholding—at face value.

39. The mean wealth of nonslaveholders was $1,791. This compares favorably with the mean wealth of nonslaveholders reported by Wright for the Cotton South, $1,781, as does the slaveholders' mean, which was $24,748 in the Cotton South. See Wright, *The Political Economy of the Cotton South*, p. 36.

40. Unlike all the other tables in this paper, the individuals in table 5.6 are all those in Charleston who had these occupations, except those who were either dependent children or relatives of the household head. In other words, the table includes basically all adults with these occupations, whether they were heads of household or lodgers. For an excellent study of the influence of planters in Charleston, see John P. Radford, "Culture, Economy, and Urban Structure in Charleston, South Carolina, 1860-1880" (Ph.D. diss., Clark University, 1974). The best analysis of the Charleston merchants in the antebellum years is Gregory Allen Greb, "Charleston, South Carolina, Merchants, 1815-1860: Urban Leadership in the Antebellum South" (Ph.D. diss., University of California, San Diego, 1978). For the best overview of antebellum Charleston, see George C. Rogers, Jr., *Charleston in the Age of the Pinckneys* (Norman: University of Oklahoma Press, 1969).

41. Quoted in the report of the court of general sessions and common pleas in the Charleston *Courier*, January 30, 1860. Judge Withers was delivering a death sentence to Francis Michel, a young man who was convicted of aiding and assisting a runaway slave. Michel was subsequently pardoned, according to a report in the *Courier*, February 4, 1860. For an excellent comparison of the systems of criminal justice in Massachusetts and South Carolina, see Michael Stephen Hindus, "Prison and Plantation: Criminal Justice in Nineteenth Century Massachusetts and South Carolina" (Ph.D. diss., University of California, Berkeley, 1975). See also Howell Meadows Henry, *The Police Control of the Slave in South Carolina* (Emory, Virginia, 1914).

42. See the important study by Leonard P. Stavisky, "The Negro Artisan in the South Atlantic States, 1800-1860: A Study of Status and Opportunity with Special Reference to Charleston" (Ph.D. diss., Columbia University, 1958). See also Ulrich B. Phillips, "The Slave Labor Problem in the Charleston District," *Political Science Quarterly*, 22 (1907), 416-39.

43. Stevedores to editor, Charleston *Courier*, January 30, 1860. See also Richard C. Wade, *Slavery in the Cities: The South, 1820-1860* (New York: Oxford University Press, 1964), and Claudia C. Goldin, *Urban Slavery in the American South, 1820-1860: A Quantitative History* (Chicago: University of Chicago Press, 1976), esp. pp. 28-33.

44. Presentment of the grand jury, as reported in the Charleston *Courier*, January 13, 1860. The grand jury recommended that the owners of the vehicles be fined and the offending blacks and slaves "be subject to corporeal punishment." See also Wade, *Slavery in the Cities*, pp. 149-60, 258-62.

45. A "master mechanic" to editor, Charleston *Courier*, December 7, 1860. The writer believed that if "the negro [were] placed in his true position . . . under a master workman . . . a closer bond of union would exist between the various classes of our citizens, and thus they would be strongly united in the support and defence of our Southern institutions."

6

SOCIAL STRUCTURE AND URBAN FORM: CHARLESTON, 1860–1880

John P. Radford

Urban geographers normally view their field as focusing on spatial relationships within and between cities.[1] These spatial relationships may be economic, cultural, political, social, or morphological. Although they may be studied at any point in time, only a minority of urban geographers have been interested in investigating them for periods other than the present.

This paper will attempt to assess the contribution that urban geographical evidence can make to our understanding of Charleston's society and its internal arrangement before and after the Civil War. Such evidence may cast light on some of the long-standing controversies surrounding the period: Was the planter presence dominant within the late antebellum city? Did the planter influence collapse with the Civil War? What was the nature of antebellum class and racial residential segregation? Was racial segregation imposed immediately after the Civil War? Did it await the last decade of the nineteenth century? Was the Civil War a devastating experience for Charleston? Did Reconstruction produce a major disruption of its social structure? Was this period as a whole a major turning point in the city's history?

There is no suggestion here, of course, that spatial evidence offers the key to a full understanding of the city during this period. However, when regarded as a manifestation of social processes, a city's spatial arrangement often provides tangible evidence of its social organization, and even the ideology of its people. Neither is it suggested that geographers have a monopoly on spatial studies. One look at the literature of human ecology,[2] or (to take a more current sociological theme) of territoriality,[3] is sufficient to dismiss such a notion. Further, two of the spatial ideas mentioned later were first presented by historians. Yet geographers, more than others, tend to "think spatially"; it is the spatial aspects of a problem that command their attention, and for many, the spatial theme provides the definition of their discipline.

Two types of spatial evidence will be considered here. First, attention will focus briefly on the nature of the distribution of class and racial variables within the city in 1860 and 1880. These variables constitute an important part of what can be called the "social geography" of the city. Second, consideration will be given to some aspects of Charleston's morphology, that is, the spatial aspects of its physical form. Finally, an attempt will be made to evaluate the contribution of this kind of evidence to our understanding of mid-nineteenth-century Charleston.

Social Geography

The nearest thing that exists to a dynamic spatial model for nineteenth-century North American cities postulates a reversal in the direction of the social gradient. The main cause of this is usually taken to be the flight of the wealthy away from the center toward the periphery, to be replaced by inmigrant poor. This is seen as having resulted, on the one hand, from the *push* of factory and warehouse proliferation near the city center, the expansion of the central business district, and the extension of immigrant reception areas and, on the other hand, from the *pull* of a pleasant suburban environment with lower per unit rents. Sam Bass Warner has described such a process in Philadelphia and has suggested that it "has been repeated, with minor variations, again and again across the nation."[4] Much emphasis has been placed on the role of innovations in intraurban transportation in this progression, particularly the horsecar from the 1850s and the electric streetcar from the late 1880s. However, the relatively high fares compared with daily wages, together with cases where a reversal largely predated transportation innovation, suggest that the role of transportation was permissive rather than determinative.[5]

In association with this reversal, geographers in particular have emphasized changes in the orientation of the city away from a single multifaceted center, as well as an increase in the functional specialization of land use, as indicated by increasing functional homogeneity of small areas within the city.[6] The transformation as a whole has sometimes been presented in theoretical terms as a transition from Gideon Sjoberg's model of the preindustrial city[7] to Ernest Burgess' model of the "modern" city based on Chicago in the 1920s. Many reservations have been expressed about the applicability of this particular interpretation in the North American context.[8] However, there is general agreement that such a transformation occurred and that its effects were felt widely by the 1850s and almost universally by 1880.

Where does nineteenth-century Charleston fit into such a scheme? Did Charleston undergo a transformation of this kind? Did social changes occasioned by the events of the 1860s and 1870s transform old sociospatial patterns into "modern" ones? Briefly, the situation may be summarized as follows.[9] Charleston in 1860 conformed in many respects to the preindustrial model, probably more so than any other major American city, but at the same time, it possessed many of the features of the North American commercial city, a city neither industrialized nor preindustrial.[10] Although the direction of the social gradient was broadly from center to periphery, there were poor as well as rich near the center, not all of them employed in domestic service, and some of the most notable areas of the wealthy were at the periphery, especially those close to the Ashley and Cooper rivers. At the citywide scale, there was a high degree of intermixture of occupational classes. The level of functional specialization of land use was quite high, with pronounced clustering of commission merchants, law offices, banks, and other mercantile functions and a specialized retailing strip on King Street. The city's detailed racial geography was extremely complex, but at the broad scale, the most striking feature of the residential patterns was one of intermixture of black and white.

Considering the drastic events of the Civil War and Reconstruction, this situation had changed remarkably little by 1880. The functional districts were by and large as they had been before the war. There is no evidence of any reversal of the social gradient. Even the new freedmen, including several thousand who had come to the city from the surrounding districts, appear to have been absorbed within the overall racial residential structure of the city, although there is evidence that alleys that were uninhabited in 1860 now housed significant numbers of blacks.

The dominant impression that one gets, then, is of little change. This is of significance in terms of the simple dynamic model of change in the nineteenth-century North American city presented earlier. Charleston showed no signs in 1880 of having begun to modernize its spatial patterns. At least three sets of reasons could be given to account for this. A catastrophic view would blame the war and Reconstruction for impeding "progress." A functional view might point to the lag of modernization processes dating from before the Civil War: transportation innovation was late and fitful, factory industry made few inroads, immigration rates were low, and expansion of the central business district was insignificant. Finally, a value-orientation approach might note this lag but seek its causes in the underlying value systems of key decision makers. These alternatives will be evaluated following a discussion of some of the morphological aspects of Charleston's spatial structure.

Morphology

It is generally accepted that the architecture of the major public buildings and the finest houses of antebellum Charleston is noteworthy for the way in which it reflected the dominant tastes of a leisured elite. Less widely recognized is the influence of this elite in shaping more generally the physical form of the city. This is perhaps most clearly seen in the allocation of Charleston's residential space. In preempting the choice residential sites within the city, the elite determined the broad outlines of its residential geography. Space for the expression of elegance and taste, riverine vistas, exposure to salubrious sea breezes, remoteness as far as possible from the perceived unhealthy areas of the city, and proximity to social institutions seem to have been the main priorities influencing the location of the upper-class residential areas.[11] Once the choicest sites had been occupied, the remaining population fitted in where it could, usually on the worst drained land, in crowded alleys, or near the wharves. Occasionally, the result was the creation of areas of uniform house types. More frequently, it gave rise to closely spaced but finely differentiated mixtures of styles and qualities of housing. Large, elegant houses were found on the same streets as more modest structures and even tarpaper shacks.

The predominance of such mixed patterns is, of course, closely related to the variegated social patterns described earlier. Neither set of patterns is evidence of any closeness or equality between classes and racial groups. Social distance and spatial distance are two quite different concepts. Careful design often allows the retention of one despite the necessity or even the desirability of the other. The result is the morphological expression of the social values of the dominant group. No better illustration of this can be found in Charleston than the slave yards. Here the requirements of the major slaveowners determined the form of one of the most important building blocks of the morphology of the city. Slave accommodation was provided on the same lot as the main house in a style that Richard C. Wade has called "the urban equivalent of the plantation."[12] The slave yard provides a powerful example of the role of ideology in urban morphology. Thus, what may appear at a broad scale to be a pattern of scattering or even intermixture is in reality the replication throughout much of the city of a carefully defined pattern of small-scale separation.

The role of elite values also can be seen in the provision of places of leisure in Charleston. Perhaps the best example is the Battery. "On this battery," observed one visitor in 1856, "in summer, from half past six until dark, you may see almost anyone of any notability in Charleston."[13] An exaggeration, perhaps, but contemporary letters to the newspapers, as well as the mayor's reports, bear evidence of the stress that many prominent Charlestonians placed on the preservation and enhancement of this outdoor environment. In the late 1830s several houses at the edge of the gardens were removed, and the area was provided with "broad and serpentine walks" and "beautiful pagodas."[14] Throughout the antebellum era, demands continued to be made for further extensions. Reaction was strong in

1860, when the city council narrowly voted to sell off some lots on the margins of the gardens rather than to enlarge the grounds. The area was valued as an environment that provided "pure air and agreeable outdoor exercise."[15]

Certain institutional buildings within the city attracted even stronger attention from the elite. Some of the buildings, in a time of increasing apprehension about the future, assumed a powerful symbolic value. Although pressures toward an efficient, rational allocation of land certainly existed, they were frequently countered by the subtle forces of aesthetics. This conflict between rationalism and sentiment in land-use allocation in Charleston is aptly demonstrated by the events following the burning of St. Philip's Church in 1835. The city surveyor recommended that the opportunity be taken to move the site of the church forty-eight feet to the east, thereby allowing Church Street to be straightened. In response to protests, a committee appointed by the city council investigated the problem and ridiculed the plan, saying that the injuries done to the graveyard and to the aesthetics of the city would not compensate for the increased convenience provided by the straightening of the street:

Your committee are not aware that since the erection of the Church, any accident, or evil has arisen from the narrowness of the Street . . . and surely the time that would be saved in passing over it, by changing the short curve that has existed for more than one hundred years, into a straight line, cannot well form an adequate motive. . . . Moreover were the Church to be recessed . . . the view would only be extended for a short distance to the end of the Street at the site of the Old Orphan House, and in viewing the Street from its most favorable aspect, where it crosses Broad Street, your Committee would submit; whether the . . . Portico of a Church would not be a more beautiful object than a private residence of ordinary appearance.[16]

The most intense sentiment, however, was directed toward the symbolic center of the city. The intersection of Broad and Meeting streets, sharply removed from the mercantile center on East Bay and the retailers of King Street, provided the focal point of the antebellum city. St. Michael's Church on the southeast corner provided the major orientation. From it, the watch was kept and curfew and reveille sounded. The guard house was the seat of law and order, and the courthouse that of law. Completing the picture on the northeast corner of the intersection, a formerly misplaced bank had long since been made into the city hall. All four major institutions of social control were thus housed at this intersection, making it the undisputed nerve center of the city and the chief locus of social, especially racial, control.[17]

This evidence is fully in keeping with a view of antebellum Charleston that argues the dominance of a leisured elite not only over the design of the major houses but also over the form of the city as a whole. Although the historian's preoccupation with slavery and the plantation can justly be blamed for the relative neglect of the nineteenth-century Southern city, it is no help to deny the influence of these powerful institutions on the urban South. Certainly in Charleston, the mind of the antebellum city seems to have been set by an elite that dominated an unusually deferential (for the United States) rank and file. Relatively firm and coherent notions of class and caste were shared by the majority of the city's population and given on occasion a spatial expression. Forces regarded as potentially disruptive to the status quo were tenaciously opposed, including the powerful modernizing force of industrialization (even on the limited scale persuasively argued for by William Gregg) as well as abolitionism. In short, it is more than ever apparent that the familiar themes and controversies of antebellum historiography cannot be regarded as foreign to Charleston. On the contrary, they must be seen as essential to its experience as an urban place.[18]

Given this antebellum situation, the central question is whether or not the city was radically altered by the events of 1860-80. The Civil War and Reconstruction, usually (and appropriately) viewed as political and social events, also were in Charleston developments of considerable morphological significance. The fire of 1860 and the subsequent bombardments destroyed large areas of the city, and after the war, the military regime sought to impose structural changes. The morphological response of the city to these events can provide valuable evidence on the nature of its society.

It may be useful to consider this question within a rather broader framework than has hitherto been employed. Several broad types of morphological response to urban catastrophe can be recognized. In the first place, reconstruction can conform to a master plan, as had been the case in many of the bombed cities of Europe following World War II. There are many more examples where a plan has been drawn up but then overtaken by circumstances, the classic example being the fate of the plans (most notably that by Christopher Wren) for the reconstruction of London after the fire of 1666.[19] The course actually taken here was a laissez-faire response, with the designs of the merchant being uppermost. Such a laissez-faire, rational, market approach predominated after the fires that occurred in most American cities. The recovery of Chicago after 1871 was rapid, and the new morphology reflected the business needs of the age. A detailed study of San Francisco following the earthquake and fire of 1906 shows a clear sequence in the colonization of the burned area, with the banks leading the way.[20] In few cases in the modern Western urban experience has the dominant desire been to put the clock back, to restore the morphology of the predisaster era. The Old Town of Warsaw, as restored since 1945 on the basis of a general plan, is an outstanding example.

The morphological response of Charlestonians to fire, bombardment, and what Jacob Schirmer angrily called "acts of vandalism" by "our Military Task Masters"[21] fits none of these models. It is no surprise that there was no adherence to a plan. Yet neither was there a widespread ordering of the city according to the precepts of the urban land market. This refusal to make concessions toward the American norm is most instructive. There can be little doubt that the main desire in postbellum Charleston was less for Reconstruction than for restoration. The quasi-restoration that eventually did take place was achieved piece by piece according to individual decision and opportunity and was patterned on outdated models. It was clear by 1880 that what was slowly emerging from the ruins of Charleston was a morphological anachronism.

Discussion and Conclusion

On the eve of the Civil War, a correspondent for the *New York Journal of Commerce* wrote:

Excepting in those characteristics peculiar to Southern cities, we can conceive the present aspect of Charleston to bear a resemblance to the New York of thirty years ago; before palatial stores of marble and freestone had usurped the places of humbler structures and when aristocratic dwellings and fragrant gardens occupied localities now surrendered to the demands of business.[22]

We are still far from understanding the fundamental causes of Charleston's reluctance to transform itself into a city with "modern" social and morphological patterns. The key probably lies in determining whether the role of the elite was an active or a passive one. To the functionalist, including most urban geographers, the persistence of an elite in the center of the city would appear to be merely a symptom of relative stagnation. Charleston's small size and slow rate of growth created little demand for commercial and industrial expression and no immigrant labor force requiring housing. There was little land-use competition and no stimulus for the kinds of changes in organization that were taking place in more rapidly growing centers. In this view, the persistence of the central elite was just one more symptom of a stagnation caused by Charleston's outdated location in relation to the realities of the economic structure of the United States in the mid-nineteenth century. Lack of growth appears almost as an independent variable.

An opposite view is at least plausible. It was the authority of an entrenched elite—noncommercial in orientation and unalterably opposed to the social changes represented by such forces as industrialization—that was primarily responsible for the persistence of land-use patterns that, by the standards of other important U.S. cities, were increasingly outdated. The elite imposed on the city the values of the plantation, which became so deeply ingrained within the population as a whole that they survived even the onslaughts of the war and Reconstruction. In this view, the elite is an active agent, and lack of growth itself becomes a symptom.

The question is essentially one of interests versus values as the major determinant of land-use allocation, a topic that has received its classical treatment in the work of Walter Firey.[23] Were the patterns extant in Charleston primarily a result of the operation of market forces or of the activities of a largely nonmercantile elite? As always, the truth lies somewhere in between these two polarities. Yet the degree to which the reality tends toward one pole or the other is of considerable importance to our understanding of Charleston's distinctiveness or otherwise within nineteenth-century urban America. Spatial evidence shares with several other types of evidence the disadvantage of being largely derived from results or end products, and as such can rarely be regarded as conclusive. Nevertheless, in this case, it contains sufficient substance to be regarded as a serious contribution to our understanding of Charleston's social and economic structure. All indications suggest that it was the influence of a conservative elite that was the decisive factor in creating the distinctive morphology of mid-nineteenth-century Charleston. This is not to suggest that every line and angle was arbitrated by the upper class. It is to argue that a comparatively small group of planters, professionals, and merchants were the prime morphological movers in the city. It was their tastes, their motives, their perceptions that retarded the process of modernization in Charleston, thereby setting it apart from the trends portrayed in Warner's evolutionary scaffolding.

On the more specific question of the nature of Charleston's transition from the Old South to the New, the spatial evidence is unequivocal in its support of the view that the era was not one of radical change. If the close racial proximity of antebellum South Carolina was immediately replaced by rigid segregation, as Joel Williamson has argued,[24] one might expect this to be manifested in the rise of segregated residential districts in Charleston by 1880. This did not occur.[25] While blacks in some Southern cities appear to have undergone some clustering,[26] Charleston's residential patterns in 1880 seemed to reflect those crosscurrents and contradictions resulting from the meeting of old and new models of behavior that C. Vann Woodward has described.[27] Equally, it might be expected that progress would have been made toward modernization of city services. Yet despite increased recognition of the problems caused by bad sanitary arrangements, these remained largely unchanged. The volume of "Social Statistics of Cities" prepared from data collected in 1880 shows how unfavorably Charleston compared with most other cities in this respect.[28] The waterworks were privately owned and not subject to inspection. Privy vaults, some of them watertight, were still the norm, as was the practice of removing night soil to the edge of the city. Water closets were still a novelty, and the sewers led only to tidal drains, many of which were defective and stopped up. Garbage and carcasses were sold to farmers or dumped in the marshes of the Neck. Neither, finally, was there any great change in the distribution of functions within the city. The city directories show that the functional districts of 1880 were substantially those of 1860. Although all of the banks had failed during the war, their successors still hugged the intersection of Broad and East Bay streets. The Bank of Charleston retained both its name and site. Others showed less persistence, but some migrated outside the core area.[29]

Charleston society was not therefore turned "bottom side up" between 1860 and 1880,[30] nor was its social geography or its morphology. The era of war and Reconstruction, for all its personal trauma, was structurally less notable for change than for continuity.

Notes

1. The distinction between the interurban and the intraurban scales of analysis is made solely for convenience. The spatial theme is not the only one emphasized in the literature of the discipline, but it is by far the most important.

2. Beginning with *The City* by Robert E. Park and Ernest W. Burgess and extending through the work of such "neo-ecologists" as the Duncans and the Taeubers.

3. For example, the work of Gerald Suttles, especially *The Social Order of the Slum* (Chicago: University of Chicago Press, 1968).

4. Sam Bass Warner, *The Private City: Philadelphia in Three Stages of Its Growth* (Philadelphia: University of Pennsylvania Press, 1968), p. xi. See also Warner's paper, "If All the World Were Philadelphia: A Scaffolding for Urban History, 1774-1930," *American Historical Review* 74 (1968), 26-43.

5. Stephan Thernstrom describes an early reversal in the case of Newburyport, Mass. *Poverty and Progress* (Cambridge: Harvard University Press, 1964).

6. One of the most comprehensive treatments of these themes is: Peter Goheen, *Victorian Toronto: 1850 to 1900* (Chicago: University of Chicago, Department of Geography, Research Paper No. 127, 1970).

7. Gideon Sjoberg, *The Preindustrial City: Past and Present* (New York: The Free Press, 1960).

8. See, for example, discussion in a recent paper on Pittsburgh: John Swauger, "Pittsburgh's Residential Pattern in 1815," *Annals of the Association of American Geographers* 68 (1978), 265-77.

9. The features of Charleston's social geography that are touched on here are considered more fully in three earlier papers: "Race, Residence and Ideology: Charleston, S.C., in the Mid-Nineteenth Century," *Journal of Historical Geography* 2 (1976), 329-46; "Delicate Space: Race and Residence in Charleston, S.C., 1860-1880," West Georgia College *Studies in the Social Sciences* 16 (1977), 17-37; "Testing the Model of the Preindustrial City: The Case of Charleston, S.C.," *Transactions of the Institute of British Geographers* 4, no. 3 (1979), pp. 392-410.

10. A good case for the existence of such a type appears in Ian Davey and Michael Doucet, "The Social Geography of a Commercial City ca. 1853," Appendix to

Michael B. Katz, *The People of Hamilton, Canada West* (Cambridge: M.I.T. Press, 1975).

11. A fuller documentation of these points is given in John P. Radford, "The Planters of Charleston in 1860," *South Carolina Historical Magazine* 77 (October 1976), 227-35. Rogers has discussed the factors influencing the location of the summer houses of the Georgetown planters in Charleston: George C. Rogers, Jr., *The History of Georgetown County, South Carolina* (Columbia: University of South Carolina Press, 1970), pp. 318-23. Joseph Ioor Waring, *A History of Medicine in South Carolina, 1825-1900* (Columbia: South Carolina Medical Association, 1967), provides some useful observations on disease perception.

12. Richard C. Wade, *Slavery in the Cities: The South 1820-1860* (New York: Oxford University Press, 1964), p. 61.

13. William Ferguson, *America by River and Rail: Notes by the Way on the New World and Its People* (London: James Nisbet and Co., 1856), p. 114.

14. Charleston City Council, The Mayor's Report of the Proceedings of the City Authorities from the 4th September, 1837 to the 1st August 1838 (Charleston, 1838), p. 15.

15. Charleston *Courier*, March 1, 1860.

16. Minutes of the Board of Commissioners for Streets and Lamps and for Opening and Widening Alleys, June 6, 1835.

17. Radford, "Race, Residence and Ideology," p. 333.

18. This view of Charleston deviates sharply from that of the antebellum Southern city presented by David R. Goldfield, "Pursuing the American Dream: Cities in the Old South," in Blaine A. Brownell and David R. Goldfield, *The City in Southern History* (Port Washington, N.Y.: Kennikat Press, 1977), pp. 51-91.

19. James E. Vance, Jr., *This Scene of Man: The Role and Structure of the City in the Geography of Western Civilization* (New York: Harper and Row, 1977), pp. 231-39.

20. Martyn J. Bowden, "Reconstruction Following Catastrophe: The Laissez-Faire Rebuilding of Downtown San Francisco After the Earthquake and Fire of 1906," *Proceedings of the Association of American Geographers* 2 (1970), 22-26.

21. Diary of Jacob Schirmer, March 11, 1868 (S.C.H.S.).

22. "C. H." "Letters from the South: No. 4, Charleston, S.C.," New York *Journal of Commerce* (January 1860). Reprinted in the Charleston *Courier*, February 11, 1860.

23. The classic statement of this conflict is Walter Firey's *Land Use in Central Boston* (Cambridge: Harvard University Press, 1946). An instance of the problem in miniature is provided by the "squaring of Circleville" (Ohio) between 1837 and 1856. Reps presents sound economic reasons for this shift, but Harold Carter suggests that the changes were made because "radial-concentric plans were not consonant with the cultural background of the settlers." John W. Reps, *The Making of Urban America* (Princeton: Princeton University Press, 1965), pp. 484-90; Harold Carter, *The Study of Urban Geography* (London: Edward Arnold, 1975), pp. 161-63.

24. Joel Williamson, *After Slavery: The Negro in South Carolina during Reconstruction, 1861-1877* (Chapel Hill: University of North Carolina Press, 1965), pp. 274-99.

25. Radford, "Race, Residence and Ideology," pp. 341-46.

26. Howard N. Rabinowitz, *Race Relations in the Urban South: 1865-1890* (New York: Oxford University Press, 1978), pp. 97-124.

27. C. Vann Woodward, *The Strange Career of Jim Crow*, 2d ed. rev. (New York: Oxford University Press, 1966), pp. 25-26. See also George Brown Tindall, *South Carolina Negroes: 1877-1900* (Columbia: University of South Carolina Press, 1952).

28. George E. Waring, Jr., *Report on the Social Statistics of Cities, Part II: The Southern and Western States* (Washington, D.C.: U.S. Government Printing Office, 1887), pp. 100-103. See also "City Registrar's Report," *Annual Reports of the Officers of the City Government to the City Council of Charleston* (Charleston, 1871), p. 40.

29. Maps showing the distributions of functions within the city in 1860 and 1880 are provided in my Ph.D. diss., "Culture, Economy and Urban Structure in Charleston, S.C., 1860-1880" (Clark University, 1974).

30. As argued in the once popular but now discredited view of James S. Pike, *The Prostrate State*, 2d ed. (New York: Harper and Row, 1968), p. 12.

7

LEADERSHIP AND DECLINE IN POSTWAR CHARLESTON, 1865–1910

Don H. Doyle

In 1884, the Charleston Chamber of Commerce commissioned a mercenary Yankee booster, Jonathan Land, to come south and whip some enthusiasm into the business community of the "ancient and hospitable city." Land, the author of several promotional pamphlets with immodest titles like *Chicago: The Future Metropolis of the New World*, was practiced in the art of commercial hyperbole. He promised to "infuse a spirit of energy and enterprise" in Charleston and to sweep away the city's "stigma of inertness or masterly inactivity." Mounds of statistics demonstrated Charleston's progress, maps displayed its strategic position in world commerce, and streams of purple prose all buoyed up Land's image of Charleston as a wide-awake New South city.

Here she stands at the very portal of one of the finest cotton and rice producing regions in the world; on the one hand is her mighty ocean system giving her transportation as free as the winds that blow to every clime; on the other lies her railways radiating in many directions throughout the State and adjacent States, and pouring into her lap an immense commerce. Already the largest city by far in such close proximity to the ocean, it seems that nature and civilization have conspired to make her in the not far distant future the greatest city in the South.[1]

After all the hot air was expended, however, the "City by the Sea" continued a discouraging pattern of stagnation. What had been one of the premier cities of early America had slid from sixth (in 1830) to twenty-sixth rank among U.S. cities by 1870, then steadily down to ninety-first place in 1910. The population grew slowly, from 49,000 to 59,000 between 1870 and 1910, not enough to keep up with the frenetic pace of younger interior cities in the New South and with the growth of Northern industrial centers. Whatever the natural advantages that Charleston enjoyed, they alone were not enough. As the local economy creaked along, many of the city's upper-class families slipped into a life of genteel poverty in decaying mansions south of Broad Street that, along with their pride, were all many of them had left of the wealth and power the city once commanded. "Clearly we are on the descending scale," lamented one Charlestonian in 1868; "our merchants are gloomy, trade is stagnant, and every interest is suffering."[2]

A series of external forces obstructed Charleston's growth in these years, many of them well beyond the control of local business leaders. The city remained heavily dependent on staple exports, especially cotton; and railroad expansion, combined with a policy of rate discrimination, channeled much of the up-country trade northward, bypassing the "City by the Sea." Sea trade was hampered by a shallow harbor unsuited to the newer deep draft vessels, and the federal government remained none too eager to assist the "cradle of the confederacy" beyond giving a series of stingy allotments. The turmoil of the Civil War and the destruction of slavery helped to undermine the once prosperous rice and Sea Island cotton plantations in Charleston's immediate hinterland, leaving a wide band of unprosperous land almost devoid of satellite towns that were essential to generating growth in Charleston. The municipal government, saddled with an enormous debt during Reconstruction and a declining tax base, was unable to surmount critical problems of water supply and public health that damaged the city's reputation. The tourist and hotel industry, which might have helped offset losses in other sectors of the local economy, was crippled by state temperance legislation supported by a pious up-country that had little sympathy for Charleston. Finally, Charleston experienced more than its fair share of natural disasters, the most notable being the earthquake of 1886.[3]

Any one of these factors might have frustrated the most eager city boosters; yet many within Charleston's business community fought consistently to overcome each of these obstacles. Not all of their efforts were in vain, but most failed, and Charleston's stagnation continued.

It would be seriously misleading, however, to explain Charleston's decline in the New South simply as the failure of struggling city boosters to overcome obstacles to growth, and equally misleading to identify all of those obstacles as external forces beyond local control. Without dismissing the importance of these outside barriers, I will argue here that a number of local conditions internal to Charleston's social structure, and the ideology of its upper class, helped to thwart an effective response to the economic challenges Charleston faced. Implicit in this line of argument is the notion that many of Charleston's upper class resisted (although perhaps not always consciously) the opportunities for growth and the economic changes growth required. If this analysis is correct, we may better understand Charleston's relative decline, not as the failure of frustrated bourgeoisie to promote their city, but as a quiet triumph of a conservative local aristocracy to preserve their city and their social status within it.

This interpretation of Charleston is based on the early results of a long-term research project in which I have compared the economic elites of four New South cities. These include Mobile, which like Charleston suffered decline after the war, and two rising interior cities, Atlanta and Nashville, which benefited from the expansion of railroads and manufacturing in the New South. This comparative framework allows certain characteristics of Charleston's economic leadership to be measured against those of other Southern cities. Data on almost 500 economic leaders (145 in Charleston) identified as directors of boards and as commercial association officers were gathered mostly from city directories of around 1880. The most important results of this collective biographical analysis with respect to Charleston can be summarized briefly.[4]

First, Charleston's economic leaders were older men who were entrenched in the local antebellum economy. Close to 40 percent were over sixty years of age, and most of the rest were in their fifties. (Atlanta, in contrast, had less than a quarter over sixty; one-fifth were under forty.) Fully 80 percent of Charleston's economic elite in 1880 could be found listed in the 1860 city directory, and only a few of the remainder appear to be "new men" who came from outside the city since the war (only 31 percent of Atlanta's elite were listed in 1860). The family names of Charleston's elite also testify to the remarkable continuity of this old city's upper class in the New South. Names like DeSaussure, Gibbes, Huger, Middleton, Pinckney, Ravenel, Rhett, and others among the 1880 elite all had deep roots in Charleston's colonial past.

Second, Charleston's economic leadership in 1880, like that of Mobile, was loaded with cotton factors, who constituted about 30 percent of the leadership. Far less well represented, in comparison to Atlanta and Nashville, were dry goods and other wholesale jobbers, railroad entrepreneurs, and manufacturers—occupations that were more in tune with the new economic order of the postwar South. Instead, the wealth, prestige, and economic power that company directorships and official positions in commercial associations signified were firmly in the hands of men strongly tied to the old order of staple exports. These were men who were probably less able to flexibly accommodate to the demands of new economic challenges. More important, I would argue, they were not *inclined* to pursue an aggressive course of change that would threaten their entrenched positions.

The characteristics of these men give us some idea of the exclusive, conservative nature of Charleston's economic leadership. This was reflected more generally in the social organization and ideology of the city's upper class in particular. To a remarkable degree, Charleston remained a society stratified by traditional ascriptive criteria. Above all, it was a society that revolved around the family and its lineage as the measure of social status. In Boston, it is said, a man is assessed by asking, "What does he know?"; in

New York, "How much is he worth?"; in Charleston, "Who was his grand-father?"[5] This jest was not entirely fanciful. It was precisely this filial piety that allowed so many older men to continue in positions of economic leadership. It left younger men frustrated (those with ambition at least) and led William L. Trenholm to decry Charleston's tendency to "defer to senil-ity."[6]

A multitude of clubs and associations, most of them with roots in the colonial era, served (in addition to genealogy) as a means of demarcating social status in Charleston. But few of these functioned like modern volun-tary associations, which cut across social and economic boundaries and honored the achieved status of "new men." Instead, Charleston's clubs tended to reinforce the system of assigning status by birth, thereby exclud-ing interlopers. A series of ethnic heritage societies provided one mechanism of underlining family genealogy. The Huguenot Society for French descen-dants, the Hibernian Society for Irish, the St. Andrews Society for Scotch, the St. Georges Society for English, and the South Carolina Society for those with colonial ancestors all passed on prestigious memberships from father to son.[7]

The most elegantly exclusive of Charleston's clubs was the St. Cecilia Society, founded in 1737. Membership and activities have been preciously guarded secrets, but there is no question that an invitation to a St. Cecilia Ball was the signal of arrival in Charleston society. The invitation lists were made up secretly by a board of managers, selected to be "representative of each large family connection in the city." Many came to the balls in frayed tuxedos and moth-bitten gowns, but it was family status not wealth that the society honored. Membership was carefully controlled by a system of inter-nal references and blackballing. The sons and grandsons of members were generally accepted at the proper age with little trouble. Those outside the circle would have to pass a more exacting test of social acceptability. Dinner parties, club activities, and guest invitations to the St. Cecilia Balls all of-fered opportunity to examine whether a prospective member had the proper family background, breeding, and attitude to fit the St. Cecilia mold.[8]

DuBose Heyward's novel, *Mamba's Daughters*, includes a fascinating ac-count of the rites of passage in Charleston society. Mrs. George P. Atkin-son, the wife of a Yankee cotton seed oil manufacturer (who bears a strong resemblance to George Babbitt), desperately wants to be accepted by the "social gods" of Charleston. For several years, she tries to ply local matrons with luncheons, bridge parties, and afternoon teas in her home on Legaré Street. But she uses these occasions to display her husband's new wealth in an effort to impress. The "straitened circumstances" of the city's "old fami-lies," Heyward explains, makes this seem gauche, and she is kept "outside the fatal line [where] one was always . . . a stranger stopping temporarily in the city." The way to a St. Cecilia invitation, the Atkinsons learn, was not over a lady's teacup, but over a glass of cold bourbon served down at the Yacht Club. Mr. Atkinson lingers at the club after work and learns that the social ladder in Charleston is not ascended by wealth or achievement, but by conforming to the gentle social graces that, if anything, discourage ambition.[9]

My point is not that anything of profound importance to Charleston's economic future was ever decided at a St. Cecilia Ball, only the certification of status among the city's social elite. But the society embodied the ideology of an upper class that awarded prestige to an exclusive line of heirs and to a few select outsiders who conformed to the code. New men of ambition and wealth appeared in Charleston but were unable to erect any lasting associational structures to establish an alternative system of stratification.

Within this closed, patriarchal community evolved a culture of leisure and a disdain for certain occupations, values that fitted perfectly the system of ascriptive status. Visiting businessmen were annoyed by the fact that most Charleston merchants never opened their doors before 9:00 A.M. and were appalled by the lingering mid-morning breaks taken at the coffee-houses and taverns along Broad Street. This strenuous work day was again interrupted by the dinner bells that called the men home for the traditional midday dinner, a full meal with the family, often accompanied by ample wine and liquor.[10]

This leisurely pace of work was well fitted to the cotton factor, whose role required frequent entertainment of visiting planters. It also was rooted in Charleston's tradition as a resort for planters when they came to town to enjoy a constant round of horse races, cock fights, and fancy balls, all accompanied by plenty to eat and drink. Although it may not have permeated all elements of the business community, this culture of leisure set the tone for the city's upper class, and all those who aspired to enter it.[11]

This meant also that only certain occupations could be pursued by Charlestonian gentlemen, "without a sacrifice of family dignity." Outside the professions, there were cotton trading, banking, and other brokerage jobs in the commercial houses along Broad and East Bay. "The honest truth," admitted Trenholm, "is that commerce was never heartily appreciated in Charleston. . . . As soon as a merchant acquired a fortune in Charleston, he invested it in lands and negroes, became a planter, and devoted his sons to the learned professions." Other successful merchants left, Trenholm argued, because Charleston was not a city that "cherishes their presence and retains their affection." With their departure, the local pool of experienced entrepreneurs who could advise, promote, and capitalize new commercial and industrial enterprises was reduced.[12]

This tone of aristocratic disdain for bourgeois striving might have been overcome by powerful commercial associations. They could give Charleston's businessmen a collective voice to promote commercial values and push for their city's advantage in the race for economic expansion. Above all, commercial associations in other New South cities linked the interests and ambitions of individual businessmen to the collective destiny of the city. But Charleston's commercial associations often seemed to reinforce rather than to combat the ambivalence toward enterprise and growth that pervaded the city.

The Charleston Chamber of Commerce was founded in 1784 and claimed to be the oldest continuous chamber in the United States. This venerable institution was dominated by older merchants (particularly cotton factors) who spent an inordinate amount of time congratulating the chamber on its ancient history and eulogizing dead members with long-winded tributes to their noble ancestry. In 1868, the chamber issued a memorial to Congress urging it to preserve the old Customs House as a home for a new Merchants Exchange. "We hope that the tide of prosperity is again setting upon us, and we wish in every way to establish and strengthen the Commercial character of Charleston." The Customs House, "consecrated by many memories," would, they argued with unintended irony, serve as an ideal home for Charleston's commercial spirit. There also was a good deal of serious business at the chamber's meetings: petitions to governments, reports on trade, debates over commercial policy, and the like. But one of the central attractions of the chamber was its club room, well-stocked with liquor and wine, where even on Sundays the members could retreat to mix business and pleasure in the best Charleston tradition.[13]

Immediately after the war a new organization, the Board of Trade, sprang up, and for a time, it offered a vigorous challenge to the chamber. "Sitting down upon the crumbling ruins of our ancient City with our arms folded and complaining of our lot will not give our children bread," proclaimed the new board's leaders. This new organization, led by wholesale jobbers, opened its doors to all merchants who would pay dues and abandoned the stuffy system of blackballing used by the Chamber of Commerce. Within a few years, its membership rose to 250. Meeting in spartan quarters in a rented room of the Charleston Hotel, the board pursued an energetic course attacking each of the city's commercial problems, with special attention to the railroad connections to the up-country and Midwest. The board also became actively involved in the national Board of Trade, and local delegates to the annual convention reported with enthusiasm on Charleston's future in a national economy. The spirit was fully in accord with the New South creed: "We are no longer sectional. Our interests are identical with every Northern and Western State." Everything was done to appeal to Northern capitalists and to advertise the opportunities for profit in Charleston. The board made strenuous efforts to repeal legislation, like the bankruptcy and usury laws, and the local practice of jailing visiting debtors that discouraged outside investment in Charleston. Railroad rate discrimination, high wharf and warehouse rates, and other obstacles to trade also were investigated and attacked by the board. The board cheered on innovative enterprises, new steamboat lines and phosphate works, that joined "the race for the golden prize." It also tried with limited success to awaken the "ancient Chamber of Commerce" to the need for "concerted action" in all these matters.[14]

As the Board of Trade matured and attracted more members from the old families of Charleston, it began to take on the familiar characteristics of Charleston club life. A building was purchased, originally for a telegraph office and reading room. But it soon included a dining room, club room, and billiards room complete with "elegant furniture and other appurtenances." Rules on gambling, drinking, and smoking appear to have been honored in the breach. A faction that pushed to keep the club rooms open on Sunday did not give business duties as their reason. (A compromise allowed the rooms to be open all day, except from 2:00 to 5:00 P.M., a concession to the two o'clock dinner.) New amendments to the rules also introduced a system of blackballing new members. The expenses of the club rooms put the board into debt, and as dues were raised and the amenities of the club rooms cut back, members began dropping out. By May 1872, the board, which began with such eager promise just six years before, apparently declared bankruptcy and disbanded.[15]

A new organization, the Charleston Exchange, emerged in the wake of the board's demise in 1872 and tried to revive the New South spirit in Charleston. Although affiliated with the National Cotton Exchange, the local organization was designed to attract support from all of Charleston's wholesale export sectors. The exchange boldly made plans for a new building near Adger's Wharf, hired a full-time superintendent, and sent him to New York City to "acquire a knowledge of the interior management and detail of the kindred Institutions of the great Commercial Metropolis." The superintendent came back from New York brimming with new ideas, and the exchange eagerly followed suggestions to build a vigorous commercial body on the Northern model. But the membership grew slowly, then fell due to a high entrance fee, the depression of 1873, and a stubborn indifference among many of the cotton factors and commission merchants along East Bay.[16] By 1884, when the "ancient Chamber of Commerce" celebrated its centennial with testimonials to its glorious years of colonial prosperity and illustrious membership, that venerable old body had regained the mantle of commercial leadership in Charleston without challenge.[17]

One of the constant complaints of Charleston's boosters was that businessmen pursued private prosperity at the expense of collective efforts to promote Charleston's commonwealth. This lack of public spirit was evident enough, but it would be misleading to blame it on a privatistic obsession with individual wealth. As the daily work habits alluded to earlier would suggest, individual enterprise was hardly more aggressive than collective ef-forts to boost Charleston. In a community that awarded status according to lineage and social grace, striving profit-seekers were not encouraged.

With some notable exceptions, business practices in Charleston were anti-quated, even by late nineteenth-century standards. In comparison with cities like Atlanta and Nashville, business firms were significantly smaller in scale, in terms of both the capital invested and the numbers of employees and partners involved. In part, this tendency toward smaller firms was due to a tenacious loyalty to family and kinship as the basis of business organi-zation. A closed system of nepotism was rife even within large organiza-tions, such as the South Carolina Railroad. According to one critic: "A man of merit and capacity had no chance to get employment, unless he was a relation. . . ."[18] The smallness of Charleston's business firms also was due to a whole tradition-bound cast of mind that rejected the risk and strange-ness of large-scale enterprise involving aggressive innovations in capital formation, labor organization, technology, and marketing. In a declining economic environment, this conservative tendency led many merchants to take a comfortable profit on a small volume of trade, rather than to com-pete with low per unit profits for a larger share of commerce. As the rail-roads opened competition among cities, planters and up-country merchants could more easily seek more competitive prices elsewhere. But Charleston businessmen seemed slow to respond to the call for commercial innova-tion.[19]

Linked to this was an outdated assumption that trade would naturally flow to the doorstep of the "City by the Sea." As drummers from Baltimore, and other northern rivals, invaded the up-country, Charleston merchants seemed content to rely on their geographic proximity to draw trade and re-fused to answer up-country pleas for competitive bidding.[20]

There were occasional criticisms of "old fogeyism" in Charleston, like F. W. Dawson's blast in 1886: "There are changes in the modes of trans-acting business which are incompatible with the easy-going method of the fathers and grandfathers of the present generation." But within Charleston's small firms, business practices continued to be passed down from one gen-eration to the next. Few new models of modern large-scale enterprise in-truded, and no educational institutions devoted to business training emerged to seriously disrupt the transmission of the old ways.[21]

The conservative frame of mind in Charleston's business community re-vealed itself most clearly in several instances when promising opportunities for bold new departures were confronted. The first of these came in 1867, when rich deposits of phosphate were discovered in the riverbeds just outside the city. Here was a source of fertilizer desperately needed by Southern cot-ton planters and an ideal occasion for Charleston to diversify its economic base. There was something poignantly appropriate in the idea that an opportunity for industrial take-off in a New South Charleston would take form in mining the ancient fossil remains of prehistoric dinosaurs. The phosphate beds, in fact, had been discovered four decades earlier, but were appreciated only for their fossil remains until 1867, when the full value of their potential as fertilizer was realized by two scientists, Dr. N. A. Pratt of Georgia and Francis Holmes, a professor at the College of Charleston. These men were later accused of keeping their discovery a secret from Charleston capitalists, and Holmes made a full account of the events that followed the discovery. Holmes insisted he took his findings to the leading men of Charleston's business community and "exerted himself beyond measure, vainly endeavoring to induce . . . the citizens of Charleston, especially her merchants and men of wealth, to avail themselves of this great discovery. He walked Broad Street almost daily for six weeks, explaining everything and urging upon everyone who heard him to beware that the golden opportunity be not lost—to grasp it at once, or foreign or Northern capitalists would certainly take it up." Ultimately, Holmes and Pratt went North to Philadelphia. Within mere hours, they attracted the interest of capitalists and formed a company with $1 million paid in capital.[22]

Local investors followed this initial Northern venture into the phosphate industry, and their money financed several small firms that survived and even prospered but that were not always able to take advantage of the economies of scale in machinery, labor training, and research to perfect techniques of mining, preparing the phosphate rock, or going into the manufacture of fertilizers. By 1880, twenty-one phosphate mining companies had entered the field, most of them capitalized and managed by Charleston investors. With all the profits that were made in this phosphate boom in its early years, surprisingly little progress was made in developing more sophisticated techniques of mining and manufacturing. Most companies still depended on local blacks to perform crude manual labor with pick and shovel on land and to dredge by hand from small boats in the rivers. By 1881, only one company, owned by outside interests, was "thoroughly equipped" with three heavy dredges, steam tugs, and a fleet of barges and small boats. By the 1890s, new phosphate discoveries were made in Florida and Tennessee, and Charleston's phosphate industry, which formerly enjoyed a monopoly, slowly sunk in the face of competition. The easy land and river mining was by this time completed, and further extraction would have required heavy equipment, which most firms did not have. Governor Tillman's policy of enforcing state claims on river phosphate royalties only hastened the collapse of this once promising industry in Charleston.[23]

A more telling example of Charleston's reluctance toward innovation and urban growth came in the late 1880s, when an opportunity arose to build a prosperous tourist industry. With the opening of large tourist hotels in Florida in the 1880s, streams of Northerners came South to enjoy the climate and indulge their health. Charleston was nicely situated to catch some of this traffic, if only as a stop-off en route to Florida. Besides its warm winter climate, Charleston's numerous historic sites and colonial architecture catered to a growing public appetite for history, particularly Civil War history. Here it seemed was an ideal way to join Charleston's conservatism to a New South boosterism.

But tourist accommodations were limited to the Charleston Hotel, built in 1839 and down at the heels by the 1880s, along with a number of other equally old, small hotels. None of them was suited in size and luxury to the taste of the new tourists coming South. Models for the modern resort hotel of the times were built in Florida and were rapidly being imitated in Savannah and other cities eager to compete for the tourist dollar.[24]

In 1888, one of Charleston's most progressive business leaders, George W. Williams, joined by F. J. Pelzer and F. W. Wagener, led the campaign for a $1 million modern tourist hotel in Charleston. At first, the public response was fervently enthusiastic, particularly among the city's young men. At a mass meeting, a series of speeches foretold a new day for Charleston and cleverly linked that new day to the glory of the past that was charmingly preserved and waiting for tourists to discover. When Williams closed his speech with a pledge of $50,000, followed by pledges from Pelzer, Wagener, and others totaling over $117,000, the audience, according to F. W. Dawson's account, "went simply wild with enthusiasm. They shouted and applauded and rose from their chairs and waved their hats. . . ." The band played "Dixie," and "there was another furor."[25]

When it came to risking capital in the new venture, Charleston's wealthy citizens were far less enthusiastic. A hotel company was formed but was barely able to raise $250,000. Landowners near the Battery refused to sell land for a hotel site, and others held out for ridiculously inflated prices. Discouraged by fading local support, Williams reluctantly went North to raise capital but found little interest. "If he will send some of his enthusiasm to Mars," The *News and Courier* advised Williams, the hotel "can be built there much quicker than it will be built in Charleston." Other, more modest hotel projects followed the campaign of 1888, but soon fizzled amid the apathy of local capitalists.[26] It would be a long while before "America's best kept secret" was revealed and made accessible to large numbers of tourists.

A third example of Charleston's ambivalence toward economic progress in the New South came with the South Carolina Interstate and West Indian Exposition in 1901-02. During the 1890s, the city reached the low point in its postwar economic doldrums. The phosphate industry collapsed, tourism fell off with the depression and with the enforcement of state temperance law, and cotton trade and railroad interests continued to suffer. Many of the city's leading businessmen left for opportunities elsewhere and were joined by a stream of young men—the "flower of Charleston's youth," lamented one of those remaining.[27]

The idea for the exposition was inspired by the success of those in Nashville and Atlanta. The Young Men's Business League first urged Charleston to follow these New South models. Soon the idea was tied to an enticing dream of reviving the Caribbean trade that once supported Charleston's colonial prosperity. After a slow start, the exposition began to attract public interest, especially among the "young men" whose last names suggested few connections with the city's aristocracy. Leading the movement was Frederick W. Wagener, a German-born industrialist with an iron determination to make the exposition the starting point for a new Charleston.[28]

There was broad but shallow support for the exposition in many quarters of Charleston. Subscription sales of over $116,000 came mainly from small contributions. Wealthy individuals, business firms, and banks showed little faith in the movement and did little to encourage it. Solicitations of Northern capital met with limited success, in part due to the weak show at home. Wagener was forced to put his personal credit behind a bond issued by the exposition company before local banks would purchase it. The "indifference" of local business leaders and the distrust of outside interests combined with bad weather, construction delays, Republican opposition in Congress, and the "indifference" of local blacks to spell serious trouble for the exposition. When gate receipts failed to generate sufficient capital, local creditors took their claims to court. Rumors of impending financial disaster smudged the "Ivory City" in the public eye, hurt attendance, and frightened creditors. Again, only Wagener's personal financial backing kept the exposition from collapsing altogether.[29]

The exposition, the official report said in 1902, "opened the 'door to opportunity' to our own people, and to those who would come into this land of promise." The door had been pried open, but many of those who counted most in deciding whether or not Charleston would walk through it, as one visitor put it, "slammed its door in Progress' face and resisted the modern with fiery determination."[30] Part of the exposition grounds, designed as the starting point for a New South Charleston, was turned into a new campus for The Citadel, which embodied the city's most cherished traditions of military honor.

Charleston's slow growth has been explained by apologists who blame external forces, from railroad discrimination and political corruption to natural disasters. These obstacles, the argument goes, were beyond the control of a courageous group of tireless civic leaders whose efforts matched their frustration. A corollary to this interpretation explains that a tone of aristocratic disdain for the New South parvenues was little more than a defense mechanism against such frustrations—the idea being that "one cannot lose, if one never admits to having played the game."[31]

My purpose here has not been to dismiss certain external, and some truly uncontrollable, obstacles to Charleston's growth. Nor do I mean to deny the importance of an ongoing effort by local boosters to fight those external obstacles and to generate new sources of local economic growth. My research suggests, however, that one of the most formidable barriers to economic innovation and growth was internal. It was the often passive resistance of the city's wealthy upper-class families to specific movements and the pervasive ideology they projected that discouraged a progressive form of capitalism from taking firm root in Charleston. This resistance was not due to mere selfish privatism, not just to dreamy romanticism, not simply to lethargic indifference. These were terms that a frustrated bourgeoisie, immersed in the New South ideal, hurled at an entrenched upper class that held fast to different ideals. The resistance to growth in Charleston was rooted in the unwillingness of the upper class to surrender its ideals and the whole system of social organization that was integrally connected to that ideology. Charleston's failure to grow rapidly after the Civil War was, in truth, the failure of the New South and the failure of its rising urban middle class to take full control of the wealth, power, and public ideals that would determine Charleston's future. Amid all the poverty and economic decay that plagued Charleston was the undeniable success of an upper class that managed to fend off the assault of the New South within its local domain. It also succeeded in preserving a city that continued to give testimony to the beauty and grace that the Old South fought to save with less success outside Charleston.

Notes

The author wishes to thank the Vanderbilt University Research Council, ACLS, and the American Philosophical Society for support of this research.

1. Jonathan E. Land, *Charleston: Her Trade, Commerce and Industries, 1883-4* (Charleston: Published by the author, 1884), p. 12.

2. Quoted in Francis Butler Simkins and Robert Hilliard Woody, *South Carolina During Reconstruction* (Chapel Hill: University of North Carolina Press, 1932), p. 282.

3. Robert Goodwyn Rhett, *Charleston: An Epic of Carolina* (Richmond: Garrett and Massie, 1940), pp. 305-16, 324-35.

4. A fuller description of the method and conclusions of this study can be found in my "Urbanization and Southern Culture: Economic Elites in Four New South Cities (Atlanta, Nashville, Charleston, Mobile), 1865-1910," in Vernon Burton and Robert C. McMath, eds., *Toward a New South?: Studies in Post-Civil War Southern Communities* (Westport, Conn.: Greenwood Press, forthcoming).

5. E. Merton Coulter, *George Walton Williams: The Life of a Southern Merchant and Banker, 1820-1903* (Athens, Ga.: Hibriten Press, 1976), p. 30.

6. William Lee Trenholm, *The South: An Address delivered . . . on the Third*

Anniversary of the Charleston Board of Trade . . . (Charleston: Walker, Evans & Cogwell, 1869), p. 9.

7. Rules and membership lists for these organizations can be found in the South Caroliniana Library, South Carolina Historical Society, and the Charleston Library Society.

8. Joseph W. Barnwell, "Life and Recollections," pp. 364-86, typescript in Barnwell Papers, South Carolina Historical Society, Charleston (SCHS); Mrs. St. Julien Ravenel, *Charleston: The Place and the People* (New York: Macmillan, 1925), pp. 426-30; Anne Rittenhouse, "America's Social House of Peers," *Ainslee's Magazine* 16 (October 1905), 76-84; *Rules of the St. Cecilia Society* . . . (Charleston: Walker, Evans & Cogwell, 1843), in SCHS.

9. DuBose Heyward, *Mamba's Daughters* (New York: Grosset & Dunlap, 1929), pp. 115-21.

10. Coulter, *Williams*, p. 30; Louis B. Wright, *South Carolina: A Bicentennial History* (New York: W. W. Norton, 1976), pp. 7-8. See also Albert Goldman's biting contemporary account of work habits in "Charleston! Charleston!" *Esquire* (June 1977).

11. Ravenel, *Charleston*, pp. 385-86; Harold D. Woodman, *King Cotton and His Retainers* (Lexington, Ky.: University of Kentucky Press, 1968), pp. 3-71.

12. Heyward, *Mamba's Daughters*, p. 43; William L. Trenholm, *The Centennial Address Before the Charleston Chamber of Commerce* . . . (Charleston: Charleston, S.C. Chamber of Commerce, 1884), p. 27.

13. Charleston Chamber of Commerce, "Minutes, 1866-78," p. 96, October 14, 1870; p. 176, February 2, 1872, MS in SCHS.

14. Charleston Board of Trade, "Minutes, 1866-72," passim, MS in South Carolina Archives, Columbia. See also the board's published *Proceedings* for 1867 and 1871.

15. Board of Trade, "Minutes," February 2, April 6, May 4, June 1, 1870; April 5, 1871; January 3, 10, February 7, March 6, 1872.

16. Charleston Cotton Exchange, "Proceedings of the Association, Board of Directors and Committees, 1872-88," October 17, 1872; February 15, 1879; 2 vols., MS in SCHS.

17. See, for example, Trenholm, *The South*, p. 5.

18. G. A. Neuffer, *Treatise on the Trade of Charleston* (Charleston: Courier Book and Job Presses, 1870) p. 20.

19. Trenholm, *Centennial Address*, p. 38.

20. Neuffer, *Treatise*, p. 18; J. C. and E. Bailey to Messrs. N. Hunt & Son, Greenville, S.C., September 8, 1876, in Nathaniel A. Hunt Papers, file 7, MS in South Caroliniana Library, Columbia.

21. *News and Courier* (Charleston), September 1, 1886. The Charleston Business College and Short Hand Institute opened around 1890, but the choice of most proper Charlestonians was the College of Charleston, which continued its classical curriculum well into the twentieth century.

22. Francis S. Holmes, "The Carolina Phosphates: How, When, and by Whom Discovered, and Their Commercial Value Ascertained," handbill, August [?] 1878, in William Ashmead Courtenay Papers, vol. 1, South Caroliniana Library (this

handbill is in the form of a letter to the editor of the *News and Courier*, but was apparently never published as such in the newspaper).

23. State Board of Agriculture, S.C., *South Carolina: Resources and Population, Institutions and Industries* (Charleston: Walker, Evans & Cogwell, 1883), p. 51; State Department of Agriculture, Commerce, and Immigration, S.C., *Handbook of South Carolina: Resources, Institutions and Industries of the State* (Columbia: The State Company, 1908), p. 398; D. D. Wallace, *The History of South Carolina* (New York: American Historical Society, 1934), vol. 3, p. 355; Coulter, *Williams*, pp. 151-62. This subject has been explored more fully in Tom W. Schick and Don H. Doyle, "Labor, Capital, and Politics in South Carolina: The Low Country Phosphate Industry, 1869-1920," (unpublished manuscript).

24. Coulter, *Williams*, pp. 207-08.

25. *News and Courier*, June 2 (8:3), 1888, quoted in Coulter, *Williams*, p. 209.

26. *News and Courier*, December 21 (1:3), 1888, quoted in Coulter, *Williams*, p. 215.

27. Rhett, *Charleston*, p. 322.

28. J. C. Hemphill, "A Short History of the South Carolina Interstate and West Indian Exposition," in *Year Book, 1902, City of Charleston, S.C.* (Charleston: Walker, Evans & Cogwell, 1903), appendix, pp. 107-71. See also *The Exposition* (Charleston: n. p. 1900-02), 2 vols., in SCHS.

29. Hemphill, "Short History," especially pp. 146-53.

30. Mildred Cram, *Old Seaport Towns of the South* (New York: Dodd, Mead & Co., 1917), p. 125, quoted in Blaine A. Brownell, *The Urban Ethos in the South, 1920-1930* (Baton Rouge: Louisiana State University Press, 1975), p. 30.

31. Ernest Culpepper Clark, "Francis Warrington Dawson in the Era of South Carolina's Conservative-Democratic Restoration, 1874-1889" (Ph.D. diss., University of North Carolina, 1974), pp. 220-22, includes a good discussion of Dawson's leadership in Charleston's promotional activities and his ambivalence toward the New South. Rhett, *Charleston*, pp. 305-55, also interprets the city's beleaguered history with an emphasis on the external obstacles to growth.

IV

LAW AND DISORDER: CASE STUDIES IN GEORGIA

Many Southern historians believe that another phenomenon to survive the transition from the Old South to the New was the region's excessive proclivity for crime and violence. The following two articles examine new approaches to this old issue.

In his article "Law and Disorder in the Old South: The Situation in Georgia, 1830–1860," David J. Bodenhamer enters the debate on whether or not the antebellum South was a prebourgeois or a modern society. His approach to answering this question is unique: an examination of Southern criminal justice for whites in four Georgia counties that, as a unit, represent "in microcosm the economic and demographic diversity of the Old South." In the more rural counties, Bodenhamer finds that the pattern of criminal justice supports the contentions of those historians who view the antebellum South as a premodern society. In the "town counties," however, the criminal justice pattern paralleled those of the North, and were similar to the criminal justice systems of modern societies. He argues, then, that the real distinction in nineteenth-century criminal justice may not be between the North and South, but rather between rural and urban areas. If this is so, Bodenhamer hypothesizes "the Southern response to white crime would be unique only because the South was more rural than the North and not because it clung stubbornly and desperately to a prebourgeois order."

In contrast to Bodenhamer's essay, William F. Holmes's examination of one aspect of postbellum violence in Georgia emphasizes sectional differences rather than similarities. Holmes's article, "Whitecapping in Late Nine-

teenth-Century Georgia," is a pioneering study of moonshine violence in which he describes how making "bootleg"
whiskey was a vital, traditional part of the socioeconomic
life of northwest Georgia. Attempts by federal law enforcement officers to suppress this activity provoked native whites into forming paramilitary "whitecapping" units
that used flogging, firebombing, and murder to stop the in-
trusions of federal revenue agents and their informers.
Holmes admits that group violence "dedicated to maintaining traditional community values" was prevalent throughout
the nation during the late nineteenth century. However,
Holmes argues, a broader pattern of this type of collective
violence existed in the South in the face of threats that originated outside the region.

8

LAW AND DISORDER IN THE OLD SOUTH: THE SITUATION IN GEORGIA, 1830–1860

David J. Bodenhamer

In recent years, historians have revived the perennial argument over the uniqueness of Southern civilization with their discussions of whether the Old South was a modern or a premodern society. Eugene Genovese and his disciples consistently identify the South as prebourgeois in its economic and social structure. Works by cliometricians, on the other hand, rebut the image of a paternalistic, suffocating aristocracy by insisting that the South was a rational and economically dynamic, hence modern, society.[1]

Problems exist with both positions, however. First, studies of Southern modernization or the lack of it in the prewar decades focus almost exclusively on slavery and the plantation system. This is regrettable because most Southerners did not own slaves, and it is unclear whether they adopted all or even most of the values of a slave-holding aristocracy. Moreover, scholars have examined only infrequently the extent to which institutions not connected with slavery—family, commerce, law, church—exhibited values associated with modernization. Another problem with previous studies is their failure to analyze values and behavior in a local setting. While this appears to be changing, historians of the Old South have shown a distressing tendency to examine society at a level no lower than that of a state. Often, this approach simply aggregates behavior and masks real distinctions in the stereotypical Southern personality.

This essay will test the assumption that Southern society remained unaffected by modernization before the Civil War by analyzing its response to the problem of white crime. Perhaps no institution of the Old South has received less attention from scholars than the legal system, especially its criminal process. This is ironic because few institutions reflect social values as clearly as does criminal justice. Joel P. Bishop, a major nineteenth-century theorist of criminal law, recognized this when he remarked that "criminal law sustains a more intimate relation to the everyday life of the community than any other division of law."[2] It establishes standards of behavior within which each citizen is to conduct himself, and by silence, it implies the citizen's freedom in areas not regulated. It also reflects the attitudes of the community toward both offense and offender.[3] Thus, an examination of Southern criminal justice should allow historians to locate important values of the antebellum South and to gauge whether they were modern or traditional.

Fortunately, scholars have provided a model of criminal justice in modern societies against which antebellum Southern justice can be compared. In modernizing areas—and in the United States modernization is usually synonymous with the commercial/industrial city—dominant social values are order, predictability, and security of property. This undoubtedly reflects the nature of the urban environment, with its social stratification, cosmopolitanism, and anomie. Because traditional institutions of authority are weak or nonexistent in the city, law must control threatening behavior. So in modern societies, the criminal justice system concerns itself with prosecuting those crimes that threaten order and property and attempts to ensure predictability and efficiency in punishment.[4]

In order to judge the modernity of antebellum Southern justice, information was gathered on over 4,500 criminal cases from four Georgia counties, of which this study examined a stratified random sample of 10 percent.[5] The data were used to construct a profile of crime and justice in this part of the Old South. Two caveats are necessary, however. Only crimes committed by whites are examined because only those offenses received routine attention from the legal system. Moreover, the data offered represent only illegal acts noted by an official body charged with law enforcement. It is impossible to determine the true amount of crime in any society; even with modern methods of reporting, criminologists estimate that less than half of all crimes are detected. Still, the data offered here are useful for illustrating broad patterns of crime and justice in this Southern state.

Georgia was studied because it represents in microcosm the economic and demographic diversity of the Old South, and each of the counties chosen for this study represents a major element of that diversity. Two of the counties—Liberty and Murray—were rural and agricultural but of different types. Liberty County was a stable society that experienced an extremely slow population growth. Located in the tidewater region below Savannah, the county had a well-developed plantation economy, with an emphasis on the cash crops of cotton and rice and a heavy use of slave labor.[6] Murray County, on the other hand, was in a rapidly growing area dominated by independent white farmers. With only a small black population, self-sufficient agriculture was the economic mainstay of this mountain county situated on the state's northwestern boundary with Tennessee.[7]

Bibb and Muscogee counties, the other two areas studied, represent the incipient modernization of antebellum Southern society. Both counties were demographically and economically dynamic. Each county practiced an extensive cotton agriculture; yet each also was a commercial center with an emerging urban culture. There were important differences between them, however. Bibb County, with its seat at Macon, was located in the center of the state's cotton-growing region, and its expansion depended heavily on the activities of cotton factors.[8] Muscogee County had a more balanced economy. Columbus, the county seat, touted itself as the "Lowell of the South" because of its textile mills, and navigation on the Chattahoochee River gave the county a direct link with the Gulf of Mexico and beyond. But Columbus was also a boom town on the state's last frontier. Its reputation for rowdiness and a less-than-genteel culture contrasted vividly with the more urbane society of Macon and Bibb County.[9]

There was a curiously divided attitude toward crime among the four counties surveyed. In planter-dominated Liberty County, crime was not a matter of public concern. Not once did grand jurors voice any fear of increased criminal activity. Instead, they repeatedly expressed satisfaction with the efforts of county law enforcement officers. With great pleasure, jurors would announce that they could find "no public violations of law requiring our interference."[10]

In rural Murray County, with its preponderance of yeoman farmers, a similar attitude toward crime prevailed throughout the antebellum period. Despite an occasional concern that there was a "looseness in the morals of our county," grand jurors usually congratulated citizens on their "general good order, sobriety and morality."[11] When jurors did notice an increase in criminal activity, they deplored the incovenience it caused for those who had to attend its prosecution, but they also interpreted the increase as an inevitable result of population growth. Still, the suppression of disorder was considered necessary in order to strengthen the bonds of society and to secure to the county an advantage equal to climate, railroads, and soil in its efforts to maintain economic growth.[12]

On occasion, grand juries in Bibb and Muscogee counties would subscribe to the belief that criminal activity posed no threat to their communities; far more often, however, they expressed alarm over its ability to invade the entire society. "Crime in various forms is stalking through the county in seeming defiance of the laws," one Muscogee jury warned, while another concluded that "vice is abroad in our community."[13] Bibb jurors joined the refrain by lamenting that they "were exposed to a continuance of vice, licentiousness, degradation and depravity."[14] Newspapers, too, reported that crime, especially serious crime, was becoming a major social problem. The comment of a Macon editor was typical: murders, he claimed, were "rife throughout the county," and "flagrant violations of the public peace" were increasingly troublesome.[15] Twelve years later, another editor even wondered whether the population of his city could be "governed at all or not?"[16]

The patterns of criminal prosecution appear to justify the different perceptions of grand juries and newspapers. Over 80 percent of all prosecutions originated in Bibb and Muscogee counties, while less than 4 percent began in the plantation society of Liberty County, and only 14 percent were from Murray County. These percentages did not change much over time, even though the average number of prosecutions per year increased each decade. This was especially true in Bibb County, where the number of criminal cases doubled from the 1840s to the 1850s. Liberty and Murray counties, on the other hand, experienced stability, and even a slight decline, in prosecutions before local courts.

Not surprisingly, the volume and percentage of serious crime varied by county. For the predominantly rural counties, serious crime remained an infrequent occurrence. With the exception of two years in Murray County, felonies never exceeded 20 percent of the criminal case load, and the total number of these crimes declined from the 1840s to the 1850s. At times, the lack of serious crime in rural areas could be striking. In Liberty County, for example, felonies committed by whites were almost nonexistent, with prosecutions for these crimes indicated in the sample for only three of the thirty years examined.[17]

The town counties of Bibb and Muscogee had somewhat different experiences with serious crime.[18] In each county, felonies and misdemeanors alike became more numerous, especially in the 1850s. But in Bibb County, the ratio of serious to nonserious crime declined sharply from the 1830s to the 1850s, a trend that probably reflects an end to a period of rapid growth and the development of an effective city police in Macon. In Muscogee County, the population boom continued well into the 1850s; yet Columbus relied on a night watch and city marshal to keep order. One consequence was a dramatic rise in felony crime until it constituted one-third of the criminal docket by 1860.[19]

A breakdown of felonies into specific crimes reveals that most prosecutions were for nonviolent property crimes, such as larceny. No county had a disproportionate share of theft-related offenses, but the types of property crime did vary according to the economic structure of the county. For example, indictments for forgery, the fraudulent conversion of banknotes or bills of exchange, or larceny after a trust had been delegated were rare outside the commercial centers of Columbus and Macon. On the other hand, theft of livestock was more common in predominantly rural areas.

Of course, violent crime and not theft gave the Old South its image as a lawless region. Tales of duels, murder, and assault were stock items in scores of contemporary travel accounts, newspaper stories, and grand jury presentments. Modern historians also have credited the Southerner with a readiness to settle private disputes with fists, dirks, or even pistols. An examination of felony indictments seems to confirm this conclusion. Over 40 percent of all such prosecutions involved violence, and 10 percent were for murder. When misdemeanors, such as simple assault or assault and battery, are considered, the percentages change only slightly. One of every three criminal cases included some degree of violence.

But violent crime did not plague every county, nor was it a constant problem for the legal system. Serious crime in the rural counties of Liberty and Murray was remarkably nonviolent; over 90 percent of all felonious assaults, including murder, occurred in counties with rapidly expanding urban centers. Muscogee County, and especially Columbus, was notorious for its gunplay and barroom stabbings,[20] and not without reason. This county alone prosecuted almost half of the violent felonies in the sample, even though court minutes record cases only from 1838. Yet even in town counties, the pattern of violent crime was not constant over time. There were brief crime waves, but no sustained increase. Violence erupted suddenly and ended quickly. More important, felonies involving violence actually decreased somewhat in relation to population growth.

Given the incidence of violence, it is not surprising to discover that crime against persons was one of the most frequently prosecuted categories (31.3 percent). In fact, the method of prosecution in antebellum Georgia actually encouraged victims of these offenses to seek a remedy within the legal system. The criminal process usually depended on injured parties to initiate prosecutions; this happened when a victim swore out a complaint before a local magistrate. This testimony was enough to cause the accused party to be arrested and subjected to a preliminary examination. Upon finding sufficient cause to proceed, the magistrate would bind the defendant over to the grand jury. Only at that time did the prosecutor have to put up a bond to ensure that his complaint was serious. Even then, the prosecutor forfeited his bond only if the grand or petty jury found that his prosecution was malicious. This was not a likely result. Thus, by making prosecution so accessible and with so little risk to the complainant, the legal system tried to ensure that the resolution of violent crime would remain solely in the hands of the state.[21]

It is not surprising to discover that crimes against persons appeared regularly on criminal dockets: every study of Southern justice has reached the same conclusion. But these studies do not lead us to expect that one of every three prosecutions was for a violation of the moral order. Yet this was what happened in antebellum Georgia, where gaming, liquor-related offenses, and sexual immorality were frequent crimes before the superior courts. This suggests a modification of recent interpretations that nineteenth-century criminal process paid progressively more attention to property and to economic crimes and placed less emphasis on the prosecution of immorality.[22] Such crime as theft may have replaced sin in the codes of Georgia and elsewhere, but the local court evidently concerned itself with maintaining a common morality.

The data also reveal moral-order offenses to be crimes of the city. Ninety percent of all such crimes occurred in counties with well-defined urban populations; 65 percent of the total belongs to Bibb County alone. This finding should not surprise us: cities for a long time had been viewed as cesspools of sin and crime; many people were convinced that the wealth and anonymity of cities nurtured criminals. In an urban environment, violations of public morality were especially threatening because they led to moral dissipation and to more serious crime. To residents of the city, then, the frequent occurrence of such crimes signaled the emergence of a more dangerous criminal element.[23]

This is not to say that prosecutions for immorality represented a consensus on moral values. An opposite conclusion is more accurate. Pressure to establish legal norms often appears greatest where consensus is least attainable. In other words, the detection and punishment of immorality may have signaled an official effort to define the limits of proper public conduct.[24] Indeed, the failure of many prosecutions to reach a verdict and the light fines imposed on convicted offenders indicate that enforcement of moral law was more symbolic than substantive. Faced with a rapidly changing environment and without social institutions capable of affecting any large measure of moral stability, men relied on criminal law to guarantee order. In doing so, they followed a practice similar to urbanizing areas in non-Southern states.[25]

These patterns of prosecution strongly indicate that criminal justice in antebellum Georgia differed according to whether the county was predominantly rural or urban. This conclusion must still be tested more rigorously, but it is clear that counties with urban populations not only prosecuted more crime but also that felonies, violent crimes, and offenses against moral order were especially crimes of these counties. Conversely, rural areas experienced a greater percentage of minor crimes, less serious crimes of violence, and many fewer prosecutions for immorality.

Differences in local criminal justice extended beyond the stage of accusation; they also can be seen in the effectiveness with which courts pursued indictments to a conclusion.[26] There can be no question that courts in Georgia were not very effective in bringing accused persons to trial and a verdict. Of all prosecutions brought before grand juries, only 25 percent ever reached a decision on the merits of the accusation. The remaining cases resulted either in a finding of "no bill" or in a decision by the prosecutor not to proceed, or as happened in a majority of indictments, the case simply disappeared from the criminal docket. Felonies were carried to trial far more often than misdemeanors, as were property crimes and crimes against persons—after all, these crimes had readily identifiable persons who could press for prosecution—but even here, verdicts resulted in less than half the cases.

The ability of courts to prosecute to a verdict differed by county. Courts in Muscogee and Bibb counties were almost twice as effective as their rural counterparts in moving indictments to trial and in securing convictions on those indictments. The character of verdicts varied by county also. Town counties witnessed a significantly higher percentage of guilty verdicts, while results of not guilty and even decisions to prosecute further were more frequent in rural areas.

Ironically, the relative effectiveness of courts in Muscogee and Bibb counties did little to assuage the city-dwellers' fear of criminal activity. A belief that crime was on the increase and that it threatened social order continued to mount in the prewar decades. In urban areas, moreover, crime was no longer perceived as the product of errant individuals; now, criminals were defined in terms of class.[27] These attitudes produced a demand that the criminal justice system control crime more effectively, with such specific reforms proposed as new criminal courts, a professional police, more stringent punishments, and a strengthened jury system.[28]

Pressure for such reforms was noticeably absent in rural counties. There, traditional institutions remained strong. As a result, prosecution alone was often sufficient to reinforce societal norms. Trial and punishment were resorted to only for those who fell outside the informal network of authority or who challenged in some fundamental way the structure of society. But change and anomie characterized the urban environment; men in the city led isolated and fragmented lives.[29] The population had grown and diversified beyond the ability of traditional institutions to guarantee order; yet disorder could not be tolerated because of the fragile interdependence of people and the requirements of a commercial economy. So, men depended on criminal law to provide the necessary stability.

If the preceding interpretation of the data is correct, then criminal justice for whites, at least as practiced in some parts of antebellum Georgia, may not have been so different from non-Southern states as has been supposed. To be sure, in rural areas, the legal system lacked the efficiency and even the prosecutorial patterns associated with modern societies. In such counties, the strength of traditional institutions made the vigorous pursuit of criminals unnecessary. Judging from the failure of rural citizens to demand changes, moreover, no one expected criminal law to play more than a secondary role in maintaining order.

This was not the case in urban counties. There, the emphasis on moral order and the security of persons and property, as well as the demand that criminal justice become more efficient, paralleled the experience of antebellum Northern cities.[30] Perhaps this similarity should be expected. Criminal justice, like all law, responds to the needs and expectations of the society in which it operates. In urbanizing areas, North and South, the requirement of order was paramount. If anything, it was the ability to achieve order that differed. Most antebellum Southern cities did not have the professional police forces of New York or Boston, nor did they have an efficient, bureaucratic system of courts and prosecutors.

But to say that is to obscure essential similarities both in perceptions and in the desired and actual response to disorder. While it must remain only a tentative conclusion at present, a comparative study of a Southern city with a Northern area in a similar stage of development would probably reveal in each the likeness of criminal justice for white citizens. The real distinction in nineteenth-century criminal justice, in other words, might not be between a traditional or a premodern South and a modern North but between rural and urban areas. If so, the Southern response to white crime would be unique only because the South was more rural than the North and not because the South clung stubbornly and desperately to a prebourgeois order.

Notes

1. For examples of Eugene Genovese's work, see *The Political Economy of Slavery* (New York: Pantheon Books, 1965), and *The World the Slaveholders Made* (New York: Pantheon Books, 1969). For the cliometrician's position, see Robert W. Fogel and Stanley L. Engerman, *Time on the Cross: The Economics of American Slavery*, 2 vols. (Boston: Little, Brown & Co., 1974), and Stanley L. Engerman, "A Reconsideration of Southern Economic Growth, 1770-1860," *Agricultural History* XLIX (April 1975), 343-61.

2. Joel P. Bishop, *Commentaries on Criminal Law*, 4th ed. (Boston, 1858), p. xi.

3. For a general statement on the relationship between criminal law and social attitudes toward crime, see Leon Radzinowicz, *Ideology and Crime* (New York: Columbia University Press, 1966).

4. A discussion of criminal justice and modernization may be found in Michael Hindus, "The Social Context of Crime in Massachusetts and South Carolina, 1760-1873: Theoretical and Quantitative Perspectives," *Newberry Papers in Family and Community History* 75-3 (September 10, 1976), 3-6. Also see Marc Galanter, "The Modernization of Law," in Myron Weiner, ed., *Modernization: The Dynamics of Growth* (New York: Basic Books, 1966), pp. 153-65. For a discussion of the impact of modernization on the antebellum United States, see Robert D. Brown, *Modernization: The Transformation of American Life, 1600-1865* (New York: Hill and Wang, 1976).

5. Minute books of the county superior courts were sources for the data used in this study. These courts had sole jurisdiction over all felonies and most misde-

meanors committed by whites. Inclusive dates of minute books examined for this study are: Murray County, 1833-60 (5 vols.); Liberty County, 1830-60 (3 vols.); Muscogee County, 1838-60 (11 vols.); Bibb County, 1830-60 (12 vols.). All volumes are microfilmed and are available in the Georgia Department of Archives and History, Atlanta. The sample was obtained by use of a computer-generated table of random digits; the margin of error was ± 4. Computer programs contained in Norman H. Nie et al., *Statistical Package for the Social Sciences*, 2nd ed. (New York: McGraw-Hill, Inc., 1975), aided the analysis of data.

6. From 1830 to 1840, slaves in Liberty County grew from 53 percent to 77 percent of the total population of approximately 7,200 persons. All demographic and economic information on counties is based on data from compendiums of the federal censuses from 1830 to 1860.

7. Murray County had a population of 4,700 in 1840, of which 17 percent were slaves. By the Civil War, the county's population had reached 12,000, but the percentage of slaves remained constant.

8. James H. Stone, "Economic Conditions in Macon in the 1830s," *Georgia Historical Quarterly* LIV (1970), 209-25; John A. Eisterhold, "Commercial, Financial, and Industrial Macon during the 1840s," *Georgia Historical Quarterly* LIII (1969), 424-41.

9. Columbus grew from 27 percent of the county's population in 1840 to over 53 percent by 1860. For more on the economy of Muscogee County, see James McDonald, "Economic History of Columbus to the Civil War" (master's thesis, Auburn University, 1944). Also see John H. Martin, *Columbus, Georgia, From Its Selection as a Trading Town in 1827 to Its Partial Destruction by Wilson's Raid in 1865* (Columbus: T. Gilbert & Co., 1874).

10. Grand Jury Presentment, Liberty County Superior Court, *Minute Book 1845-1859*, p. 15. Also see ibid., p. 153.

11. Grand Jury Presentment, Murray County Superior Court, *Minute Book 1841-1845*, p. 388.

12. Grand Jury Presentment, Murray County Superior Court, *Minute Book 1851-1858*, pp. 62-63. Also see *Minute Book 1841-1845*, p. 443.

13. Grand Jury Presentment, Muscogee County Superior Court, *Minute Book*, vol. 1, p. 388. Also, *Minute Book*, vol. A, p. 229.

14. Grand Jury Presentment, Bibb County Superior Court, *Minute Book*, vol. 0, p. 360.

15. Macon *Telegraph*, October 10, 1846.

16. Columbus *Tri-Weekly Times and Sentinel*, November 26, 1853.

17. Of all prosecutions in Muscogee, 26.62 percent were for felonies; in Bibb, 20.23 percent; in Murray, 19.97 percent; and in Liberty, 17.65 percent. But Muscogee and Bibb counties experienced many more prosecutions for felonies than did the other two counties. Of the four-county total for such prosecutions, Bibb had 45.92 percent; Muscogee, 37.76 percent; Murray, 13.27 percent; Liberty, 3.06 percent.

18. Town or urban counties are defined as those with more than 30 percent of their populations living in a town or city. Bibb and Muscogee counties meet this definition, and they also exhibit the diversity of economic and social function associated with urbanizing areas.

19. In Bibb County, the population doubled from 1840 to 1860, but felony crime rose by only 20 percent. For Muscogee County, the population more than tripled, but serious crime increased by only 70 percent.

20. A famous traveler to Columbus in 1855 noted the less-than-genteel environment: "I had seen in no place, since I left Washington, such gambling, intoxication, and cruel treatment of servants in public, as in Columbus. . . ." Frederick Law Olmstead, *Journey in the Seaboard Slave States, with Remarks on Their Economy* (New York: Dix and Edwards, 1856), p. 548.

21. The procedure for criminal prosecution is set forth in T. R. R. Cobb, *Digest of Statute Laws of Georgia*, pp. 832-45.

22. For recent interpretations that nineteenth-century criminal justice, especially in the Old South, paid little attention to moral-order crime, see William E. Nelson, *Americanization of Common Law: The Impact of Legal Change on Massachusetts Society, 1760-1830* (Cambridge: Harvard University Press, 1975), pp. 109-16, and Jack K. Williams, *Vogues in Villainy: Crime and Retribution in Ante-Bellum South Carolina* (Columbia: University of South Carolina Press, 1959), p. 53.

23. For the belief that cities bred criminals, see Lucretia and Morton White, *Intellectuals versus the City: From Thomas Jefferson to Frank Lloyd Wright* (Cambridge: Harvard University Press, 1963), pp. 6-36. This notion was echoed in Columbus when an editor contrasted the openness of homes in the country with the locked doors of the city. Columbus [weekly] *Enquirer*, February 22, 1847.

24. This interpretation is suggested by Joseph Gusfield, "Moral Passage: The Symbolic Process in Public Designations of Deviance," *Social Problems* XV (Fall 1967), p. 188.

25. Michael S. Hindus presents evidence that this was true in urban areas of Massachusetts in "The Contours of Crime and Justice in Massachusetts and South Carolina, 1767-1878," *American Journal of Legal History* XXI (July 1977), pp. 212-37. And I argue that the concern with prosecuting immorality also was prevalent in antebellum Indianapolis. David J. Bodenhamer, "Crime and Criminal Justice in Antebellum Indiana: Marion County as a Case Study" (Ph.D. diss., Indiana University, 1977), pp. 168-87.

26. This study measures the effectiveness of criminal justice as a ratio of verdicts to all cases handled by the legal system rather than the more simple (and less meaningful) ratio of convictions to the total of convictions and acquittals. For a discussion of both measures, see Hindus, "Social Context of Crime: Theoretical Perspectives," p. 15.

27. One editor warned that "our county is filled . . . with banditti and bands of rogues," Columbus *Times*, August 5, 1846. Others warned of gangs of thieves and gamblers. See Columbus *Enquirer*, March 27, 1847; Macon *Georgia Messenger*, June 11, 1853.

28. Examples of calls for a professional police are found in Columbus *Weekly Times & Sentinel*, January 24, 1854; Columbus *Tri-Weekly Times and Sentinel*, November 26, 1853; and Macon *Georgia Citizen*, June 18, 1853. The need for new courts: Grand Jury Presentment, Bibb Superior Court, *Minute Book*, vol. 6, p. 336; Columbus *Enquirer*, May 13, 1856; Columbus *Tri-Weekly Times & Sentinel*, October 22, 1853 and January 11, 1856. Reorganization of the jury system: Message of Governor Charles J. McDonald as reported in Columbus *Times*, November 11,

1843; Columbus *Weekly Enquirer*, June 28, 1843 and June 3, 1851; Grand Jury Presentment, Bibb Superior Court, *Minute Book*, vol. 3, p. 540.

29. A newspaper editor in Columbus seemed to recognize this when he complained that in the city "nothing is done to humanize the youth. . . . Each family lives alone and shirks the amenities of life. The father confines himself to his counter and mother to her household chores. No thought is given to social intercourse. . . . This is unquestionably all wrong. . . . [W]ithout a heartier and habitual social intercourse, we have no hope that our future will be any brighter than our present," Columbus *Tri-Weekly Times & Sentinel*, April 22, 1853.

30. Studies that examine various aspects of local criminal justice in the North are Roger Lane, "Crime and Criminal Statistics in Nineteenth-Century Massachusetts," *Journal of Social History* II (1968); Michael S. Hindus, *Prison and Plantation: Crime, Justice and Authority in Massachusetts and South Carolina, 1767-1878* (Chapel Hill: University of North Carolina Press, 1980); Bodenhamer, "Crime and Criminal Justice in Antebellum Indiana"; James F. Richardson, *The New York Police: Colonial Times to 1901* (New York: Oxford University Press, 1970).

9

WHITECAPPING IN LATE NINETEENTH-CENTURY GEORGIA

William F. Holmes

A high rate of violence has long been recognized as a feature distinguishing the South from other sections of the nation.[1] Two phases of Southern violence have received little scholarly attention: the first, moonshine violence, arose in the late nineteenth century and was concentrated mostly in the southern Appalachians; the second, whitecapping, was a term that became widely used in America between 1887 and 1920 to describe vigilante-type raids conducted by bands of disguised men.[2] While whitecapping occurred through the country in response to a variety of circumstances, many instances of it centered in the South. This paper will examine an outbreak of whitecapping that was directly related to conflicts between federal revenue agents and moonshiners in four north Georgia counties in the 1890s. It represents an initial investigation into the history of moonshine violence in the South.

Except for the Federalist era and for a few years during the War of 1812, the nation did not impose a tax on liquor distillers until the Civil War. Beginning in 1862, federal law required that distillers purchase a license and pay a tax on each gallon they produced. Following the war, the taxes in a slightly modified form remained in vogue.[3] In north Georgia, as in other parts of the southern Appalachians, the taxes gave rise to widespread problems because they were in conflict with a way of life that had long prevailed. Throughout the country, people viewed the new revenue laws as taxing a luxury item, but many farmers in the upper piedmont and mountains of Georgia considered home brewing a matter of economic necessity. Cotton had not become a major staple, by that time, but grain crops had. For years, many had converted part of their corn crop into liquor, which they sold at nearby markets. The profits that some home brewers derived from selling liquor—although an important part of their income—was so small that they would actually lose money by purchasing licenses and paying the new taxes. In addition to economic considerations, they opposed the new taxes for other reasons. Not only did many enjoy drinking home-made whiskey, but in a region that had few doctors and druggists, whiskey was used for medicinal purposes. Finally, the rural mountaineers, a people with an intense sense of individualism, resented the attempts of outside agents to stop their practice of home brewing.[4] The fact remained that as a result of the new taxes a practice that had long been legal became illegal. Distillers who did not pay the taxes became moonshiners.[5]

Federal officials had the responsibility to collect the taxes, and they realized that the total quantity of liquor produced by home brewers represented a large amount of uncollected revenue.[6] Thus, the stage was set for an inevitable clash between federal authorities and moonshiners. Serious conflicts did not begin until 1877, when the commissioner of internal revenue reported that the thousands of illicit stills operating in the southern Appalachians caused the government to lose thousands of dollars annually. In response to that report, federal officials launched an intense campaign against moonshiners.[7] In north Georgia, violence quickly followed. Federal troops from Atlanta's Fort McPherson went into some mountain counties to assist revenue agents. On one occasion, a group of moonshiners, consisting of men and women, ambushed a detachment of soldiers in Fannin County and killed one lieutenant. The troops retaliated by killing three moonshiners.[8] Soldiers did not assist revenue agents in Georgia after 1877, but violence continued. In Hall County, for example, a fight occurred in 1884 between revenue agents and moonshiners that lasted twenty-four hours, occasionally involved hand-to-hand combat, and resulted in at least two deaths.[9]

As years passed, a sense of grievance developed among the residents of north Georgia. In addition to opposing the taxes on distilled liquor, many became convinced that they were victims of an unfair revenue system. Since U.S. commissioners, marshals, and deputy marshals—all of whom played roles in enforcing the revenue laws—were paid on a fee basis, they were suspected of frequently arresting innocent people "for the purpose of reaping pecuniary benefits" or "to gratify some personal animosity." Some attributed much of the trouble to the kinds of people employed as marshals and deputy marshals; they urged that men of integrity be appointed to enforce the revenue laws.[10] The practice that federal officials had of paying fees to witnesses who disclosed the locations of illicit stills contributed to a sense of mistrust in local communities. Sometimes witnesses were moonshiners who informed on other distillers in the hopes of escaping prosecution. Mountaineers accused revenue agents of unnecessarily resorting to violence, and over the years, many stories contributed to a tradition of police brutality. Finally, they objected to moonshiners' being taken to Atlanta, far from their home counties, to be tried and if convicted to be sentenced to federal penitentiaries outside the state. While men served prison sentences, their families frequently depended on friends and relatives to support them, adding an additional burden to the community.[11]

Federal officials realized that the sentiment of the mountain people ran strongly against them, but they blamed the moonshiners for perpetrating the violence. In 1886, U.S. Marshal John W. Nelms charged that conditions had become so dangerous in some mountain counties that his deputies would enter only in pairs. During the past two years, he reported, moonshiners had killed two deputies, shot at four others, and stabbed one. They also had killed four guides.[12]

While a great deal of violence resulted from battles between individual moonshiners and revenue agents, there were instances of concerted action on the part of moonshiners. During Reconstruction, the Ku Klux Klan in some counties attacked people suspected of testifying against distillers.[13] In the late 1870s and early 1880s, groups of moonshiners occasionally banded together to protect themselves by violently attacking revenue agents and informers. It does not appear, however, that such groups lasted long or were widespread; instead, small groups of moonshiners would temporarily join forces when authorities attempted to seize their stills.[14]

That pattern changed in the winter of 1888-89, when a larger and better organized group, the "Distillers Union," was formed in Murray County, from which it subsequently spread into the neighboring counties of Gilmer, Whitfield, and Gordon. In Gilmer County, they took the name "Workingmen's Friend Protective Organization"; in Gordon County, they were known as the "Gordon County Grangers." This secret, oathbound organization, whose members became popularly known as whitecaps, probably because they wore disguises similar to those used earlier by the Klan, had the original objective of protecting distillers. Members took an oath, signed in blood, promising to supply alibis for fellow members arrested for moonshining. They also agreed to whip witnesses and to drive them out of the region; witnesses who refused to leave would be killed, as would members who violated their oath.[15] As the whitecap organization grew, it became subdivided within each county into local clubs over which a captain presided. The clubs developed a communications network, for occasionally whitecaps from one county would be called into a neighboring county to whip witnesses.[16] The clubs originally consisted of distillers, the first being those in the Cohutta Mountains of Murray County; later, distillers from surrounding counties joined. These men appear to have been small farmers who faced a hard struggle in supporting themselves and their families. Later, the clubs included men who were not distillers but who sympathized with the distillers in their battles against federal agents. Others joined to protect themselves against the suspicion that they were informers. Eventually, the whitecap clubs won the support of well-to-do farmers, ministers, physicians, county office holders, and at least one federal deputy marshal.

By 1894, the combined membership in the four counties was estimated to be between 800 and 1,000.[17]

Violence quickly followed the organization of the whitecap clubs, as members beat and shot people whom they suspected of testifying against distillers. They struck at men and women, sometimes attacking entire families. They also burned barns and homes and destroyed crops. There is no way to know the exact number of their victims. For the years 1892 through 1894, authorities estimated that they beat over 150 persons and killed as many as twenty.[18]

The general pattern of whitecap violence was illustrated by an incident that occurred in the fall of 1893. At that time, George Terry, a resident of Gilmer County, revealed the location of his still to Thomas A. McIntyre, a neighbor who lived a short distance away in Murray County. The two men were life-long acquaintances; years earlier, McIntyre had taught Terry to write. In exchange for a two-dollar fee, McIntyre told a deputy marshal where to find the still. Before the marshal took action, Terry learned that McIntyre had betrayed him and hastily removed his still. On a cold night two week later, a band of disguised whitecaps surrounded McIntyre's home and called for him to come out. He refused, and the whitecaps knocked down his front door and threw flaming cotton balls into the dark house. As several whitecaps seized McIntyre, he was struck across the head with a shotgun and in the face with a pistol. Then they dragged him outside to a plum orchard. While kneeling on the ground in his nightshirt, McIntyre admitted that he had reported Terry's still. The spokesman for the whitecaps asked if the informer deserved one hundred licks on the back. McIntyre replied, "I guess so." A night rider then broke a limb from a plum tree and lashed McIntyre's back. Although the incident occurred 200 yards from McIntyre's home, his wife, who remained in bed during the attack, heard the beating.[19]

Whitecap violence began to intensify in the fall of 1893, when federal authorities stepped up their raids on illicit distillers. In addition to continuing their attacks on informers, the whitecaps then struck directly at federal officers by threatening the life of a U.S. commissioner, burning the barns of two deputy marshals, and dynamiting a fire box of a third deputy marshal.[20] Since federal action against moonshiners did not decline, whitecap violence became bolder and more widespread during the first half of 1894. On New Year's night, a band of fifty men rode into Calhoun, in Gordon County, broke open a railroad boxcar containing two stills recently seized by federal authorities, and quickly departed with the stills in tow.[21]

It was at this time of increasing conflict between whitecaps and federal authorities that Henry M. Tankersley of Murray County made himself famous in north Georgia. After spying a group of revenue men passing his home, Tankersley mounted a mule known for its speed, got ahead of the revenue men, and then rode for thirty miles, shouting as he passed mountain cabins, "Look out! The revenoorers is a-coming." In his wake, men quickly removed their stills. Tankersley was subsequently arrested for obstructing officers in the performance of their duty, but the grand jury refused to indict him, declaring it did not see anything criminal about a man's riding a fast mule.[22]

Local authorities faced a difficult task in attempting to stop the terrorism. In the affected counties, many residents sympathized with the whitecaps; others were afraid to testify against them, as well they should be since whitecaps sometimes drove potential witnesses from the region. Whitecaps offered alibis for fellow members who were tried in state courts, and it is quite likely that some whitecaps served on juries. As a result, state officials were unsuccessful in their early attempts to prosecute whitecaps, and federal officials eventually assumed responsibility for ending the lawlessness. Beginning in the fall of 1893, when a few men arrested on the charge of moonshining began to reveal the secrets of the whitecap clubs, the U.S. attorney and marshal for north Georgia became convinced that the terrorists could be stopped only by convicting them in federal court on the charge of conspiring to violate the civil rights of citizens who testified against moonshiners. But the early efforts of federal authorities proved almost as ineffective as had the efforts of state authorities. For one thing, it was difficult to find people who would testify against the night riders. The reason was quite simple: the whitecaps tried to kill them. Soon after Jim Chastain and W. I. Hammick of Murray County told federal officials about the workings of the whitecap clubs, Chastain disappeared, and Hammick was permanently crippled as a result of being shot four times in the hip.[23]

Far more sensational was the story of Henry Worley, a resident of Gilmar County who was indicted for participating in a whitecap raid that resulted in the beating of Hood Nailer. Since the evidence against Worley was strong and since authorities in Gilmer County were trying hard to end whitecapping, Worley fled to Texas. He soon returned and in the hopes of having the charges against him dropped began telling federal authorities about the locations of some illicit stills and also divulged information about the whitecap clubs of which he had been a member. On the night of April 7, 1894, a group of thirty whitecaps dragged Worley from his home, strapped him to a mule, and took him into neighboring Murray County. There they hanged him. After the whitecaps departed, Worley managed to wrap his legs around the trunk of the tree from which he was hanging, untied his hands, and with a pocketknife cut himself free. He was either a very brave or a very stupid man because he returned to his home. There, as he worked in a field two weeks later, whitecaps shot and killed him.[24] That murder served as a warning to others not to testify against the whitecaps.

Following the acquittal of three men accused of beating revenue informers in Gordon County, the federal attorney for north Georgia wrote to the attorney general describing the power of the whitecap clubs in the four-county region:

From all I can gather they have almost absolute control over that portion of our state. I receive almost daily appeals from the law abiding citizens of that section to put a stop to these nefarious crimes. . . . Those who write to me, a great many of them, do so under assumed names, saying that if their identity was known they would be killed and their property destroyed.

Under the present circumstances, he concluded, federal and state officials were "powerless to do anything with them. . . ."[25]

The turning point in the campaign against the whitecaps came the following summer. In retaliation against Will Roper, a farm laborer, for having testified against two moonshiners in Murray County, five whitecaps seized him on June 11, 1894, and took him on a two-hour ride to the site of an abandoned copper pit. Along the way, they drank whiskey from a "pepper sauce" bottle and convinced Roper to drink some too, declaring it would be his last. By the time they arrived at their destination, they were in such good spirits that they removed their masks. On being told that he was about to die, Roper knelt at the edge of the pit and prayed. The whitecaps then shot him, and he fell into the pit, some sixty feet deep. Six days later, two boys looking for stray cattle discovered Roper, who was still alive. He was rescued, taken by federal officials to Atlanta, and nursed back to health. He signed affidavits naming W. R. Morrison, A. P. Duncan, J. W. Redd, J. T. Morrison, and J. M. Morrison as the men who had attacked him. In federal court in Atlanta the following November, they were tried and convicted of trying to violate Roper's right to testify against illegal distillers. The court imposed ten-year prison sentences and $1,000 fines on four of them; it sentenced W. R. Morrison to eight years and a $500 fine.[26] Marshal Samuel S. Dunlap declared that it was the "most valuable verdict ever rendered in this district."[27]

As far as ending whitecapping, Dunlap was correct. By that time, an increasingly large number of people in north Georgia had become convinced that the terrorism had become too widespread and should be checked. During the winter of 1894-95, sentiment against the whitecaps mounted. Some state newspapers published lengthy reports on the seriousness of the problem. A few individuals spoke out against the whitecaps, and groups of citizens in some communities held public meetings calling for an end to whitecapping.[28] Rebecca Latimer Felton, wife of a former congressman from the district, called for vigorous prosecution of the whitecaps: "I am an old resident of this Cong[ressional] Dist[rict] . . . but I have never beheld such a state of affairs in all my life. . . . It is a disgrace to civilization."[29]

In Gilmer County, Superior Court Judge George F. Gober and solicitor George Brown initiated strong action against the whitecaps in the fall of 1894. By carefully eliminating all suspected whitecaps and their sympathizers from the juries, Gober and Brown secured the convictions of three whitecaps. The following year, several other whitecaps were convicted in Murray County.[30]

Most of the convictions came in the Atlanta federal court between November 1894 and April 1895. Altogether, federal prosecutors obtained a total of twenty convictions, but they represented only a small portion of the whitecaps. A number of conditions accounted for the low number of convictions. The more well-to-do were defended by able attorneys who frequently proved superior to the federal prosecutors. In one case, in which a former state legislator, a justice of the peace, and a physician were positively identified by witnesses as having been part of the group that beat Robert Hooker, the defense called attention to a clerical error in the bill of indictment; as a result, the judge ordered the jury to render a verdict of not guilty.[31] Later, when two men were tried for hanging Henry Worley, the prosecution erred badly by joining a felony and a misdemeanor in the same count of the indictment.[32] In view of the poor performance by federal prosecutors, it is not surprising that the Justice Department was unwilling to spend more money to convict additional whitecaps. Even as things stood, by the spring of 1895 the federal government had already spent a large amount of money in securing the twenty convictions. Those convictions had contributed to the demise of the whitecap clubs, which by that time had ceased operating. Over the next six years, charges against those who had been indicted but not tried were gradually dropped, some because of insufficient evidence, others because "the ends of public justice do not require further prosecution. . . ."[33]

To understand why this episode of whitecapping occurred, a number of conditions must be considered. For one thing, this region had a well-established history of violence. It was originally part of the Cherokee nation, and during the 1830s, vigilante groups, state militiamen, and federal soldiers drove the Indians from the region. During the Civil War, Whitfield and Gordon counties, both in the direct line of Sherman's army, experienced a great deal of fighting. Gilmer County, whose people were sharply divided between Union and Confederate sympathizers, experienced so much violence that vigilante groups arose to restore order. During Reconstruction, Murray County had an active Ku Klux Klan.[34] Following Reconstruction, groups of night riders occasionally appeared in the region: in Whitfield County in 1879, a group of armed men killed a Mormon elder who was considered "obnoxious" by some local residents;[35] in that same county in 1885, fifty masked horsemen rode into Dalton and attacked people whom they accused of being prostitutes, miscegenationists, thieves, and lazy men unwilling to work;[36] several weeks later in Murray County, night riders flogged a black man for "his calumnious language concerning several young white ladies. . . ."[37] Thus, the whitecaps had many examples of violence to emulate.

Some insight into this era of violence can be gained by considering the identity of the terrorists and their victims, as well as the reaction of the local community to the violence. The whitecaps who were convicted of committing acts of violence were mostly poor men who ran small distilleries. This was well illustrated in the Henry Worley case. Although twenty-eight men were indicted for hanging Worley, only two were tried and convicted: John Quarles, a blacksmith and father of fourteen children, and David Butler, a small farmer and father of eight children. Soon after entering the federal penitentiary in Columbus, Ohio, Quarles contracted meningitis and died. His widow and children then moved to Dalton, where some went to work at a cotton factory, others at a cannery.[38] Whitecap victims came from similar backgrounds, for they were usually farm laborers, tenants, and small landowners. The whitecaps also enjoyed the active support of many well-to-do farmers and townspeople because they tried to uphold the long-established tradition of home brewing. Those who violated the tradition by cooperating with federal agents were considered disloyal to their own people. When the whitecaps asked Henry Worley's mother if she wanted to see him one last time before they hanged him, she replied: "I never want to lay eyes on the traitor. Take him along."[39]

Personal feuds, some of long duration, occasionally affected the community's response to whitecapping. Dr. E. O. Stafford, a leading physician in Murray County, had served as a Confederate soldier and led the local Ku Klux Klan during Reconstruction. But in the 1890s, he became a leading critic of the whitecaps, whom he labeled as bushwackers who attacked innocent people. He accused John Edmondson, one of Murray's wealthiest farmers, of being a leader of the whitecaps. The feud between the two men went back to the Civil War, for Edmondson had opposed the war and had served as a county judge to escape military service. Although Edmondson denied being a whitecap, he sympathized with them and denounced the revenue system that "made the moonshiner a hermit and a cave dweller in his own land in order to escape the shotgun of the officer . . . who seemed to take fiendish delight in pursuing his brother man." Stafford and Edmondson had many loyal friends, and their dispute contributed to a polarization in Murray County between supporters and opponents of the whitecaps.[40]

More than anything else, the conflict between the established values of the local community and the operation of the federal revenue system caused this episode of whitecapping. Many people in north Georgia believed that the federal taxes were designed to benefit large commercial distillers by driving the small operators out of business. They deeply resented federal authorities coming into their counties for the purpose of seizing and destroying stills. They believed, moreover, that some federal officials were unscrupulous men who used unfair methods to enforce the revenue laws. P. J. Moran, a reporter for the Atlanta *Constitution*, learned from talking to hundreds of people in the whitecap counties in 1894 that since the Civil War a huge backlog of grievances had built up against the revenue system. Some people who became whitecaps, Moran concluded, were goaded by the memories of "atrocities which would drive the most conservative people into revolution."[41]

A Justice Department investigator, S. B. Sheibley, made discoveries that supported Moran's assertions. Early in 1895, he reported that four deputy marshals operating in the whitecap counties—William M. Mauldin, J. T. Lewis, Thomas M. Wright, and Charles S. Kellett—had knowingly arrested innocent people and even received payoffs for protecting illicit distillers. In addition, they had falsified accounts for mileage, meals furnished to prisoners, and expenses incurred in serving subpoenas. "A large measure of the recent reign of terrorism [whitecapping] in this District was due," Sheibley concluded, "to these unscrupulous officers of the law, who 'trumped up' charges against innocent parties for the purpose of making fees, and protected illicit distillers in their violations of the internal-revenue laws."[42] Sheibley's finding contributed to the dismissal of the four deputies and spurred prosecuting attorneys to try only those moonshining cases in which the evidence was strong enough to give them a good chance to obtain convictions. While these reforms in the operation of the revenue system eliminated one grievance that had caused some people to become whitecaps, it would be a mistake to conclude that the whitecaps disbanded simply because they had called attention to corruption on the part of some deputy marshals. Violent conflicts between federal authorities and moonshiners would continue for many years after 1895.

Whitecapping arose among a people who had low levels of income and education. With a strong sense of grievance against tax collectors, they were a prepolitical people who used violence as a way to protest the federal revenue system. This episode of whitecapping did, of course, coincide with a major political protest movement—Populism. Only one episode suggests a possible connection between whitecapping and Populism. On the night of October 23, 1892, a band of approximately 150 armed horsemen rode into Dalton and killed one black man and severely beat another. They gave no reason for the attack. Two things stand out about this raid. First, the local white community reacted strongly in condemning the murder of a black man who enjoyed a good reputation among the whites. During the 1880s and 1890s, no other episode of violence in the four-county region was denounced so strongly by the local whites. Second, people who knew the murdered man reported that he had always voted the Democratic ticket; their remarks implied that the night riders were Populists.[43] But there also is reason to believe that the whitecaps were Democrats. Several years later, a leading defender of the night riders claimed that every member of the white-caps was a Democrat; he labeled the leading critics of the terrorists as Popu-lists.[44] There is, in short, no evidence to link whitecapping to Populism.

This outbreak of whitecapping represented a collective response aimed at maintaining a right that people had once enjoyed but that had become threatened. As such, it was a reactionary form of violence. This does not mean that the whitecaps were trying to escape reality, for they were react-ing to problems that for them were real. Distilling had long played an im-portant part in their lives. This movement, like other instances of reaction-ary violence, was short lived and did not prevail. Group violence dedicated to maintaining traditional community values occurred in many sections of the nation in the late nineteenth century. In the South, however, it appears that there was a broader pattern of this type of collective violence. Some ex-amples that come readily to mind include the Klan of Reconstruction, the Klan of the 1920s, and the Klan-type activities of the 1950s and 1960s di-rected against civil rights activists. Whitecapping appears to have belonged to a broad pattern of collective violence in the South that was conservative and dedicated to maintaining traditional community values.

Notes

1. See, for example, H. V. Redfield, *Homicide: North and South* (Philadelphia: J. B. Lippincott & Co., 1880); H. C. Brearley, "The Pattern of Violence," *Culture in the South*, W. T. Couch, ed. (Chapel Hill: The University of North Carolina Press, 1934), pp. 678-92; John Hope Franklin, *The Militant South, 1800-1861* (Cambridge: Harvard University Press, 1956); Sheldon Hackney, "Southern Violence," *Violence in America*, Hugh Davis Graham and Ted Robert Gurr, eds. (New York: Bantam Books, 1969), pp. 479-500; Raymond D. Gastil, "Homicide and a Regional Culture of Violence," *American Sociological Review* 36 (June 1971), pp. 412-27; John Shelton Reed, "To Live—and Die—in Dixie: A Contribution to the Study of Southern Violence," *Political Science Quarterly* 81 (September 1971), pp. 429-43.

2. William F. Holmes, "Whitecapping: Agrarian Violence in Mississippi, 1902-1906," *Journal of Southern History* 25 (May 1969), pp. 165-85; William F. Holmes, "Whitecapping in Mississippi: Agrarian Violence in the Populist Era," *Mid-America* 55 (April 1973), pp. 134-48; Madeleine M. Noble, "The White Caps of Harrison and Crawford County, Indiana: A Study in the Violent Enforcement of Morality" (Ph.D. diss., University of Michigan, 1973).

3. Sidney Ratner, *American Taxation: Its History as a Social Force in Democracy* (New York: W. W. Norton & Co., 1942), pp. 27, 32, 35, 82, 116, 238-39; 12 *United State Statutes at Large* (1863), pp. 446-59; 13 *United States Statutes at Large* (1865), pp. 303-04; 14 *United States Statutes at Large* (1867), pp. 480-84.

4. Atlanta *Constitution*, January 12, 1895; Horace Kephart, *Our Southern High-landers* (New York: Outing, 1913), pp. 110-90; John C. Campbell, *The Southern High-lander and His Homeland* (New York: Russell Sage Foundation, 1921), pp. 103-10.

5. Georgia became a leading state in moonshining during the last quarter of the nineteenth century. Beginning in 1877, when the commissioner of internal revenue

began publishing detailed reports on the problem, Georgia consistently ranked among the top two states in the number of stills seized and the number of persons arrested for working those stills. See the annual *Report of the Commissioner of Internal Revenue, 1877-1900.* Each report has a table giving the number of stills seized, persons arrested, and officers killed and wounded. See also Edward C. Wade to Green B. Raum, March 18, 1878, in Treasury Department, Collectors Letters, Box 907, National Archives, Washington, D.C.

6. Atlanta *Constitution*, February 12, 1895.

7. *Annual Report of the Commissioner of Internal Revenue for Fiscal Year Ending June 30, 1877* (Washington, D.C., 1877), pp. xxx-xxxiii.

8. Atlanta *Constitution*, January 23, February 13, March 1, 2, 3, 1877; Dahlonega *Signal and Advent*, March 2, 16, 30, 1877; Georgia *House Journal*, 1876, pp. 226, 259, 272; Georgia *House Journal*, 1877, pp. 582-83, 609-11.

9. Atlanta *Constitution*, December 18, 1884.

10. J. E. Alsobrook to Alfred H. Colquitt, March 13, 1877, in Alfred H. Colquitt Executive Department Papers, Georgia Department of Archives and History, Atlanta, Georgia. The fee system was recognized as a source of potential corruption. See *Annual Report of the Attorney General of the United States, 1885* (Washington, D.C.: Government Printing Office, 1885), p. 12; *Annual Report of the Attorney General of the United States, 1895* (Washington, D.C.: Government Printing Office, 1895), pp. 5-6.

11. Calhoun *Times*, August 18, 1877, June 6, 1894; Atlanta *Constitution*, December 23, 1894, January 11, 1895; Dalton *North Georgia Citizen*, December 6, 20, 1894; Greensboro *Herald-Journal*, February 17, 1888, September 1, 1894.

12. John W. Nelms to A. H. Garland, April 8, June 29, 1886, May 12, 1887, Folded File No. 9415, Justice Department Records, Record Group 60, National Archives, Washington, D.C. (hereafter cited as Justice Department Records).

13. *Report of Joint Select Committee to Inquire into the Condition of Affairs in the Late Insurrectionary States*, 13 vols. (Washington, D.C.: Government Printing Office, 1872), House Reports, 42d Cong., 2d sess., No. 22, Georgia, I, pp. 445, 464-65, 467, 499, 509-10, 525; II, 601, 749, 751, 812, 1126, 1130-31.

14. Greensboro *Herald*, December 25, 1879; John W. Nelms to A. H. Garland, November 14, 1885, file No. 9415, Justice Department Records.

15. Atlanta *Constitution*, December 23, 1894, January 11, 1895; Calhoun *Times*, September 28, 1893; Atlanta *Journal*, April 27, 1894; S. J. James to Attorney General, May 2, 1894, Year File No. 7112-1886, Justice Department Records.

16. *U.S. v. George W. Terry*, no. 6821, U.S. Circuit Court of Northern District of Georgia, October term, 1894, Federal Records Center, East Point, Georgia; Atlanta *Constitution*, April 11, 1895.

17. Atlanta *Constitution*, December 14, 15, 23, 1894; S. J. James to Attorney General, December 15, 1894, Year File No. 7112-1886, Justice Department Records.

18. S. J. James to Attorney General, December 15, 1894.

19. *U.S. v. George W. Terry*, no. 6821; Atlanta *Constitution*, February 6, 1895.

20. Samuel S. Dunlap to Attorney General, January 24, 1894, Year File No. 7112-1886, Justice Department Records; Calhoun *Times*, November 9, 1893; Cartersville *Courant-American*, November 9, 1893.

21. Calhoun *Times*, January 14, 1894.

22. Atlanta *Constitution*, December 23, 1894.

23. Ibid., December 23, 1894, January 11, 1895; S. J. James to Attorney General, May 2, 1894, Year File No. 7112-1886, Justice Department Records.

24. Atlanta *Constitution*, January 12, 1895, April 10, 11, 12, 14, 1895; Dalton *Argus*, April 21, 1894.

25. S. J. James to Attorney General, May 2, 1894, Year File No. 7112-1886, Justice Department Records.

26. Atlanta *Constitution*, November 13, 14, 15, 1894; Dalton *Argus*, June 23, 1894; Samuel C. Dunlap to attorney general, August 15, 1894, Year File No. 7112-1886, Justice Department Records; *U.S. v. W. R. Morrison et al.*, No. 6791, U.S. Circuit Court of Northern District of Georgia, October term, 1894, Federal Records Center.

27. Samuel C. Dunlap to Attorney General, November 16, 1894, Year File No. 6525-1893, Justice Department Records.

28. Atlanta *Constitution*, January 3, 5, 31, 1895.

29. Mrs. W. H. Felton to Attorney General, December 24, 1894, Year File No. 7112-1886, Justice Department Records.

30. Atlanta *Constitution*, November 10, 12, 1894; Calhoun *Times*, September 18, 1895.

31. Atlanta *Constitution*, February 7, 8, 9, 1895. Green Treadwell was a former state senator; Frank Kilgore was a justice of the peace; and Dr. Sam Brown was a prominent physician in Murray County. *U.S. v. Sam Brown et al.*, No. 7444, and *U.S. v. Green Treadwell et al.*, No. 7457, U.S. Circuit Court for Northern District of Georgia, March term, 1895, Federal Records Center.

32. Atlanta *Constitution*, April 2, 1895.

33. Dalton *Argus*, February 23, 1895; S. J. James to Attorney General, April 17, 1895, June 10, 1895, Year File No. 7112-1886, Justice Department Records; Atlanta *Constitution*, November 10, 12, 1894; *U.S. v. Tobe Smith et al.*, No. 8739, U.S. Circuit Court for Northern District of Georgia, October term, 1894, Federal Records Center.

34. George Gordon Ward, *The Annals of Upper Georgia: Centered in Gilmer County* (Carrollton, Ga.: Printed by Thomasson Print & Office Equipment Co., 1965), 340-49; Whitfield County History Commission, *Official History of Whitfield County, Georgia* (Dalton, Ga.: A. J. Showalter Company, 1936), pp. 55-66; Burton J. Bell, ed., *1976 Bicentennial History of Gordon County* (Calhoun, Ga.: Gordon County Historical Society, 1976), p. 261; Atlanta *Constitution*, December 23, 1894.

35. Calhoun *Times*, July 31, 1879.

36. Dalton *Argus*, August 22, 29, 1885.

37. Calhoun *Times*, September 10, 1885.

38. Atlanta *Constitution*, April 12, 17, 1895; Dalton *Argus*, August 17, 1895.

39. Atlanta *Constitution*, January 12, 1895. See also *Constitution*, December 23, 1894, February 7, 8, 1895; S. J. James to Attorney General, May 2, 1894, Year File No. 7112-1886, Justice Department Records.

40. Atlanta *Constitution*, December 23, 1894, January 2, 12, 1895.

41. Ibid., December 23, 1894.

42. S. B. Sheibley to Attorney General, March 4, 1895, Year File No. 6525-1893, Justice Department Records.

43. Dalton *North Georgia Citizen*, October 27, 1892.

44. Atlanta *Constitution*, December 23, 1894.

V

SOUTHERN MYTHOLOGY: FICTION AND FILM

For many years, historians have recognized that myth can be as important as reality in shaping the attitudes and actions of people. The following two essays demonstrate how myth has influenced certain aspects of Southern history and culture since the Civil War.

In his article, "Southern Writers and the Image of Johnny Reb: Reflections of Regional Change Since Appomattox," Professor Stephen Davis argues that myth is seldom static. By examining the works of Southern fiction writers who created lasting images of the common Confederate soldier and reflected contemporary attitudes, Davis discovers four major shifts in how Johnny Reb has been perceived. He maintains that changing cultural attitudes during the 1860s, 1890s, 1930s, and 1950s were responsible for these shifting images. Accordingly, he concludes that the study of myth is important not only because it shapes our perceptions of the past but also because it serves as an index to the era in which the myth originated.

Davis' conclusion is supported by Edward D. C. Campbell, Jr. in his article, "Gone With the Wind: Film as Myth and Message." Much to Margaret Mitchell's chagrin, Campbell argues, David O. Selznick overromanticized the film version of GWTW in order to exploit the popular image of the South. Depression era and World War II audiences were receptive especially to that image because it portrayed another civilization that had triumphed over adversity. But Campbell notes that, by becoming "a national epic of contemporary meaning," the movie also verified the myth of Southern life-styles and stereotyped the black man. The acceptance of such legends by audiences nationwide, Campbell believes, retarded progress in race relations and clouded insights into the South's past and problems.

10

SOUTHERN WRITERS AND THE IMAGE OF JOHNNY REB: REFLECTIONS OF REGIONAL CHANGE SINCE APPOMATTOX

Stephen Davis

A decade and a half ago, George Tindall suggested that Southern historians begin to explore myth as a fruitful field of study. As he defined it, myth was not necessarily a set of falsehoods to be disproved or debunked by the careful scholar. Rather, a popular myth represented a people's intellectual and emotional response to its history. It was the aim of such study, therefore, to define these perceptions of the past—elaborating the distinction between history as it actually happened, on the one hand, and history as it was popularly perceived, on the other.

Scholars before Tindall's writing recognized the historical significance of myth; but in the last few years, there has appeared an increasing number of works in the field. Frequently, such studies have concentrated on a particular "image" around which popular attitudes seem to form. Thus, in Civil War scholarship, we have recently had Lincoln's image in the South treated by Michael Davis; Thomas Connelly has similarly traced Robert E. Lee's image since the war. Both works indicate the wide range of materials available to the myth-oriented historian: novels, poetry, popular journalism, as well as more traditional sources. And recently, Jack Temple Kirby has examined modern media to elaborate an image of Southern identity. Each of these cases suggests that an image study may reflect cultural attitudes. In Davis' case, for instance, Southerners' changing perceptions of Lincoln reflected the gradual development of a reconciliatory spirit in the South after Appomattox.[1]

I intend to show how Southerners' changing perceptions of the common Confederate soldier—the central figure in their war for independence—reflect various currents in regional culture since the war. In the main, these popular perceptions have drawn on the work of different image-makers—novelists, poets, journalists, illustrators, orators, sculptors, and historians. Here I will deal with Southern fiction writers of the last century, not only because of their importance in articulating contemporary attitudes, but also because of their role in creating a durable image of Johnny Reb.

Throughout this body of literature, one sees four general themes. First, when the war began and early volunteers turned out, Johnny Reb was hailed as a strong and manly champion of a virtuous cause. By this idealistic view, Confederate soldiers were defenders of morality, liberty, and progress. In battle, they assumed the righteousness of Old Testament heroes, as poet Henry Lynden Flash wrote:

> Marshalled 'neath the Right's broad banner,
>> Forward rush these volunteers,
> Beating olden wrong away
>> From the fast advancing years.

At the same time, Confederates championed the advancement of civilization. "Let us rise and join the legion," Flash continues,

> Ever foremost in the fray —
> Battling in the name of Progress
> For the nobler, purer day.

A second prominent theme among wartime writers was the Confederate's defense of political liberty. Many Southern spokesmen likened the Confederate soldier to the patriot of 1776, as they termed their struggle the "second American Revolution." Thus, poet John R. Thompson asserted that Southerners were combating the same form of coercion as oppressed the patriots at Yorktown and King's Mountain. In the same spirit, another bard paraphrased Jefferson's immortal line to set forth Confederate aims: "Peal, bannered host, the proud decree/Which from your fathers went,/'No earthly power can rule the free/But by their own consent!' "[2]

In this way, Southern soldiers were seen as defenders of morality, liberty, and progress. In contrast, Federal troops were generally depicted as agents of immorality, tyranny, and degradation. In one poem, William Gilmore Simms characterized Northerners as "Tyranny's minions" and "heathen" bent on desecrating the South. Like other Confederate bards, Paul Hamilton Hayne found use for the term "horde" to describe the enemy. The word could have several applications. First, it connoted the foe as so many Goths and Vandals seeking to destroy the citadel of culture and decency. Then, too, "horde" suggested both the enemy's superior numbers and the diverse composition of its armies, which came to include foreign immigrants and former slaves. Finally, the word had mechanical uses: "horde" provided the poet with a convenient rhyme when coupled with "sword." (In similar style, Henry Timrod, "poet laureate of the Confederacy," urged his countrymen to "Fling down thy gauntlet to the Huns,/And roar the challenge from thy guns."[3])

Writing these kinds of lines, poets not only reflected wartime Southerners' patriotic idealism but also expressed a romantic concept of war, in which martial combat pitted virtuous warriors against a wicked and vengeful foe. Serving both of these functions was the best-selling novel by a Confederate author, *Macaria* by Augusta Jane Evans. The author's introduction makes clear that she shared the patriotic sentiments of other Southern partisans, as she dedicated her work to Confederate soldiers "who have delivered the South from despotism, and who have won for generations yet unborn the precious guerdon of Constitutional Republican Liberty." These noble principles seem to impel Southern soldiers to remarkable feats of valor—as at Gaines' Mill, where Federal troops try to defend earthworks that, according to Evans, "none but Confederate soldiers could successfully have assaulted."[4]

Yet the Southern writer who best exemplified romanticism in Confederate literature was not a female behind the lines, but John Esten Cooke, who served in Lee's army. After Appomattox, he collected a number of his articles written during the war and published them in 1867 as *Wearing of the Gray*. Here Johnny Reb frequently appears as chivalrous gentleman and gallant cavalier. When he fights, it is with a "gay and chivalric courage"; when he dies, it is for "knightly faith and truth." One infantry captain is hailed as "the soul of chivalry and honor," "a 'good knight' of old days," whom "neither monster nor magician, giant nor winged dragon could frighten."[5]

Eventually, however, both forms of idealism—patriotic and romantic—faded amid the wreckage of total war. After the surrender, the humiliation and ache of defeat declined slowly, but in Southern novels toward the end of the century, one sees the growth of reconciliatory spirit. This attitude, quite different from that of wartime, forms a second type of imagery for Johnny Reb. Deprecation of the enemy, for example, now gave way to a more charitable outlook that praised the soldiers of both armies. Joel Chandler Harris was only one Southern writer who perceived the Confederate soldier as not too different from his enemy in blue. Soldiers of both sides in fact seem to share a commendable Americanism that Harris saw as the source of soldierly valor. In one of his stories, he describes a small engagement in which Federal troops launch a surprise attack on unsuspecting Southerners. The latter quickly recover, Harris explains, because "American troops have a way of getting over their astonishment, as was abundantly demonstrated on both sides of the war."[6]

George Washington Cable's two war novels exemplify even more the harmony of North and South at the turn of the century. Although a former Confederate, Cable stressed that heroism had not rested solely with Southerners. Thus, in *The Cavalier* (1901), Federal Captain Jewett is every bit as brave and chivalrous as Confederate Lieutenant Ferry. Each soldier does his duty as he sees it and is therefore honorable. At the other extreme is the individual who owes allegiance to neither side. Such is the villainous Oliver, who deserts the Confederates and whose treachery ultimately leads to banishment by the Federals as well. In the end, Captain Jewett dies a hero's death (with sword upraised as a lady nearby sings "The Star-Spangled Banner"), but Oliver's bullet-riddled body is consumed by fire with no mourners at hand. Even this death is pronounced too fine by a vengeful Confederate, who would have had Oliver crushed alive by a cotton press.[7]

Yet even while the South entered the national mainstream, some writers felt disillusioned with American technological progress and material enrichment. Thus, in the 1920s and 1930s, there developed a third image of the Southern fighting man—the opponent of modern complacency and crassness. Ellen Glasgow, for example, pondered the meaning of the Confederate experience and perceived in it the effort of Southerners to maintain a chivalric code against the rise of a materialistic way of life. "Not the fortunes of war, not the moral order of the universe," she wrote, "but economic necessity doomed the South to defeat. In the coming industrial conquest, the aristocratic tradition could survive only as an archaic memorial."[8]

The Confederate soldier, symbol of old and valued tradition, thus stood in contrast to all that was going on in the New South. Not all Southerners shared this opinion, of course. But many had misgivings about the loss of conventional values that increasing urbanization and industrialization brought to the region. To these critics, modern times represented the hectic pursuit of profit and the vulgar taste for conformity. Sometimes those expressing this viewpoint were not characteristically Southern writers at all. H. L. Mencken, for instance, claimed in 1930 that Appomattox represented "a victory of what we now call Babbitts over what used to be called gentlemen." Similarly, Lawrence Stallings, speaking in Charleston, avowed admiration for South Carolinians who realized that Lincoln's election was part of a plot to "put the country into Arrow Collars." Even Hemingway was quoted as having said that Southern defeat had ended the days of carefree living; after 1865, all of life's pleasures, he said, began to cost money.[9]

In Southern war novels, the Northern soldier accordingly comes to represent the sordid hustle for riches while the Confederate is high-minded and manly. Such stereotypes were not new: as Michael C. C. Adams has shown, they existed even during the war. But one sees this imagery predominant in such fiction as Clifford Dowdey's *Bugles Blow No More* (1937). In this novel, a Virginian proclaims at the start of the war: "There's a lot of hate behind this. Don't forget that in the North they've had to break their backs in toil and sour their lives in money grubbing, and they've developed a harsh philosophy which values only the dollar." "And that's where we'll beat them," shouts another; "while they've been mucking for those dollars we've been making men out of ourselves." "I'm afraid that's the test," the speaker concludes, ". . . our men against their money."[10]

Donald Davidson and Allen Tate, members of the group of Nashville poets called the Fugitives, made even further use of Johnny Reb in their critique of modern America. In "The Deserter: A Christmas Eclogue," Davidson views postwar society through the eyes of two former Confederates. They find that Nashville in the 1880s is overcast by clouds of sooty factory smoke and overrun by greedy businessmen and self-seeking politicians. In contrast, the poet's two Confederates represent a social code in which a man was known for his honor, not for his wealth. Time has clearly passed them by, but they secretly plan to carry on their fight against the hostile new order. As one of the Rebels confides to his friend. "Nashville was occupied by Federal troops/In eighteen sixty two. THEY HOLD IT STILL!"[11]

An aged Confederate also figures in Tate's "To the Lacedemonians." Here an old veteran attending a soldiers' reunion held at Richmond in 1932 finds that the young city-dwellers cannot comprehend the meaning of the soldiers' sacrifices. Rather, they are caught up in a frantic existence characterized more by motion than by direction. Indeed, life has grown "sullen and immense"; it has lost its passion and "lusts after immunity to pain." The aged Rebel sees all of this—"the seventy years of night"—as ushered in by his defeat in 1865. But unlike the two old men in Davidson's poem, Tate's veteran does not fight back. "We shall not fight again," he says to himself, "the Yankees with our guns well-aimed and rammed—/All are born Yankees of the race of men/And this, too, now the country of the damned."[12]

Tate's old Confederate thus determines to carry his secret to the grave, at least partly because modern Southerners seem unable to comprehend his meaning. This also is the theme of Tate's most famous poem, "Ode to the Confederate Dead." In this work, a visitor to a Confederate cemetery finds it impossible to understand the purpose and principle that had driven these men to sacrifice themselves. For his part, Tate was able to look understandably on the past; he also was able to see the present and recognize that tradition was fading. This "looking both ways," as he called it, was the perspective of Southern writers after World War I. It was thus the perspective of William Faulkner when he considered the Southern past. To the Confederate soldier in particular, Faulkner responded with admiration when he viewed Johnny Reb's record of valor and endurance. In *Absalom, Absalom!*, for example, he alleges that Southerners sustained the highest casualties in military history, adding that "to talk about wounds in the Confederate army in 1865 would be like coal miners talking about soot."[13]

At the same time, Faulkner saw that the South was fighting nobly to maintain an ignoble social and economic system. In such a paradoxical struggle, monstrous men like Thomas Sutpen could bring home from the war Lee's personal citation for bravery. Apparently, Faulkner recognized that the Confederacy had been enshrouded in a deceptive veil of romance, obscuring the violence and depravity on which the antebellum South had founded its economic structure. Although the romantic outlook had seen its day two generations before, Faulkner dealt it its death blow. In one story, "My Grandmother Millard and General Bedford Forrest and The Battle of

Harrykin Creek," a young Confederate cavalry officer embodies the whole knightly tradition. This gallant singlehandedly charges a group of Yankees in order to rescue a defenseless family's silver; he leads reckless charges with the seeming intention of suicide, that he might prove himself to his lady fair, Melisandre—a name straight out of the romance of Roland. Yet his own surname is hardly chivalrous: it is Backhouse, synonym for privy.

The two lovers are wed only after a practical-minded Bedford Forrest re-arranges the spelling of the bridegroom's last name. The general simply writes a report stating that Lieutenant P. S. Backhouse has been killed in action and that Philip St-Just Backus is promoted to replace him. The new name evidently sticks, for a "Melisandre Backus" appears in another of Faulkner's works.[14]

Perhaps Johnny Reb's image had thrived on romance; when it was stripped away, he seemed to lose his vitality. Thus, the fourth and most recent image of the Confederate is that of an old grizzled veteran, the outdated relic and somewhat quaint antique that Flannery O'Connor describes in her story, "A Late Encounter With the Enemy" (1953). Here she shows a Confederate veteran, not at the time of the war, but three generations later. He is a crotchety 104-year-old amnesiac who is wheeled out to be gawked at by crowds at the premiere of *Gone With the Wind*. He provides the audience with its only authentic link to the Civil War, but he himself cannot remember a thing about it.

More recently, John William Corrington's story, "Reunion" (1968), treats Confederate veterans not at the Battle of Gettysburg but at the fiftieth commemoration of the engagement. There the old Rebels in attendance find that the younger generation has lost all comprehension of the war's meaning. To spark enthusiasm in the crowds, a program director naively suggests that the Southerners reenact Pickett's Charge. But at just the thought of reliving the terrible assault, one old soldier keels over dead.[15]

The aging of Johnny Reb signifies the aging of the Confederate experience as a whole and a waning of the Confederate myth. But the changing image of the Southern soldier also suggests that popular myth is seldom static; it alters in response to changes in cultural attitudes. We have seen how Johnny Reb has come to reflect the fervent idealism of the war years; the bounding nationalism of the late nineteenth century; unsettling transformations in regional social and economic patterns; and finally the emergence of the South into the modern century, in which little memory is retained of a conflict fought so long ago. Thus, I think we may say that as myth serves as an index of the various eras of the past so it becomes a fitting subject for historical study. We may hope to see this subject more fully explored in the future.

Notes

1. George B. Tindall, "Mythology: A New Frontier in Southern History," in Nicholas Cords and Patrick Gerster, eds., *Myth and Southern History* (Chicago:

Rand McNally College Publishing Company, 1974); Michael Davis, *The Image of Lincoln in the South* (Knoxville: University of Tennessee Press, 1971); Thomas L. Connelly, *The Marble Man: Robert E. Lee and His Image in American Society* (New York: Alfred A. Knopf, 1977); Jack Temple Kirby, *Media-Made Dixie: The South in the American Imagination* (Baton Rouge: Louisiana State University Press, 1978).

2. Henry Lynden Flash, "The Legion of Honor," John R. Thompson, "Coercion: A Poem for Then and Now," and A. J. Requier, "Our Faith in '61," in William Gilmore Simms, ed., *War Poetry of the South* (New York: Richardson & Company, 1867), pp. 41, 60, 167-68.

3. William Gilmore Simms, "Ode—'Do Ye Quail?' " Paul Hamilton Hayne, "My Mother Land," and Henry Timrod, "A Cry to Arms," in ibid., pp. 50, 118, 252-53.

4. Augusta Jane Evans, *Macaria; or, Altars of Sacrifice* (New York: John Bradburn, Publishers, 1864), introduction, p. 449.

5. John Esten Cooke, *Wearing of the Gray*, ed. by Philip Van Doren Stern (Bloomington: Indiana University Press, 1959), pp. 150-51, 352.

6. Joel Chandler Harris, "The Troubles of Martin Coy," in *On the Wing of Occasions* (New York: Doubleday, Page & Company, 1903), p. 93.

7. George Washington Cable, *The Cavalier* (New York: Charles Scribner's Sons, 1901), pp. 181, 304.

8. Ellen Glasgow, *A Certain Measure* (New York: Harcourt, Brace and Company, 1938), p. 13.

9. H. L. Mencken, "The Calamity of Appomattox," *American Mercury* XXI (1930), p. 29; Donald Davidson, "Still Rebels, Still Yankees," in *Still Rebels, Still Yankees and Other Essays* (Baton Rouge: Louisiana State University Press, 1957), p. 231; Allen Tate to Donald Davidson, December 12, 1929, in John Tyree Fain and Thomas Daniel Young, eds., *The Literary Correspondence of Donald Davidson and Allen Tate* (Athens: University of Georgia Press, 1974), p. 245.

10. Michael C. C. Adams, *Our Masters the Rebels: A Speculation on Union Military Failure in the East 1861-1865* (Cambridge: Harvard University Press, 1978); Clifford Dowdey, *Bugles Blow No More* (Boston: Little, Brown and Company, 1937), pp. 12-13.

11. Donald Davidson, "The Deserter: A Christmas Eclogue," in *Lee in the Mountains and Other Poems* (New York: Charles Scribner's Sons, 1949), pp. 15-22.

12. Allen Tate, "To the Lacedemonians," in *Poems* (Chicago: The Swallow Press, Inc., 1960), pp. 14-18. See also Donald Davidson, "The Meaning of War: A Note on Allen Tate's 'To the Lacedemonians,' " *Southern Review* I (1965), pp. 720-30.

13. Louis D. Rubin, "The Historical Image of Modern Southern Writing," *Journal of Southern History* XXII (1956), pp. 147–66; William Faulkner, *Absalom, Absalom!* (New York: Random House, 1936), pp. 189, 344.

14. William Faulkner, "My Grandmother Millard and General Bedford Forrest and The Battle of Harrykin Creek," in *Collected Short Stories of William Faulkner* (London: Chatto and Winders, 1958), vol. I, pp. 271-91.

15. Flannery O'Connor, "A Late Encounter With the Enemy," in *The Complete Stories* (New York: Farrar, Straus and Giroux, 1971), pp. 134–44; John William Corrington, "Reunion," in Allen F. Stein and Thomas N. Walters, eds., *The Southern Experience in Short Fiction* (Glenview, Ill.: Scott, Foresman and Company, 1971), pp. 124-35.

11

GONE WITH THE WIND: FILM AS MYTH AND MESSAGE
Edward D. C. Campbell, Jr.

Emerging from a theater after viewing *Gone With the Wind*, an aged Confederate veteran could only exclaim: "it's the gol-darndest thing I ever saw."[1] But the production was far more than that. When Margaret Mitchell's novel was published in 1936, the United States was still in the midst of the Great Depression. By the film's premiere in December 1939, the nation was fully aware of the political and military ravages in Europe. The world and domestic scene was no better during the picture's second distribution, in 1941.

In watching *GWTW*, as it became popularly known, the nation as a whole saw an example of the fortitude and ideals of another civilization that also had faced monumental uncertainties and had in spirit survived. Although excessive, the film presented an example for depression-era audiences that few could ignore. As a result, the image of the vanquished took on a new luster. The picture became a national epic of contemporary meaning.[2]

The United States was not alone in perceiving the film's power and significance. In wartorn London, for instance, it played during most of World War II, enthralling appreciative audiences cognizant of *Gone With the Wind*'s encouraging message of a society's emergence from the destruction of war. In 1945, liberated areas of Europe were wildly excited to view a film of spiritual survival at any cost. Even though many of the prints were still in English and without subtitles, the movie was nonetheless a broadly popular tale to which people could relate with ease.

Of course, as the culmination of the pictures of the 1930s with an antebellum theme, the film was no less romantic and ornately produced in its praise of the prewar South than its predecessors. The decade began with productions of the musicals *Hearts in Dixie* in 1929 and *Dixiana* in 1930. Other popular films included *Mississippi* in 1935 with Bing Crosby and *So Red the*

Rose, also in 1935, with Randolph Scott and Margaret Sullivan. *Jezebel* in 1938, starring Bette Davis and Henry Fonda, played heavily on the advance publicity of *GWTW*. *Way Down South*, in 1939, with the male counterpart of Shirley Temple, Bobby Breen, continued the tradition of ornate films with a conservative slant. The productions were escapist entertainment, to be sure, but within each lurked significant biased interpretations on many issues, such as the racial hierarchy, for example.

Better than previous movies, *GWTW* pointed to the utility, and the dangers, of the plantation theme as more than entertainment. And the film was eagerly awaited. A Gallup poll of December 1939 estimated that 56.5 million people planned to attend the release.[3]

Once David O. Selznick had purchased, for $50,000, the film rights to the novel, he determined that the film would be a magnificent effort to portray the South as accurately as possible—at least as he saw it.[4] He began appropriately enough. At the recommendation of Margaret Mitchell herself, Selznick hired various technical advisors to oversee production details. Will A. Price checked the cast's Southern accents. A noted expert on antebellum social customs—Susan Myrick, "the Emily Post of the South"—was employed. In addition, artist and historian Wilbur G. Kurtz aided in verifying historical details.

However, the problem—and one common to pictures of the Old South— was that the studio's penchant for accurate detail extended only so far. Whether oral thermometers could be used for the hospital scene had to be confirmed, but Selznick's sweeping conception of the antebellum South was another matter entirely.[5] And few could interfere with his perceptions. Margaret Mitchell had stipulated in her contract with Selznick International Pictures, much to the producer's chagrin, that she wanted no part of the film adaptation once she had granted the rights to her story. She was determined to remain aloof in the event the production disappointed her fellow Southerners. More importantly, sudden fame and the accompanying attention had altered her life so much that she did not wish to court further interruptions by working for Hollywood. As a result, though, Selznick had relatively free rein over the general romanticism of the picture despite the criticism of his advisors.[6]

The producer's overwhelming romantic conceptions of the antebellum region were particularly evident in his instructions for the construction of the Tara set. Although researchers closely studied period photographs as well as sketches and other documents to achieve the right architecture for the forty-acre set of 1864 Atlanta, the prewar O'Hara mansion owed more to imagination than to research. Consequently, the set reflected the mythology built up by previous films and seemingly accepted without question by a filmmaker whose preciseness of detail had helped establish his reputation.

In the novel, Tara was not the grand seat of plantation wealth and power but the home of a not particularly wealthy planter. In other words, it was a fairly ordinary home, especially in light of the cinematic presentations of the Southern houses. But Selznick fully realized that such a structure comported neither with his idealization of the section nor—and far more importantly—with the public's.

For the movie, Tara became hardly representative of the class of which Miss Mitchell wrote, although she had admittedly given the O'Hara property an avenue of cedars and neatly ordered, white-washed slave quarters. But by the writer's own admission, it was quite "hard to make people understand that North Georgia wasn't all white columns and singing darkies and magnolias. . . ." Southerners even questioned her as to why the novel's setting was not the mansion that they had come to expect. At least in the picture, the romantic depiction was achieved for those disturbed at the book's lack of splendor on that point.

Selznick, his production designer William Cameron Menzies, and art director Lyle Wheeler instead presented an architecturally grand house of white columns, handsome vistas, and blossoming dogwoods. It was hardly the small plantation common to north Georgia in 1861. In fact, searching through Clayton County, which the author had used for the novel's setting, Miss Mitchell found but one columned house from the prewar era. But Selznick knew the nation desired the grandiose image, and the South would embrace it wholeheartedly, even to the extent of claiming that Tara or Twelve Oaks was "just like the mansion my grandpappy had that Sherman burned."[7]

Although she persisted in refusing to interfere directly, Miss Mitchell did on occasion express her fears to Susan Myrick. Realizing Selznick's unbounded enthusiasm and how the South itself would warmly receive the nostalgic romanticism he was so carefully creating, she regretted the excessiveness. She especially feared that the opening scenes would include field hands suddenly erupting in joyous song, as they had in so many films. Both she and her husband, John Marsh, were weary "at seeing the combined Tuskegee and Fisk Jubilee Choirs bounce out at the most inopportune times and in the most inopportune places . . ." as such groups had done from *Hearts in Dixie* in 1929 to *Jezebel* the year before. Worse than the singing would be "the inevitable wavings in the air of several hundred pairs of hands . . ." a characteristic born as early as the Thomas Edison Company's 1903 version of *Uncle Tom's Cabin*.[8] She was not far wrong, for although the movie contained no mass chorales every other stock ingredient was included.[9]

As the first part of the picture attempted to demonstrate, the South was, in Melanie Hamilton's words, "a whole world that only wants to be graceful and beautiful." If the region's physical beauty was to be destroyed, the changes wrought would be so significant as to threaten the South's very ideals. And throughout the remainder of the film, the audiences were vividly shown the alternative when a society's very foundations were crumbled. The analogy to the viewers' own times was not easily missed. As a result, the South's argument took on even more force.

The latter half of *Gone With the Wind*, including the years of Reconstruction, repeatedly accentuated the differences between the plantation world and the postwar society. One of the recurring symbols of the changes brought by the war was the use of the staircases of Twelve Oaks, Tara, and Rhett and Scarlett's postwar Victorian home.

The grand, wide, beautifully curving stairway of the Wilkes home represented all that was gracious in the Old South. The passage was sparkling white, airy, full of the ebb and flow of refined society. There, Rhett first spied Scarlett on the staircase; Scarlett herself ensnared some of her admirers on the steps. The stairwell area was the meeting place of bowing servants and their supposed betters. There, Melanie displayed her Christian charity in defending her cousin Scarlett's designs; there too, Ashley Wilkes ecountered the flirtatious Scarlett. One of the widely used publicity stills pictured the stairs full of belles descending to meet awaiting gentlemen. It was the plantation world at its best.

But such would not last, for the war would change it all. The movie refrained from showing much of the actual fighting, confining the war to only panoramic shots of a subdued or burning Atlanta or of Scarlett driving a wagon across a field strewn with the dead and military debris. But all the horror and destruction of war were nonetheless powerfully captured in the scene of Scarlett, cornered on the staircase of Tara, repelling the Yankee looter. In that moment, the horrifying extent of the culture's altercation was depicted.

The region was no longer the same. Tara's once-graceful interior was but a shell of its former self. Scarlett stood on a stairway, appearing confused within its war-ravaged condition. The symbolic structure was dark, weakened, narrow and led to only further darkness and ruin in the once-proud estate. At its bottom waited what appeared to her as the cause of all the destruction. The ensuing shot echoed the South's frustration; whatever price was exacted on the enemy, the culture's fate had already been sealed.

But the script emphasized that perseverance would bring eventual recovery. Even though Scarlett and Rhett maintained a fortune built on the former's newfound entrepreneurial talents and the latter's wartime blockade running, the life-style they enjoyed could never match that which had been so recently destroyed. Their new mansion did not reflect the refinement of the South, but instead the crass materialism of a commercial society with which the cinematic South had been for so long unfamiliar. The red brick, Victorian-style house seemed out of place, and dominating its interior was a wide, dark-stained, garish red-carpeted staircase leading from a gloomy, foreboding hallway up to what often appeared total darkness. The comparative crassness of the new, overdone, and heavily ornate grandeur was in pointed contrast to the splendor of, say, Twelve Oaks. It was the stairway over which raged many an argument, and it was the passage down which Scarlett rushed in pursuit of Rhett, who had declared that even he, who was once viewed as a prewar oddity for his callous disregard of conventions, was "going back to Charleston, back where I belong" to find if there was not "something left in life of charm and grace." Down the stairs, he retreated to a past. In the end, Scarlett would follow the same course. She went home to Tara, to the land, still dominated by a mansion and still tended by Hollywood's ever-present faithful blacks.

Audiences, North and South, flocked to the theaters to view the eagerly awaited epic. Particularly in the South was there a sense of pride, even of vindication. At the December 15, 1939, Atlanta premiere, 1 million people streamed into the city for what the governor had declared as an official state holiday.

GWTW was hailed in the Georgia capital as a giant step in the healing of sectional wounds. In an editorial in the Atlanta *Constitution*, Robert Quillen exclaimed that the story of the Old South, "by the simple expedient of telling the truth, has won the admiration and affection of all America." Forgiven and finally understood, the spirit of the region would "march through all America, conquering hearts as it goes." A later editorial praised the tale's refraining "from caricature, either the romantic exaggeration of Southern partiality or the impossible nobility of visionary Northerners." As a result, the production would be viewed "as the historic recording of its place and time." The editor of the Atlanta *Journal*, the newspaper for which Miss Mitchell had once worked, agreed completely. The film chronicled an age that "seems never to have died—or, rather, to have died and risen in new strength and beauty."[10] Margaret Mitchell's fears of modern Southern romanticism had been well grounded.

Consistently, regional critics viewed the picture as a "superlative effort" that would withstand close scrutiny and the test of time. A Richmond commentator was especially pleased with the treatment of the slavery issue, as it was "in accord with all the stories and legends of slavery-time Negroes" and accurately depicted the planters and their ladies. Thus, *GWTW*, as one reviewer phrased it, "should give the dream reality."[11]

Although one reviewer pointed to the issue of slavery and warned that, in light of the world economic and political situation in the late 1930s, the master-slave relationship was not necessarily a dead issue, such critical insights were rare. For example, several critics perceived Scarlett's excessive business greed built on sprawling urban growth as appalling. Henry Martin, a Memphis reporter, viewed Vivien Leigh's change in character as one that served as a "study of the South's descent into Gethsemane and its return from Calvary." And Clark Gable's final awareness of the culture's significance was the "personification of man's regeneration through belated awakening to the call of a cause greater than one's own self."[12]

Although Southerners such as Mrs. W. D. Lamar, president-general of the United Daughters of the Confederacy, believed *GWTW* was "wonderfully faithful to the traditions" of the section, for national import the production had to prove popular and meaningful in the North and West as well.[13] Popular it certainly was. In Boston, for instance, a record crowd of 17,000 persons viewed the film on its first day; the line for tickets had formed at 6:00 A.M., and by the second day, over 50,000 advance bookings had been sold.[14] But did non-Southerners grasp the theme of the plantation ideal and of spiritual survival?

Indeed, the reception was unanimous. In Los Angeles, the critics were particularly pleased with the background color. A San Francisco commentator also marveled at the society and at its demise, at "how completely the gracious, patrician life of the Old South, the life of Tara and Twelve Oaks, has been shattered, never to be reclaimed." At times, there seemed genuine sorrow that such culture had to die. Although regretting what he interpreted as the film's bitterness against Northerners, a Chicago reviewer remarked that the war was "in pathetic and terrible contrast to episodes of the lazy, carefree prewar era in a South of Cavaliers and ladies and gracious living. . . ."[15]

Particularly noteworthy about these reviews was the consistent perception of the South as a section overflowing with wealth and refinement, that Tara was indicative of the up-country, middle-class planter existence, and that the cotton planter class itself was representative of the region's populace as a whole. A Midwestern critic labeled the film as accurate; the atmosphere was "faithful" and "startingly beautiful in pastoral scenes." Remarkably, practically all described the production's view as perfect in its recreation of the plantation setting as a "graceful culture" or a gorgeous panorama." The myth was becoming harder to distinguish from the fact. As the film was overdone, so too was the acceptance of the "magnolia-scented days of the Old South." To non-Southerners, the society was without doubt one of "wealth and distinction," with the attendant "hospitable manners, broad acres, beautiful women and chivalrous men and the faithful old mammies who served them."[16]

If the life-style had become so laudable, so fantastically alluring, it was then but a short step to grieve at its passing, to regret its treatment by the victors, and finally to praise its determination and example. It was quite a turnabout, only seventy-five years after the nation's bloodiest conflict. The romantic films could take a great deal of responsibility for the change.

Movies aided enormously the affirmation of the South as the most distinctive region of the country with a rural character that increasingly served as an alternative to recall with fondness. So attractive was the section, especially as seen in *GWTW*, that non-Southerners continued to embrace the films' viewpoint with little hesitation or awareness of the social repercussions.

Many reviewers, as one in Topeka, insisted that *GWTW* presented its theme without undue favoritism toward the South, a judgment that revealed the extent of the mythology's credibility. *Gone With the Wind* and its predecessors strongly argued that the South was not solely responsible for the war, that slavery was not so evil, and that both sides were defending life-styles, modes of society. Pictures of the antebellum period made the point, as a Connecticut writer phrased it, that people "merely misunderstood the motives underlying two completely different types of people," of two "contrasting sets of ideals." Once the sincerity of the Confederate cause was understood and its way of life so lovingly recreated, even a Northerner could—as a Boston writer postulated—"rise up and whistle 'Dixie' along with rabid Yankee-hating Georgians." The film in its presentation of "the finest qualities of the Old South" indeed constituted a moving argument that the section was misunderstood.[17]

What a Midwesterner termed the region's "dreamy appeal of the baronial magnificence" became a vision for Depression audiences. Viewers too faced what the defeated South had encountered: "the rise of a new and unhappy age," as a Cleveland writer described it. And in the defeated people's very survival as a unique part of the nation lay the lesson. A Philadelphia critic believed strongly that the example merited considerable attention, that "even a dyed-in-the-wool Yankee must—and can afford to—give a rebel yell for *Gone With the Wind*." The epic had magnificently served to demonstrate that one "courageously, stubbornly, and painfully built upon the ashes of crushed hopes and ruined lands . . ." a feat many hoped to duplicate.[18]

The romantic films of the Old South during the 1930s of course did not alone ameliorate the low spirits of numerous viewers, but the contribution toward such an end was evident. Moreover, and more importantly, such releases as *GWTW* that praised the fortitude of the South furnished a popular example for the country of recovery from adversity. For the region itself, the movies of the 1930s verified legend and presented an apologia more sweeping than any section had constructed. By the outbreak of World War II, the many myths and the racial and cultural conservatism had reached an apex of cinematic reevaluation begun so humbly and unintentionally in 1903 with *Uncle Tom's Cabin*. The marvel was that the process was still so much one of innocence; the stories often were simply the studios' reflection of popular taste that craved films of romance and flair. But what a message the surface innocence of pictures as *GWTW* bore; their very acceptance revealed the persistence of a legend that decreed an opulent South, and its beliefs were to be praised at the expense of progress nationally in race relations and in a more accurate perception of the South's past and problems.

Notes

1. New Orleans *Times-Picayune*, January 27, 1940. See also Memphis *Commercial Appeal*, January 27, 1940; *Nashville Banner*, December 16, 1939.

2. As one Eastern reviewer stated, "the story of the Old South with its Cavaliers and cotton has given America its most eloquent and grandest film narrative." A Midwestern critic remarked that the drama of the planter culture was for all since it was a "story of great events in American history," not merely Southern. See Wilmington (Del.) *Journal-Every Evening*, January 27, 1940; *St. Louis Post-Dispatch*, January 28, 1940.

3. *The New York Times*, December 20, 1939.

4. For the best overview of the novel's creation, see Finis Farr, *Margaret Mitchell of Atlanta* (New York: Morrow, 1965), especially pp. 25-26, 99-147; see also Richard Harwell, ed., *Margaret Mitchell's Gone With the Wind Letters, 1936-1949* (New York: Macmillan, 1976), especially pp. 1-2, 5-6, 61-62, 65-66, 71-72, 111, 118-20, 132, 219, 298-300, 357-58, 406. For the background of the adaptation to film, see Rudy Behlmer, ed., *Memo from David O. Selznick* (New York: Viking, 1972), pp. 143, 159, 206, 235; Gavin Lambert, *GWTW: The Making of Gone With the Wind* (Boston: Little, Brown, 1973), pp. 16–17, 31–36; Roland Flamini, *Scarlett, Rhett and a Cast of Thousands: The Filming of Gone With the Wind* (New York: Macmillan, 1975), pp. 3-5, 8-9, 12-13, 16; see also Bob Thomas, *Selznick* (New York: Doubleday, 1970), p. 155.

5. The anecdotes of the lengths to which the exactness of detail was carried are many; see, for example, Studio Press Book for *Gone With the Wind* (1954, rerelease), in Museum of Modern Art Film Study Center, New York; Studio Press Book (1961, rerelease), in Library of Congress Motion Picture Section Box C-109, cited hereafter as LC-MPS. See also Souvenir Booklet (1967, rerelease), in LC-MPS Box C-41; and Studio Press Book (1967, rerelease), in LC-MPS Box C-19.

6. Behlmer, *Memo*, p. 202; Harwell, *Gone With the Wind Letters*, pp. 36, 137, 249-50, 358, 406-07; see also Lambert, *GWTW*, pp. 69-70; and Flamini, *Scarlett, Rhett, and a Cast of Thousands*, pp. 146, 148, 210.

7. Harwell, *Gone With the Wind Letters*, pp. 271-72; see also pp. 406-07.

8. Ibid.; see also Richard Harwell, ed., "Technical Adviser: The Making of *Gone With the Wind*, The Hollywood Journals of Wilbur G. Kurtz," *Atlanta Historical Journal*, XXII (Summer 1978), pp. 7-131.

9. See Dialogue and Cutting Continuity of *Gone With the Wind* (1939), in LC-MPS Copyright File LP-9390. The romantic aura of the Old South also was brought out in the advertising, which pictured belles, gentlemen, and officers. See, for example, Baltimore *Sun*, January 26, 1940; *St. Louis Post-Dispatch*, January 24, 1940;

Detroit Free Press, January 24, 1940; *Meridian* (Miss.) *Star*, March 24, 1940; *Manchester* (N.H.) *Union*, February 9, 1940; *Santa Fe New Mexican*, February 20, 1940; *Newark Star-Ledger*, January 25, 1940; Portland *Oregon Daily Journal*, January 21, 1940; *Seattle Post-Intelligencer*, January 24, 1940; *Providence* (R.I.) *Journal*, January 25, 1940; Sioux Falls *Daily Argus Leader*, February 25, 1940; Memphis *Commercial Appeal*, January 26, 1940; *Pittsburgh Press*, January 25, 1940. The more well known poster of Rhett carrying Scarlett was actually developed for the later releases; see Poster for *Gone With the Wind* (n.d., rerelease), in Library of Congress Prints and Photographs Division.

10. Atlanta *Constitution*, December 13, 14, 15, 16, 1939; Atlanta *Journal*, December 14, 15, 1939.

11. See, for example, *Richmond Times-Dispatch*, February 3, 1940; *Birmingham News*, February 4, 1940; *Montogomery Advertiser*, January 28, 29, 1940; Little Rock *Arkansas Democrat*, February 25, 1940; *Meridian* (Miss.) *Star*, March 24, 1940; Raleigh *News and Observer*, February 11, 18, 1940; *Dallas Morning News*, February 7, 1940; *Miami Herald*, January 18, 1940; *Charlotte Observer*, January 30, 1940; Louisville *Courier-Journal*, January 27, 1940.

12. *Dallas Morning News*, February 8, 1940; *Houston Post*, February 11, 1940; Memphis *Commercial Appeal*, January 27, 1940.

13. *Nashville Banner*, December 16, 1939.

14. *Boston Daily Globe*, December 22, 1939; see also *Indianapolis News*, January 27, 1940; Butte *Montana Standard*, February 22, 1940; *Newark Star-Ledger*, January 26, 1940.

15. *Los Angeles Times*, January 1, 1940; *San Francisco Chronicle*, January 26, 1940; *Chicago Daily Tribune*, January 26, 1940.

16. *Cleveland Plain Dealer*, January 27, 1940; *Portland* (Me.) *Press Herald*, February 9, 1940; *Detroit Free Press*, January 24, 1940; Portland *Oregon Daily Journal*, January 26, 1940; *Salt Lake Tribune*, January 29, 1940; *Seattle Post-Intelligencer*, January 26, 1940.

17. *Topeka Daily Capital*, February 21, 1940; *Hartford* (Conn.) *Times*, February 3, 1940; *Boston Daily Globe*, December 22, 1939.

18. *St. Louis Post-Dispatch*, January 28, 1940; *Cleveland Plain Dealer*, January 27, 1940; *Philadelphia Inquirer*, January 19, 1940; see also *Pittsburgh Press*, January 27, 1940.

VI

FOLLOWING THE COLOR LINE: QUESTIONS OF RACE RELATIONS

Within the last few years, an intensified reinvestigation has been made of how the black community made the transition from slavery to freedom. Offering new evidence in this inquiry is Ronald L. F. Davis in his article "Labor Dependency Among Freedmen, 1865–1880." Focusing on several "representative" Deep South Cotton Belt counties in the Natchez district of Mississippi and Louisiana, Davis contends that the findings of cliometricians on the origins and nature of black dependency in sharecropping in the postwar South may be "misleading." Blacks preferred sharecropping to a wage system because it afforded them greater freedom from white supervision and hence gave them more autonomy over their lives. Therefore, Davis argues, planters of the Natchez district had to accept sharecropping on decentralized plantations as a labor system because the freedmen insisted on it. He also finds that the supply merchants did not hold a "territorial monopoly" over the black croppers. Most storekeepers competed with one another for the freedmen's business, affording the croppers more leverage within the system than some historians have recognized. Despite the facts that eventually sharecropping did become "an economic trap" and that a caste society did evolve, Davis concludes that there was enough flexibility initially within the labor system to ensure that the black sharecroppers of the Natchez district did not become simply an "obsequent and subservient people."

The extent to which the caste system alluded to by Davis had evolved in the South by the early twentieth century and the willingness of whites to use violence to maintain this pattern of race relations are vividly demonstrated by James A. Burran in his essay, "Urban Racial Violence in the South During World War II: A Comparative Overview." Burran points out that wartime riots in Northern cities were instigated primarily by blacks who did not live under a rigidly enforced caste system; whereas simultaneous race riots in Southern cities were initiated primarily by whites who feared that the war might bring changes that would threaten the South's system of white supremacy. In sum, Burran concludes that during the 1940s the South's Jim Crow policies, vigorously enforced by hostile whites, effectively inhibited any show of assertiveness on the part of Southern blacks. Burran's thesis challenges the interpretations of those historians who have argued that the Southern black militancy of the "Second Reconstruction" originated during the years of World War II.

12

LABOR DEPENDENCY AMONG FREEDMEN, 1865–1880

Ronald L. F. Davis

The most basic change that occurred with slavery's end in the American South was the separation of blacks from their white masters. This is self-evident. Yet it also is clear that freedom for black people in the social economy of Southern agriculture soon meant a new kind of dependency that may have been slavery in all but name. Sociologists and anthropologists writing in the 1930s have detailed the extent to which rural Southern blacks, the majority of the South's black population, were bound by the rigors of a caste system that deprived them of the legal, political, and social protections afforded whites by the U.S. Constitution. This caste system went beyond the plight of an impoverished people in that blacks not only were poor but also were unable to protest their poverty in demonstrations, in movements, or in organized but democratic resistance without breaking the all powerful color line that kept them entrapped.[1] The South's single crop economy, the crop lien system, and the lack of job opportunities outside the plantation economy meant that there was no real escape for the black masses until the great migrations North in the twentieth century.[2]

The caste and economic box in which blacks found themselves during the first generations after slavery meant that they were forced to continue, as in slavery, their deferring role in life as an entrapped and dependent people. The extent, however, of their dependency is unclear. Indeed, the bent of the most recent literature on slavery suggests that much remains to be discovered about the autonomy of black people before as well as after the Civil War. In Eugene Genovese's view of slavery, the dominance of plantation masters shaped the black's world in a complex system of reciprocal relations. The determinant of that world was the planter's all-engulfing power demonstrated in random terror and paternalism. Within the interstices of the plantation community, blacks won for themselves a sense of meaning and identity insofar as their dependency and deference enabled masters to take pride in their mastery and to treat their slaves as peculiar members of their extended families. Econometricians Robert Fogel and Stanley Engerman agree, in their own way, that plantation slavery, due to the rationality of the masters' drive to maximize profits that offered definite rewards and incentives to black workers, resulted in both good and faithful laborers as well as in a community of well-adjusted slaves.[3]

Yet the work of Herbert Gutman suggests that there may be more to be said about the autonomy of black people. In Gutman's study of the black family, we see evidence of a world apart from that of the master's. The very resiliency and inner directedness of the slave family's ties and structure suggest that black slaves not only resisted planter domination but also created a viable world of their own out of resources beyond the master's control. If this were so in slavery, what about in freedom?[4]

The purpose of this paper is to look briefly at the nature of black dependency in sharecropping as found in the Natchez district of Mississippi and Louisiana in the years 1864 and 1880. The district, consisting of Adams County, Mississippi, and Concordia Parish, Louisiana, was one of the richest of the plantation areas of the Deep South. Its slave population was spread over several hundred plantations, with one hundred slaves the average number on each place. Its plantation elite was notorious among the antebellum upper class for its wealth, society, and plantation mansions. Many of these plantation "nabobs" owned several plantations, often one in the less fertile uplands of Adams County and a second or third in the fertile bottom lands of Concordia Parish, and mansions in Natchez. When slavery ended in the Natchez district, a world ended as well.[5]

The first indication that Natchez blacks meant to have a meaningful freedom may be seen in the origins of sharecropping in the district. Most of the scholarship on the transition from slavery to sharecropping sees the period as one of initial flux followed by gradual stabilization as labor and capital struck a bargain on the conditions of working. The general view is that sharecropping, or that system wherein freedmen either worked for a share of the crop for their wages or else paid a share of their crops in rent, was mutually attractive to both planters and freedmen as both saw in the system the possibilities of sharing with one another the risks of production. In the bargain that was struck, blacks gained independence from the gang labor system of slavery, while planters and landlords remained in control of the crucial decisions of crop management. In time, according to this view, blacks farmed on relatively decentralized plantations in family arrangements, while planters became merchants and merchants became planters.[6]

Much of this interpretation is misleading. In the Natchez district, planters, Yankees, and local Southern whites were forced to adopt sharecropping by the freedmen's refusal to work under any other system. The emancipated slaves had tried wages only to find themselves subject to such flagrant abuses as to render the wage system totally unacceptable. Immediately after the first appearance of Northern troops in the Natchez district, blacks flocked to the Union lines. Grant, the commanding general in the area, placed the refugees back on the plantations as wage laborers. In his mind, the freedmen would thus learn the meaning of a contract, earn their keep, and free the military from the problems of heavily populated refugee camps.

The program was a disaster on all accounts. What the refugee slaves learned is that the Yankee whites were not to be trusted. For one thing, the wage system was so low as to mean no wages at all once their subsistence was deducted. After the war, the Freedmen's Bureau, unable to distribute lands to the freedmen, urged blacks to return to the plantations as wage laborers. Similar to Grant's reasoning, the agents of the bureau thought it reasonable and just for Southern blacks to sell their labor to the highest bidders, to work at their jobs as long and hard and well as disciplined wage hands, and thereby to accumulate enough capital from their earnings eventually to buy small family farms of their own. Forced to haggle and bargain for their wages in a free economy, moreover, the former slaves would soon develop, according to this reasoning, and insofar as each individual was able, the one requirement of the free labor system: self-motivated ambition.[7]

At first, few Southern planters believed blacks capable of working without the whip as their chief incentive. But in time, mainly due to the competition for black labor by Northern lessees of neighborhood land, most landlords abandoned their "black code" attempts at slavery and hired blacks for wages. Blacks soon learned, however, that set wages tied them to the direction and dictation of their white employers as much as had been the case in slavery. While they might not be sold or beaten, blacks found themselves disciplined to slavelike obedience on the plantation through the loss of wages due to loosely defined insubordination. In the hundreds of wage contracts signed between planters and freedmen in the early postwar period, the most common stipulation bound blacks to provide their employers with "good and faithful labor." And it was this promise that planters most often accused their hired wage slaves of breaking. For most local planters, "good and faithful labor" on the part of blacks meant subservient labor as had once existed in slavery. Yankee employers, those who had rented plantations and hired blacks to work them, were less concerned with subservient labor but nevertheless used the wage system to punish freedmen for practices ranging from labor shirking to feigned illnesses.[8]

As a result of this peculiar form of wage arrangement, blacks demanded a system wherein they would be free from the particular direction of their lives by white landlords. Under no circumstances would they agree to contract for planters under a wage system. What they demanded, rather, was a system that enabled them to labor under their own direction, in their own time, and in family arrangements. They insisted, as a minimum condition, that no landlord or supervisor work with them in a labor-directed sense. Agents of the landlord might visit, might hire wage hands to supplement the family labor at the family's expense, and might make regular rounds to check on the crop. But no boss would be allowed on the place in the sense of daily supervision. Indeed, most freedmen wanted the planter to even abandon the plantation house if at all possible.[9]

Looking back on this practice, several historical economists tell us that planters agreed to the move from wages to family sharecropping because it was cheaper for them to supervise the freedmen's work and because the share system provided freedmen with the proper incentive for effective labor. Viewing both planters and freedmen as rational hedonists (that is, as individuals motivated to minimize risks and maximize incomes), these scholars tell us that the move reflected the risk aversion possibilities of the system, the lower supervision costs, and the option by labor to therein shift their income efforts among agriculture, fishing, hunting, and other remunerative activities.[10] While all of these are sound theoretical justifications for sharecropping, the historical facts are that freedmen demanded sharecropping because it provided them the independence allowed by no other system. Planters were dragged kicking and screaming into the system because blacks refused to work in any other system of labor.

To be sure, the system that finally replaced slavery was an economic trap for blacks. But it was not slavery. Indeed, one of the main reasons why the caste system emerged so dramatically in the South may be due to the very failure of Southern planters to survive as a class of active plantation managers in control of a centralized system of plantation blacks. This is not to say that by 1880 the district's antebellum planters vanished from the scene as planter elites. In Adams County, nearly one-half of its antebellum planter families survived as holders of plantation estates in 1870. More may have survived but remain hidden due to the nature of the records. Of those families surviving, their total holdings also survived basically intact as plantation estates, although 15 percent fewer acres appeared in the improved acreage records in the manuscript census records. Moreover, when studied in categories of size defined by acres improved, we see that the largest of the antebellum estates experienced the greatest decline in land under cultivation as well as the greater incidence of loss. The smallest holdings in 1860 actually experienced a 78 percent gain in acreage as a group, although even here the typical family had lost acreage. What this suggests is that at least one out of two planter families survived the war as landowners. But most, nearly 65 percent, lost over half their acreage improved in 1860; those who gained, some 29 percent of the surviving families, gained significantly, nearly doubling their 1860 acreage improved.[11]

In Concordia Parish, by taking the tax records, the manuscript census tracts, and local documents ranging from courthouse records to plantation manuscripts, we were able to identify seventy of its 134 antebellum plantations as to owners, names of estates, acreage owned, and approximate locations for both 1860 and 1881. Of these seventy, 54 percent remained in the same family hands a generation after the Civil War. As in the case of Adams County a decade earlier, the persistence was accompanied by a 19 percent loss of total acreage. The bulk of these surviving plantations were large estates, but the typical place had lost more than one-fourth of its antebellum acreage. Those gaining, although fewer, enjoyed similar percentage increase in size—one-fourth.[12]

One thing is certain: few surviving antebellum planters, although they continued to own plantation estates, were planters in the antebellum sense of the term. For some, especially those who had functioned as absentee owners before the war, the new era meant replacing the overseer-manager with the merchant-manager. For others, the antebellum resident planters, their survival as landowners saw them giving up their resident planter status. A great many left the neighborhood to live in St. Louis or in New Orleans or in Memphis, with their plantations leased to others. When the antebellum planter William F. Miller, for instance, agreed to lease his Park and Dumbarton plantations to Natchez merchants in 1869, he fully understood that his tenants would then contract with freedmen to work the plantations as sharecroppers and that neither he nor his merchant-tenants would live on the place. He also understood that such a deal gave the merchants a lien on the cotton due to the freedmen for supplies advanced and the right to a share of the freedmen's crop as rent, thus combining for the merchants the advantages of landlord and supplier with but a minimum of capital investment and without actually owning the land. Miller had retained his ownership of the plantations, but he was no longer a planter.[13]

The displacement of the planter as an active resident manager of the plantation accompanied the general decentralization of the plantation. A crucial feature of this new plantation was the role of the merchant as the chief source of supply to Southern freedmen sharecroppers and tenants. The general literature on this subject sees merchants assuming new dictatorial powers over freedmen as they came to hold the legal power over the freedmen's very food and credit. In return for merchant credit, the sharecroppers gave the merchant a lien on their crops. In short time, this credit lien system entrapped black and white sharecroppers alike in a system of high credit prices, high interest advances, and perpetual debts as cotton prices spiraled downward. Recently, economists Roger Ransom and Richard Sutch have argued that individual merchants actually held a territorial monopoly on their customer accounts that reinforced the rigidity of the system.[14]

Much of the above was true as well of the Natchez district. But some important differences existed that, if they were common for the South as a whole, modify at least initially the system of dependency engulfing freedmen sharecroppers. For one thing, while it is true that merchants came to dominate the supply business of freedmen within a few years after the war, it would be mistaken to assume that such domination meant that merchants took an active role in the direction of blacks as farmers on the decentralized plantations. Although the typical planter in 1880 leased his lands to local merchants, the typical merchant then subleased his rented lands to freedmen. The terms of the lease generally specified the crops to be planted as well as the rent or the share wages. No insistence by the merchant to have supervisory people on the place as work directors occurred. The nature of the farming enabled the merchant to check on the crop's progress in weekly trips, and the terms of the contract usually included the merchant's right to bring in hired workers at the cropper's expense if the crops fell behind.[15]

More importantly, the lien records, housed in the district courthouses, for the generation after slavery indicate that merchants were involved in keen competition for the freedmen's business. Indeed, liens were often piled on top of liens in the drive for the freedmen's business. While it is doubtful that merchants wished to advance money or supplies to freedmen heavily in debt to others, it did happen enough to show the extent of merchant competitiveness. Some merchants, especially the most successful, often held accounts with freedmen on the same plantations. Isaac Friedler, for one example, shared accounts on Helena plantation in 1873 with merchant James Pendleton, did the same on Whitehall with John Mackin, and on Shamrock with merchant J. H. Scott. These competing merchants had no real territorial monopolies, although once an account was established it most likely continued to run for several years. The procedure was simple enough. Freedmen consumers of mercantile credit seldom shopped around to compare prices, haggled over interest rates, or changed creditors due to promotions or merchant offerings of advantages. The typical freedmen, rather, shopped for the amount of advances they might obtain over the year. Merchants competed on their record or promises of advances to be had and, at least initially, by their attitude regarding supervision. In time, these terms of credit and policy of plantation management became quite well established. For the merchant, such promises and accommodations were easy terms to meet since sums and supplies advanced carried heavy interest rates and specification of crops to be planted. In the Natchez district, at least, if merchants held freedmen in a monopolistic grip, it was the hold of a system of competitive merchants rather than the clasp of a single store, although the economic effects of such competition eventually bound freedmen to a long-enduring status of debtor poverty.[16]

What the foregoing suggests is that sharecropping and the decentralized plantation of the postbellum South, if the Natchez district is a good example, originated largely due to the freedmen's insistence on it. These demands for family farms and autonomy in their working lives were not the demands of slaves reduced to childlike dependence. That much is certain. Whether or not these demands rested on a viable Afro-American slave culture of its own, one created in the wake of plantation hegemony or one in which past "capitalistic" experiences made freedmen ready to maximize their opportunities, must await further research. In any case, freedmen came to sharecropping independently of planters and soldiers. They came to it on their own.

Once sharecropping and its crop lien system settled on the South, the latter growing up as the necessary and sufficient means by which the free market provided expensive credit for Southern farmers in the wake of declining cotton prices and in the absence of government intervention on the side of equality and justice, freedmen indeed lost the independent status that had enabled them to obtain sharecropping in the first place. Historian U. B. Phillips deplored the new state of affairs as absurd. Not only was the plantation decentralized, according to Phillips, but the modern landlord, in sharecropping, lost the main advantage of free labor: the ability to deal ruthlessly and quickly through firings with antagonistic, shirking, undisciplined, lazy, or incompetent workers. In Phillips' mind, sharecropping fastened to the New South the old antebellum disadvantage of cultivating cotton with dependent labor since freedmen contracted in families on a yearly basis and were generally linked to the place by the bonds of sentiment, sympathy, and debt, without the old antebellum advantage of efficient organization, centralized planning, and intensive supervision.[17]

The outcome of this new mode of production was the caste system mentioned earlier. From the standpoint of white and black relationships, few freedmen openly challenged the system. Even the Colored Alliance of Populism was organized by whites and only covertly by blacks.[18] From the outside looking in, the successful black seemed to be the deferential black, with success defined as property ownership, while those disruptive in any way were set on with violence. Too, according to the recent writings of economist Jay Mandle, few avenues of escape were available, what with meaningful jobs nonexistent in the Northern states until the new century.[19]

Yet in spite of all this, it is not true that blacks in sharecropping were simply reduced to an obsequent and subservient people. The fact that they had successfully demanded and obtained freedom from direct supervision and overlording in their work meant that they were at least as autonomous in freedom as they had been in slavery. Indeed, the manuscript census records for the Natchez district in 1880 vividly demonstrate the persistence among blacks of the family system of farming. Although it is true that they were threatened with eviction for undesirable behavior, the definition of what was undesirable is not very clear. Landlords, having abandoned intensive supervision with sharecropping, sought to at least guarantee both "faithful labor" and steady labor by a supply arrangement wherein sharecroppers were kept in debt. Tenants, it seems, were not easily evicted in the Natchez district because their replacements were not easily obtained. In the 1870s, for instance, hundreds of the district's freedmen stopped their work and prepared to journey to Kansas in what amounted to a mass strike at the economic trap in which they had found themselves. It was only after tremendous propaganda, coordinated violence, and the promise by supply men and planters to write off all back debts that the disgruntled freedmen agreed to abandon the Kansas dream and return to work. Thereafter, freedmen in the district worked in families of continuous and persistent structure.[20]

Indicative, too, of their relative autonomy is the fact that district blacks often refused to set themselves up as croppers. Although the matter is uncertain, the data analyzed suggest that perhaps one-fourth of the adult black population in the district lived and worked as what might be called casual laborers in the cotton economy. It seems that hundreds of freedmen worked only as pickers or as hands occasionally brought in for cash wages to supplement a cropper's labor force at times of emergency.[21] One explanation for this surplus of labor is that slavery's end also had ended the South's need to keep the entire black population at work. The matter was simple enough. Blacks in 1860 were not only laborers but also sources of credit and valuable commodities, and thus provided planters with an incentive to own as many slaves as possible as long as the returns from planting covered the expenses of production, interest on loans, and costs of living. But with blacks no longer commodities in 1880, there was less incentive for planters to work the marginal lands or to expand their operations to cover the costs of owning slaves. In this context, landlords and planters may have contracted with only the best (most faithful) hands and worked only the best soils in 1880 in recognition that (1) a large surplus of workers existed for hire as seasonal pickers and (2) the expenses of cultivating marginal lands were no longer offset by the income (either cash or credit) derived from owning slaves.

But the fact that planter-landlords were always short of labor suggests that some, possibly many, of these so-called casual laborers actually preferred such seasonal work over the life of a cropper in debt to the store. Indeed, cash wages three months out of the year, supplemented by a little fishing, woodcutting, odd jobs, and hunting, may have provided incomes for some that equaled the incomes of the sharecroppers. Although the choice threatened its takers with insecurity and was thus unavailable to the majority of black families in the district, the fact that blacks en masse had once refused to work unless there was no white supervision and the fact that sharecropping had reduced hundreds of blacks to paupers suggests that the choice was not farfetched. The low returns for their labor, rather than the landlord's refusal to employ them, and their status as free men and women mindful of their past and determined not to become slaves again may have combined in creating a people hardly best described as "good and faithful laborers."

Notes

1. See Allison Davis, Burleigh B. Gardner, and Mary R. Gardner, *Deep South: A Social and Anthropological Study of Caste and Class* (Chicago: University of Chicago Press, 1941); Gunnar Myrdal, *An American Dilemma: The Negro Problem and Modern Democracy* (New York: Harper and Brothers, 1944); Hortense Powdermaker, *After Freedom: A Cultural Study in the Deep South* (New York: Atheneum Press, 1968); Arthur F. Raper, *Preface to Peasantry, A Tale of Blackbelt Counties* (Chapel Hill: University of North Carolina Press, 1935); and Morton Rubin, *Plantation County* (Chapel Hill: University of North Carolina Press, 1951).

2. See Jay R. Mandle's *The Roots of Black Poverty: The Southern Plantation Economy After the Civil War* (Durham, N.C.: Duke University Press, 1978); and Daniel A. Novak's *The Wheel of Servitude: Black Forced Labor after Slavery* (Lexington: University Press of Kentucky, 1978), for two different but insightful interpretations of the nature of black entrapment in the post-Civil War South.

3. Eugene D. Genovese, *Roll, Jordan, Roll: The World the Slaves Made* (New York: Pantheon Books, 1974); and Robert William Fogel and Stanley L. Engerman, *Time on the Cross: The Economics of American Negro Slavery* (Boston: Little, Brown and Company, 1974).

4. Herbert G. Gutman, *The Black Family in Slavery and Freedom, 1750-1925* (New York: Pantheon Books, 1976).

5. The bulk of the research for this paper is drawn from my study on the origins of sharecropping, now being submitted for consideration for publication. That work is entitled *Good and Faithful Labor: A Study in the Origins, Economics, and Society of Sharecropping, 1863-1890.*

6. See especially Stephen J. DeCanio, *Agriculture in the Postbellum South: The Economics of Production and Supply* (Cambridge: MIT Press, 1974); Robert Higgs, *Competition and Coercion: Blacks in the American Economy, 1865-1914* (New York: Cambridge University Press, 1977), "Did Southern Farmers Discriminate?" *Agricultural History* XLVI (April 1972), "Patterns of Farm Rental in the Georgia Cotton Belt, 1880-1900," *The Journal of Economic History* XXXIV (June 1974), pp. 468-82, "Race, Tenure, and Resource Allocation in Southern Agriculture, 1910," *The Journal of Economic History* XXXIII (March 1973), pp. 149-69; Roger L. Ransom and Richard Sutch, *One Kind of Freedom: The Economic Consequences of Emancipation* (Cambridge, Eng. and New York: Cambridge University Press, 1977); Joseph D. Reid, "Sharecropping and Agricultural Uncertainty," *Economic Development and Cultural Change* XXIV (April 1976), pp. 549-76, "Sharecropping as an Un-

derstandable Market Response: The Post-Bellum South," *The Journal of Economic History* XXXIII (March 1973), pp. 106-30, "Sharecropping in History and Theory," *Agricultural History* XLIX (April 1975), pp. 426-40; Ralph Shlomowitz, "The Transition from Slave to Freedman: Labor Arrangements in Southern Agriculture, 1865-1870" (Ph.D. diss., Department of Economics, University of Chicago, 1978); Richard Sutch and Roger Ransom, "The Ex-Slave in the Post-Bellum South: A Study of the Economic Impact of Racism in a Market Economy," *The Journal of Economic History* XXXIII (March 1973), pp. 131-38.

7. See Chapter IV of my work referred to above as well as my article entitled "The U.S. Army and the Origins of Sharecropping in the Natchez District—A Case Study," *Journal of Negro History* LXII (January 1977), pp. 60-80.

8. See the records of the Bureau of Refugees, Freedman and Abandoned Lands, Record Group 105, National Archives, Washington, D.C. and the hundreds of lien records housed in the courthouses of Adams County, Mississippi, and Concordia Parish, Louisiana.

9. The main sources for this interpretation are the following plantation records: L. P. Conner Papers; J. A. Gillespie Papers; William Newton Mercer Papers, Louisiana State University, Baton Rouge, Louisiana.

10. See note 6 above and Harold D. Woodman, "Sequel to Slavery: The New History Views the Postbellum South," *The Journal of Southern History* XLIII (November 1977), pp. 524-54.

11. Lien and Mortgage Records, 1865-75, Adams County, Mississippi, Office of Records, Natchez, Mississippi; Probate Records, 1870-80, Mississippi, Office of Records, Natchez, Mississippi; U.S. Census (1860), Manuscript Population, Agriculture, and Slave Schedules, Adams County, Mississippi; U.S. Census (1870), Manuscript Population and Agricultural Schedules, Adams County, Mississippi. The definition of planter includes the immediate family as well as such members as could be determined.

12. Liens and Mortgage Records, 1860-90, Concordia Parish, Louisiana, Office of Records, Vidalia, Louisiana; Manuscript Tax Rolls (1861-96), Concordia Parish, Louisiana, Office of Records, Vidalia, Louisiana; Police Jury Minutes, October 5, 1885, Concordia Parish, Louisiana, Office of Records, Vidalia, Louisiana; U.S. Census (1860), Manuscript Population, Agriculture, and Slave Schedules, Concordia Parish, Louisiana; U.S. Census (1870 and 1880), Manuscript Population and Agricultural Schedules, Concordia Parish, Louisiana. See also Roger Shuggs, *Origins of Class Struggle in Louisiana* (Baton Rouge: Louisiana State University Press, 1968), pp. 234-73.

13. Liens and Mortgage Records, November 9, 1869, Concordia Parish, Louisiana, Office of Records, Vidalia, Louisiana.

14. Ransom and Sutch, *One Kind of Freedom*, pp. 126-48.

15. See Chapter V of my work referred to above.

16. Liens and Mortgage Records, February 18, 1870; April 19, 1874; August 13, 1874; August 11, 1880, Concordia Parish, Louisiana, Office of Records, Vidalia, Louisiana.

17. See U. B. Phillips, "Plantations with Slave Labor and Free,"*American Historical Review* XXX (July 1925), pp. 738-53, "The Decadence of the Plantation System," American Academy of Political Science, *Annals* XXXV (January 1910), pp. 37-58,

"The Economics of the Plantation," *The South Atlantic Quarterly* II (July 1903), pp. 231-36.

18. See Lawrence Goodwyn, *The Populist Movement* (New York: Oxford University Press, 1978).

19. See Mandle, *The Roots of Black Poverty*.

20. See Chapter VI of my work referred to above.

21. Of the approximately 22,000 blacks living in the Natchez district in 1880, only about 600 to 800 were themselves, or the family of, owner-operators of farms. Another 2,000 people—men, women, and children—were full-time wage hands. Some 4,683 people were employed as casual wage hands for no more than six weeks at one dollar per day. The remaining population was composed of sharecroppers of one sort or another. See Chapter VI of my work referred to above.

13

URBAN RACIAL VIOLENCE IN THE SOUTH DURING WORLD WAR II: A COMPARATIVE OVERVIEW

James A. Burran

In the past few years, historians have elevated a previously "neglected" topic, Afro-Americans in World War II, to new levels of importance. The works of Richard Dalfiume, Ulysses Lee, Harvard Sitkoff, and more recently of Lee Finkle, Neil Wynn, and A. Russell Buchanan stand as proof of a surge in interest surrounding this topic. In relation to other American wars, however, studies of race relations during World War II remain scarce and, at best, offer only the barest outline of the total picture. This paper is an attempt to delineate another section of that outline.[1]

Total war tests, alters, perhaps crumbles seemingly invincible institutions, and it acts as a catalyst in the emergence of sensitive issues. Of the Civil War South, James Roark has observed that "the intensity of extreme situations triggers primary values. Ideology, which in normal times often remains obscured, is thrust to the surface." Primary values became no less evident in the years from 1940 to 1947, when in race relations the South suffered the collision of tradition with change. That this collision occurred is generally recognized, but a debate has developed over its results. Most writers have agreed that the war brought to both North and South the beginnings of the "Second Reconstruction" and that a new and prevailing militancy by blacks sprang from the confusion of war to set the stage for future minority advances. That this militance arose is without dispute, as the March on Washington Movement (MOWM) and the "Double V" slogan so visibly attest. Yet this militance was for the most part not evident in the South; the Southern black experience during World War II proved to be sharply limited by the region's rigidly enforced caste system. Dixie blacks simply did not have the freedom enjoyed by those elsewhere. When they tried to shake off the white South's comprehensive cloud of oppression, as they haltingly attempted prior to mid-1943, white majority resentment built into violent reaction. It is this violence that most clearly shows the divergence in regional black life during the war.[2]

The repressive nature of Southern race relations appeared most clearly through the urban racial violence starting in mid-1943, a year when an epidemic of discord infected the entire nation. Indeed, one observer counted 242 racial outbreaks large enough to merit newspaper coverage during those twelve months. This is not to say that the other major forms of violence that plagued the region during the period, lynching and military-related conflict in nonurban settings, were any less important. In fact, from 1940 to 1947, between thirty and fifty lynchings and about twenty military outbreaks tormented the South. Yet examining urban riots has three significant advantages. First, these episodes were the most spectacular of the various types of violence, and they merited more attention and concern than others. Because of this, more information about them is available. Second, urban areas offered more freedom to Southern blacks than did rural areas and military bases. Thus, urban violence allowed blacks to display whatever militance they internalized so that a clearer portrayal of both collective black and white behavior emerges. Finally, urban riots provided more of a common denominator for the entire nation than did lynchings or military-related violence and so furnish the clearest basis for regional comparison.[3]

In general, the significance of urban racial violence came as much from its nature as from its volume and intensity. Prior to mid-1943, there was little divergence in the character of urban riots, whether Northern or Southern. With the exception of the Harlem riot of 1935, most of the violence exhibited traditional or "Southern-style" characteristics, in that whites acted as the aggressors and rioted against real or perceived challenges to the color line. In the summer of 1943, however, Northern riots in Detroit and in New York took on the characteristics of black aggression against the most accessible symbols of their frustration, white-owned property. But in Dixie, the Alexandria, Louisiana, riot of 1942, which saw white civilian and military police attack black servicemen, and the crippling Mobile and Beaumont incidents of 1943, both of which began in shipyards and witnessed unrestrained assaults against black citizens, remained traditional in nature. As the most obvious manifestation of strained race relations, these riots showed increasing black militancy in the North, while in the South, they showed the white majority stiffening in its conviction to maintain a strong caste system. This divergence continued through the end of the war; in late 1945 and 1946, the white South again violently attempted to keep blacks from consolidating modest wartime gains in politics and employment through a rash of lynchings, accompanied by riots in Columbia, Tennessee, and Athens, Alabama, an outburst that the North did not suffer.

At the beginning of the war, many of the nation's 12.8 million blacks displayed a mixture of hope and cynicism. On the one hand, they regarded the international crisis as a golden opportunity to gain strong footholds in both the armed forces and the defense industry. Such appeared to be the case when, on the eve of the 1940 election, President Franklin D. Roosevelt made a number of symbolic appointments that included elevating Colonel Benjamin O. Davis, Sr., to brigadier general and naming William H. Hastie of Howard University as civilian aide to the secretary of war. The next year, Roosevelt succumbed to the MOWM threat and created the Fair Employment Practices Committee (FEPC), designed to oversee equal employment opportunities in the defense industry. But hope soon turned to disillusionment as the services remained rigidly segregated, the War Department proved insensitive to racial discrimination, and the FEPC turned out to be a paper tiger.[4]

The differences between hope and reality were most frustrating both for Southern blacks and for Northern blacks stationed in the South for training. In 1940, 77.1 percent of all American blacks lived in the former Confederate states, and during the war, an estimated 80 percent of all black troops received their training there. An armed black man, or worse a Northern black officer, appeared as a threat to a white South that insisted both on rigid enforcement of Jim Crow laws and customs and on the inherent inferiority of the blacks. To black GIs and the Southern black population in general, however, such views seemed hypocritical in the face of the nation's fight against a foe that preached a master race ideology. The memory of World War I and the summer of 1919 added more fuel to smouldering black cynicism; yet in Dixie, they could do little about it.[5]

Incidents of varying size and severity mounted in a gradual crescendo in the eighteen months after Pearl Harbor, driving Southern race relations "nearer and nearer the precipice." This unrest culminated in the summer of 1943. The first of five major urban riots came on May 25 in a choked war production center, Mobile, Alabama. From a metropolitan population of 115,000 in 1940, the city by the end of 1943 had swelled to 201,000, of whom 30 percent were black. This was an overall increase of 61 percent, a rate unmatched by any other city of this size. Mobile was a member of what the Committee for Congested Production Areas termed its "most critical" list, and when author John Dos Passos visited the city in March 1943, he described it as looking "trampled and battered like a city that's been taken by storm."[6]

As in other cities, much of Mobile's rapid growth was due to a huge influx of rural folk of both races. According to one observer, the citified whites were "hostile, defiant, suspicious and terrified" while the thousands of black migrants flooded into already swamped Jim Crow residential districts and tried to find work. But skilled labor usually remained all white, so the minority workers were forced to take jobs as janitors and helpers at Mobile's many industrial plants. One such plant, the mammoth Alabama Dry Dock and Shipbuilding Company (ADDSCO), counted about 7,000 blacks on its total employment list of 30,000, but of that number, none served in skilled positions.[7]

In mid-1942, at its regional hearings in Birmingham, the FEPC had singled out ADDSCO, along with several others, for an investigation of its hiring practices. From those hearings came an order to upgrade ADDSCO's employment policies toward blacks, a directive the shipyard tried to ignore for several months. Repeated efforts to coerce management finally led to the symbolic upgrading of twelve blacks to the skilled status of welders. While a carefully constructed plan for this move had been worked out by the War Manpower Commission (WMC), ADDSCO grudgingly decided to cast caution aside and, on May 24, 1943, placed the welders on the graveyard shift of its Pinto Island operations without announcing the change to its other employees.[8]

By mid-morning on May 25, word had spread throughout the yard, and the white workers, surprised and angered, took up pipes, clubs, and tools to seek revenge against federally inspired tinkering with the color line. The riot that followed showed enraged whites chasing hapless blacks around Pinto Island, while the ferries and bridge connecting the island with the city sagged with streams of workers. About fifty blacks received injuries during the fray; despite reports to the contrary, apparently no one died.

The timely arrival of state guardsmen from neighboring cities and a contingent of federal troops from Mobile's Brookley Army Air Field quelled the riot and prevented further discord. Meanwhile, businesses all over town sent their black employees home while keeping whites on the job. And ADDSCO officials sat back smugly, as if the violence had proven their contention that desegregation could not work.[9]

During the next several days, the FEPC, WMC, Maritime Commission, and the CIO, which held bargaining rights with ADDSCO, puzzled over a solution. A recent change in the FEPC's leadership contributed to the confusion. ADDSCO argued in favor of dropping the entire project, while the FEPC, under pressure from the White House, militated for a continuation of some plan for upgrading black workers. Finally, the group decided to segregate the shipways, placing both skilled and unskilled blacks on four ways at the north end of the yard while manning the other eight ways exclusively with whites. This plan was put into practice about June 1.

Civil rights proponents, from the local chapter of the NAACP to the largest Northern black newspapers, were incredulous. "Here is proof," wailed the Pittsburgh *Courier*, "that segregation ALWAYS means discrimination." It seemed insufferable that the federal agency created to oversee equal opportunities in the defense industry would accept a proposal that was clearly a hasty compromise. Yet their hands were tied. To continue protesting against such blatant segregation and discrimination could provoke further violence, while placidly accepting the ADDSCO compromise might cost valuable respect among ordinary black Americans. In the end, the compromise stood, ADDSCO made few subsequent concessions to blacks, and minority leaders were forced to turn their attention elsewhere.[10]

The Mobile episode clearly showed the force of Southern-style violence used as a tool for black repression. For whites, such action had the desired effect of forcing blacks to abandon overt assertiveness. For blacks, the riot served as confirmation of the hypocrisy inherent in America's war effort. For the South in general, the outbreak signaled the onset of a summer of disruptive racial warfare.

Southern race relations continued to degenerate with the outbreak of numerous riots and mutinies in Dixie military camps. Among others, serious incidents occurred during the summer at Camps McCain and Van Dorn, Mississippi, Camp Stewart, Georgia, Fort Bliss, Texas, and Lake Charles, Louisiana. And on June 15, in the midst of this domestic military violence, a riot erupted in another congested war center, Beaumont, Texas. In several ways, the situation in Beaumont resembled that of Mobile. Like most other American cities, Beaumont had seen rapid growth since 1940—from 59,000 to 80,000, with about a third of that population being black. Surrounding towns that helped make up the metropolitan area—Orange, Port Arthur, and Port Neches—bulged with similar population explosions. Also like Mobile, Beaumont's largest single industry was a shipyard; in this case, Pennsylvania Shipyards, which employed about 8,000 people and held government contracts in excess of $100 million per year. A second shipyard in nearby Orange counted about 20,000 workers on its rolls. Finally, Beaumont's system of race relations was based on rigid segregation, a system whites closely guarded; thus, like Mobile, the trauma and confusion of war affected interracial relations so severely that violence resulted.[11]

The discord in Beaumont had its origins in various kinds of strain on traditional patterns of race relations, including the upward mobility of blacks in employment and minority encroachments on white residential areas. But perhaps the sorest point between the races was the congested public transportation system. In the year preceding the riot, a number of blacks had fallen victim to enraged whites who sought to enforce Jim Crow restrictions on city buses, producing so volatile an atmosphere that the city administration finally created all-black and all-white coaches to minimize interracial contact. More immediately important was the rape of a young white woman by a deranged black man on June 5; only ten days later, another reported interracial rape shattered the uneasy peace.[12]

On June 15, the young wife of a Beaumont war worker reported being raped by an itinerant black man, and the news spread like wildfire through the city. At Pennsylvania Shipyards, the report was greeted with more than dismay, for around 9:00 P.M. over 2,000 white workers dropped their tools and marched en masse to the city jail some ten blocks away. The mob obviously had lynching on its mind as it demanded the reported rapist from Police Chief Ross Dickey. When Dickey convinced them that the black man was not in custody, the shipyard workers and other interested townspeople broke up into small groups, forced their way into the fringes of the city's two black districts, and wreaked havoc until dawn the next day. This was a classic example of a traditional riot, with whites reacting aggressively against the familiar rumor of interracial rape and attacking a generally defenseless black community, in contrast to Northern outbreaks of the same period where blacks responded violently to rumors of white assault.

At the end of six hours of rioting, in which an estimated 4,000 whites participated, two blacks and one white lay dead, between 200 and 400 people were injured, 2,500 had fled to the city, 231 were in jail, and portions of the town lay in shambles. By the night of June 16, 2,400 local and state law enforcement personnel had Beaumont under control, and Acting Governor A. M. Aikin had declared martial law. The violence also cost 210,000 manhours of defense work.[13]

Initial speculation blamed the violence on Axis sabotage, but a preliminary investigation by the Federal Bureau of Investigation (FBI) found "no indication" that the riot was "instigated or inspired by foreign action." The editor of the local Beaumont *Enterprise* lamely concluded that "the fault lies at home and not abroad. The chief offenders are not foes of this country but its own citizens who may think themselves just as loyal as anybody else."

An ironic footnote to the Beaumont story came when a medical examination of the white woman allegedly raped on June 15 showed that not only had she not been assaulted but that there was no sign of sexual activity during the twenty-four hours surrounding the alleged incident. Why she claimed to have been raped remained a mystery, but in any event, the truthfulness of her accusation made little difference.[14]

The summer of 1943 adversely affected not just Southern urban race relations but also those in the nation at large, as the Los Angeles "zoot suit" riots and the somewhat more spectacular Detroit and Harlem outbreaks so visibly attested. The Los Angeles riots occurred from June 3 through 7 and featured the widespread terrorization of Mexican-American youths by white residents and sailors stationed at nearby Chavez Ravine Naval Base. From June 20 through 22, the Detroit race riot took thirty-four lives and did an estimated $2 million in property damage. Heavy congestion, in-migration to the city, restrictive convenants that confined blacks to a ghetto known as "Paradise Valley," poor relations with police, and isolated but significant racial clashes provided the major factors that led to the violence. These factors closely paralleled those preceding the Mobile and Beaumont incidents, but here the major similarities end. The Detroit episode took the lives of nine whites, damaged considerable white-owned property, and on several occasions showed open aggression by blacks against whites. August Meier and Elliott Rudwick have noted this increased black aggression by observing that "it was this symbolic destruction of 'whitey' through his property that gave the Detroit holocaust the characteristic of what we may call the 'new-style' race riot." They went on to suggest that the circumstances surrounding the change from old- to new-style violence sprang from a "marked shift in the climate of race relations" that saw whites becoming more sensitive to minority oppression and blacks more militant, and an "ecological factor," meaning the creation of large, self-contained ghettos whose nature stimulated black restlessness while making white attack nearly impossible.[15]

The Harlem riot of August 1 and 2 provided an even clearer example of Meier and Rudwick's new-style riot. That black aggression boiled through Harlem hardly seemed surprising; in fact, the very first of the new-style riots had occurred there in 1935. As the largest and most influential black community in the nation, Harlem had been home to Marcus Garvey and the Harlem Renaissance, W. E. B. Du Bois, and many other leading lights in black America.

The actual violence that began on the night of August 1 consisted almost exclusively of black attacks on white-owned property in and around the area. Whether these rioters were bonafide militants or were what Walter White called the "Bigger Thomases of New York" who "passed like a cloud of locusts over the stores of Harlem" remains a point of dispute. The bottom line, however, was the destruction of $5 million worth of property, the deaths of five blacks and injuries to 400 people of both races, and the arrest of over 500 others. The violence could well have been more prolonged had not the city's feisty mayor, Fiorello La Guardia, taken expeditious and effective countermeasures.[16]

For years, historians, sociologists, and social psychologists have to some degree been occupied with the issue of why riots exploded in some cities when many others produced similar conditions but did not suffer these incidents. Models, theories, and formulas based on demography, social indices, politics, economics, and historical antecedents flowed from their pens. Certainly, an examination of the five major riots of mid-1943 provides a common variety of causal factors: the failure of interracial communication, the insensitivity of policymakers toward increasing tension, the perceived or real threats by one group against another, the labor and housing conflicts, and the racial traditions manifested themselves in the cities that underwent riots as well as in others. But rationalizing about spontaneous, semirational incidents does not provide the full explanation. Some places underwent riots because the various ingredients in the overall formula jelled at precisely the wrong time; a relatively inoffensive incident proved sufficient to ignite violence.[17]

The same general causal patterns that prevailed across the nation produced different results. In the South, the violence involved white aggression against perceived threats to the color line; in the North, the violence involved black aggression in varying degrees that stemmed from years of frustration and oppression. In explaining the sectional divergence, historical patterns of race relations emerge as crucial. For Southern blacks, life meant virtually total segregation in a rigidly enforced caste system. Because of this, little interracial understanding existed. The working, residential, religious, social, political, and intellectual lives of blacks were restricted and defined. Attempts to break out of the caste system resulted in violence, thus helping produce the tradition of violence for which the South became noted. The total experience provided Southern blacks with a restricted view and limited goals. When the war came, conditions changed enough so that blacks in the South became hopeful of permanent advancements. When they reflected this hope through assertiveness, whites felt that the color line was in peril. To maintain it, they employed violence.

For Northern blacks, the situation remained one of discrimination and oppression, but they did not suffer under a rigidly imposed caste system. Many attended good schools, read unprejudiced textbooks, rode integrated buses and trains, and enjoyed many everyday pleasures denied to most Southern blacks. Yet Northern blacks faced frustration. Despite their freedom, they remained in second-class positions. Their view was not limited by an obvious color line, so they clearly saw that, although they enjoyed more advantages than their brethren in Dixie, they remained below whites. They lived in a superficial nearness to whites and felt tolerated, never accepted. The frustration that came from this position crystallized in the Harlem riot.[18]

The urban racial violence of mid-1943 was one of the forces that acted as both cause and effect in race relations during World War II. In the South, where historically "the intensity of extreme situations triggers primary values," white reaction to threats against the color line forced embittered blacks to recognize the power of segregation and white dominance.[19] Thus, it would be a distortion to maintain, as some have, that a nationwide groundswell of militancy and aggressiveness among blacks arrived with World War II, for the system of race relations below the Mason-Dixon line changed little. While precedents for future black advancement were set or strengthened on the national level, implementing them in an area only seventy-five years removed from slavery remained a dubious proposition.

Notes

1. Richard M. Dalfiume, *Desegregation of the U.S. Armed Forces: Fighting on Two Fronts, 1939-1953* (Columbia: University of Missouri Press, 1969), and "The 'Forgotten Years' of the Negro Revolution," *Journal of American History* 55 (June 1968), pp. 90-106; Ulysses Lee, *The Employment of Negro Troops*, vol. 8: *The United States Army in World War II, Special Studies*, ed. by Stetson Conn (Washington: Government Printing Office, 1966); Harvard Sitkoff, "Racial Militancy and Interracial Violence in the Second World War," *Journal of American*

History 58 (December 1971), pp. 661-81; Lee Finkle, *Forum for Protest: The Black Press During World War II* (Rutherford Heights: Fairleigh Dickinson University Press, 1975), and "The Conservative Aims of Militant Rhetoric: Black Protest During World War II," *Journal of American History* 60 (December 1973), pp. 692-713; Neil A. Wynn, *The Afro-American and the Second World War* (London: Holmes and Meier, 1976); A. Russell Buchanan, *Black Americans in World War II* (Santa Barbara: Clio Books, 1977).

2. James L. Roark, *Masters Without Slaves: Southern Planters in the Civil War and Reconstruction* (New York: Norton, 1977), p. vii; Herbert Garfinkel, *When Negroes March: The March on Washington Movement in the Organizational Politics for FEPC* (Glencoe: Free Press, 1959); the Pittsburgh *Courier* initiated the "Double V" slogan in its February 14, 1942, issue.

3. Sitkoff, "Racial Militancy," p. 671; a discussion of the lynchings and military-related Southern violence referred to here and elsewhere in this paper is contained in James A. Burran, "Racial Violence in the South During World War II" (Ph.D. diss., University of Tennessee, Knoxville, 1977).

4. Jessie Parkhurst Guzman, ed., *Negro Year Book: A Review of Events Affecting Negro Life, 1941-1946* (Tuskegee: Tuskegee Institute, 1947), pp. 1-2; Lee, *Employment of Negro Troops*, pp. 79-80; Garfinkel, *When Negroes March*, p. 7; Louis Ruchames, *Race, Jobs, and Politics: The Story of FEPC* (New York: Columbia University Press, 1953), p. 140; U.S., President's Committee on Fair Employment Practice, *First Report, July 1943–December 1944* (Washington: Government Printing Office, 1945), p. 104-05.

5. Guzman, *Negro Year Book*, pp. 1-2; Jean Byers, "A Study of the Negro in Military Service" (Washington: Department of Defense, 1950), p. 26 [mimeographed copy in Library of Congress]; the best general summary of the race riots of 1919 is contained in Arthur I. Waskow, *From Race Riot to Sit-In: 1919 and the 1960s* (Garden City: Doubleday, 1966).

6. Virginius Dabney, "Nearer and Nearer the Precipice," *Atlantic Monthly* 171 (January 1943), pp. 94-100; U.S., Department of Commerce, Bureau of the Census, "Wartime Changes in Population and Family Characteristics, Mobile Congested Production Area: March, 1944," *Population—Special Reports*, Series CA-2, No. 1 (Washington: Government Printing Office, 1944), p. 2; "List of Areas Certified by Federal Agencies as Critically Congested," Series 14, Records Relating to Undesignated Congested Production Areas, 1943-44, Records of the Committee for Congested Production Areas, Record Group 212, National Archives (hereafter cited as CCPA Records, RG 212); John Dos Passos, *State of the Nation* (Boston: Houghton Mifflin, 1944), p. 92.

7. Agnes Meyer, *Journey Through Chaos* (New York: Harcourt, Brace, 1944), pp. 202-10; Charles S. Johnson and Clifton R. Jones, "Memorandum on Negro Internal Migration, 1940-1943," Charles S. Johnson Papers, Fisk University, Box 376; unidentified memorandum in "Negro Problems—Mobile," Series 28, Office Files of Wilfred C. Leland, Jr., Consultant, October 1943–August 1945, Records of the Committee on Fair Employment Practice, Record Group 228, National Archives (hereafter cited as FEPC Records, RG 228); "Survey of the Mobile Employment Stabilization Plan, July 26, 1943," in "Monthly Mopac Area Reports, Labor

Mobilization—Alabama," Series 11, Central Files and Monthly Mopac Area Reports, Records of the War Manpower Commission, Record Group 211, National Archives (hereafter cited as WMC Records, RG 211). The WMC records for Region VII, which includes most of the Southeast, are housed in the Federal Archives and Records Center, East Point, Georgia.

8. Lawrence M. Cramer to Alabama Shipbuilding and Drydock Corporation, November 19, 1942; "Field Investigation Report, June 8, 1943," in "Alabama Dry Dock and Shipbuilding Co.," Series 25, Central Files of the FEPC, August 1941–April 1946, FEPC Records, RG 228; Herbert Northrup, *Organized Labor and the Negro* (New York: Harper and Brothers, 1944), pp. 225-26; Merl A. Reed, "The FEPC, the Black Worker, and the Southern Shipyards," *South Atlantic Quarterly* 74 (Autumn 1975), pp. 454-55; Burton R. Morley to John Griser, May 3, 20, 1943; B. C. Knerr to Morley, May 22, 1943, in "Monthly Mopac Area Reports: Labor Mobilization and Utilization, Women, Alabama," Series 11, WMC Records, RG 211.

9. "Field Investigation Report, June 8, 1943," FEPC Records, RG 228; "Report on Riot Duty, Mobile, Alabama, June 10, 1943," in "Report—Riot Duty Mobile, 1942-45," Records of the Office of the Provost Marshal General, Record Group 389, National Archives; Mobile *Register*, May 26, 1943; *The New York Times*, May 26, 1943, p. 25.

10. Mobile *Register*, May 27, 28, 29, 1943; June 8, 1943; *The New York Times*, June 13, 1943, p. 34; Pittsburgh *Courier*, June 19, 1943; John LeFlore to Francis J. Haas, June 11, 1943, in "Alabama Dry Dock and Shipbuilding Co.," Series 25; G. F. Floyd to John A. Davis, February 10, 1944, in "Negro Problems—Mobile," Series 28; "Field Investigation Report, June 8, 1943," FEPC Records, RG 228; Ruchames, *Race, Jobs, and Politics*, pp. 56, 58-59; Morley to Griser, May 26, 1943; "Report on the Situation at Alabama Drydock and Shipbuilding Company," in "Monthly Mopac Area Reports: Labor Mobilization and Utilization, Women, Alabama," Series 11, WMC Records, RG 211; Reed, "Black Worker and Southern Shipyards," pp. 456-57; "Along the NAACP Battlefront," *Crisis* 50 (July 1943), p. 212.

11. Lee, *Employment of Negro Troops*, p. 366; "Report on Adequacy of Services and Facilities in the Orange-Beaumont Area, Texas, November 15, 1943," in "Orange-Beaumont, Texas—Report on Conditions"; "Report on Orange, Texas, March 7, 1944," in "Port Neches, Texas—Report on Conditions," Series 13, Records Relating to the Operation of the Area Offices, 1943-44, CCPA Records, RG 212; Meyer, *Journey Through Chaos*, pp. 174-75; Frederick C. Lane, *Ships for Victory: A History of Shipbuilding Under the U.S. Maritime Commission in World War II* (Baltimore: Johns Hopkins University Press, 1951), pp. 34-35.

12. Houston *Informer*, August 1, 1942; Beaumont *Enterprise*, July 1, 2, 3, 15, 28, 1942; August 15, 20, 1942; January 23, 1943; June 6, 7, 1943; Beaumont *Journal*, June 5, 7, 1943; Memorandum, Houston FBI to Frank L. Welch, June 16, 1943, Records of the Federal Bureau of Investigation, Department of Justice (hereafter cited as FBI Records). The FBI maintains separate files from the Justice Department. Access to these records requires a Freedom of Information Act request.

13. Beaumont *Enterprise*, June 16, 17, 22, 1943; October 6, 1943; Beaumont *Journal*, June 16, 1943; Houston *Post*, June 17, 1943; Houston *Informer*, June 19, 26, 1943; Chicago *Defender*, June 26, 1943; War Department memorandum, Office of

the Director of Intelligence Division, Eighth Service Command, Dallas, Texas, July 1, 1943; J. Edgar Hoover to Wendell Berge, July 9, 1943, FBI Records.

14. Beaumont *Enterprise*, June 17, 18, 1943; July 9, 1943; Dallas *Morning News*, June 18, 1943; Pittsburgh *Courier*, June 26, 1943; Hoover to Berge, July 9, 1943, FBI Records; New York *PM*, June 18, 1943; anonymous Jefferson County official to H. C. Galloway, September 25, 1943, in "Beaumont Texas Riots," General Office File, Papers of the National Association for the Advancement of Colored People, Library of Congress.

15. The latest discussion of the Los Angeles riots is contained in Mauricio Mazon, "Social Upheaval in World War II: 'Zoot-Suiters' and Servicemen in Los Angeles, 1943" (Ph.D. diss., University of California at Los Angeles, 1976); Harvard Sitkoff, "The Detroit Race Riot of 1943," *Michigan History* 53 (Fall 1969), pp. 183-94; August Meier and Elliott Rudwick, "Black Violence in the 20th Century: A Study in Rhetoric and Retaliation," in Hugh Davis Graham and Ted Robert Gurr, eds., *Violence in America: Historical and Comparative Perspectives* (New York: Bantam, 1969), pp. 405-06.

16. Harold Orlansky, *The Harlem Riot: A Study in Mass Frustration* (New York: Social Analysis, 1943), pp. 4-6, 12; Pittsburgh *Courier*, August 7, 1943; *The New York Times*, August 2, 1943, p. 1; August 3, 1943, pp. 1, 10; Walter White, "Behind the Harlem Riot," *New Republic*, August 16, 1943, pp. 220-22, and *A Man Called White: The Autobiography of Walter White* (Bloomington: Indiana University Press, 1948), pp. 233-41; the latest discussion of the Harlem riot is contained in Dominic J. Capeci, Jr., *The Harlem Riot of 1943* (Philadelphia: Temple University Press, 1977).

17. For a sampling of the work done on racial violence and its characteristics, see Allen D. Grimshaw, ed., *Racial Violence in the United States* (Chicago: Aldine, 1969); James F. Short, Jr., and Marvin E. Wolfgang, eds., *Collective Violence* (Chicago: Aldine, 1972); Graham and Gurr, *Violence in America*; National Advisory Commission on Civil Disorders, *Report of the National Advisory Commission in Civil Disorders* (Washington: Government Printing Office, 1968).

18. Orlansky, *Harlem Riot*, p. 13.

19. Roark, *Masters Without Slaves*, p. vii.

VII

CASH'S BOOK: *THE MIND OF THE SOUTH* REVISITED

Few books on the South have provoked more recent debate than W. J. Cash's *The Mind of the South*. Mark K. Bauman in "Race and Mastery: The Debate of 1903" reappraises Cash's concept of a monolithic "savage ideal" that repressed dissent in the South. Bauman examines a regionwide newspaper controversy on the race question that occurred during the summer of 1903. He finds a remarkable diversity of opinion, from "radical" to "reactionary," on topics such as lynching, the origin of the species, and religious attitudes toward race. In the course of the debate, Bauman discerns no significant attempt to repress freedom of thought and expression. While admitting that there was repression of dissent in other instances, Bauman suggests that there was tolerance in this episode because the debate was carried on by Southerners, not by those viewed as alien and hostile to the region. Bauman argues, therefore, that Cash's model of the "savage ideal" should be altered to include "a multitude of minds of the South." "For a large number of people, Cash's model held true," Bauman concludes; "yet for so many others in a variety of different circumstances the model fails."

Bauman is one of many historians who have challenged aspects of Cash's book. Bertram Wyatt-Brown believes that such criticisms have been badly overdrawn. In "W. J. Cash and Southern Culture," Wyatt-Brown offers a rigorous defense of Cash's classic. Because of nonacademic prose and the lack of footnotes, Wyatt-Brown explains, Cash's "provocative book . . . aroused precious little provocation" among serious scholars until very recently. Wyatt-Brown then turns to analyze the criticisms of *The*

Mind of the South by Cash's most "savage critic," Eugene D. Genovese as well as other historians. He chides them for first denouncing Cash's ideas and then reintroducing his ideas as their own without citing Cash or his book. But Wyatt-Brown sees most of Cash's pioneering themes as having withstood the assaults of the last four decades. He believes that Cash's book stands now, as when first published, as one of the most important contributions to the understanding of Southern history.

14

RACE AND MASTERY: THE DEBATE OF 1903
Mark K. Bauman

Since the appearance of Wilbur J. Cash's classic study, *The Mind of the South*, historians, with some few notable exceptions,[1] have accepted the determined presence of a "savage ideal," the "ideal," in Cash's words, "whereunder dissent and variety are completely suppressed and men become, in all their attitudes, professions, and actions, virtual replicas of one another."[2] The cases of Andrew Sledd and John Spencer Bassett have been used to illustrate the rejection mechanism in practice. Sledd, a Latin professor at Emory College, wrote an article published in the *Atlantic Monthly* in July 1902, denouncing lynching and racial injustice. The article was made an issue of race orthodoxy by Rebecca Latimer Felton, an important political power in Georgia, and the president and trustees of Emory readily accepted Sledd's resignation.[3] A professor of history at Trinity College (later Duke University), Bassett developed a similar theme for the October 1903 number of the *South Atlantic Quarterly*. Bassett had the temerity to link Booker T. Washington with Robert E. Lee as the greatest men produced by the South in the previous hundred years. A storm was raised by Josephus Daniels that would have resulted in Bassett's ouster had it not been for the ardent support of Trinity president John C. Kilgo and the independence afforded his administration by Duke financial backing.[4]

Actually, an episode occurred between the Sledd and Bassett affairs that sheds a considerably different light on them and that calls into question the ascendancy of the "savage ideal," if not the very existence of one "mind of the South." In August 1903, the Atlanta newspapers began carrying a debate concerning the "problem of race." The interrelated lines of combat included the origins and creation of the black race, the causes and remedies of lynching, and the place of the Afro-American in America. The people and newspapers opposing each other were indistinguishable by class, education, or occupation. Never were the rights of people to question racial shibboleths denied, nor was there any attempt to stop dissent.

The summer of 1903 was not a calm season in which one might expect zealous dissent. Many Southerners were considering possible Democratic candidates for the upcoming presidential campaign to oppose Theodore Roosevelt, whose manner of treating Booker T. Washington and race relations had become anathema to the region. In August, Washington and his party were seated at the regular dining room when his train made a breakfast stop in a small town in North Carolina. Georgia Senator A. O. Bacon and the other white passengers refused to be seated at the makeshift facilities arranged for them. The Southern press made the incident a matter of race pride. At this time, too, South Carolina Senator Benjamin Tillman rode the chautauqua circuit debating Senator Burton of Kansas on "the Negro question" and urging the use of the shotgun to halt black rapists. Late in the season, Senator E. W. Carmack of Tennessee proposed the repeal of the Fifteenth Amendment. The young historian U. B. Phillips, spending the summer in his native state, wrote letters to the editor of the Atlanta *Constitution* advocating the strengthening of a reformed plantation system. The passage and administration of the new Calvin Vagrancy Law also were of much concern.[5]

These events contributed to the climate of opinion when, in August, a debate on lynching began on the national level. Recent atrocities in his state and region led Governor Durbin of Indiana to issue a strong condemnation of mob violence. Theodore Roosevelt agreed in a well-publicized letter. The president equated lynching with anarchy, warned that it degraded the community as well as the participants, and maintained that it induced further brutality. "[T]he mob," he wrote, "seems to lay most weight, not on the crime, but on the color of the skin of the victim." Governor Joseph Terrell of Georgia, the state that consistently led the nation in the number of lynchings, substantially concurred with the ideas expressed by Durbin and Roosevelt but emphasized that justice had to be applied swiftly to perpetrators of "that crime which most frequently excites the anger of mobs . . ." or lynch law would persist.[6]

Other governors and several judges discussed rape as a cause of lynching and the relationships between law enforcement and the prevention of lynching and between race and lynching. Supreme Court Justice David Brewer of Kansas recommended the abolition of appeals in criminal cases— they were merely devices of delay that encouraged normally law-abiding citizens to bypass the too slow legal process by taking matters into their own hands. Louisiana's executive officer William W. Heard agreed with these remarks but differed with Roosevelt's contention that race was a greater desiderata than rape in inciting Judge Lynch. To Governor Heard, rapists were "limited almost exclusively to the colored race." The usual punishment was applied to white men, too, who committed the dastardly deed—they just did it less frequently. Delaware's Chief Justice Charles B.

Lore demurred. He emphasized that less than one-third of all lynchings involved outrages of black men against white women. Furthermore, justice should not be denied for the sake of expediency. "[A] fair and full opportunity of defense" must be offered the accused, including the right to appeal. Life and liberty had to be preserved even in the face of mob action. These exchanges would be repeated and extended through the following months.[7]

Two speeches by John Temple Graves, editor of the Atlanta *News* and scion of an old Southern family tracing its roots to the Calhouns, greatly extended the form of the debate.[8] His first address, given at a New York chautauqua meeting, began by stressing the national tendencies of the lynching dilemma. Graves placed the onus of lynching on the crime of rape, which necessitated the defense of "the mothers, the wives and the daughters of the race." Lynching was an evil, but inevitable as long as the provocation continued. To solve the problem, Graves urged the separation of the races, with the blacks gradually going to a specified state. At the University of Chicago, he elaborated: two races, one strong, the other very weak, could not coexist without detrimental results. To the Anglo-Saxon Caucasian, the experiment in racial equality issuing from the Civil War wrought sectional division, hampered the South's material advance, and lowered the lot of the white laborer and made him live in fear for the safety of his women. To the Negro, it meant his inevitable loss of political rights and an inability to prosper economically or socially. Race antagonism was foreordained, argued Graves, as it was based on human nature, experience, and divine agency. The Philippines, lower California, and west Texas were suggested as black territories in which, as an inducement for immigration, only blacks could vote. In all other areas, only whites could exercise the franchise. A slow exodus lasting about eighty years would cost $400 million. As precedents to prove the practicality of the scheme, Graves pointed to England's offer of a homeland to the Jews and its payment of $500 million to pacify the Irish. The editor appealed to what he labeled "Caucasian unity" and "the imperial destiny of our mighty race" to forward the plan.

Graves's first address was part of a program on mass disturbances. Prior to his presentation, Dr. James Buckley had offered remarks that included reference to the passage, "God made of one blood all the nations of the earth." The eminent Methodist editor of the *Christian Advocate* was using the Bible to support the unity of creation of black and white people. If such a unity was accepted, it was difficult to argue biological inferiority or to advocate separation. Graves recognized the significance of the citation to his religiously oriented region. He completed the passage, "and fixed the metes and boundaries of their habitations," thereby illustrating that segregation and separation were countenanced by Scripture while social intercourse and intermarriage were proscribed.

Or were they? The few lines quoted by Buckley and Graves brought a divided religious community into the fray and of the several subtopics discussed sustained the longest interest. The Reverend Dr. J. B. Mack wrote a letter to the editor of the Atlanta *News* maintaining that God had not placed the word "blood" in the section of Acts 17:26 under consideration. Mack marshaled the authority of two Greek testaments and even the Roman Catholic version to confirm his interpretation. The Presbyterian noted that it was wrong for Christians to falsify God's word, especially when the additions allegedly provided divine support for the "Unity of Mankind." Bishop Warren A. Candler of the Methodist Episcopal Church, South, countered that, although the word "blood" was not literally a part of the original, the text in question could only be interpreted as confirming the unity of humanity as descended from Adam. To him, Mack was "merely trifling." The bishop closed with an aside concerning the lynching issue. Recent mob actions in the North, he observed, had made Northerners "more tolerant and less censorious" of Southerners. They had profited from the "wretched outbursts." The people of the South, on the other hand, had become more inured to the lynching evil. Candler warned the South: "let us keep our moral perceptions clear enough to see that lynching is always and everywhere wrong." The failure of the section to accept this would be "the greatest of all misfortunes." God, according to the bishop, believed in one race and disapproved of lynching.[9]

The two theologians exchanged a number of letters demanding of each other biblical exegesis. Mack noted the existence of Babylon in 7,000 B.C.—three centuries before Bishop Usher's date for Adam's birth, thus implying that the other races had been created prior to and separate from Adam. Noting the existence of separate races at the time of the flood, he outlined the meaning of the argument. If descended from Adam, the black was the "unfortunate brother" who had to be raised to a position of equity through education so that he could vote, hold office, and "enter our homes and our families." If of a different origin and inferior race, the granting of these privileges would be worse than folly. Future columns left little doubt as to where the Reverend Dr. Mack stood.

Other laymen and clergy took sides in this dialogue, and over forty letters were printed in the *News*. "J. G. T." of Athens asked Candler: If all mankind was of one blood, how did one account for different skin pigmentation and the variance in size and shape of the blood corpuscles? "Inquirer" wanted to know about "the flat nose, very dull black eyes, thick lips, calf of leg very high up and in a knot," the harsh odor, and even the elliptical form of Negroid hair contrasted with the cylindrical shape of the superior race.[10] Luther H. Holsey, of the Colored Methodist Episcopal Church, brought "Inquirer" to task for his pretensions. Holsey compared blacks and whites physically, morally, and intellectually and found no distinction that could not be overcome. Where the blacks had faults, so, too, did the white, and those often of a graver nature. Separate creation and race? Then how might one account for the ease and frequency of "amalgamation"? queried Bishop Holsey.[11] C. W. Humpries, supporting Candler, linked racial unity to salvation and missionary labors. The denial of joint origins placed in doubt in inherent sinfulness of the Afro-American and, thus, his need for redemption in Christ.[12]

The Bible seemed to be open to such varied analysis that perhaps "A. S. E." offered the best solution for ministerial haggling:

> If a preacher meets a preacher,
>> When nobody is by,
> Let a preacher paste a preacher,
>> Nobody will cry.[13]

As the scriptural debate continued, a series of parallel arguments concerning lynching and the law emerged. Once again, the issues were complex and interrelated. What was the cause of lynching? Who was lynched? How could it be prevented? These were the critical questions framed around Graves's initial positions.

At the onset, the Atlanta *Constitution*'s editor, Clark Howell, agreed with his competitor's contention that rape was the cause of lynching.[14] The editor of the Campbell *News* of Fairburn, Georgia, defended lynching as "the sure and best way of meteing out speedy and severe punishment to the rape fiend. . . ." He bragged, "We lynch 'em every time we catch 'em, right or wrong, and we catch 'em every time."[15] Many others accepted these opinions. Even black commentators failed to question the allegation that rape served as a catalyst for lynching. The Savannah *Tribune*, for example, editorialized: "The horrible crime charged to a certain class of our people is abhorred and we are always in favor of the guilty ones given their just deserts."[16] W. H. Heard, former American minister to Liberia, assumed the prevalence of rape when he traced the defects in some black people to the demoralizing influence of slavery with its lack of privacy and degradation of black women. John Wesley Gilbert, one of the first graduates of Paine Institute in Augusta and its first black faculty member, saw an end to mob law only after "the black pulpit preaches against the crimes that provoke lynchings. . . ." He wanted "all the rapists killed, *according to law and order*," and stood "ready to protect the women of the southern white people. . . ."[17]

Lynching could not have occurred, it was widely believed, had the legal system been capable of dealing with rape cases. Many spoke against delays and uncertain punishment in the courts, expanding on Justice Brewer's ideas. Judge William T. Gary of Augusta charged his county grand jury to consider the feasibilty of legalizing mob action. A magistrate would be called on by the mob to swear in six "reputable citizens" who would hear the case on the spot and have justice done at once. This process also would preclude the shameful scene of the innocent woman being questioned in the open courtroom.[18] Winifield B. Woolf emphasized preventive steps. Besides advocating increased police protection, he would let no white woman be left alone or even be allowed to walk in pairs without male stewardship. Every white woman should learn to shoot and protect herself—"to sell her life dearly if need be." "R" assumed the need to exculpate the crimes that were perceived to result in lynching but urged very progressive methods. Taking a sociological approach, this anonymous, transplanted Northerner believed that the crowded urban environment in which the poor lived bred lawlessness. He encouraged the provision of public works, jobs, and homes. New Zealand was cited as an example of a country in which private, unused land was condemned and purchased by the government for resale to the poor at cost. America should consider founding agricultural colonies of poor blacks and whites before expatriation was undertaken.[19]

While the majority of the participants in the debate assumed that lynching was an evil in the abstract, they tended to reject as impractical Graves's solution of racial separation. They noted the high cost of ships as well as the rapid growth rate of the black population. Blacks reproduced faster than they could be transported.[20] The editor of the Birmingham *Age-Herald* reacted to the idea with derision. He wrote, Graves "says a whole state should be assigned to the negroes. It will trouble him to pick out the state and procure the assent of the white men in it."[21] The Atlanta *Journal* wondered what would happen if "someone should suggest that the white people be deported and this country be left to the negro." Its editor satirized, "Simply repeal the fifteenth amendment; then hurry the negro aboard ship and deposit him in Africa. Presto! Change.—the problem vanished. Why these things are dead easy when you go about them right." Several Southerners even sided with the contentions of *The New York Times* that black labor was essential to the economy.[22]

Many Southern and Northern spokesmen came to the defense of Graves's plan.[23] He also received support for his separation scheme from several black leaders. Former minister W. H. Heard, then president of the Colored National Emigration and Commercial Association, requested that the *News* and *Journal* begin fundraising to pay for the repatriation of blacks to Africa. Since they had labored for 250 years without pay, it was only just that whites should finance their return home.[24] One of Heard's lecturers maintained that Afro-Americans were doomed to second-class status in America and that their ultimate destiny had to be in Africa.[25] W. H. Council, president of the Alabama Normal School at Huntsville, considered Graves's proposed settlement in the Western Hemisphere far superior to the back-to-Africa plans of Heard and Bishop Henry M. Turner since it was cheaper and easier and would allow black Americans to continue to receive the benefits of their adopted homeland.[26] The Atlanta *Age* estimated "Two-thirds of the southern negroes want to go anywhere, anywhere to get away from southland. . . ."[27]

Climactically, Bishop Candler left the biblical skirmish with J. B. Mack in the Atlanta *News* to enter the pages of the rival *Constitution* and redraw the debated propositions with a frontal assault against lynching and racial separation. In a letter entitled, "Must Put Down the Mob or Be Put Down by It," the bishop marshaled progressive Southern opinion behind black rights. After providing the usual sectional defense against considering lynching only a Southern crime, Candler denounced mob lawlessness in no uncertain terms. Echoing Roosevelt, he labeled it an "outburst of anarchy" that would lead to tyranny and the overthrow of the Republic. He challenged those who claimed rape as the cause of lynching by showing that fewer than one-fourth of all lynchings were linked to alleged rapes. The clergyman had no patience with those who justified lynching on any grounds, nor was he interested in any system of separation. "Our homes," he wrote, "are sheltered by law, and they are not shielded by lawlessness." Warren Candler did "not wish to live in any country where there are no negroes."[28]

Candler's protestations met with wide acclaim. The Atlanta *Constitution* moved decidedly away from its prior endorsement of many of Graves's contentions. It joined wholeheartedly with the bishop in a crusade against "the lynching evil." On the day after the appearance of Candler's article, the paper used a full five columns beginning on the front page for positive comments from Atlanta's clergy and leaders. Two Methodists, two Baptists, one Presbyterian, and one Jew denounced lynching as "a grave and serious menace to the moral and civil liberty of any people," as "unqualified murder," and as "abject atheism." Henry H. Proctor, an influential black Congregational minister, declared that every word in Bishop Candler's message was "worth its weight in gold." Former Governor William Northen, who had pressed for the passage of an antilynching law, urged law enforcement officials to halt mob actions and to bring lynchers to justice.[29] Governor Terrell, General Gordon, Judge Samuel B. Adams, and Judge W. A. Covington joined Candler and Northen in their call for law and order. S. P. Verner wrote from Mississippi acclaiming Candler's utterances. Both he and W. C. Dodson, another supporter, were members of former slaveowning families that denounced lynching as unjustifiable and that advocated public pressure for racial harmony. The Reverend Dr. James W. Lee, denouncing the recent comments by Southern Methodist Bishop H. C. Morrison, informed Candler that he was forwarding the latter's comments to the New York *World*, Boston *Transcript*, and St. Louis *Globe-Democrat* to counteract the image created by "John Temple Graves and old Tillman and the rest of that cheap ignorant lot."[30]

The most poignant comments came from Afro-Americans, many of whom were almost apologetic of the "poorer classes" of blacks who perpetrated rapes and other crimes. They advocated swift justice for rapists, self-improvement, and moral uplift. F. M. Gordon, head of the Georgia School for the Deaf, Negro Department, hoped that there would never be a separation of the races. He addressed 500 black men and women, urging "them to settle down to business and buy homes and become useful citizens." The Reverend Lee O'Neal, presiding elder of Albany district, forwarded a resolution to his Thomasville Convention "Setting forth their great pleasure" with Candler's stand. The associate editor of the Georgia *Baptist* expressed thanks and informed Candler that his article was being reprinted in full. The Savannah *Tribune*, also a black periodical, offered favorable editorial comment.[31] Principals of public schools, the manager of the first black-owned drugstore in Georgia, and the grand master of a black Masonic lodge expressed appreciation. Bishop Turner compared Candler to the great preacher-advocates of racial justice of previous generations and lay his "gratitude at your feet, for the manly, humane, logical and reformatory letter. . . ."[32] Finally, in November, as the debate gradually subsided, a group of thirty-eight black professionals—including Bishops Wesley Gaines and Turner, President James Anderson of Morris Brown and President W. H. Crogman of Clark, George A. Town, W. E. B. Du Bois and other faculty members from Atlanta's black colleges, doctors, and dentists—signed a letter to Candler that showered praise on their "noble champion" in a time when other "men of influence [were taking] compromising position[s] on the question of human rights. . . ."[33]

Candler's article had included a denunciation of "chautauqua platformers and performers" who agitated the race issue with "picturesque proposals" in order to attract an audience. Naturally, Graves assumed this to be a personal attack and launched an editorial assault against "The Fat Bishop and His Fainting Foes."[34] Candler, a long-time friend of Graves, wrote the latter an apologetic letter answering his charges and claiming reference to Senators Tillman and Burton rather than to the *News'* editor. He asked if Graves's article had been written in the heat of the moment. A reconciliation was achieved partly through the aid of Charles Murphy Candler, the bishop's nephew and head of the State Railway Commission. Rather weak retractions were published in their respective journals.[35] A personal exchange, this incident removed Candler and, to a lesser extent, Graves from the debate.

National interest continued, and in addition to reports throughout the South, arguments over Graves's platform appeared in newspapers in Cleveland, New York, Chicago, Baltimore, and even Omaha. Periodicals like *Collier's Weekly* also carried stories. The Atlanta *News* regularly filled its space with excerpts from these. Judge Lore was heard against and Senator Tillman for lynching once more. The third week in September at an interracial educational mass meeting to benefit Morris Brown College, Bishop Turner challenged other speakers to debate, with him supporting the positive aspects of separation. Two days later, Henry H. Proctor countered Turner's program before the National Convention of Congregational Workers Among the Colored People. Proctor was subsequently chosen to be president of the group. The lines of the influential editor of the New York *Age*, Timothy Thomas Fortune, claiming the necessity of social equality and intermarriage for political equality were recorded with grim forewarnings by the Atlanta *News*. On September 28, a group of respected black leaders, including Professor Kelly Miller and several federal officeholders, met with Dean Richmond Babbitt of Brooklyn's Church of the Epiphany to formally propose "a thorough organization of their race" at least partly in response to Graves's agitation. Holding that the number of crimes attributed to blacks had been grossly exaggerated, they advocated the collection and publication of the facts. These men looked to religion and "the just execution of the laws" to "cure" the growing prejudice. They urged the maintenance of black legal rights and the continuity of educational alternatives beyond industrial training. Carefully denying any interest in "social equality," they also requested the black clergy to preach against crime and intemperance.[36]

Although articles appeared in the *News* frequently through October and into November, the Candler-Graves altercation had done much to sidetrack the issues. The *Constitution*, as the *News* reported with condescension and glee, simply declared the debate harmful and at an end. On December 12, the *News* printed a poem by Fanny Barber Knapp that drew a curtain on this episode, a poem illustrative of the Southern racial paradox. "The Black Man's Burden" bemoaned past wrongs to America's Africans, predicted doom for the white man's future, and beseeched:

> You brought us here in bondage;
>   In freedom, take us away!
> Is there no fair warm land,
>   You will give to this hybrid race?
> In the light of the tropical sunshine,
>   Will the white stain fade away—
> We will leave you a white man's country,
>   To rule in a white man's way.

With these lines, this debate on race relations ended. The "savage ideal" had not been invoked. On the contrary, if the issues had been quashed at all, they had been by the leaders of the party with positive attitudes toward Afro-American rights in America. Through the years, other Southerners continued to denounce lynching and to advocate equal justice. The "solid South," in terms of racial ideology, was clearly rent with division. Prejudice existed. Lynchings continued. Segregation hardened. Black people found rights and opportunities narrowly circumscribed. Yet these negative realities fail to give credence to the complexities of our past.

The question remains why dissent was halted in some cases and not in others. A brief comparison of this Atlanta debate with the Sledd and Bassett cases is suggestive. In the Atlanta situation, while the Northern press carried many articles, the Southern participants with positive attitudes remained within the South, spoke predominantly to a Southern audience, came from the established class, had deep sectional ties, and were known to be loyal Democrats. Bassett, on the other hand, castigated the South before a Northern audience, and Sledd's article, although appearing in a journal edited by Bassett at Trinity, was read largely by Northerners. Both were college teachers who lacked local influence and were not well known. ·

This tentative contrast lends greater weight to other causal factors beyond intellectual repression in the invocation of the "savage ideal." Animosity between Rebecca Felton and Sledd's father-in-law, Warren Candler, and local North Carolina politics and conflict between Josephus Daniels and the Trinity administration loom larger in this scenario. Sectional pride and personal ambition gain greater emphasis. Tillman and Graves were concerned with gate receipts, as Candler stated. Both also harbored political ambitions and, in Graves's case, a desire to increase his newspaper's circulation.[37] Rather than viewing the Atlanta debate as a feared breach in Southern racial solidarity, they welcomed the publicity of a heated altercation. Apparently, then, the "savage ideal" was a tool of the opportunist.

Years ago, Perry Miller created a paradigm of the "New England Mind." During the last two decades, it has become clear that, although the image was suggestive and informed, it was a generalization that constrained research and knowledge because it failed to give acknowledgment to nuance and variety. We are beginning to reach the same conclusion with Wilbur Cash's construct of the Southern mind as well. For a large number of people, Cash's model held true; yet for so many others in a variety of different circumstances, the model fails. In the cases of Bassett, Sledd, Candler, and their supporters, and in the case of those in the supposedly "silent South," we can discern a number of varied attitudes toward race and mastery—a multitude of minds of the South.

Notes

1. Morton Sosna, *In Search of the Silent South: Southern Liberals and the Race Issue* (New York: Columbia University Press, 1977); Carl Degler, *The Other South: Southern Dissenters in the Nineteenth Century* (New York: Harper and Row, 1974); Charles E. Wynes, ed., *Forgotten Voices: Dissenting Southerners in an Age of Conformity* (Baton Rouge: Louisiana State University Press, 1967). Wynes's anthology includes the articles by Sledd and Bassett cited below. Even these authors

view dissent as an aberration rather than as the norm. The *South Atlantic Quarterly* (Autumn 1978) reprinted Bassett's article on its seventy-fifth anniversary.

2. Wilbur J. Cash, *The Mind of the South* (New York: Vintage Books, n.d. [originally published 1941]), pp. 93-94. See also Bruce Clayton, *The Savage Ideal: Intolerance and Intellectual Leadership in the South, 1890-1914* (Baltimore: Johns Hopkins University Press, 1972); and H. Shelton Smith, *In His Image, But . . . Racism in Southern Religion, 1780-1910* (Durham: Duke University Press, 1972).

3. Henry Y. Warnock, "Andrew Sledd, Southern Methodists, and the Negro: A Case History," *Journal of Southern History* XXXI (August 1965), pp. 251-71; John E. Talmadge, *Rebecca Latimer Felton: Nine Stormy Decades* (Athens: University of Georgia Press, 1960), Chapter 13; Albert E. Barnett, *Andrew Sledd—His Life and Work* (n.p., n.d.); Raymond H. Firth, "The Life of Andrew Sledd" (B.D. Thesis, Emory University, 1940).

4. Earl W. Porter, *Trinity and Duke, 1892-1924* (Durham: Duke University Press, 1964); Paul N. Garber, *John Carlisle Kilgo: President of Trinity College, 1894-1910* (Durham: Duke University Press, 1937); Joseph L. Morrison, *Josephus Daniels Savs* (Chapel Hill: University of North Carolina Press, 1962); Earl W. Porter, "The Bassett Affair: Something to Remember," *South Atlantic Quarterly* LXXII (Autumn 1973), pp. 451-60. The facts noted later in this paper are from these sources and those cited in note 3, above. My interpretation alters the emphasis but draws heavily from the inferences in Morrison.

5. All of the incidents cited were covered by the Atlanta *Journal*, the Atlanta *Constitution*, and the Atlanta *News* between July and August 1903. I. A. Newby states for the period 1900-30: "These were the years in which anti-Negro thought reached its zenith. . . ." Newby, *Jim Crow's Defense: Anti-Negro Thought in America, 1900-1930* (Baton Rouge: Louisiana State University Press, 1965), p. xi. The arguments that follow were not unique. Historians have traced most of them through the nineteenth century and into the twentieth. What is unusual is the concentration of the issues in one incident. For comparison, see Newby, *Jim Crow's Defense*; George M. Fredrickson, *The Black Image in the White Mind: The Debate on Afro-American Character and Destiny, 1817-1914* (New York: Harper and Row, 1971); Claude H. Nolan, *The Negro's Image in the South* (Lexington: University of Kentucky Press, 1967); George W. Stocking, Jr., *Race, Culture, and Evolution* (New York: Free Press, 1967), pp. 42-68; William L. Stanton, *The Leopard's Spots: Scientific Attitudes Toward Race in America, 1818-1859* (Chicago: University of Chicago Press, 1960); John S. Haller, Jr., *Outcasts from Evolution: Scientific Attitudes of Racial Inferiority, 1859-1900* (Urbana: University of Illinois Press, 1971).

6. These letters were reprinted widely. See, for example, Atlanta *Constitution*, August 10, 11, 1903.

7. Atlanta *Constitution*, August 11, 20, 29, September 25, 1903.

8. Atlanta *News*, August 18, 21, September 4, 1903.

9. Ibid., August 21, 25, 1903. The Mack-Candler letters appeared from August 21 to November 11, 1903. The *Literary Digest* requested these for reprinting (September 24, 1903). For Candler's concept of race, see Mark K. Bauman, *Warren Akin Candler: Conservative as Idealist* (Metuchen, N.J.: Scarecrow, forthcoming). For other views on the biblical theme, see Dwight W. Hoover, *The Red and the Black* (Chicago: Rand, McNally, 1976), pp. 176-78. On the most vocal advocate of

colonization to the Philippines, see Joseph O. Baylen and J. Hammond Moore, "Senator John Tyler Moore and Negro Colonization in the Philippines, 1901-1902," *Phylon XXIX* (Spring 1968), pp. 65–75.

10. Atlanta *News*, August 27, September 1, November 6, 1903.

11. Ibid., September 14, 1903.

12. Ibid., September 7, 1903.

13. Ibid., September 9, 1903.

14. Atlanta *Constitution*, August 2, 12, September 4, 1903.

15. September 26, 1903. See also comments quoted in this paper from Crawfordsville *Advocate-Times*, August 21, 1903, and Augusta *Chronicle*, October 2, 1903. Rebecca Felton, wife of the Independent party leader of Georgia, sometime ally of Tom Watson and perennial political operative, placed the onus for the rise of rape on the leaders of Reconstruction who encouraged the idea of "absolute equality" and "amalgamation" through the passage of the Fourteenth and Fifteenth Amendments. In so doing, they unleashed "the lustful ferocity of humanized orang-ou-tangs." She supported lynching. Atlanta *Journal*, October 19, 1903.

16. September 26, 1903.

17. Atlanta *News*, August 28, 1903; Gilbert to Candler, September 11, 1903, Warren A. Candler Papers, Woodruff Library, Emory University (italics in original).

18. Atlanta *News*, August 29, 1903 (reprinted from Augusta *Chronicle*). The Darien *Gazette* editor wrote, "Judge Lynch knows no such thing as a shyster lawyer in his courts" (August 15, 1903). "We know that way down in the heart of Judge Lynch he feels that it is wrong but what is he to do when the courts fail to act promptly" (August 22, 1903). See also Atlanta *Journal*, October 21, 30, 1903.

19. Atlanta *News*, August 14, 1903. Woolf noted, "She should know that because of physiological laws, if she resists and fights bravely, she may indeed die, but, unless she loses consciousness, she cannot be made to suffer the least disgrace." Ibid., September 2, 1903.

20. See, for example, Atlanta *Constitution*, September 13, 1903; Columbus *Enquirer-Sun*, September 11, 16, 1903.

21. Quoted in Americus *Times-Recorder*, September 13, 1903.

22. Atlanta *Journal*, September 10, 24, 1903; *The New York Times*, September 7, 1903.

23. The Chicago *Tribune* and Chicago *Journal* differed over the separation issue and offered an interesting minor skirmish in a Northern city. Raymond Patterson, the *Tribune's* Washington correspondent, toured the South in August. Excerpts from his articles and comments appeared in the Atlanta *News* and *Constitution*. For the Chicago *Journal*, see Atlanta *News*, September 7, 1903.

24. Atlanta *News*, August 28, 1903. Bishop Henry M. Turner was chancellor of this organization.

25. W. Harwick Davis, ibid., September 3, 1903.

26. Ibid., September 9, 1903. Endorsing Council's letter, Graves called him "the greatest American Negro" (Atlanta *News*, September 9, 1903). The Savannah *Tribune* (October 17, 1903) referred to the tribute with scorn. Elsewhere in this issue, its editor wrote, "Bishop Turner stands for migration to Africa, Bishop Holsey for segregation and Booker Washington for fighting it out in this country. The bulk of the people stand with Booker on this question." On Turner, see Edwin S. Redkey, "Bishop Turner's African Dream," *Journal of American History* LIV (September

1967), pp. 271–90; Edwin S. Redkey, ed., *Respect Black: The Writings and Speeches of Henry McNeal Turner* (New York: Arno Press, 1971), especially pp. 194-95. The Columbus *Enquirer-Sun*, September 13, 1903, editorialized, "One trouble with the Hon. John Temple Graves' idea of separating the races is that no one agrees with him except Bishop Turner. And it is noticeable that the latter sticks mighty close to Georgia." A colonization scheme of Georgia blacks to Liberia met an unsuccessful end in November 1903. See Atlanta *Constitution*, November 7, 1903; and John Dittmer, *Black Georgia in the Progressive Era, 1900-1921* (Urbana: University of Illinois Press, 1977), p. 176. Dittmer's excellent account provides fine sketches of many black participants in this debate.

27. Cited in Atlanta *News*, September 18, 1903.

28. Atlanta *Constitution*, September 9, 1903, reprinted in *The Possibilities of the Negro in Symposium*, Willis B. Parks, compiler (Atlanta: Franklin Printing Company, 1904). This collection included Graves's Chicago speech and addresses by Holsey, Turner, Candler, and others. Its publication was probably the result of this debate. For the background on Candler's article, see Mark K. Bauman, "A Famous Atlantan Speaks Out Against Lynching: Bishop Warren Akin Candler and Social Justice," *Atlanta Historical Bulletin* XX (Spring 1976), pp. 24-32.

29. Atlanta *Constitution*, September 9, 10, 13, 1903; Atlanta *Journal*, September 23, October 3, 1903.

30. Box 11, 1902, June—1903, Candler Papers. Excerpts reprinted in Atlanta *Constitution*, September 15, 1903.

31. Ibid., Savannah *Tribune*, September 12, 26, 1903.

32. Turner to Candler, September 9, 1903, Candler Papers.

33. H. A. Rucker et al. to Candler, November 20, 1903, Candler Papers.

34. Atlanta *News*, August 25, September 10, 1903; Atlanta *Constitution*, September 9, 1903.

35. Candler to Graves, September 10, 1903, Graves to Candler, September 11, 15, 1903, C. M. Candler to W. A. Candler, September 12, 13, 1903, Candler Papers; Atlanta *Constitution*, September 11, 15, 1903; Atlanta *News*, September 15, 1903.

36. The comments and meetings can be found in the *News* and *Constitution* from opposing perspectives. For divisions among black leaders, see Hoover, *The Red and the Black*, pp. 253-56.

37. The Augusta *Chronicle* opined that Graves's Chicago speech resulted in the suggestion that Graves run for governor (noted with derision in Americus *Times-Recorder*, September 15, 1903). The Sparta *Ishmaelite* (September 18, 1903), thought "That speech ought to put him in the U.S. Senate." Graves did run for the vice-presidency in 1908 on the National Independence ticket. In 1906, Hoke Smith, former editor of the Atlanta *Journal*, ran for the governorship of Georgia on a "progressive" slate with emphasis on black disenfranchisement. The Atlanta newspapers joined in a sensational racist campaign that has been credited with fomenting the Atlanta race riot of 1906. Cash placed the blame for this hysteria on Graves (*Mind of the South*, p. 309). Again, the link between newspaper circulation, editors, and politics is most important and deserves further study. On the riot, see Charles Crowe, "Racial Violence and Social Reform—Origins of the Atlanta Race Riot of 1906," *Journal of Negro History* LII (July 1968), pp. 234-56; Crowe, "Racial Massacre in Atlanta, September 22, 1906," *Journal of Negro History* LIV (April 1969), pp. 150-73; Dittmer, *Black Georgia*, pp. 123-32.

15 _____

W. J. CASH AND SOUTHERN CULTURE
Bertram Wyatt-Brown

With Wilbur J. Cash specifically in mind, C. Vann Woodward once observed, "In America, historians, like politicians, are out as soon as they are down. There is no comfortable back bench, no House of Lords for them."[1] Woodward's sentiment indeed applies to the famous North Carolina journalist and author of *The Mind of the South*. Cash was once a thinker to be reckoned with. Such is no longer the case.

When Carl N. Degler wrote *Place over Time: The Continuity of Southern Distinctiveness*, he felt no compulsion to analyze Cash's themes of "continuity" and "distinctiveness." Yet it was Cash who had laid the ground rules for the debate to which Degler addressed himself. When Eugene D. Genovese wrote a thoughtful essay on "Yeoman Farmers in a Slaveholders' Democracy," he never referred to *The Mind of the South*. Yet his own perceptions of white class structure reflected Cash's influence.

Condescension is the prevailing mood whenever Cash's name does appear. Sheldon Hackney has called him "the South's foremost mythmaker," a dubious compliment for one who had hoped to dispel, not create, illusions. According to a recent critic, "One may not be able to save the book as a primer for students of the southern past, but one can learn a little from its declining prestige."[2]

Perhaps the explanation for the current ill favor of Cash's *Mind of the South* can be found in its former popularity, particularly with the general reader. After all, as Woodward has observed, Cash's pungent words entered common usage: the "Proto-dorian" consensus of white supremacy; the "Man at the Center," Cash's typical, ill-educated yeoman farmer; "the lily-pure maid of Astolat," a rendering of the mythical Southern belle. Indeed, the style was catching. Woodward himself added similar tags to the storehouse of Southernisms that Cash had begun: "Bulldozer Revolution," the "Man on the Cliff," "Jim Crow," forever unsegregatable from a "Strange

Career," and the alliterative "Reunion and Reaction." "Irony," "Burden," and "Forgotten Alternatives" are vintage Woodward. They belong, though, to the same genre as "Savage Ideal," "hell-of-a-fellow" complex, terms of a similar evocative power from *The Mind of the South*.[3] Like Woodward himself, Cash simply became part of a Southern scholar's world, a fixture that can no more be expelled completely from memory than the author of the *Origins of the New South* can be. Both Cash and Woodward belong to a great tradition, now coming to a close.

Unfortunately, as Sigmund Freud explained long ago, filial indebtedness inspires little gratitude. In fact, Harold Bloom, the literary critic, claims that formidable precursors can be vexing to later artists. They repudiate past giants in an "anxiety of influence" out of a fear of being intellectually overwhelmed. "In every work of genius we recognize our own rejected thoughts—they come back to us with a certain alienated majesty," Bloom remarks.[4] If Cash exercised that sort of power over successors, none save Woodward and Genovese have bothered to denounce him in the way T. S. Elliot assaulted the allegedly baneful influence of John Milton. Instead, the common way of handling Cash's ideas was to praise them, then to ignore their ramifications. The historiography of the South is somewhat the poorer for that pious but essentially unfruitful response.

To be sure, *The Mind of the South* enjoyed an enviable repute from the start. Even so, Donald Davidson, a major literary critic and English professor at Vanderbilt University, greeted the work with a review that by comparison made later criticisms seem gracious. Rhetorically, the Vanderbilt scholar invited Cash to be the object of an ill-humored lynching party, fit penalty, Davidson implied, for one who had so maligned Southern character. A conservative and former member of the "Agrarian" school of Southern intellectuals, Davidson meant no genuine harm. He dispersed the fictional mob before Cash was made the subject of its customary persecutions. He closed cheerily with the admonition: "Stonewall, don't forget you left that jug in the hollow beech-tree." If Cash had not taken his own life, the essay might have been a minor classic in the reviewing art. (Stricken by the news of Cash's death, Davidson tried to withdraw it from the *Southern Review*, but the journal had gone to press.) Despite his later regret, Davidson clearly bristled at Cash's portrait of a primitive, anti-intellectual South, yet somehow exemplified, even in his satire, what Cash had called the "savage ideal"—that touchiness and celebration of gut feeling so typical of the section.[5]

Academic Southern liberals were not wholly convinced by the book, although unwilling to lambaste him in the way that Davidson had. In an otherwise appreciative review, Woodward, already recognized as the South's most promising young scholar, pointed out in 1941 that Cash had "chosen a literary and imaginative rather than a scholarly approach. He has not attempted to write intellectual history, and must be forgiven for ignoring some of the South's most important minds in writing about the mind of the South." The fault was apparently forgiven, but not forgotten. Cash's approach was unsettling. It was indeed unusual for a work on the Southern past to forget the usual genuflections toward Monticello and Mount Vernon. Not even wrongheaded geniuses like John C. Calhoun and George Fitzhugh received the attention customarily due their standing. As if to defy the cloister, the Tar Heel journalist supplied no bibliography, not a single footnote. When mentioned at all, academicians and historians like John Spencer Bassett appeared only to illustrate Southern persecutions of independent minds, not to support a particular piece of information or interpretation.

But in fact, Cash was not at all divorced from academic sources. He was greatly swayed by Howard W. Odum, the dynamic sociologist at Chapel Hill. Although Cash did not place himself firmly in the European behaviorist tradition, which Odum had introduced to Southern social science, he might well have done so. Max Weber had employed the typological style in *The Protestant Ethic and the Spirit of Capitalism*, and Cash undertook the same mission, a delineation of social ideals. In the opening pages, Cash proposed to describe "a fairly definite mental pattern, associated with a fairly definite social pattern—a complex of established relationships and habits of thought, sentiments, prejudices, standards and values, and associations of ideas, which, if it is not common strictly to every group of white people in the South, is still common in one appreciable measure or another, and in some part or another, to all but relatively negligible ones." Thus, he understood the significance of Weber's concept of generalized rules by which individuals judge themselves and others. Cash did not admire the Southern whites' moral standards. With evangelical zeal, he wished to describe Southern usages in hope of banishing them—without, however, resorting to condemnation or apology. His attitude resembled Weber's "value-free" approach (an obective always out of reach). Yet historians worked with different assumptions, derived from political rather than anthropological thought. In 1960, Dewey Grantham gently chided Cash for not making "known to the reader the historical rubric or conceptual framework out of which he wrote."[6] Cash was innocent of the obligation. The amenities were not being observed.

When history advisors, particularly at Southern universities, spurred their graduate students toward historical topics, few if any urged them to challenge or test *The Mind of the South*. Issues that suggested the continuity and solidarity of Southern life went begging. Except for John Hope Franklin's rather conventional but useful study of violence, Cash's Savage

Ideal and its outcroppings gained no fresh recruits for examining the evidence. In fact, Cash became an excuse for *not* probing, except for the most superficial renderings, such themes as lynching, sexual violations of the race bar, and personal violence. No one challenged or defended his understanding of Southern honor and its sociological sources. For a provocative book, *The Mind of the South* aroused precious little provocation. For instance, Cash showed nothing but contempt for Southern politics—"a theater for the play of the purely personal" that often "caught the very meanest white up out of his tiny legend into the gorgeous fabric of this or that great hero." The observation was not superficial, and it explained more about Southern leadership than a host of dissertations on bank war politics and tariff policies. Only recently have the cultural aspects of partisanship regained attention. Yet in the years following Cash's publication, scholars did not make practical use of his observations on politics or anything else. Woodward later complained of this uncritical attitude toward the work but failed to add that adjectives of praise had become a substitute for hard thinking about Cash's themes.[7]

Of course, when sweeping generalizations required backing, *The Mind of the South* filled the intellectual void of many an author. Yet in classrooms, it had to be treated as informed journalism, an intellectual study of some sort, with intellectuals omitted. The title itself was confusing, especially since Perry Miller, a contemporary historian, had employed the term in a more familiar way in *The New England Mind*. The contrast between the rigorous cerebrations of Miller's divines and Cash's parvenu planters was distressing. In spirited retort, Woodward later contended that "if he were convinced that the Southerner had a 'temperament' but no 'mind,' that he 'felt' but did not 'think,' he might have more accurately entitled his book 'The Temperament of the South,' 'The Feelings of the South,' or more literally, 'The Mindlessness of the South.' "[8] Woodward subscribed to the convention that culture was simply the artistic and philosophical treasure-house of a society. Cash conceived of culture as the rules of conduct that guide individuals as social creatures. So wide a discrepancy between these approaches might not have been bridged even if Cash had employed the term "ethic" rather than "mind" of the South.

Woodward's misinterpretation should not be blamed on semantic confusion. Cash's own style contributed to the problem. He sought a large audience that could only be reached through popular, journalistic means, for he saw himself as a changer of attitudes, not just their expositor. Unburdening himself to Odum as early as 1929, Cash remarked, "I have sometimes hesitated over writing the book at all just because of the fear that the literary demand for simplification might result in a wholly inadequate representation of the South."[9] Undoubtedly, the style betrayed the author's own nervousness about dissenting from Southern orthodoxies. Smashing household gods, as Cash often said, was not the preferred role of the Southern intellectual. The struggle cut the dissenter from his roots and threatened intellectual exhaustion.

Bravely, Cash welcomed the risks, unmasking some cherished deceptions about Old South aristocracy while holding fast to other ideas that fellow liberals were abandoning. For instance, he did not join the assault on that venerable minor deity, the Solid South. As early as 1941, Davidson noticed the discrepancy between Cash's consensual South and the liberals' insistence on the "many Souths."[10] Moreover, Cash found little substance to an alleged tradition of liberal dissidence arising from these "many Souths."[11] In dealing with the Civil War, Cash stressed the horrors of Yankee Reconstruction. Other intellectuals were dismantling the myth of a "Reign of Terror" and fashioning a new legend about abolitionist, freedman, and scalawag purity.[12] Yet Cash's unwillingness to part with the old outrage against black rule had a beneficial side. It enabled him to perceive that, like Ireland, Poland, Finland, Bohemia, and other exploited lands, the South found a new unity in the fury of war and the resentment of defeat. The example of Union rule imposed a sense of common destiny that was reflected in the reinstallation of old Confederate leaders to bridge past glory with present misery. Like the Celtic Fringe of Great Britain, the former slave states were compelled to assume the peripheral, subordinate role assigned agrarian outlands in relation to rich metropolitan centers. Cash was blind to the merits of Republican partisanship, but he correctly believed that after the war economic and cultural dependency and the angry rattling of Yankee shackles aggravated racial hatreds. White savagery against blacks served as compensation for a sense of regional inferiority. Rather than progress, the South retreated into race primitivism as its colonial status became more evident.[13]

In contrast, Woodward questioned Cash's view of racist continuity that linked slavery, black peonage, lynch mobs, and, finally, disfranchisement and Jim Crow segregation at the turn of the century. Said Woodward, "Lacking the tradition of historical continuity possessed by their fellow countrymen, Southerners have less reason to expect the indefinite duration of any set of social institutions." Emancipation, Woodward argued, opened up various approaches to race relations so that whites in reconstructed states were not "so united" on the status of blacks "as has been generally assumed." Likewise, Grady McWhiney also discovered a redeemable South. The whites, he announced, were willing in early Reconstruction "to accept a large measure of democratization, including a goodly dose of colorblind democracy" for the sake of moving down "the progress road."[14] According to Southern scholars after World War II, race repression a hundred years before was not the foundation of Southern culture, at least not one on which they cared to dwell. Rather, race prejudice was a device to be hauled out or shelved as politicians or New South robber barons found appropriate for diverting class antagonisms.

In contrast, Cash was wholly unaware of a pliable and self-scrutinizing mood among planters as they watched former slaves move off and Union troops—many of them black—move in. Nor did he detect a revolution in social and political leadership during the Bourbon Restoration. But a generation of academicians after World War II assured the scholarly world that Whigs replaced Democrats, capitalists swept aside cavaliers, town-dwellers put country folk firmly in their social place. Cash's concept of political continuity has once again reappeared, if in more sophisticated and convincing form. In the late 1950s and early 1960s, however, Cash's utility on this and other points was greeted with increasing skepticism, voiced in the classroom if not in print.[15]

In the customary way of historians, present prospects seemed to prompt appropriately congenial views of the past. The South, most everyone agreed, had to break the chains of racial and sectional parochialism. Thus, in 1960, history was made to conform to current expectations of national consensus when the Southern scholar Charles G. Sellers, Jr., declared: "The traditional emphasis on the South's differentness . . . is wrong histori-cally," making it all the "harder for the South to understand both its Southernism and its Americanism, and hence escape the defensiveness, prejudice, and belligerence of its regional self-preoccupation. . . ."[16] Venturing below his customary haunts, Perry Miller smoothed out sectional discrepancies by locating strongly puritanical, Yankeelike habits in un-suspected corners of seventeeth-century Tidewater. Puritans and Vir-ginians had sprung from the same English "pious, hard-working, middle class ranks," Miller contended. In surveying the eighteenth-century terrain, Edmund S. Morgan agreed that Southerners swore allegiance to the "puritan ethic," thus making possible the common front against British vice and oppression in 1776. Woodward demurred from Morgan's homogeniz-ings. Yet his cautions were not enough to halt attempts to shove the South higgledy-piggledy into the Great American Melting Pot.[17]

Further divergences from Cash's position appeared even on a topic about which there was supposed to be agreement: the sense of guilt over slave-holding. Cash explained that Southerners well knew both the innate brutality and the worldwide infamy of American slavery. In uneasy conscience, he argued, they reacted with such "defense mechanisms" as the comic "banjo-playing, heel-flinging hi-yi-ing happy jack of the levees" and the formal proslavery logic to "prettify the institution" and "boast of its own Great Heart." In the 1960s, however, "guilt" took on different meaning. "The Travail of Slavery," historian Sellers and others argued, weighed heavily on white souls. It was a therapeutic release when the white man's yoke of slavery finally lifted in 1865. The argument hinted of wishful thinking. Genovese, rather unfairly, attacked Cash for this lugubrious explanation, whereas Cash had more Freudian and darker notions of guilt than his successors. In any case, by Genovese's 1969 attack on what he derisively called "guiltomania" in planter ranks, the spell of critical silence on Cash had been thoroughly broken.[18]

The reason for the delay had less to do with a lively appreciation for Cash's themes of continuity and consensus than the popularity of the literary mode in which *The Mind of the South* had been written. It was the pioneer book in what came to be called American Studies. The genre, which encompassed such disparate works as David Riesman's *Lonely Crowd*, Woodward's *Burden of Southern History*, and Stanley Elkins's *Slavery*, was concerned with American social and racial concepts and their delusiveness or validity. The authors sought to explain American identity through chiefly literary typologies, like Riesman's "inner-directed" man and Elkins' "Sambo." Differences among the writers existed, however, for Cash believed myth and reality were indistinguishable since aspiration and ideal were part of a cultural whole. Woodward and others, however, treated myths as manipulations, false, and therefore temporary. Yet the Plantation Legend, the Lost Cause, White Supremacy, as Cash well understood, were rationales for conduct and therefore inseparable from Southern identity. Cash was close enough to such myths to know their power; later writers in this mode were not. Yet all were preoccupied with the moral durabilities of the American experiment.[19]

By the mid-1960s, the American Studies concept was intellectually exhausted. Fine-tuning on ethical matters gave way to belligerent certainties; irony, as literary attitude, fell victim to dogma. Cash and American Studies were out. Marx and Malcolm X were in. Slavery and race became the sole preoccupations of the leading scholars whenever they turned southward. Much was written about slave insurrections, such as they were. Even secession was explained as reaction to the threat of servile rebellion. Genovese epitomized the mood of the decade when he announced that antebellum slavery had created "an organic relationship so complex and ambivalent that neither [white nor black] could express the simplest human feelings without reference to the other."[20] Cash could not have anticipated these changes of emphasis. Although Cash had specifically limited his topic to the ethic of the white Southerner, Woodward observed in 1967, "in view of the enormous impact slavery had on the mind of both whites and blacks, he cannot be excused for brushing over the Peculiar Institution as lightly as he did."[21] Woodward's challenge, however, reflected the mood of the moment as much as it did a deficiency on Cash's part. Slavery, much more than race itself, was the focus of historical attention. Cash, however, had maintained that the prime issue was white supremacy. What form it took—slavery, Klan, Jim Crow—mattered much less than the symbols, gestures, and habits to vouchsafe black subjection and white overlordship.

In the last few years, however, the historical landscape has been shifting once again. There seems to be a greater appreciation of how deep the roots of white arrogance have always been—deeper than slavery. The continuity underlies the changing institutional arrangements that Woodward chronicled in *The Strange Career of Jim Crow*. Moreover, young scholars have rediscovered that the South, even the colonial South, conformed neither in culture nor in demography to the eastern settlements. Owing to these changes as well as to the growing influence of the *Annales* school, the typological approach that Cash had applied could well enter a second period of acceptance. For all its faults—among them a tendency to underestimate social change—the use of the Ideal Type may provide answers in social and ethical history not amenable to other modes. As the pioneering work in the method, *The Mind of the South* bears directly on future efforts along these channels. For that reason, the book is relevant despite its age and curious history.

As an exercise in social analysis, Cash's work proposed three major elements as the foundation of the Southern ethic of *mentalité*. The first was the persistence of frontier conditions and attitudes; second, the agrarian style of class unconsciousness; and third, race hierarchy as a sacrosanct principle. None was peculiar to Cash's vision alone; rather, his insight was to trace the organic interrelationship of these elements, one to the other.

In regard to the first issue, there is a tendency to mistake Cash's frontier with that of the Turnerians, who romantically described the blessings of democracy, good cheer, and neighborliness. Southern individualism, Cash maintained, was hardy, but not necessarily healthy. Whereas Frederick Jackson Turner and his disciples conceived of natural abundance as a source of character building and self-reliance, Cash detected grounds for skepticism. In fact, ethnic origins, he claimed, had as much to do with Southern habit as the availability of land. The "man at the center," as Cash identified his typical settler, "had much in common with the half-wild Scotch and Irish clansmen of the seventeenth and eighteenth centuries whose blood he so often shared."[22] Curiously, we now accept the notion that there were substantial continuities in African and black American culture, but we are less willing to see such continuities in the oral, primitive, and traditionalistic patterns of the Southern whites.

Cash argued that the environment simply *preserved* but did not create the customs of the past. In almost Faulknerian prose, he observed that the frontiersman's "way of life was his . . . not because he himself or his ancestors or his class had deliberately chosen it as against something else, not even because it had been tested through the centuries and found to be good, but because, given his origins, it was the most natural outcome of the conditions in which he found himself."[23]

On this score, Cash and Genovese were agreed. Both interpreted the South as an organic, primordial society in the midst of dynamic, worldwide change. For both writers, too, the trans-Atlantic community and the North offered implied but not specific contrast. Their vision was completely at odds with the popular academic notion of a profit-making, bourgeois planter class, a concept that later received fullest expression in the work of Stanley Engerman and Robert Fogel. The chief difference between Genovese and Cash was the former's admiration of the self-confidence, commitment, and integrity of the slaveholding rulers. "It is rather hard to assert that class responsibility is the highest test of morality," said Genovese, rebutting the Old South's liberal critics, "and then to condemn as immoral those who behave responsibly toward their class instead of someone else's." On the other hand, Cash, like Allen Tate in *The Fathers*, thought that there was something incomplete about the Southern white male, a grievous simplicity or innocence that was much more dangerous and self-destructive than outright evil. But the two writers recognized that there was nothing hypocritical or manipulative in the manner by which white leaders assumed command, won lower-class loyalty, and exercised power. Like Genovese, Cash described a hegemonic relationship between leader and follower. Even after long years of settlement, Cash asserted, that primal, institutionless sense of communal oneness called democracy endured. The bonds lasted because neither a growth of cities, a disciplined educational system, a commanding church order, nor a vast flow of alien peoples appeared in the slave states to disrupt "a world in which horses, dogs, guns, not books, and ideas and art"—and cotton and slaves—were "the normal and absorbing interests."[24]

In describing this uncomplex style, Cash said next to nothing about its colonial roots. Like U. B. Phillips, Elkins, Kenneth Stampp, Genovese, Herbert Gutman, and other leading students of slavery, Cash dealt chiefly with the last thirty years before the Civil War. Unfortunately, he helped to accentuate the shameful neglect of prerevolutionary Southern social history. But at least he had good reason to do so. Cash set out to expose old fallacies about gentility, not add to its grandeur. The historical scholarship to which he had access in the 1930s sought to prove the long genealogy of Southern bourgeois origins and habits. Thomas Jefferson Wertenbaker of Virginia and others had transformed the early Chesapeake "cavaliers" into sober, industrious, hard-working souls. When not practicing good burgher virtues, though, they were engaged in developing a sturdy set of gentry traits—love of liberty and the classics. These admirable credentials were compatible with liberal, "New South" hopes for a march into twentieth-century progress, while the dreams of ancient nobility were cast behind. Cash accepted the new Progressive dogmas of colonial history but hastened on as quickly as he could. The myth of a planter bourgeoisie, in tie-wig and stiff Jeffersonian monumentality, did not square with the raw, downright rummy style that Cash sought to portray. Not until recently have historians begun to realize that Monticello and Nomini Hall were scarcely representative of Virginia life. A much bawdier, death-haunted, compulsive gentry class has at last begun to appear as a link between Cash's frontier vision and the colonial past.[25]

Although criticized for not examining the South's colonial roots, Cash proved no sentimentalist in beginning with the romantic, frontier era of Turner's "common man." He reconciled a contradiction that Turnerians and others refused to admit: the apparent discrepency between pioneer individualism and the demands for a general social conformity. In Cash's view, Southern individualism was not directed toward civic ends, that is, toward the building of community, the humanizing of social relations, the founding of powerful institutions. Such goals would have destroyed the elemental character of the society itself. Instead, individualism was most often synonymous with manliness. The ability to defend oneself received public applause. The *habitus* of masculinity contrasted with the impulse for other kinds of self-assertion—such as literary accomplishment, spiritual fulfillment, scientific discovery. Cash did not deny the existence of individuals who did aspire to other criteria—Matthew Fontaine Maury, Langdon Cheves, William Gilmore Simms—"and beneath these were others: occasional planters, lawyers, doctors, country schoolmasters, parsons, who, on a more humble scale, sincerely cared for intellectual and aesthetic values and served them as well they might." The trouble was that they were lost in a wilderness of mediocrity. Instead, the cultural aims were embodied in the "chip on the shoulder swagger and brag of a boy," the "boast" that the possessor could "knock hell out of whoever dared to cross him." This ideal masculinity so seldom clashed with conventional values that the most "independent" of men was the one who best met ancient standards of manhood and personal assertiveness. The Southern individualist whom peers admired was not the bookish eccentric or the spiritual pilgrim. Never was he an ideological maverick opposed to existing social fundamentals, but simply the most exemplary of conformists, however exotic his personal habits. The eccentric could be tolerated as long as he did not repudiate existing communal beliefs.[26]

Whereas Turnerians found frontier ideals praiseworthy, Cash detected backwardness, a luxuriating in the needlessness of mental exertion. The Savage Ideal of manly aggression discouraged other activities. Those few who were cursed with intellectual gifts, he noted sympathetically, had to suffer alone, even those in his own literary generation. Referring to Faulkner, Wolfe, and Caldwell, he said, "they hated [the South] with the exasperated hate of a lover who cannot persuade the object of his affections to his desire." With rare insight, he elaborated that "their hate and anger against the South was both a defense mechanism against the inner uneasiness created by that conflict and a sort of reverse embodiment of the old sentimentality itself." The anti-intellectuality of the region revealed that in strictly utilitarian terms the society had "little need or desire" for heavy cerebral toil. The general public was not only indifferent to the pronouncements of its intellectual tyros and sages but also sensitive about even a breath of criticism, from home or abroad. Cash did not rejoice in Southern hedonism, and he criticized his Southern literary contemporaries, the contributors to *I'll Take My Stand* for taking too little notice of "the underdog proper, the tenants and sharecroppers, industrial labor, and the Negroes as a group." But the dismal record, he thought, could not be denied by forever hauling out the Revolutionary Fathers, the founding of the University of Virginia, and *Uncle Remus.*[27]

The Savage Ideal of frontier derivation with its anti-intellectual results was closely connected with Cash's second major theme: the relative absence of class consciousness. On this issue, despite the discernible agreement mentioned earlier, Genovese has been Cash's most savage critic. (Woodward, on the other hand, accepted Cash's insight about how the anxieties of race blinded the poor to their "real interests.") To be sure, Cash, as Genovese claimed, was vulnerable. He did misunderstand aristocracy. Despite myths to the contrary, Cash said, cotton snobs were neither gracious, genteel, nor well-born. But he was mistaken in thinking that aristocracy was defined by such pleasant characteristics. He confused *gentility* as a social ideal with aristocracy as a class designation. Yet it does not illuminate the issue to say that Cash had, according to Genovese, "a pathetic fascination with the romance of aristocracy." The effort to break free of such long-standing ideals might seem "pathetic" a score of years after Cash's suicide, but his creativity, in fact the creativity of his literary generation in the South, owed much to just that wrenching free from the paternal grasp of old doctrine. By challenging the tales told him in childhood, Cash captured the essence of planter life. His image of the Carolina Irishman who started as a one-mule squatter and ended his days as "a gentleman of the old school" provided an insight that still has vitality. Genovese's criticism seems rather beside the point. The authors agree that gentlemen were not very gentlemanly in those days.[28]

We must assume, however, that Genovese's quarrel goes deeper than a semantic quibbling over the nature of gentility. Cash, he claims, simply did not understand the seigneurial hegemony that slaveholders exercised over the rest of Southern society. The problem with Genovese's emphasis on the power of the planter class is that it does not really reflect the fluidity and subtlety of leader-follower relationships. One has the impression that Genovese's masters, like Raimondo Luraghi's in a recent study, were a fixed, all-powerful set. They more or less fit the European model of rural overlords, particularly as Genovese portrayed them in *The Political Economy of Slavery*. In a sense, this representation is closer to the stereotype of the Southern grandee (with some features of Simon Legree thrown in) than to Cash's peasant-turned-pseudo-gentleman. Although stressing continuity of ideals, Cash insists on the expansionary trend and changing personnel of the slaveholding element. Power went to those who seized it, not to a static, well-born elite, simply out of sentiment or irrational deference. Within individual families, Cash maintained, there could be substantial discrepancies of wealth and poverty. They separated brother and sister, parent and offspring, uncle and nephew. At the same time, these kinship ties strengthened consensus and checked class consciousness. Cash overdid the polemics against the cavalier myth, as Genovese claims, but in its place, he constructed a better model.

Genovese reveals his own misunderstanding of Southern hierarchy when he argues that Cash was embarrassed by his portrayal of a "frontier bred" and "parvenu ruling class." Under these circumstances, Genovese asks, "how . . . does one account for the obvious hegemony exercised by the planters over the yeomen, especially in view of the colonial period's evidence of rebelliousness toward authority?" Cash offered the best reply to this conundrum ever devised. Sensitive to the personal, oral, and almost tactile character of Southern social exchange, he found significance in the manners and conventions that bridged the gaps of wealth and poverty, education and illiteracy. During the post-Jeffersonian era, Cash said, "rank had not yet hardened into caste." Probably it never did, at least in the short span before the Civil War, except in lowland South Carolina, southern Louisiana, the Sea Islands, and a few other well-known but not representative neighborhoods.[29] In any event, simple bonds of common locale, common ancestry, common commonness, as it were, brought yeoman and planter together—not in sustained, unchanging harmony, but in agreement about fundamentals of social order and ideal. On this issue, Odum, Cash's North Carolinian mentor, had, as early as 1929, advised him well: "I should not draw the lines too closely between the different cultural groups of the South. That is, the line between your old-time romantic gentlemen of the South and other types. Many of the southerners who were reputed to have a plantation and leisure still ate dinner in their shirtsleeves and washed on the back porch and let the chickens roost in the tops of the trees in the yard."[30]

The ultimate triumph for an author so severely handled is to have his perceptions adopted even by his critics. Thus, Genovese in 1975, some years after the publication of his original complaints, reintroduced Cash's interpretation of class bondings, although he did not mention Cash's name or book. Genovese even peopled his account with Cash-derived archetypes: "Josh Venable," the poor, independent-minded forty-acre cousin of "Jefferson Venable," his condescending but helpful neighbor at the "Big House," with broad acres and well-stocked slave cabins. Cash's parallel-figure, "Cousin Wash Venable," would feel pretty much at home in the World Genovese Made, sharing, as he does, the same patronym. In short, Genovese repackages what Cash had explained a quarter century before. Ironically, Genovese's "Yeoman Farmers in a Slaveholder's Democracy" is a convincing short piece because it acknowledges the class unawareness and the personal, familial nature of Southern hierarchy, a world away from his class-minded themes in earlier works.[31]

Cash's penetration, however, went beyond the simplicities of some sort of frontier democracy. Unfortunately, he called the style "paternal." Even so, he recognized the inadequacy of the designation. "I call the term [paternalism] inaccurate," said he, "because its almost inevitable connotation is the relationship of Roman *patron* and *client*; it suggests with a force that has led to much confusion, that there existed on the one hand an essential dependence, and on the other a prescriptive right—that it operated through command . . . and rested . . . on compulsion."[32] Such was not the case. "Cousin Wash" or "the man at the center" expected and received respect for his individuality and resented any infringement on his independence, his honor, or his desires. Yet he accorded deference to those whose power awed him, as long as some mutuality of personal exchange existed.

On this point, Cash and William Faulkner shared the same vision of historical reality. Take, for example, Thomas Sutpen and Wash Jones in *Absalom! Absalom!*, John Sartoris (and then son Bayard) and George Wyatt in *The Unvanquished*, or, when matters did go very sour, Major De Spain and Abner Snopes. Cash explained that there was no contradiction between the primitive individualism he had sketched and a required subordination to leaders publicly invested with the mystique of power. This preference for charismatic chieftains was based on the commoner's assumption that the men who gained command could never, said Cash, "run counter to his aims and desires."[33] When that expectation was betrayed, however, the result was utter fury, as if a backlog of jealousies, malice, guilts, and grievances never self-examined had erupted all at once. Cash, like Genovese, never quite penetrated the nature of the power still vested in the followers. The unspoken rules of conduct so easily over-stepped, the dangers of pressing elitist innovations too hard, the helplessness of the rich when the ordinary folk assailed their slaves during alleged insurrectionary panics, the petty harassments of court suits initiated by poor folk against richer neighbors—these also were part of the social structure. They did not destroy consensus, but they helped to make acts of violence, both great and small, a means of enforcing the ways of the poor, as it were, on the wealthy, the hedonism of the unrefined on the sensibilities of the respectable. Neither Cash nor Genovese moved his argument about upper-class hegemony into these rather uncharted areas of social experience. Nevertheless, Cash provided an excellent starting point.

In connection with the feelings of the disreputable toward their social betters, as Cash outlined them, one could do no better than to recall the example of Faulkner's Colonel Sutpen and Wash Jones. In his remorseless determination to found a dynasty, Sutpen seduces Milly, daughter of the useless Wash, caretaker of Sutpen's Hundred. After the war was over, Milly gives birth in the stable straw to a daughter, not the son Sutpen so desperately sought to immortalize himself. In his disappointment and callousness, Sutpen tells her, "Well, Milly; too bad you're not a mare too. Then I could give you a decent stall in the stable." By community standards, Wash Jones is poor white trash, friendless, only marginally independent. Inwardly, he knows his position, too. But the colonel had never forced him to confront his worthlessness, had never driven him to self-humiliation before. The brutish remark shows how matters really stand. In mad reprisal, Jones seizes a scythe and decapitates his chief. Then he sits passively to await the inevitable arrest.

The scene dramatizes Cash's point almost precisely. Social interchanges between gentry and yeoman, sometimes even between those connected by blood or marriage, included such primitive and violent events. Moreover, it should be recalled that Sutpen himself rose out of the same obscurity and shiftlessness as Wash Jones. As a young lad down from the hills of Virginia, Sutpen had met rebuff at the front door of a big planter's mansion. The black porter ordered him to knock at the back. Numb but unaware of inner fury, Sutpen translated outrage into cold ambition, not into class resentment. Sutpen was determined to be that master to whom the likes of Wash Jones and the Virginia house slave would have to defer. Yet as Faulkner, and Cash as well, makes clear, those in command must meet their obligations in command, subtle rules that Sutpen failed to learn.[34]

Superficially, it appeared that planter sway, as Faulkner and Cash depicted it by literary means, resembled the style of father to son. Cash, however, correctly saw the fallacy but had no other term to apply than "paternalism." Instead, he might have adopted "fraternalism." In the bonding of one white to another, each of differing standing, the style was a combination of the democracy inherent in that familial form and the hierarchy of male siblings, too. In this analogy, all white brothers were equal in having the same parentage and roughly the same upbringing; yet they did not share equally the places of honor in the family order. Thus, the eldest brother, or possibly the one with the greatest drive and promise, assumed control or had conferred on him the advantage of education, better lands, or some other marks of preference. For instance, Thomas Jefferson, the eldest son, obtained the best properties and slaves, as well as the boarding school and college education. His younger brother Peter as well as his undereducated sister Lucy fell far behind. Yet all three were born and raised under the same roof.

This form of familial hierarchy and distinctiveness had its counterpart in society at large, a connection not simply coincidental. Often enough, brothers, nephews, and cousins served in militia units headed by a recognized kinsman who had built on preferments granted by the patriarch of the previous generation. At election time, as Cash so vividly described, these lesser kinsfolk enjoyed the casual hand on the shoulder, the confidential whisper about the upcoming election, the conviviality of the cider barrel. "If the common white," Cash says, "was likely to carry a haughtiness like that of the Spanish peasant . . . very well, so far from challenging and trampling on that, his planter neighbors in effect allowed it, gave it boundless room—nay, even encouraged it and invited it on to growth."[35]

Finally, on matters of race, Cash proposed the Proto-Dorian Convention. In a highly sophisticated way, it has lately reappeared as *Herrenvolk Democracy*, a term of George M. Fredrickson's coining. As Genovese has forcefully observed, nonslaveholders were seldom "political marshmallows," easily gulled with talk of racial threats to their standing. Cash did not make this error. Yet his Proto-Dorian theme was a cornerstone of Southern "fraternalism," that mixture of democracy and hierarchy that was so organic to the regional style. Fear of the contamination of blood lineage was not purely a sexual fear, but was a dread of loss of race command, the nightmare of impotence, both physical and social. As a result, Cash observes, "any assertion of any kind on the part of the Negro constituted in a perfectly real manner on attack on Southern Woman." The imperative of a brother to defend a sister's purity found expression in "Would you have your sister marry one?" The query was not rhetorical but overladen with the most visceral of emotions. "Fraternalism," then, not only bonded white men together; it also made whites brothers in the guarding of sisterly "perfection." Again, the theme found unusual resonance in the work of Faulkner, who also perceived the significance of intense sibling feelings— brother to brother, sister to brother—and equally strained emotions about race and family integrity. Unlike Faulkner, Cash was not altogether aware of the complexities of psychology and social behavior that were involved. Yet intuitively, he came much closer to grasping these interconnections than many who followed after his pioneer labors.[36]

As it turned out, Cash wrote just at the closing of what could be called the Classic South. Had he lived into the era of sweeping Supreme Court interventions, Martin Luther King, Jr., and the Voting Rights Act; had he watched the progress of a "Bulldozer Revolution" with an accompaniment of fried chicken stands and freedom, at last, from cotton if not from sin, he would have been tempted to tinker with the text. Cash suspected, but he did not know for certain, that the triptych of frontier traits, democratic hierarchy or fraternalism, and white supremacy was soon to fall. As it was, he wrote when it was still possible to puncture the hedonistic pretentiousness of Atlanta's lofty skyline over the clay hills of north Georgia: "Softly, do you not hear behind that the gallop of Jeb Stuart's cavalrymen?" Faulkner, too, was a child of that transitional period, when the Confederate past was still remembered but distantly enough to permit a new-found detachment. Harold Bloom's "anxiety of influence" stirred these writers to demolish paternal myth, but the power of legend drove them forward. In Faulkner's *Intruder in the Dust* (1948), Charles Mallison, fourteen years old, could still relive the dusty afternoon "when Pickett himself is looking up the hill waiting for Longstreet to give the word and it's all in the balance" on that slope near Gettysburg.[37] The metaphor of legendary hoofbeats ringing against the concrete walls of Atlanta's modernity may today require a leap of imagination. On the far side of the greatest of all Southern fault lines, World War II, it took much less insight to grasp Cash's meaning. How ludicrously, Cash was saying, Southerners held to outworn beliefs and incorporated them in a world of shifting values and innovation. After all, Gene Talmadge was governor of Georgia then. With rhetoric and galluses ablaze, Talmadge kept alive the politicis of nostalgia, even as his cracker constituency hankered after the good things. Tacky romanticism, violence, shouts against the wind—matters that Cash had so well depicted and mourned—were still part of a durable South. Only lately, in the last quarter century, has it shrunk beyond easy recognition. We have Cash's study to thank for describing a fast-receding Southern way that *The Mind of the South* helped to speed on its unregretted departure.

Notes

I am grateful to the Guggenheim Foundation and the Davis Center (Princeton) for the assistance given in the writing of this essay and to Professors David Van Tassel, Lawrence Friedman, and William L. Marbury for their close reading of the text.

1. C. Vann Woodward, "W. J. Cash Reconsidered," *New York Review of Books* (hereinafter, *NYRB*), December 4, 1969, p. 34.

2. Carl N. Degler, *Place over Time: The Continuity of Southern Distinctiveness* (Baton Rouge: Louisiana State University Press, 1977); Michael O'Brien, "W. J. Cash, Hegel and the South," *Journal of Southern History* XLIV (August 1978), pp. 379-98; W. J. Cash, *The Mind of the South* (New York: Alfred A. Knopf, 1941); Sheldon Hackney, "Origins of the New South in Retrospect," *Journal of Southern History* XXXVIII (May 1972), p. 201.

3. C. Vann Woodward, *The Burden of Southern History* (Baton Rouge: Louisiana State University Press, 1960), *Origins of the New South, 1877-1913* (Baton Rouge: Louisiana State University Press, 1953), *The Strange Career of Jim Crow* (New York: Oxford University Press, 1958), "The Elusive Mind of the South," in Woodward, *American Counterpoint: Slavery and Racism in the North-South Dialogue* (Boston: Little, Brown, 1971), p. 262, *Reunion and Reaction: The Compromise of 1877 and The End of Reconstruction* (Boston: Little, Brown, 1951).

4. Harold Bloom, *The Anxiety of Influence: A Theory of Poetry* (New York: Oxford University Press, 1970), p. 30.

5. Donald Davidson, "Mr. Cash and the Proto-Dorian South," *Southern Review* VII (Summer 1941), pp. 4-5, 20; C. Vann Woodward, review of *The Mind of the South,* in *Journal of Southern History* VII (August 1941), p. 400.

6. Woodward, review of *Mind of the South,* p. 400; Cash, *Mind of the South,* pp. viii, 283, 332-33, 383; Reinhard Bendix and Guenther Roth, *Scholarship and Partisanship: Essays on Max Weber* (Berkeley: University of California Press, 1971), pp. 253-65; Max Weber, *The Protestant Ethic and the Spirit of Capitalism,* trans. by Talcott Parsons (New York: Charles Scribner's Sons, 1958); Dewey W. Grantham, Jr., "Mr. Cash Writes a Book," *Progressive* XXV (December 1961), p. 41.

7. John Hope Franklin, *The Militant South, 1800-1861* (Cambridge: Harvard University Press, 1956); Clement Eaton, *The Freedom of Thought in the Old South* (Durham: Duke University Press, 1940); Davidson, "Mr. Cash," p. 13; see also, Charles S. Sydnor, *The Development of Southern Sectionalism, 1819-1848* (Baton Rouge: Louisiana State University Press, 1948), p. 316. Ronald P. Formisano, "Deferential-Participant Politics: The Early Republic's Political Culture, 1789-1840," *American Political Science Review* LXVIII (June 1974), pp. 473-87; J. Mills Thornton, *Politics and Power in a Slave Society: Alabama, 1800-1860* (Baton Rouge: Louisiana State University Press, 1977); William J. Cooper, Jr., *The South and the Politics of Slavery, 1828-1856* (Baton Rouge: Louisiana State University Press, 1978); Daniel J. Kraska, "The First Reconstruction: Andrew Johnson and Southern Response" (Ph.D. diss., Case Western Reserve University, 1979). These last three citations suggest some new approaches to political history and interpretation. On the adjectival praise for Cash, see, for instance, Arthur S. Link and Rembert W. Patrick, eds., *Writing Southern History . . .* (Baton Rouge: Louisiana State University Press, 1965), pp. 359, 384, 442.

8. Woodward, *American Counterpoint,* pp. 263, 265; O'Brien, "W. J. Cash," p. 379; Woodward, review of *Mind of the South,* pp. 400-01.

9. Richard King, "The Mind of the South: Narcissus Grown Analytical," *New South* XXVII (Winter 1972), pp. 16-18; quotation, Wilbur J. Cash to Howard W. Odum, November 22, 1929, Howard W. Odum MSS, Southern Historical Collection, University of North Carolina, Chapel Hill (hereinafter *SHC*). The Odum-Cash correspondence was brought to my attention very kindly by Daniel J. Singal of Tulane University.

10. Davidson, "Mr. Cash," p. 1.

11. Cash, *Mind of the South,* pp. 92, 250, 253; Kenneth M. Stampp, "The Fate of the Southern Antislavery Movement," *Journal of Negro History* XXVIII (January 1943), pp. 10-22; David Donald, "Mississippi Scalawags Revisited," *Journal of Southern History* (November 1944), pp. 447-60; Woodward, *Origins of the New*

South; C. Vann Woodward, *Tom Watson: Agrarian Rebel* (New York: MacMillan, 1938).

12. Cash, *Mind of the South,* p. 106; Carl V. Harris, "Right Fork or Left Fork? The Section Party Alignment of Southern Democrats in Congress, 1873-1897," *Journal of Southern History XLII* (November 1976), p. 471; William B. Hesseltine, *Confederate Leaders in the New South* (Baton Rouge: Louisiana State University Press, 1950); Clement Eaton, *The Waning of the Old South Civilization* (Athens: University of Georgia Press, 1968). On the matter of political continuity, see also a very effective argument in Degler, *Place over Time,* pp. 104-14. David Potter in *The Impending Crisis, 1848-1861* (New York: Harper & Row, 1976), p. 469, also thought that the war, far from chastening Johnny Reb as the Republicans unrealistically expected, "did far more to produce a southern nationalism which flourished in the cult of the Lost Cause than southern nationalism did to produce the war."

13. Cash, *Mind of the South,* pp. 105-08; Woodward, *Origins of the New South,* pp. 291-320. On Reconstruction revisionism, see Eric L. McKitrick, *Andrew Johnson and Reconstruction* (Chicago: University of Chicago Press, 1960), pp. 32-35; Eric L. McKitrick, ed., *Andrew Johnson* (New York: Hill and Wang, 1969), pp. viii-xxiii. Michael L. Benedict, *The Impeachment of Andrew Johnson* (New York: W. W. Norton, 1973); but see, for a more Cash-like interpretation of the Johnsonian era of Reconstruction, Hans L. Trefousse, *Impeachment of a President: Andrew Johnson, the Blacks and Reconstruction* (Knoxville: University of Tennessee Press, 1975). On internal colonialism, see Michael Hechter, *Internal Colonialism: The Celtic Fringe in British National Development, 1536-1966* (London: Routledge & Kegan Paul, 1975); Raimundo Luraghi, *The Rise and Fall of the Plantation South* (New York: Franklin Watts, 1978); and a fine review of the colonial theme in actuality and intellectual conceptualization, George B. Tindall, *The Ethnic Southerners* (Baton Rouge: Louisiana State University Press, 1976), pp. 109-23.

14. Grady McWhiney, "Reconstruction: Index to Americanism," in Charles S. Sellers, Jr., ed., *The Southerner as American* (Chapel Hill: University of North Carolina Press, 1960), p. 95; Woodward, *Strange Career,* pp. 6, 7; Ulrich B. Phillips, "The Central Theme of Southern History," *American Historical Review XXXIV* (October 1928), pp. 30-43.

15. William J. Cooper, Jr., *The Conservative Regime: South Carolina, 1877-1900* (Baltimore: Johns Hopkins University Press, 1968); for an excellent perspective on this issue, see James T. Moore, "Redeemers Reconsidered: Change and Continuity in the Democratic South, 1870-1900," *Journal of Southern History XLIV* (August 1978), pp. 357-78. John V. Mering, "Persistent Whiggery in the Confederate South: A Reconsideration," *South Atlantic Quarterly LXIX* (Winter 1970), pp. 124-43; Allen W. Moger, *Virginia: Bourbonism to Byrd, 1870-1925* (Charlottesville: University of Virginia Press, 1968); Harris, "Right Fork," pp. 471-506. David Potter, it must be added, took a more cautionary approach than did Woodward: see Woodward, "The Strange Career of a Historical Controversy," in *American Counterpoint,* pp. 234-60; David Potter, "C. Vann Woodward," in Marcus Cunliffe and Robin W. Winks, eds., *Pastmasters: Some Essays on American Historians* (New York: Harper & Row, 1969), pp. 375-407, esp. pp. 402-05; Michael O'Brien, "C. Vann Woodward and the Burden of Southern Liberalism," *American Historical Review LXXVIII* (June 1973), pp. 589-604; Joseph L. Morrison, "W. J. Cash: The Summing Up," *South Atlantic Quarterly* 76 (Autumn 1977), p. 508.

16. Kenneth M. Stampp, "The Southern Road to Appomattox," *Cotton Memorial Papers*, No. 4, University of Texas at El Paso (February 1969), pp. 3-22; Sellers, ed., *Southerner as American*, pp. v-vi; Howard Zinn, *The Southern Mystique* (New York: Simon & Schuster, 1972); F. Garvin Davenport, Jr., *The Myth of Southern History: Historical Consciousness in Twentieth Century Southern Literature* (Nashville: Vanderbilt University Press, 1970), p. 112.

17. William R. Taylor, *Cavalier and Yankee: The Old South and the American National Character* (New York: George Braziller, 1961); Stanley M. Elkins, *Slavery: A Problem in American Institutional and Intellectual History* (Chicago: University of Chicago Press, 1959); Perry Miller, *Errand into the Wilderness* (Cambridge: Harvard University Press, 1956), pp. 108, 138; Edmund S. Morgan, "The Puritan Ethic and the American Revolution," *William and Mary Quarterly*, 3d ser., XXIX (January 1967), pp. 3-43; Woodward, *American Counterpoint*, pp. 13-46; Morgan qualified his positions considerably in *American Slavery, American Freedom*.

18. Cash, *Mind of the South*, pp. 31, 99; Eugene D. Genovese, *Red and Black: Marxian Explorations in Southern and Afro-American History* (New York: Random House, 1972), p. 342, *The World the Slaveholders Made* (New York: Pantheon, 1969), pp. 130-54.

19. Ray Mathis, "Mythology and Mind of the New South," *Georgia Historical Quarterly* LX (Fall 1976), pp. 228-38: as perceptive though this article is, I disagree with Mathis that the South's distinctiveness is itself a myth; otherwise, his points are unusually persuasive. See on these questions the brilliant article of Robert F. Berkhofer, Jr., "Clio and the Culture Concept: Some Impressions of a Changing Relationship in American Historiography," in Louis Schneider and Charles M. Bonjean, eds., *The Idea of Culture in the Social Sciences* (Cambridge, Eng.: Cambridge University Press, 1973), pp. 77-100; Elkins, *Slavery*; Louis Hartz, *The American Liberal Tradition* (New York: Alfred A. Knopf, 1955); David Reisman et al., *The Lonely Crowd: A Study of Changing American Character* (New Haven: Yale University Press, 1950); Henry Nash Smith, *Virgin Land: The American West as Symbol and Myth* (Cambridge: Harvard University Press, 1950); Taylor, *Cavalier and Yankee*; David M. Potter, *People of Plenty: Economic Abundance and American Character* (Chicago: University of Chicago Press, 1954). C. Vann Woodward, "The Search for Southern Identity," in *Burden*, first published in *Virginia Quarterly Review* XXXIV (Summer 1958), pp. 321-38.

20. Eugene D. Genovese, *Roll, Jordan, Roll: The World the Slaves Made* (New York: Pantheon, 1974), p. 4. Cash, however, declared that the relationship between the races was "nothing less than organic. Negro entered into white man as profoundly as white entered into Negro," *Mind of the South*, p. 51. He did not, however, follow up the insight. See also, Cash to Odum, November 13, 1929, Odum MSS, SHC.

21. C. Vann Woodward, "White Man, White Mind." *The New Republic*, December 9, 1976, p. 9.

22. Cash, *Mind of the South*, p. 30; Grady McWhiney and Forest McDonald, "The Antebellum Southern Herdsmen: A Reinterpretation," *Journal of Southern History* XLI (May 1975), pp. 147-66.

23. Cash, *Mind of the South*, p. 31.

24. Ibid., p. 99; Genovese, *Red and Black*, p. 342; Allen Tate, *The Fathers* (Chicago: Swallow, 1938).

25. Boynton Merrill, Jr., *Jefferson's Nephews: A Frontier Tragedy* (Princeton: Princeton University Press, 1976); Michael Zuckerman, "An Amusement in This Silent Country: The Family Life of William Byrd of Eighteenth Century Virginia," unpublished paper, Armington Program on Values in Children, Case Western Reserve University, Fall 1978; Daniel B. Smith, "Mortality and Family in the Colonial Chesapeake," *Journal of Interdisciplinary History* VIII (Winter 1978), pp. 403-27; Rhys Isaac, "Evangelical Revolt: The Nature of the Baptists' Challenge to the Traditional Order in Virginia, 1765 to 1775," *William and Mary Quarterly*, 3d ser., XXXI (July 1974), pp. 345-68. On the liberal and New South leanings of that generation, see Daniel J. Singal, "Ulrich B. Phillips: The Old South as the New," *Journal of American History* LXIII (March 1974), pp. 871-91. See also, Aubrey C. Land et al., eds., *Law, Society, and Politics in Early Maryland: Essays in Honor of Morris Leon Radoff* (Baltimore: Johns Hopkins University Press, 1977); Timothy H. Breen, "Horses and Gentlemen: The Cultural Significance of Gambling Among the Gentry of Virginia," *William and Mary Quarterly*, 3d ser., XXXIV (April 1977), pp. 239-57.

26. Cash, *Mind of the South*, pp. 44, 97.

27. Ibid., pp. 386-87, 147, 392; cf. Woodward, *American Counterpoint*, p. 266.

28. Woodward, *American Counterpoint*, p. 273; Genovese, *World Slaveholders Made*, p. 140; Cash, *Mind of the South*, Book I.

29. Genovese, *World Slaveholders Made*, pp. 139-40, and *The Political Economy of Slavery: Studies in the Economy and Society on the Slave South* (New York: Pantheon, 1965); Cash, *Mind of the South*, p. 8; Luraghi, *The Rise and Fall of the Plantation South*.

30. Odum to Cash, November 20, 1929, Odum MSS, SHC.

31. Genovese, "Yeoman Farmers," *Agricultural History* XLVI (April 1975), pp. 331-42; Cash, *Mind of the South*, pp. 28-29.

32. Cash, *Mind of the South*, p. 54.

33. Ibid., p. 115.

34. William Faulkner, *Absalom! Absalom!* (New York: Random House, 1972), pp. 286 ff.

35. Cash, *Mind of the South*, p. 43.

36. George M. Fredrickson, *Black Image in the White Mind: The Debate on Afro-American Character and Destiny, 1817-1914* (New York: Harper & Row, 1971); Cash, *Mind of the South*, p. 119. See esp. John T. Irwin, *Doubling & Incest Repetition and Revenge: A Speculative Reading of Faulkner* (Baltimore: Johns Hopkins University Press, 1975).

37. Cash, *Mind of the South*, pp. 224, 225; William Faulkner, *Intruder in the Dust* (New York: Random House, 1948), p. 194.

VIII

MIND OR MINDLESSNESS, PERSISTENCE OR PARADOX?: CURRENTS OF SOUTHERN THOUGHT

Involved in nearly all of the preceding essays are direct or indirect assessments of the "Southern mind." This perennially debated topic is explored more thoroughly by the authors of the final four articles in this volume.

In "Slavery and Confederate Nationalism," Steven A. Channing addresses an old question: Was Confederate nationalism prior to 1861 a myth or a reality? Channing surveys the literature on this topic from Kenneth Stampp, who argued that no deep-seated national consciousness existed, to Eugene Genovese and Raimondo Luraghi, who, using a neo-Marxist analysis, contended that a deep-seated nationalism filtered from the planters downward to encompass all of Southern society. Channing, however, argues that both views are shot through with "internal contradictions." Although Channing believes that a high degree of Southern nationalism existed by 1861, he does not think it resulted simply from the machinations of a master class of planters. Rather, Channing contends, a distinctive Southern nationalism was the product of "a complex interplay of international, regional, class, and religious inputs" played out against the background of an all-important "creative interaction" between blacks and whites. "This matrix of race, class, and cultural consciousness," Channing concludes, "consitituted a sort of protonationalism . . . that was susceptible to political exploitation by . . . the slaveholders" into a full-bred nationalism when the first battles were fought in 1861.

Lawrence Goodwyn, in "Hierarchy and Democracy: The Paradox of Southern Experience," focuses on Southern reformers and their legacies of paradox. He believes that the ultimate contradiction of Southern history is that its individual episodes of paradox have served only to strengthen what may be the South's most persistent feature. Goodwyn identifies this feature as the perpetuation of social, economic, and political hierarchies that have been able consistently to co-opt reform traditions for their own purposes and thus to prevent the emergence of a genuinely "new," "democratic" South. Given this historical record, Goodwyn wistfully asks if present-day Southerners can reasonably expect to be more successful than their predecessors in forging a radically New South based on democracy rather than hierarchy. Goodwyn himself remains only "cautiously hopeful."

Paradoxical episodes in Southern history often have come from the actions of singular individuals who have challenged those traditions that have persisted from the Old South to the New. Among the most dramatic instances are those in which the strict racial orthodoxy of the region has been defied by attempts at improving race relations. The concluding two articles in this volume tell the stories of two of these Southerners.

In his article on racial reformers, "Dorothy Tilly and the Fellowship of the Concerned," Arnold Shankman focuses on the important role played by Southern women in general and Dorothy Tilly in particular. Shankman contends that Tilly's liberalism, like that of many women reformers, sprang from her childhood experiences in the Methodist Church and her belief in the concept of Christian equality. Her racial dissent was manifested by her leadership in such organizations as the Commission on Interracial Cooperation, the Association of Southern Women for the Prevention of Lynching, and the Southern Regional Council. But the climax of Tilly's lifelong crusade for racial reform came in 1949, when she organized the Fellowship of the Concerned as a women's adjunct to the Southern Regional Council. While recounting the harassment, threats, and obscene telephone calls to which they were subjected, Shankman describes how Tilly, and the 4,000 white women who joined her organization, monitored courtroom proceedings, accompanied black voters to the polls, denounced lynching, and campaigned for desegregation. Although the Fellowship of the Concerned did not revolutionize Southern race relations, it did help to protect black legal rights, decrease lynchings, and smooth the way for the desegregation process of the 1960s. Through such efforts, Shankman concludes, Tilly and white women like her helped to vindicate the belief that Southerners could "ease the tensions of our section and make it a proving ground for democracy."

Equally committed to this belief was Dorothy Tilly's contemporary and the subject of Robert M. Randolph's article, "James McBride Dabbs: Spokesman for Racial Liberalism." Dabbs was perhaps more representative of the "typical" white Southern liberal than Tilly in that his commitment to racial equality took much longer to evolve and emerged only after a rigorous period of self-examination. The paternalistic ideas inherited from his family, the intellectual stimulus of college life, and the death of his beloved wife all profoundly influenced Dabbs. By the time Dabbs reached middle age, in the late 1940s, these experiences had led him to believe that Southern Society had to be reformed and that the basic ingredient in achieving that task was the improvement of race relations. Dabbs pursued his quest in the 1950s and 1960s as a writer, president of the Southern Regional Council, and eventual advocate of the Black Power movement. Randolph concludes that Dabbs's greatest contribution to racial reform was as a prophet who was dedicated to the idea that the South would lead the nation in improving race relations and who proved that it was possible to be both a loyal white Southerner and a racial liberal.

16

SLAVERY AND CONFEDERATE NATIONALISM

Steven A. Channing

One of the most venerable historical chestnuts in Southern history concerns Confederate nationalism: myth or reality. Considering the prolonged and often brilliantly fought paper war that has been waged over the issue, one would have to be at least a bit foolhardy to enter this ancient fray. But I've been feeling a little impetuous of late, and so I would like to share some thoughts and observations, mostly speculations about the question of how broadly and deeply Confederate Southerners held a system of beliefs that united them in nationalism.

If we could discover them, the answers would apply not only to the issue of popular support for secession and war but also for the very nature and distinctiveness of Southern society and culture long before and after the Civil War.

One obvious problem the historian has in generalizing about Confederate sentiment is that the process of the war continuously generated deeply personal evaluations and reevaluations of attitudes in the minds of the participants, changing attitudes toward the war, the Confederate government, and Southern national identity itself. Suppose we consider an early and crucial illustration of that experience—the First Battle of Manassas.

The scene, as Richmond journalist Edward Pollard later recalled it, was extraordinary. Members of the federal Congress, their wives, and friends by the hundreds had gathered, champagne and picnic baskets at hand, to witness the first and presumably conclusive battle to subdue the rebellion of certain treasonous slaveholders. A splendid vista lay before them: woods and fields extending toward the warm haze of the Blue Ridge Mountains to the west. Hours passed. The field obscured by bluish clouds, the air punctured by the clatter of shots, bursts of bugle calls. Overhead, a July sun glared down, turning cool morning into scorched afternoon. Then . . . shouts of "We are whipped." Retreat became a stumbling, headlong rout, civilians, horses, and carts, pushing wildly toward the refuge of Washington.

By telegraph, newspaper, and word-of-mouth the story spread rapidly. The hastily assembled forces of the new Confederate State government had *defeated* the grand federal army. This was no mere rhetoric, no blustering pronouncement from the politicians. This was an *event*, and to a people disposed to see the Divine hand at work amidst the deeds of men, it was an event fraught with meaning. Not a narrow victory, but an entire army broken and driven to flight! As Pollard remembered:

We had, indeed, won a splendid victory, to judge from the fruits within the limits of the battlefield. The events of the Battle of Manassas were glorious for our people, and were thought to be of crushing effect upon the morale of our hitherto confident and overweening adversary.[1]

What an astonishing endorsement of Southern nationalist illusions! Truly, it seemed the very best of times. The government of the slave states set up only months before, trembling on the brink of disintegration, had apparently destroyed the army of its foe—and on the Sabbath! What better way to confirm a vast body of assumptions about the nature of the South, the meaning of the war, and the inevitability of Confederate victory? That the South was as vast and impregnable as Mother Russia. That it would fight even more intensely to defend home and family, states, and nation. That it enjoyed all the tactical and strategic advantages of the defensive position. And that the South possessed—in slavery, in the plantation, and in its chivalrous elite and pure, stouthearted common folk—a cultural harmony, stability, and superiority that would surely spell victory over the decadent North.

Or so these notions were endlessly reiterated by spokesmen for the new nation. Secession, constitution making, war, and now the glorious triumph at Manassas all appeared to moot the question of whether claims to cultural singularity were based more on wish than on fact. Of course, we often have been warned by students of nationalism to guard against such claims, for they are often tissues of rationalization. They serve to obscure the pursuit of special interests and to create a misleading sense of national solidarity. In his superb essay on the uses of nationalism, David Potter noted how easy it was to find cultural underpinnings for every successful national movement, where oftentimes few of these actually existed prior to the revolution. And certainly, it is easy to see that some assertions of Southern cultural distinctiveness were contrived and manipulated by secessionists.[2]

Still, I think that this criticism can be carried too far. While we can argue about the *degree* of sectional difference before 1861, the existence of an independent Southern nation is a great and challenging fact.

The problem is: What to *make* of that fact? Did it signify the existence of "true" nationalist feelings, whatever that means? Did it prove that sufficient numbers of Southern whites had come to believe in their own difference from and even superiority to the people of the North?

How have historians dealt with the issue? The question of divergent culture has always seemed central. Like the contestants in 1861, the two principal historical lines of interpretation—those who accept and those who reject the validity of Southern nationalism—seem to divide on this point: Did Americans in the slave states share a materially distinctive regional culture?

Those who describe Southern nationalism as fraudulent emphasize the absence of a natural frontier, of a distinctive demographic stock, of political and religious traditions. They assert that the Confederate States of America was essentially the product of manipulated hysteria and anger, that it was not the result of deep-seated and persistent cultural differences from the North. This view, expressed most conveniently in Kenneth Stampp's essay, "The Southern Road to Appomattox," tells us that secession was an abberation, the climax of a generation of increasingly irrational politics, of gnawing self-doubt, of a frustration-aggression syndrome arising from conflicting liberal and illiberal values that had their roots finally in misgivings over slavery. Regardless of economic and manpower deficiencies, then, the Confederacy was doomed to political bickering and impotence. "The history of the Confederacy," Stampp writes, "is not that of a people with a sense of deep commitment to their cause—a feeling that without victory there is no future—for too many of them declined to make the all-out effort that victory would have required."[3]

On the other hand, those historians who have made the most persuasive claims for the "two civilizations" tell us that a unique social and political culture did in fact arise out of the peculiar economic substructure generated by slaveholding itself, with tendencies toward ideological separatism displayed like badges after First Manassas. It follows from this interpretation that the Confederacy was the logical creation of self-conscious slaveowners and whatever whites endorsed or acquiesced in their views. The strongest arguments along these lines in recent years have come from the pens of neo-Marxist writers unconcerned with the obligation to delineate a crude dialectical materialism arising from inevitable worker-capitalist conflict. The works of such men as Eugene Genovese and Raimondo Luraghi, drawing especially on the analysis of the early twentieth-century Italian theorist Antonio Gramsci, assume that all mature societies have their own "bosses," the men of wealth and therefore power. This social class, together with the fundamental economic relations that obtain in that society, eventually determine moral and legal standards of behavior, political and social attitudes, in short, its ideology.[4]

Social power, according to this interpretation, is not rapidly acquired or brutally exploited. The protodominant class slowly rises above simple economic self-interest and into a fuller political sense of itself and its potential authority. An ideology or world-view is gradually articulated that comes to permeate and shape virtually all relationships. Initially, this takes place in the realm of economics and social interactions, Luraghi explains, "then interests, feelings, traditions, even prejudices" are melded "into a concrete ideology which transforms diverging (and frequently contrasting) interests into an 'historic bloc' "—in our context, a potential nation. Through its intimate relationship to the prevailing ideology, a dominant social class "succeeds in exercising its hegemony" over that society. Dissensions, interest conflicts, and the like are in time synthesized or smothered, with the resulting patterns of thought and behavior verified by time and experience, becoming at last habitual.[5] Crude abuses of power and instances of stark conflict between groups are largely edited out of this scenario. It is consensus Marxism. As Genovese writes: "A ruling class consolidates its hegemony precisely by presenting itself as the guardian, even the embodiment, of a moral code, much of which represents the interests and sentiments of *all* classes, and by disguising the purely exploitative and manipulative features of the prevailing code."[6] This process supposedly went forward in the South in behalf of the planters and presumably in the North as well, although there the emerging industrial-capitalist class, with its individualistic values, was in marked contrast to the "premodern" ethos of Dixie. And so the war came, in neo-Marxian fashion.

The historian's recourse to "splitting the difference," to "truth lies somewhere in the middle" logic, appears hopeless as a device for reconciling this debate. The two positions seem to have a mutual exclusivity about them, divided on the culture frontier. Equally troubling is the fact that both interpretations exhibit internal contradictions. For example, if Stampp is correct, and the anxiety-ridden South blundered almost willfully into a self-destructive war, are we then to assume that claims of cultural singularity and nationalism were mere psychic placebos, no matter how vigorously and consistently expressed? And how, on the other side, do we reconcile with the neo-Marxian view the profound *tensions* within Southern society, tensions reflecting interest conflict not only between planter and hill country nonslaveholder but also within the "ruling class," indeed, within the minds of individual slaveholders and their families. Was that all, then, "false consciousness," or some nineteenth-century Southern version of "bourgeois revisionism"? If the slaveholders had reached the apex of their political and ideological maturity and self-awareness at the advent of their own destruction, as Luraghi suggests, then that social consciousness exhibited a mystifying degree of vacillation and flaccidity, of unanticipated and ultimately fatal limits.

We are reminded again of Potter's warnings about the uses of nationalism. Hindsight tells some of us that secession did take place, that the

Confederacy *was* created, and therefore that Southern nationalism was bona fide, with all that implies. Hindsight tells others that the Confederacy collapsed into defeat and that nationalist claims were therefore a fraud. We have lost the sense of contingency, of possibility inherent in the course of events as they unraveled. This is not to suggest that if the Confederacy had successfully established its independence we would not be writing studies about the internal weaknesses of Northern nationalism (Unionism). Rather, it is to offer the possibility that our knowledge of the sequence of historical events prevents us from fully appreciating the dynamics of the situation. In a political revolution that subjects the personal identities and loyalties of millions to an excruciating test, the revolution itself becomes a formative factor.

No one can doubt that the South was marked by serious cultural ambivalence. Whites were certainly aware of the tensions between the larger American liberal democratic ethos and slaveholding, regardless of the convenience of *herrenvolk* racism. Many were sensitive to the latent and apparent abuses of slavery. Still more were torn by conflicting loyalties to plantation, state, region, nation. And there was sharp awareness of the potential for internal discord involving persistent Unionism, the cities, industry, women, nonslaveholders, and the fragility of black subordination. Only the most naive and ardent young "southron" would have suggested that a perfect unity of viewpoints existed, even in the blush of First Manassas enthusiasm, even in the minds of the planters themselves.

Yet where has perfect unity or anything resembling it ever existed in the realm of social and cultural values, outside of small, homogeneous pre-industrial societies? Even if it *had* existed in the South, would that unity have precluded sharp disagreements over the appropriate political (or military) *strategies* needed to protect the social order? The range of such disagreements might extend all the way from the debate over whether secession was justified or wise, to issues of military tactics. Political bickering in itself does not disprove the possibility that there was an ideological core sustaining a latent cultural nationalism, as the bitter political and military divisions in *Lincoln's* government and army suggest.

Two and a half centuries of contact between whites and blacks, masters and slaves, planters and nonslaveholders had exerted a profound influence on the Southern people. Distinctive regional variations on American attitudes toward sexuality and family, land and work, politics and the realm of God had evolved in the special context of the presence of plantations and African slaves. But the regional culture also evolved under influences apart from "ruling-class hegemony." There was an unusually long contact with the frontier and the Indian. There was the deep influence of American democratic ideals and institutions (which endlessly challenged the ingenuity of conservative planters). Many nonslaveholding whites lived in proximity to the Black Belts, but many others did not. At the same moment that these whites treasured notions of "leveling upwards," they also cultivated a strong sense of independence. English wartime correspondent William Howard Russell remarked on an aspect of this while visiting Montgomery:

There are, so far as I have seen, no rustics, no peasantry in America; men dress after the same type, differing only in finer or coarser material; every man would wear, if he could, a black satin waistcoat and a large diamond pin stuck in the front of his shirt. . . . The mean white affects the style of the large proprietor of slaves or capital as closely as he can; he reads his papers . . . and he takes his drink with the same air—takes up as much room, and speaks a good deal in the same fashion.[7]

This speaks both to the influence of the elite and to a mechanism employed by the hoi polloi to turn things to their better advantage. Cultural values were not merely molded, masked, and handed down by the planters; they emerged out of a complex interplay of international, regional, class, and religious inputs (although the primary influence of the planters in the provincial and isolated world of the early South was obvious).

Above all, the drama of white culture was played out against the reality of the presence of the Negro. Black people in their own rich cultural variety and creative interaction with whites, deeply affected the emerging regional culture—its foods, dress, language, religion, labor attitudes, and entire psychology—in ways still only partially explored and understood. Between the founding of the Republic and secession—the lifetime of a man—the white population of the South had multiplied five times and had expanded westward and southward across the Mississippi delta into Texas. But blacks had multiplied nearly as rapidly, an unparalleled New World phenomenon. Except for the relatively few whites subsisting in real mountain isolation from these tides of growth, Southern whites lived in physical, or at least ideological, proximity to black people and their bondage.

The implications of this were felt at the deepest level of social consciousness. It was in their perception of black folk that whites ultimately perceived and understood their own nature. From the earliest days of American interracial history, as Winthrop Jordan has shown, Southern whites have identified themselves in terms of the Negro, have forced the slave to embody their fantasies, to represent and act out a life in counterpoint.[8] In part, whites cultivated a keen sense of superiority, their "chivalry and high sense of honor," by comparison with the alleged moral inferiority of the slaves—a mechanism of race relations designed to place maximum status distance between white and black.[9] But this intimate psychological symbiosis was more than an instrument of social apartheid. The black man was, after all, called on to embody, not only *despised* qualities (including private lusts), but also admirable, even unattainably elevated "feminine" *virtues* as well: loyalty, devotion, earthly fatalism, humility—the very qualities of the idealized Christian that whites were entreated to cultivate within themselves. As the slave was perceived as possessing basic moral failings *and* virtues, the white self-image was reinforced in all its arrogance and Christian guilt. To be sure, the Negro was perpetually the outsider, barred from real community within the tight kinship circles that knit Southern rural society. At the same moment, it was certain that without black men and women there would have been no distinctive Southern culture and social psychology such as presented itself to the North in 1860.

This matrix of race, class, and cultural consciousness constituted a sort of protonationalism, a sense of regional singularity and anxiety, that was susceptible to political exploitation by its most self-aware and endangered element, the slaveholders. It may well be argued that before February 8, 1861, Southern nationalism was a doctrinal abstraction. With the creation of the Confederacy on that day, and the subsequent outbreak of civil war, however, the concept rapidly gained substance. A sufficiently distinctive core of ideas was believed to exist. The majority of whites in the slave states were for the moment convinced emotionally and/or intellectually that concrete and immediate interests were at stake—broadly speaking, the survival of their way of life. And the effects of contingency came into play in a hundred ways: South Carolina's clever haste, President Buchanan's vacillation, misconceptions of Lincoln's radicalism, events leading to the stand at Fort Sumter, and, above all, the existence of the new Southern nation as a legal and constitutional entity that now aroused grudging or wholehearted sympathy, wounded or vain pride, love of home and family now threatened, honor, masculinity, and all the rest.

In the midst of continuing anguish and uncertainty within the slave states about whether separation and independence were either wise or necessary, news of the First Battle of Manassas struck a resonant chord. The bridge seemed to have been burned, and the steadiest men and women soon realized that a prolonged and terrible war was unavoidable. "[William Henry] Trescot says this victory will be our ruin," South Carolina diarist Mary Boykin Chesnut wrote. "It lulls us into a fools paradise of conceit at our superior virtue, and the shameful farce of their flight will wake every inch of their manhood."[10] The real test of self-identity and political loyalty now lay ahead. Historian Luraghi has stressed that, if an ideology is concrete and real, all members of that society "must be convinced of the truth and the moral valor of a given ideology . . . otherwise the 'historic bloc' would melt away and nobody would fight."[11] The coming hard months would begin to melt fantasy from true belief. But surely many fought—and died.

Notes

1. Edward A. Pollard, *The First Year of the War* (Richmond, Va.: West & Johnston, 1862), p. 133.

2. David M. Potter, "The Historian's Use of Nationalism and Vice Versa," in *The South and the Sectional Conflict* (Baton Rouge: Louisiana State University Press, 1968), pp. 47-49.

3. Kenneth Stampp, "The Southern Road to Appomattox," Cotton Memorial Papers, No. 4 (El Paso: The University of Texas Press, 1969), p. 18.

4. Raimondo Luraghi, "The Civil War and the Modernization of American Society: Social Structure and the Industrial Revolution in the Old South before and during the War," *Civil War History* 18 (September 1972), pp. 230-50; Eugene Genovese, *Roll, Jordan, Roll: The World the Slaves Made* (New York: Pantheon, 1974), p. 608.

5. Luraghi, "The Civil War," pp. 241-42.

6. Genovese, *Roll, Jordan, Roll*, p. 608.

7. William Howard Russell, *My Diary North and South* (Boston: T.O.H.P. Burnham, 1863), pp. 162-63.

8. Winthrop Jordan, *White over Black: American Attitudes Toward the Negro, 1550-1812* (Chapel Hill: University of North Carolina Press, 1968).

9. *DeBow's Review* 31 (September 1861), p. 301.

10. Mary Boykin Chesnut, *A Diary from Dixie*, ed. Ben Ames Williams (Boston: Houghton Mifflin, 1949), p. 91.

11. Luraghi, "The Civil War," p. 239.

17

HIERARCHY AND DEMOCRACY: THE PARADOX OF THE SOUTHERN EXPERIENCE
Lawrence Goodwyn

The tragic discontinuities of the Southern heritage beckon to poets with vivid signals of paradox: whip and whippoorwill, triumph and disaster, hauteur and hookworm. Taken in all its parts, it seems a marvelous, forested landscape through which the novelist, the balladeer, the folklorist may pick his way, knowing in advance that, whatever he seeks, his findings promise to be rich in two highly serviceable ingredients: "symbol" and "myth." Marvelous—because in such a country of clashing elements, it is not essential to understand the whole; it is necessary merely to exploit the pieces at one's selective pleasure. Or so it seems.

How we historians envy our colleagues across the campus, ensconced in their English seminars, all aflower in metaphor and symbol. We puzzle over the disparity: while our literary counterparts seem to exploit Southern materials without pausing to sort them out, the poor historian is forced to sort them out before he can deal with them at all. How grotesquely unfair! To be burdened with such a muddle of a forest. To be silenced until orderly dynamics are perceived among the trees. To be under the imperative, not to glory in the celebration of the foliage, but to explain the relationship of the leaves. Not to exploit paradox, but to make sense of it.

Envy, yes. And its product, trepidation. How cautiously we historians tiptoe into the dense underbrush, with only the contradictions of Southern memory to guide us, uncertain whether we are fatally compromised because we have only one eye and thus are without depth perception or (perhaps beguiled by the thought that we may be the true pathfinders) because we are one-eyed men in the country of the blind. A foolish calling then, to be such a regional antiquarian, a seeker without adequate lenses, an investigator compromised in his premise, a practitioner of a futile pastime: the Historian of the South.

For long years, he was a social type not greatly to be courted outside the region because his prose appeared deadened by limp passages of apologetics: such a mode of discourse transparently did not lend itself to mighty themes. The judgment, however unwanted, seemed particularly vivid should Southern historical literature be compared to the rhythms of William Faulkner and Richard Wright or to those of Ralph Ellison and Katherine Anne Porter. In contrast to the region's renowned novelists, the offerings of Southern historians appeared timid and woodenly defensive, differing only in the minor variations they provided on the theme of apology. Perhaps most distressing of all, they seemed to stalk only safe and familiar trails through the forest. They thus were vulnerable to a most grave literary indictment—they repeated one another.[1]

On rare occasions—they were very few and they were greatly spaced in time—a voice would appear from the academy that would be perceived as aberrant. A lonely scholar, writing in the first decade of the twentieth century, offered an essay entitled "Reconstruction and Its Benefits." His was a curious vision, deeply threatening if anyone were to take it seriously, but not so, it quickly became apparent, because no one did take it seriously. Learned battalions, their Dunningite drums arrayed rank upon rank, rendered the solitary voice almost inaudible. Its cadenced arguments faded and, to many, seemed to disappear entirely.

Two generations later, another aberrant sound became audible, rising clearly and surprisingly out of that most tentative of expositions, a Ph.D. dissertation. This second toiler also seemed to find something of value in the departed Reconstruction era, although his focus was on a later time. In his graduate student days, he laid his vision before us in a superb biography of a forgotten and unlamented Southern dissenter and, in so doing, unveiled one of the central insights that thenceforth would inform his scholarly labor: the South was not a state of mind or a distinctive memory that needed to be evoked or apologized for; rather, the South was a land alive with variety. Indeed, the voices he found were so numerous and so diverse that it required a bit of analysis to uncover what they had in common. Our scholar supplied the analysis and thus enabled us to see that his varied people shared two elemental characteristics: they stood against the triumphant, defensive memory, and they were indiscriminately suppressed by that memory.

The probings of this second artisan produced a powerful exploratory work of scholarship. As the years passed and his researches penetrated ever-broadening areas of Southern life, he offered us, a decade later, his mature conclusions in a study equally as brilliant as his earlier effort, but now augmented by the broad rhythmic strokes of the great creative scholar. His chapter headings confronted not only the mighty themes of race, social conflict, and human striving and tragedy but also set the themes against a national canvas rather than a provincial one: Chapter II: "The Forked Road to Reunion"; Chapter XII: "The Mississippi Plan as the American Way";

Chapter XVI: "Bonds of Body and Spirit"; and for the concluding chapter, a gem of irony and understatement, the simple title: "The Return of the South."

How he must have puzzled over precisely what to call his mature work. The time of slavery had been the Old South. With the formal ending of slavery, many Americans saw, or thought they should see, a New South. But our scholar understood that the New South was much more like the old one than either influential Americans or influential Southerners were willing to acknowledge. With millions of people, white as well as black, yoked to the land in a degrading system of peonage, a process he detailed for us with irony and controlled indignation and sadness, he understood full well the culminating irony of the phrase, New South. So be it.

As a student of the South, he accepted irony as his handmaiden. He would explain in his introductory pages that the New South of his time was anchored firmly in the inherited power relationships of the old. He would suggest that, in the decades stretching beyond the limits of his own study, even more New Souths would be proclaimed by optimistic boosters and that they, too, would find their way into history books and into the region's self-understanding. And finally, he would gently suggest that only the incorrigibly romantic would accept these new appraisals as being more accurate than the old ones. But ironist that he was, he also would accept the fact that a great number of his readers would, in fact, be incorrigible romantics and would, therefore, misunderstand his book. Perhaps one should not stride too far in advance of one's own culture, lest one's voice grow not only faint but pass beyond hearing. Perhaps he thought of his predecessor. We cannot know. We can only be sure that, his tragic sense fully intact, he accepted these realities, powerful as they were and so deeply sanctioned as they were by the Southern orthodoxies from which he himself stood apart. The ironist named his book *Origins of the New South*.

Two discrete voices, one describing the years of Reconstruction, a voice unsanctioned, too "early" as the saying goes, and, accordingly, one that failed to penetrate into the national consciousness. The second, reaching its full power forty years later, describing the years after Reconstruction, a voice original but no longer wholly isolated and one inflected with subtlety and literary power, a voice, therefore, that, if it did not fully transform every nuance of the culture, nevertheless could not be ignored because, quite simply, its controlling rhythms and haunting ironies would not go away.

Du Bois and Woodward. They so pervasively hover over historians of the New South that we can scarcely find the words to do them credit.[2] It is not merely that they, more than anyone else, have made the scales fall from our eyes; not merely that we stand on their shoulders to see whatever it is we think we are seeing. To be content with such an explanation would be to participate in an insular historical tradition and in a language of self-congratulation that each of them, for different reasons, held in sober contempt. Rather, they hover over contemporary Southern historians because, as participants in the American historical tradition, they, like we, have had scant impact on the very American culture the study of which is our chosen pursuit. They hover over historians of the South because they stood isolated from the levers of cultural power in the common homeland. While Du Bois presumably would have been consoled and Woodward presumably is consoled by the thought that modern historians treasure their pioneering intuitions, neither, surely, has ever been much consoled by the very narrow limitations that describe that influence. Rather, one suspects, both have, each in his own time, fully appreciated the deeper irony that, in affecting their fellow scholars, they in no seminal way affected the larger American culture. And sharpest irony of all, they did not even decisively affect the culture in which their scholarly descendants labored. Both doubtless speedily and routinely noted the continuing irony of our continued illusions, even as we at various times over the years have gone about the business of honoring them. For while it is evident that Du Bois sought and Woodward continues to seek a historical language, and a conceptual framework to support such language, that would enable them to make their unsanctioned ideas fully comprehensible to their fellow Americans, it is equally evident that this objective has continued to prove maddeningly elusive. The fact points less readily to identifiable shortcomings on their part than to the power and narrowness of the received assumptions against which they have labored. Since one of them was, or at least became, a believing Marxist, and the other has remained not-so-believing, the constraints imbedded in modern languages of politics and social analysis may be suggested—if not made immediately self-evident. We can merely observe in passing that the received languages of politics did not arm either with the power to penetrate and alter that body of complacent assumptions that, in the aggregate, undergird contemporary American culture. In any case, the business-dominated and racially stratified New South of the post-Reconstruction era was, as Du Bois knew in 1910, of potentially long life; it was, as Woodward knew, still intact when *Origins* was first published in 1951. That the modes of racial hierarchy have since 1951 altered, in form if not yet in underlying substance, is, perhaps needless to emphasize, not because we Americans suddenly found a way to hear these scholars' words. In terms of political consciousness and the underlying assumptions informing the culture itself, both Du Bois and Woodward continue to be, as they were in 1910 and 1951, respectively, voices that we have not yet fully heard.

The alterations in interracial social etiquette in recent years grew out of the dynamics of the civil rights movement of the 1960s. Two indigenous elements, the Southern black church and a certain youthful militancy, plus one external influence, the philosophical and tactical teachings of Mahatma Gandhi, combined to have far more to do with the shaping of this movement than were the scholarly insights of either Du Bois or Woodward. On the other hand, in terms of underlying economic power relationships not organically intertwined with questions of caste—power relationships that have been the objects of prolonged inquiry by both Du Bois and Woodward—the civil rights movement, like the larger society within which it existed, cannot be said to have been creatively analytical in ways these two men would respect.

Rather, what has happened in recent years is that many of the ideas of Woodward and Du Bois, like many of the ideas of the civil rights movement, have simply been incorporated into the received culture of America in ways that preserve the structures of power and privilege, including racial privilege, than inform that culture. These relationships are hierarchical rather than democratic. On this conclusion, Du Bois, Woodward, and fervent participants in the civil rights movement would doubtless all have agreed. Indeed, the fact is probably their strongest point of contact.[3]

Thus, while we can acknowledge the existence of aberrant autonomous scholarship within the Southern historical tradition—and aberrant, democratic social conduct during the years of Reconstruction, Populism, and the civil rights movement—we are forced at the same time to acknowledge the continuing power of the inherited hierarchical culture of America itself.[4]

Where, it is fair to ask, does yet another conference on the New South fit into such a national pattern of historical experience? How can such a conference be remotely relevant to the realities of contemporary life, contemporary culture, or even contemporary scholarship beyond regional limits? How can such a conference avoid the fatal preoccupations with Southern distinctiveness that have served as a sanctioned device through which, for these many generations, more organic problems of social analysis have been skirted? Can such a conference avoid being fatally provincial in geographical interest and narrow in intellectual range? Can such a conference address matters of interest to America, much less the world? In short, can a conference on the South be at one and the same time two things: Southern and creative? Or are we doomed to rehashing the metaphors of paradox that, in our time, have become the settled apologetic tradition of white Southern historical writing?

These are all fair, if awkward, questions. I, for one, think they can be given an affirmative answer, although, for reasons I shall endeavor to offer, an affirmative answer necessarily must at this juncture remain heavily qualified.

We may begin by looking into the origins of what I have called "the settled apologetic tradition of white Southern historical writing." Where did it begin? In the broadest sense, it has been with us as long as the South has had a racial caste system and a corresponding psychological need to rationalize that system. For many generations, this meant that "Southern history" existed principally as a literary form that had the political effect of defending slavery. But since the Civil War, particularly since the 1890s, when historical research and writing first became professionalized, the theme of distinctiveness necessary to defend the peculiar institution has been broadened to include states' rights in politics, graceful manners and a sense of community in social relations, the plantation as a centerpiece of economic interpretation, and finally (and as part of various excursions into what might be described as geographical determinism) even the uniqueness of the climate. It may be observed, parenthetically, that all of these approaches have provided ways for beleaguered white Southern authors to step gingerly around the minefield of race. All provide evidence of the varieties of hierarchical ways of thinking in the homeland. Consciously or unconsciously, all express white supremacist modes of thought.

The emergence of this broader tradition of apologetics predates the emergence of professional historical writing in the region. Although it would not be easy to fix that moment in time precisely, I believe it can be fixed in a cultural sense: one need only borrow from the Southern literary tradition and, in so doing, gain permission to employ a useful symbol. I hope, therefore, to be granted scholarly leave to encase the ensuing historical assessment within the boundaries of a metaphor. Worse than that, a rather elaborate metaphor running several pages in length. And worse than *that*, a metaphor so engrained in Southern memory, so familiar, so encrusted with romanticism and nostalgia, so old timey, as to have soared quite beyond categories of historical allegory into realms of simple cliché. I ask indulgence because I have in mind that time so long ago, well over a century now, when a certain war had gone on for much longer than anybody had feared, when the casualty lists had become enormous, even as the outcome remained shrouded in uncertainty: in short, that day, that very last day, when, as William Faulkner once put it, "it all had not happened yet."

It is July 3, 1863, and the wooded area that is our setting is near that small town in Pennsylvania. Like most modern wars—and this is one of the first of the modern wars—the specific cause of the conflict is being blown away by the savagery of conflict itself. Everyone knows, although many will not yet concede, that the war is over black slavery. For reasons of national self-interest and perceived idealism, one side has promulgated a document of emancipation. And very quickly as historical time is measured, the leaders of the other side, for reasons of national self-interest and perceived idealism, will promulgate another document of emancipation. We hold this irony in our hand, inspect human dogmatism and human frailty, put the irony aside. From this day forward to the final curtain, the intensity of the struggle will increase and the slaughter will be greater even as the precipitating cause becomes more remote. In our metaphor, as in the historical moment it seeks to describe, no one knows these things. It is July 3, 1863, and it has all "not happened yet." The night before, an argument takes place between the two ranking generals of this most remarkable of armies that peoples our metaphor. One general, a man "ahead of his time," has concluded from two years of mayhem that the traditional rules of war have changed radically. He has concluded from what he has seen that massed infantry—even infantry whose officers believe to be the best in the world—cannot charge concentrations of massed artillery that modern industry has begun to fashion. Fifty-one years later, in 1914, French generals, who do not see what James Longstreet sees, will try the traditional way one more time, and thousands of working-class French soldiers and middle-class French officers will die providing their leaders with a schoolbook example. The French generals have little excuse in 1914; perhaps, in 1863, the other Southern general does. Robert E. Lee is the most successful leader in the war, and on this night before July 3, he and Longstreet, alone in a tent, disagree a final time. The attack, by those incomparable brigades of Southern infantry, will come across a mile of open field. At the end are heights. Atop the heights are brigades of excellent Union infantry. Among them and behind them is the best artillery in the war, commanded by the most competent artillery officers in the war. The attack—across the open field, up these heights, into this infantry and artillery—will be on the center of the Union line. Longstreet shakes his head, points out the hazards, proposes to Lee a flank movement as an alternative to frontal assault. They talk respectfully to each other while in disagreement. Lee says, finally, "They will break."

And so, on July 3, the Southern troops emerge from the woods into the open terrain, some forty regiments in nine brigades and, in the van, thirteen regiments in three brigades—thousands of youngsters, almost all of them between the ages of seventeen and twenty-five, lining up shoulder to shoulder in massed formations that stretch a mile across the open plain, their light blue regimental flags of Virginia fluttering in a Pennsylvania wind. Longstreet, in his anxiety and foreboding, has seen to it that the ground has been studied carefully, down to the smallest detail. A depression juts diagonally across the line of march. It will destroy the order of the formations. Care must be taken that the ranks are reformed when the regiments emerge on the far side. It will not be easy. The commanders agree on how it will be done. The Confederate bombardment is heavy, but not so heavy as the one that is yet to answer it. When the Southern guns fall silent, the allocated ammunition exhausted, the word is given, and the massed regiments move forward. It is all right. As everyone knows, in both armies, infantry is the backbone of this army of our metaphor. Not even the Union general in the West, the one named Grant, can mount the kind of massed infantry assaults that have made the Army of Northern Virginia the most fearsome force of the war. This army is a brotherhood, the kind that can only be built on repeated success. It is, therefore, a brotherhood rare in war; the officers deeply confident in their men; the men, ably led and knowing it, deeply confident in their wartime community. They, like their leader, Lee, are sure the enemy will "break." Hasn't it always? Forward the van then, under the confident young major general whose long hair bangs in ringlets; forward also under three brigade commanders, thirteen regimental colonels, and hundreds of company commanders, the thousands of people go.

Historical memory hurries over the next part. Massed infantry regiments, marching slowly, so slowly, across an open field: a proper target for artillery canister. The ranks are torn open, quickly filled by able men, quickly dressed by able officers. But when the depression is reached, the formations are badly askew. And then a sight that makes anxious observers on both sides hold their breath in wonder, in fear, in admiration. The regiments are seen to be halted now, halted under artillery fire, the ranks reforming, under fire, the blue flags lining up again (some say as on a parade ground; what poise this army has!) and then forward once more, into the canister, into rolling musketry, up the heights, into whatever it is that constitutes the Army of the Potomac.

It is happening now, the metaphor at its extreme limit, the high tide of the Confederacy, Pickett's charge at Gettysburg. Images form that romantics will paint into the memory of a people: Brigadier General Armistead at the head of his brigade atop Cemetery Ridge, one hand on a Union field gun, his other hand holding a raised sword that calls for its surrender. Armistead near the moment of his death, a symbol of the cause, the one not quite lost. It is, indeed, a symbolic moment, for somehow a faith is being born. Many of those who participated in the moment of its birth, however, will not even know, for they are gone. The three brigade commanders of the van are dead. Of the thirteen regimental commanders, thirteen are down—seven dead, six wounded. At the head of them all, Pickett, alone of the senior commanders, escapes being hit. He will never again be the same: his division dying around him, his faith in Lee shattered and never to be fully restored, his elan for the assault forever used up at the very moment his name becomes mythically linked to the very idea of offensive warfare. Symbols aside, he will never again lead a charge to glory across ruined fields. Nor will Lee. The Army of Northern Virginia, henceforth, will fight on the defensive—fatal for an army whose glory was assault and whose ranks contained shrinking reserves.

Lost Causes, like other causes, require a usable past. The army of the South, and the society it represented, impaled itself on the guns of Cemetary Ridge, on a present it could not understand, on a future it could not contemplate, because it had renounced the essential ingredient of contemplation: the capacity for critical reflection. It was one of those tragic junctures in human history when people died because they could not think. This understanding rises unsought from the eerie battlefield silence that followed Pickett's charge. Unmistakably, it provides a "usable past." But it is too strange; it is too much. The logic is perceived to be un-Southern. So fatefully, it is laid aside. The white South therefore looks elsewhere for a usable past. Our metaphor necessarily nears its completion in another formulation: from this moment, the South was to be defended, not appraised. The Lost Cause, and the customs that undergirded it, needed to be honored, not retrospectively considered. In keeping with the stirring brush strokes that gave heroic, if rigid, character to the painting of Armistead, a folk loyalty took rigid definition after the surrender at Appomatox: independent thought was unpatriotic. The rock foundation of racial hierarchy having been sundered, the cause required the defense of the hierarchy itself. One defended one's captains. A fearful dynamic was set loose on the younger generation and on the unborn generations. In politics, after Appomattox, the army of the Confederacy remained a monolith—the party of the Confederacy, the party of white supremacy.

With stubborn consistency, Longstreet, surviving the war, continued to acknowledge radically altered conditions and endeavored to face them with the only tool he had: the force of an independent mind. He joined the interracial Southern Republican party. In keeping with the new dynamics of Southern patriotism, he was, perforce, ostracized by many of his former comrades-in-arms. A new military orthodoxy quickly took form and held for as long as there lived Southerners who knew the personalities who had fought the war: Longstreet, not Lee, lost Gettysburg. In time, this orthodoxy lost its force, but the deeper emotional and social rhythms sustaining the rigid new faith of regional loyalty did not lose force. Increasingly, the white Southern custom of tribal loyalty and political hierarchy completely supplanted the older, more complex, and more democratic rhythms that had animated Thomas Jefferson in less beleaguered times. Conformity in thought inevitably produced a ritual of sloganeering, mobilized with martial simplicity and power. Lee's "They will break," having failed the test of historical serviceability, had to be laid aside. Later slogans would meet a similar fate. In Reconstruction, the Democratic party would look to the past, its sloganized name becoming, quite simply, the party of redemption. The phrase had only a brief moment of tenuous applicability, if only because the restored leadership was so palpably different from the remembered inheritance. The "redeemers" who repelled the interracial society of Reconstruction became, in the next generation, the businessmen who repelled the democratic ideas of Populism. The new party of business dusted off the now-dated Reconstruction slogans of "Negro domination" and employed them to overwhelm the agrarian democrats. Hierarchy, in economics as in social relations, was preserved; the old captains were honored and followed, even when they became new captains.

The slogans changed, the economic structure evolved, but the rigidity of the old hierarchical ways of thinking that undergirded both did not change. The incipiently egalitarian views of Jefferson, not unflawed but easily capable of expansion, withered into a cramped defense of the Lost Cause, a tribal faith that, through ceaseless repetition and elaboration, fashioned new modes of social and intellectual deference throughout the fabric of Southern society. If the new structures of conformity were not quite so ritualized as in the bygone centuries of feudalism, they were in no sense compatible with the kind of freewheeling intellectual life so organic to a truly vital democratic society. After the Populists went down in the 1890s, seemingly taking with them the possibilities of serious public consideration of serious democratic evolution of the society, the number of Southern progressives decreased. More importantly, their hopes shrank, too. Small changes—even the appearance of small changes, sometimes even the *hope* of small changes—became the basis for yet another public proclamation of a new "New South." While impoverished white Southerners in each generation adopted, tested, and were forced to abandon each New South creed, black Southerners in each generation hailed the appearance of the "New Negro." Although progress in this latter area was marginally more visible than in the sundry New Souths, the underlying structures of hierarchy, in both thought and social organization, proved remarkably well equipped to withstand all the New Souths and New Negroes. The rigidity of inherited power relationships infected every area of social and intellectual exchange—in the universities, in the churches, and—always—in race and economic relations.

To independent and creative observers—and by definition the new social order produced very few of them—the stirring up of racial animosities among the laboring people of the region became a most serviceable and repeatedly employed tactic of Southern business. Despite a formidable mass of evidence surfacing to this effect in each generation of the twentieth century, the remarkably close-knit social and economic hierarchies within Southern society have been characterized as being composed of racial "moderates"—in Southern textbooks written by Southern historians laboring in Southern universities. These "moderates" have been, and for the most part still are, portrayed as working gracefully to bring "progress" in race relations, hampered in their efforts though they have been by racial "extremists" unerringly found to reside in the white laboring population. The intellectual dynamic set loose by the Lost Cause—full of self-deception as it was in conception—may be seen to have had a long life, one that continues to the present. Despite Du Bois, despite Woodward, despite the events of history itself, the apologetic tradition of Southern historical writing remains intact, imprisoned in nostalgia and defensiveness. Inspected closely, this literary avalanche appears firmly encased in a kind of tenacious provincial romanticism that serves as a cover for a deeply ingrained pessimism about human possibility. Such pessimism is the cornerstone, and the rational defense, of all hierarchies in human societies.

Can Southerners create a New South? By a number of indicators, black Southerners appear quite willing to give the matter a real try. Impediments to aspiration and staying power seem to cluster in other quarters. Let us rephrase the question then. Can white Southerners play a significant role in creating a genuine New South? That is to say, to repeat in a more precise context the question posed at the outset, can white Southerners be at one and the same time two things: Southern and creative?

The answer, self-evidently, is "yes." But also self-evidently, the answer can scarcely be "yes" if white Southerners insist on being defensive merely to earn the credentials to call themselves "Southern." To be creative necessitates the licensing of a new tradition of critical thought rather than ritualistically honoring the tribal memory, now so highly developed some 115 years after Gettysburg, of impaling ourselves on the logic of the present and of impaling also the hopes for a future of dignity of so many millions of Southern people of diverse ancestry. Thankfully, few people still care whether Lee or Longstreet lost the Battle of Gettysburg, and growing numbers of Southerners seem less than overwhelmingly concerned that it was lost at all. This seems a helpful development.

A forebear of mine who possessed the unwieldly but distinctly Southern name of Jeremiah James Madison Bloodworth and who died of his wounds at the age of twenty-four in Richmond in 1864 would not have applauded all of these sentiments. On the other hand, I cannot say that I would have applauded what I suspect were his sentiments toward Frederick Douglass. Although I prefer to believe that Jeremiah was more or less as good a man as circumstances permitted him to be during his time on the planet, the simple historical fact is that his beliefs get in the way of our time on the planet. We do share with Jeremiah, however, one important historical coincidence: to be alive at a time when new ideas about the scope of human aspiration struggle for life in our homeland. If Jeremiah was not fully alert to these confluences, two men, Du Bois and Woodward, certainly have been. Both scholars help us to understand that the topic question of this conference, the "New South," may require a measure of clarification in its premise. The issue seems not to be about the extent to which we have another New South, but whether the most recent new one is any less hierarchical or any more democratic than all the other new ones that have been proclaimed in the past hundred years.

It seems fitting to end the metaphor where it began, with James Longstreet. He, too, is now an authentic part of the heritage, and we, like Longstreet with Lee, are once again in a rare moment of respectful internal discussion. The hierarchical tradition is real, but as Du Bois and Woodward have labored to tell us, it is not an unassailable monolith. The democratic impulse still maintains a discernible presence, and one remains cautiously hopeful. It seems merely necessary to acknowledge, then, that the apologetics of white supremacy still suffuse the latest New South—in the corporations, in the churches, in the universities, in every social class. Not much appears possible until this awkward historical reality is more widely understood. No paradox seems visible here. On the contrary, the causal relation that *is* visible has been hovering over the historical profession for a long time: the paradox is not in something called "Southern history," but rather in the way that that history has been conveyed. It would appear that we should be about our work. For as a fellow at Gettysburg had the wit to perceive, it will require more than sloganeering to climb those heights.

Notes

1. Louis D. Rubin, Jr., ed., *A Bibliographical Guide to the Study of Southern Literature* (Baton Rouge: Louisiana State University Press, 1969), provides an indispensable introduction to the region's literature. For biographical details of Southern historians who have attempted to wrestle with the concrete events that have helped to inform this literary outpouring, see Wendell Holmes Stephenson, *The South Lives in History: Southern Historians and Their Legacy* (Baton Rouge: Louisiana State University Press, 1955), and Wendell Holmes Stephenson, *Southern History in the Making: Pioneer Historians of the South* (Baton Rouge: Louisiana State University Press, 1964).

2. W. E. B. Du Bois, "Reconstruction and Its Benefits," *American Historical Review* XV (1910), pp. 781-99; W. E. B. Du Bois, *Souls of Black Folk* (Chicago: A. C. McClury & Co., 1903); C. Vann Woodward, *Tom Watson: Agrarian Rebel* (New York: Macmillan, 1938); C. Vann Woodward, *Origins of the New South* (Baton Rouge: Louisiana State University Press, 1951).

3. See, for example, C. Vann Woodward, *The Burden of Southern History*, rev. ed. (Baton Rouge: Louisiana State University Press, 1968), "The Populist Heritage and the Intellectual," pp. 141-66.

4. For example, in Richard Hofstadter's prize-winning analysis of American reform movements, *The Age of Reform*, the author presents an interpretation that differs wildly from Woodward's analysis; at the same time, Hofstadter praises Woodward's work and appears to build on it. It is now evident, after some passing years have enabled these dynamics to be assessed, that Hofstadter actually grounded

his interpretation on a number of traditional and rather complacent assumptions about the meaning of American democracy that are measurably at odds with the premises governing Woodward's study. In Hofstadter's treatment, Woodward's professional status is acknowledged while his scholarly findings, skeptical as they are about the general health of the democratic polity, are put aside. While Woodward portrays the Populists as sensibly advancing needed reforms, and therefore implicates the larger society that resists those reforms, Hofstadter portrays the agrarians as nonsensically advancing extreme ideas and, by implication, exonerates the forces of tradition from involvement in the failure of reform.

In a similar manner, the triumphs and defeats of the civil rights era are increasingly coming to be understood in terms of the success of the movement's moderates (such as Martin Luther King, Jr.) and the failure of its radicals (such as the Black Panthers). Although this assessment seems to serve the psychological needs of many white Americans, while at the same time preserving Hofstadterian complacency about the status of democratic forms in contemporary American society, it is grounded on a gross misreading of historical events: the moderates themselves were defeated. This has been clear—to the participants at least—from the moment it happened. Debbie Louis, *And We Are Not Saved: A History of the Movement as People* (New York: Doubleday, 1970); C. Eric Lincoln, *Sounds of the Struggle: Persons and Perspectives in Civil Rights* (New York: Peter Smith, 1968).

To complete the general point, while individual and widely scattered intellectual breakthroughs in interpreting power relationships in American society have been achieved by a handful of scholars, their underlying perspectives have in no sense come to inform the general culture. In terms of reflecting a comprehensive understanding of the American (or Southern) experience, inherited cultural assumptions grounded in the idea of progress prevail absolutely as if these scholars had never written a word.

18

DOROTHY TILLY AND THE FELLOWSHIP OF THE CONCERNED

Arnold Shankman

The civil rights movement of the past three decades has unquestionably brought about some of the most significant changes in Southern history. Thus far, scholars studying this movement have given inadequate attention to those white Southern women who sought "a way to ease the tensions of our section and make it a proving ground for democracy."[1] One such woman was Dorothy Eugenia Rogers Tilly (1883-1970). Frail, barely five feet tall, addicted to hats with roses, she was, at first glance, an unlikely crusader for civil rights, but few fought as hard and with as much conviction as she to better the lives of black Southerners.

Born in Hampton, Georgia, on June 30, 1883, Dorothy Tilly was the fourth of eleven children, eight of whom survived infancy. Her father, the Reverend Richard Wade Rogers, graduated in 1869 from Washington College (now Washington and Lee). He was a Methodist preacher and from 1896 to 1901 was president of Reinhardt Junior College in Waleska, Georgia. Her mother, the former Frances (Fannie) Eubank, graduated from Wesleyan College in 1876, and was a strong supporter of higher education. Both parents sought to instill in each of their children a social conscience. "As a child," Dorothy Tilly remembered:

I could not help hearing the troubles of people and the community as they flowed over our doorsteps. They hurt me deeply. . . . So through the years, I have tried to enter into the suffering of others and to translate them to others.[2]

Not surprisingly, at age twelve she was elected president of the children's missionary society of her father's church.

All eight surviving Rogers children were given a college education, and Dorothy graduated with honors from both Reinhardt (1899) and Wesleyan colleges (1901), where she majored in mathematics. In 1903, two years after graduation from Wesleyan, she married Milton Eben Tilly, a graduate of the University of Georgia and an Atlanta chemical distributor. They had one son, Eben, born in 1904. Following his birth, doctors, concerned about Dorothy Tilly's fragile health, advised her not to have any more children. Milton Tilly, whose social conscience was as sensitive as his wife's, advised her to spend her time working with church groups and taking summer school courses at various colleges.[3]

It was Dorothy Tilly's good fortune that, as she was involving herself with church work, the Methodist Episcopal Church, South, was becoming increasingly more liberal on the race question. She served on various committees for the North Georgia Conference concerned with children, tenancy, and race relations. For several years, she conducted leadership seminars at Paine College to prepare Afro-American women to accept positions of responsibility in the black religious community. She also held leadership classes for whites at Emory University, Blue Ridge, North Carolina, and at the Episcopal Leadership Training School in Richmond, Virginia. As superintendent of children's work for the church in north Georgia, she sponsored various activities that would promote tolerance so that "when our children are grown a better understanding will exist between the two races."[4]

Even though he remained in the background, Milton Tilly encouraged his wife to involve herself more in efforts to improve the lot of Afro-Americans. In fact, in the late 1920s, he would insist that, before breakfast, they ride through the Negro slums of Atlanta. Once he took her to the service entrance of Atlanta's fashionable Piedmont Hotel, where both observed hungry Afro-American children raiding garbage cans for bits of edible food. When Dorothy Tilly protested to her husband that she did not wish to see such horrible things, he responded: "If seeing [this] . . . hurts you enough, you will tell other people and they will do something." He also promised to give his wife whatever financial support she needed to "get involved."[5]

Shortly after witnessing the starving youngsters, Tilly joined the commission on Interracial Cooperation, then one of the more progressive civil rights groups in the South. In 1931, she was one of the first Georgians to become a member of the Association of Southern Women for the Prevention of Lynching (ASWPL). Within a few years, she was named to its national executive committee and was appointed secretary of its Georgia chapter. With Jessie Daniel Ames, founder and moving force behind the ASWPL, she investigated lynchings in Georgia and became increasingly aware of the plight of Negroes in the South.[6]

Perhaps the most important crusade that Dorothy Tilly led during this part of her life was one that sought to establish a state institution for the care and training of delinquent Negro girls. Governor Eugene Talmadge let it be known that he did not approve of such an institution even after black women's groups donated to the state land on which the reformatory could be built. Tilly mobilized Methodist women and others to petition their legislators to vote money for constructing and operating a delinquent girls' home. She quickly learned that there would be no training school as long as Talmadge was governor. Therefore, in 1942, in return for Ellis Arnall's support for the training school and his repudiation of lynch law justice, Tilly endorsed his candidacy for governor and persuaded hundreds of influential women to campaign in his behalf. Arnall was elected governor, and in 1943, the school opened its doors in Macon.[7]

Over the next seven years, Tilly engaged in a wide variety of activities. She served as a private lobbyist in Washington for the Farm Security Administration,[8] held high positions in the Women's Society of Christian Service of the Methodist Church, observed labor disputes in the North, served on national commissions concerned with the care of children, and visited Palestine as a member of a national church delegation trying to resolve the Arab-Jewish stalemate over the future of Jerusalem. In all of these jobs, she served with distinction, but it was to be her work for civil rights that was to be her most lasting contribution.

In December 1945, Tilly was the only white woman and one of only two Southerners appointed to President Truman's Committee on Civil Rights. Her work for the committee persuaded her that segregation was morally wrong, but she cautioned against depriving segregated schools of federal aid. Tilly and Frank Graham, the other Southern member of the committee, sought to soften the report so that the South was not the only section of the nation castigated for tolerating discrimination. This does not mean that she was reactionary or paternalistic. She heartily endorsed the forthright report of the commission, "To Secure These Rights." "I do not believe," she publicly stated, "that there is anyone in the United States, who, had he been with us and seen the things we did, would have signed his name to any less strong a report." Tilly toured all sections of the nation to win support for the recommendations of "To Secure These Rights."[9]

But as Tilly traveled about the North, Midwest, and West, she knew that her real work was in the South. She was a charter member of the Southern Regional Council (SRC), which was founded in 1944 to replace the increasingly stodgy Commission on Interracial Cooperation. In her capacity as fieldworker for the SRC, she investigated the 1946 race riot in Columbia, Tennessee, and the brutal lynching of two couples later that year in Monroe, Georgia. The ASWPL had dissolved in 1942, and it was apparent to Tilly that a new group was needed to carry on its work.[10]

SRC officials, who had forced the aggressive Jessie Daniel Ames into retirement, knew that Tilly had the leadership qualities to organize such a new group. When she had been appointed director of women's work for the SRC, she had held a number of well-received women's conferences. Tilly therefore was encouraged to schedule a meeting of women active in Southern churches and synagogues so that a new group could be formed.

More than 160 women representing the three major faiths and most Southern church groups assembled at the Wesley Memorial Church Building on September 8-9, 1949. The interracial group heard Eleanor Roosevelt speak on "The Declaration of Human Rights and the Community." Then Tilly asked the women present to take the following pledge:

I AM concerned that our constitutional freedoms are not shared by all our people; my religion convinces me that they must be and gives me courage to study, work, and lead others to the fulfillment of equal justice under the law. I will respond to calls from the Southern Regional Council to serve my faith and my community in the defense of justice.

Conference participants were told about the sorry state of law enforcement and of prison conditions in the South. They also were told that things would not change unless women used their influence to ensure that equal justice was accorded all.[11]

The organization that Tilly formed soon took on the name of the Fellowship of the Concerned (F of C). It was an unusual group. It had no officers save Tilly, charged no dues, met irregularly, and only required that its members sit in courts as observers and inform themselves of the condition of law enforcement in their communities. They also were encouraged to accompany Negroes to the polls and to work for decent educational and housing opportunities for blacks. Hundreds of pledges poured into SRC headquarters in Atlanta each month, and by February 1950, over 4,000 women had joined the F of C. Most of the early members were Georgians, but from the beginning, there were pledges from women in each of the former Confederate states and Kentucky. Tilly sent several pamphlets to members with instructions to read them and then to distribute them to their local law enforcement officers. The most widely circulated tract was entitled "Race and Law Enforcement," a brief primer on how communities could avoid racial friction.[12]

Courtroom visits by white-gloved F of C members did bring changes. Some, to be sure, were merely cosmetic. Embarrassed officials ordered that dirty rooms be cleaned and that those attending trials rise whenever the judge entered the courtroom. Among the more substantive changes were those affected by lawyers, who, conscious of the prominent, well-dressed women attentively watching the proceedings and occasionally even taking notes, became careful not to insult Negro defendants and witnesses by calling them "boy," "uncle," or "auntie." Spectators also were more circumspect in their behavior, and jurors took their jobs more seriously.[13]

An especially important goal of the F of C was the elimination of lynchings from the South. There are documented examples of incidents that might well have resulted in violence had it not been for the efforts of F of C members. Tilly was enough of a realist to know that not every situation would be resolved satisfactorily. "We may not always get justice," she admitted, "but we can get public opinion so stirred up that the same thing can't ever happen in that community again." To Tilly's great pleasure, in 1952 there were no lynchings in any of the forty-eight states.[14]

Believing that racial violence would continue to decrease, Tilly began to reorient the activities of the F of C. She anticipated that the Supreme Court would soon outlaw school segregation, and she wanted Southern women to serve as the "shock absorbers" of social change. Therefore, she decided to hold workshops for the F of C in Atlanta and elsewhere. Many of these meetings during the early years were concerned with school desegregation and justice in the courts; later workshops focused on such varied topics as the United Nations, juvenile delinquency, alcoholism, and open housing.[15]

To pay for these workshops and conferences, Tilly was given some direct assistance by the SRC, but most of the money had to come from foundations and religious organizations. Tilly developed some skill as a fund-raiser. In order that both rich and poor could come to her meetings, she sought funds to pay all or part of the expenses of those who attended. This was especially important during the years when the White Citizens' Council mobilized opposition to integration. Women chosen to attend the meetings were usually selected by church and synagogue groups. Sometimes they found it prudent not to tell their husbands that they were going to F of C workshops; rather, they said they were going shopping or were visiting relatives. "These are brave women," Tilly declared, "many going against the will of their families by their strong convictions. Their slogan is to find a conviction that will not rest, a faith that will not shrink and courage that will not waiver."[16]

Tilly was well aware that workshops had no real value unless they were followed up by action. For this reason, she was careful to correspond with workshop participants months after each of her conferences. Tilly was determined to ensure that "her" women were actively seeking to improve race relations in their communities. Women were encouraged—virtually ordered—to report on their activities. Scores of letters addressed to Tilly flooded the SRC headquarters each year from women eager to prove that they were worthy of membership in the F of C. It is notable that when Montgomery, Alabama, finally integrated its bus system F of C members were among the very first patrons of the desegregated buses.[17]

White members of the F of C found several ways to assist blacks and make themselves aware of race relations in their communities. After one F of C meeting, Kathryn Bullard, an official of the Baptist Woman's Missionary Union of North Carolina, invited for the first time an Afro-American woman to be an overnight guest in her home, spoke to an integrated group on the importance of literacy, and hired a black lady to work on her staff.[18] A middle-aged Alabamian whose husband held a state government job confessed that she could not do as much as she would like. "We own a house in Fairhope," she explained, "and have children in school and college." Nonetheless, she rejoined the local human relations group. One especially heartening response came from Loretto Chappell of Conley, Georgia:

Sent some money to a Negro youth who had been recommended to me, who was in need of help to further his education . . . his mother's home had been bombed. Visited with a racially mixed group. . . . I have been teaching one Negro woman to read, and a young man who joins us irregularly. . . . Correspond with one of the young men who was held in jail in Americus and with his mother. Went to Americus to attend his trial, only to find the date had been changed. . . . Took the opportunity of explaining to several friends the object of my visit and helped them to see the real injustices toward the Negro. . . . Have written to our congressman and senators about civil rights.[19]

Blacks also wrote to tell Tilly how her conferences had helped them. Constance Wyatt of Norfolk, Virginia, confessed that going to an F of C workshop in Atlanta "was my first trip into the deep South and quite frankly I had no previous desire to go there because I have often said, 'Lord, deliver me from any place worse than Virginia, the land where I was born.' " However, attendance at the F of C meeting caused her to reshape her ideas about whites. "Probably [I] would never believed, had I not been present, that such a meeting was possible in the South during these times. I doubted that people could come together and sit down and discuss sanely and intelligently the problem[s] which really exist in the South."[20]

At F of C workshops, the SRC remained in the background, and it made no effort to recruit members. Tilly gave minimal newspaper, radio, and television coverage to most F of C assemblies lest demonstrators harass F of C participants or Klansmen and other segregationists persecute liberal women's groups. Most politicians were too shrewd to attack church women publicly, but rabid anti-integrationists were not particular about whom they castigated. In 1958, Bill Cleghorn, a segregationist editor, sent reporters and photographers to an F of C meeting in Montgomery, Alabama, to photograph participants and to record their automobile license plates. Cleghorn subsequently published the names, addresses, and business connections of the husbands of the women at the meeting. For several weeks thereafter, F of C members in Montgomery received obscene telephone calls.[21]

Tilly was furious. She asked Cleghorn if he "realized how much you and the two men who sat outside really trampled on the basic rights guaranteed by the Constitution of the United States to all of us."[22] To her friends in Alabama, she offered these words of hope:

Reprisals have a way of striking back. I have found it al[ways] to be so. The men in the car, the uninvited guest and the editor are too *little* to intimidate praying women. Don't let them—defeat them. Don't give them that much power over your lives.[23]

Tilly was herself an object of harassment. In the late 1940s, a newspaper columnist denounced her as "a parasite who while living upon funds furnished by the Methodist Church had rendered much of her service to the cause of Socialism and Communism." An anonymous writer insisted, "You are not worthy to live in the South." Others asked the House Un-American Activities Committee to investigate her.[24]

In the 1950s and 1960s, Tilly frequently received nasty telephone calls and threatening letters. Some of her neighbors objected to her entertaining Negro guests in her home. For a while, hate mail and crank calls greatly disturbed her, "and many times," she wrote, "[I] fell in bed and prayed for strength and it always came." Later, she placed a small record player on her telephone table so that she could play the Lord's Prayer whenever she received an obscene call. "It always helps me," she declared, "and it silences the one at the other end of the phone." Once in a while, she would incessantly demand of her caller "Who is speaking?" without giving him much time to talk. If he responded Smith or Jones, she would leave the phone and not come back to it; if he gave his true name, Tilly continued to talk with him, holding a Bible in her hand.[25]

Even more menacing were threats from organized extremist groups. On at least one occasion, the Ku Klux Klan planned to bomb the Tilly residence. Fortunately, the plot was discovered before any damage could be done. Mayor William Hartsfield of Atlanta arranged for a street light to be placed in front of her house. A guard followed Tilly, and for a while, a police car cruised her street at night. J. Edgar Hoover, a personal friend of Tilly, sent FBI agents to Atlanta to investigate the situation, but no arrests were made.[26]

Such episodes were calculated to discourage Tilly, but they failed. During the decade following the *Brown* v. *Board of Education* decision, when many Southern whites threatened to resist integration no matter what the cost, Tilly continued her work. Twice in 1968 in her capacity as Southern advisor to the National Women's Committee for Civil Rights she visited Selma, Alabama, where she encouraged church women and civil rights leaders to continue their good work. She was made painfully aware how much opposition existed to civil rights when she learned that a "Dr. Dunn, who has a Rest Home, not only fired Mrs. Cecil Collins [a black] when he found she had registered [to vote] but beat her severely." In fact, hostility was so great that the Selma Ford agency was nearly "put out of business because the Ford Foundation had furnished money to aid the freedom groups." Local police watched her uneasily, and when she left Selma for the second time, lawmen followed her rented car almost as far as Montgomery.[27]

Even when Tilly could not be on the scene of racial violence, she phoned women there and wrote letters to friends asking for information on what was really going on. Dressed in fashionable clothing, she looked much like a Southern aristocrat, which, in fact, she was, and often she would visit communities in Georgia and elsewhere, talking with cabdrivers, news vendors, and even customers in markets, seeking to find out local sentiment on integration and to learn the names of potential troublemakers. At SRC headquarters, she kept file boxes full of cards listing Southern communities and names of whom to contact in times of racial stress.[28]

Because of her bravery and her determination "never for a moment to be afraid to face a truth, because it is new to me or to dig under a belief which is dearly loved by me," Tilly was admired by many. Wesleyan College made her one of its first three women trustees. Presidents Truman, Kennedy, and Johnson appointed her to various national commissions;[29] even President Nixon sought to honor her.[30] She served as an advisor for UNESCO and was named to the national boards of the Americans for Democratic Action and the American Civil Liberties Union. Of her scores of honors, perhaps the most important came in 1965, when the Women's Society of Christian Service named her the outstanding Methodist woman in the South for the quarter century that had just ended. Medals and citations came from the National Council of Negro Women, the Urban League, Paine College, the United Church Women, and Gammon Theological Seminary. Tilly accepted these awards with humility and dignity, always careful to point out that she could never have accomplished much without the help of friends. Before her husband's death, she usually credited him with giving her the courage and strength to go on.[31]

Tilly needed this strength in the 1960s. The decade was a difficult one for her. Race riots and other violence disrupted much of the nation. In 1961, her devoted husband of nearly sixty years died, and she became very upset when the funeral director refused to allow blacks to attend Milton Tilly's funeral. Moreover, the deaths of John F. Kennedy and Martin Luther King, Jr., profoundly distressed her. Militant blacks alleged that she patronized them. SRC officials more and more ignored her and other women at their policy meetings. "The men get together," she complained, "and decide everything behind closed doors and don't even *tell* us what they're doing."[32] SRC leaders also became increasingly impatient with Tilly's insistence that liquor not be served at SRC functions. "No fire and brimstone preacher," observed her friend, Margaret Long, "could excel Mrs. Tilly in abhorrence of alcohol in any of its uses, except maybe as a back rub." Worst of all, Tilly, never in great health, was troubled by various maladies that required long hospital stays.[33]

Nothing, however, could long keep her idle. When confined to a wheel-chair, she traveled to conferences by train; when on crutches or obliged to use a cane, she went by plane. When well, even though she was an octogenarian, she drove her car, ignoring the protests of her son, Eben. Finally, she was forced to slow down. At the last meeting of the F of C in the fall of 1968, Thelma Stevens recollects, "She was so ill that she was unable to be heard when she talked—*but we knew what she wanted us to do.*"[34]

Late in 1969, it was necessary for Eben Tilly to have his mother admitted to a nursing home. She died there on March 16, 1970. Paul Anthony, executive director of SRC, eulogized Tilly, taking "solace in the fact that her uniqueness reminds us all that perhaps the greatest life after death is the way in which one person can touch so many."[35]

The F of C died with Tilly. Hers was a one-woman show, and there was no logical successor to replace her. By 1970, Southern schools were integrated, and Jim Crow's defenders could no longer point to the law as sanctioning segregation. The F of C had completed much of its work.

Plainly, Dorothy Tilly was a remarkable woman. Devoutly religious, she saw her work for the SRC as an extension of what she did for blacks; she also helped to combat prejudice against Jews and Catholics and poor whites. "I am . . . concerned about the poor and outcasts of white people," she once wrote. "I was at Selma, Alabama, several times and I [was] as sorry for the poor white men as I was for the Negroes they were fighting, for they, too, had been sinned against by society."[36] Tilly's legacy was that of many other Southern white liberal contemporaries. It was, as Morton Sosna has observed, the "belief that the South would eventually resolve the race question in a manner that would surprise Americans outside the region."[37]

Notes

The writer would like to thank the Winthrop College Research Council for financial assistance that helped make possible the researching of this essay. He also would like to express appreciation to Professors Annette Cox Smith and Constance Ashton Myers for their helpful suggestions.

1. Dorothy Tilly to Mrs. W. Murdock McLeod, August 6, 1956 (copy), Dorothy Tilly and the Fellowship of the Concerned Papers, Southern Regional Council (SRC), hereafter cited as Tilly MSS, SRC. These papers are eventually to be transferred to Atlanta University. One of the few scholarly studies that consider the role of some Southern women is Morton Sosna's deservedly acclaimed *In Search of the Silent South: Southern Liberals and the Race Issue* (New York: Columbia University Press, 1977). Of great value will be Jacquelyn D. Hall's study of Jessie Daniel Ames, which will be published by Columbia University Press.

2. Tilly to Jerome Klein, July 27, 1964 (carbon), Tilly MSS, SRC; see also Helena Huntington Smith, "Mrs. Tilly's Crusade," *Colliers* CXXVI (December 30, 1950), p.

66; Eben Tilly to writer, January 28, 1978.

3. Personal interview with Eben Tilly, May 15, 1975; *Friend's Intelligencer* (Philadelphia) CV (July 24, 1948), p. 426.

4. See, for example, Tilly's report as superintendent of children's work in the *Eleventh Annual Report of the Woman's Missionary Society of the North Georgia Conference* (Gainesville, GA.: n.p., 1921), p. 29; Tilly, "Leadership School," *Wesleyan Christian Advocate* (Atlanta), May 14, 1937; ibid., September 26, 1924.

5. Thelma Stevens to writer, January [14,] 1978; Smith, "Mrs. Tilly's Crusade," p. 66.

6. Atlanta *Constitution*, November 22, 1931 (Tilly incorrectly identified in photograph as "Lilly"); Minutes of Central Council, ASWPL, November 20, 1931, ASWPL MSS, Box 13, Atlanta University; Memo on Lynching at Vienna, Georgia, on September 28, 1935, ibid., Box 17; Frances Dwyer to Tilly, June 18, 1935, ibid.

7. Ann Ellis, "The Commission on Interracial Cooperation" (Ph.D. diss., Georgia State University, 1975), pp. 178-89; Minutes of Fulton-DeKalb Committee, CIC, June 3, 1941, CIC Papers, Box 84, Atlanta University; Tilly to Mrs. H. A. Hunt, October 29, 1942 (carbon); memorandum on meeting of Tilly and Ellis Arnall, October 27, 1942, Box 35, ibid.

8. Helen Fuller, "The Invisible Congress: Lobbies on the Left," *The New Republic* CX (April 10, 1944), p. 496; *Congressional Record*, Appendix, 78th Cong., 2nd Sess. XC (May 22, 1944), p. A 2499. Tilly was lobbyist for the Emergency Committee for Food Production, which sought to save the FSA.

9. Sosna, *Silent South*, pp. 150-52; Chatauquan (New York) *Daily*, August 26, 1948; "Civil Rights," *The New York Times*, December 12, 1947, p. 56; Chattanooga *Times*, November 5, 1947.

10. Smith, "Mrs. Tilly's Crusade," p. 67; report of interview of Tilly with Governor Jim Nance McCord of Tennessee, March 6, 1946, on Columbia riot, Guy Johnson Papers, SRC.

11. "Southern Church Women Draft Action Program," *New South* IV (September 1949), pp. 2-3; "Church and Conscience in the South," ibid. VI (February 1951), pp. 1-4; *The Fellowship of the Concerned* (leaflet) (n.p., n.d.).

12. Ibid., Smith, "Mrs. Tilly's Crusade," p. 67.

13. Jessie Arndt, "Women's Crusade Spurs Fair Treatment of Negroes in Southern U.S.," *Christian Science Monitor*, January 9, 1953; Dorothy Tilly, "The Fellowship of the Concerned," *The Woman's Press* XLIII (February 1950), pp. 8-9, 19; Katherine Fisher, "Compact," *Charm Magazine* LXXIII (March 1951), p. 130.

14. "Want Human Rights in the South," *Milwaukee Journal*, October 30, 1949; Smith, "Mrs. Tilly's Crusade," p. 29; Tilly, "Citizenship," in *The People Take the Lead, a Record of Progress in Civil Rights, 1948-1958* (New York: American Jewish Committee, 1958), p. 11.

15. Tilly to Rabbi Roland Gittelsohn, July 20, 1956 (carbon), Tilly MSS, SRC; Thelma Stevens to writer, January [14,] 1978. An address presented to the F of C is reprinted in Marion Wright, *Human Rights Odyssey* (Durham: Moore, 1978), pp. 119-25.

16. Tilly to Dorothy Thompson, July 24, 1959 (carbon), Tilly MSS, SRC; George Mitchell to F. D. Patterson, October 15, 1956 (carbon), Mitchell Papers, SRC; Tilly

to Bill Cleghorn, December 5, 1958 (mimeographed), ibid.; Tilly to Charles Turck, September 11, 1959 (carbon), ibid; Ruth Collins, "We Are the Inheritors," *Response* III (July-August 1971), p. 31; Margaret Long, "Mrs. Dorothy Tilly: A Memoir," *New South* XXV (Spring 1970), p. 49.

17. William Allred, "The Southern Regional Council, 1943-1961" (master's thesis, Emory University, 1966), pp. 120, 200-201.

18. Bullard to Tilly, March 5, 1964, Tilly MSS, SRC.

19. Reports of 1963 Workshop Participants (mimeographed), ibid.; Mrs. John Bishop to Tilly, March 9, 1964, ibid.; Chappell to Tilly, February 25, 1964, ibid.

20. Wyatt to Tilly, February 1, 1965, ibid.

21. Forence Robin, "Honeychile at the Barricades," *Harper's* CCXXV (October 1962), p. 174; Tilly to Dear Friends [in Alabama,] December 17, 1958 (mimeographed), Tilly MSS, SRC.

22. Tilly to Bill Cleghorn, December 5, 1958 (mimeographed), ibid.

23. Tilly to Dear Friends [in Alabama,] December 17, 1958, ibid.

24. Franklin Acker, "The New Attack," Anderson (S.C.) *Independent*, November 17, 1947; anonymous letter sent to Tilly in February 1948, Tilly MSS, Emory University; Dow Kirkpatrick to M. G. Lowman, January 19, 1959 (copy), Tilly MSS, SRC; Thomas Wolanin, *Presidential Advisory Commissions* (Madison: University of Wisconsin Press, 1945), p. 40.

25. Tilly to Dear Friends [in Alabama,] December 17, 1958, Tilly MSS, SRC; John Wicklein, "Birmingham Resists Church Integration," *The New York Times*, July 7, 1959, p. 30; personal interview with Ruth Alexander Vick, July 29, 1975.

26. Tilly to Mrs. Page Wilson, April 10, 1964 (carbon), Tilly MSS, SRC; Chester Davis, "Capturing the Strategic Foothills," Winston-Salem *Journal and Sentinel*, February 22, 1953, hereafter cited as Davis, "Foothills."

27. Tilly, "[First] Visit to Selma, October 7, 1963" (mimeograph) and "My Second Visit to Selma, October 31, 1963" (mimeograph), Tilly MSS, SRC.

28. Smith, "Mrs. Tilly's Crusade," p. 67; personal interview with Ruth Vick, July 29, 1975; Davis, "Foothills."

29. Tilly was especially impressed with John Kennedy. Tilly to Thelma Stevens, May 13, 1963 (carbon), Tilly MSS, SRC; Tilly to Dear Friends [in Alabama,] July 24, 1963 (mimeograph), ibid.; Sarah Cunningham, "A Woman Beyond Her Times," *The Church Woman* XXXII (December 1966), pp. 11-12; form for 1959 F of C Workshop in Florida, Tilly MSS, SRC.

30. Nixon, unaware that Tilly had died two months before, sought to honor her in May 1970. The episode greatly surprised Eben Tilly. James Keough to Tilly, May 2, 1970, and commendation from Nixon, May 6, 1970, both in Tilly MSS, Emory University; personal interview with Eben Tilly, May 15, 1975.

31. Milton Tilly died on August 19, 1961. Eben Tilly to writer, January 28, 1978; Thelma Stevens to writer, January [14,] 1978; Beulah MacKay, "Dorothy Tilly, Pioneer," *The Church Woman* XXX (March 1964), p. 18.

32. Long, "Tilly," pp. 46-48. Tilly was not imagining this. Marion Wright, the distinguished civil rights crusader and twice president of the Southern Regional Council, recollected that "George Mitchell [who was one of the executive directors of the SRC] had great difficulty getting along with women members of the staff. I think he would probably have to have been one of the original male chauvinists."

Interview with Marion Wright by Jacquelyn Hall, March 8, 1978, Southern Oral History Program Collection, Southern Historical Collection, University of North Carolina at Chapel Hill, p. 20; personal interview with Ruth Vick, July 29, 1975.

33. Long, "Tilly," pp. 46-48; personal interview with Janet Smith, July 24, 1975; personal interview with Ruth Vick, July 29, 1975.

34. Long, "Tilly," p. 43; Collins, "Inheritors," p. 32; Stevens to writer, January [14,] 1978.

35. Paul Anthony to Mrs. Kenneth Law, May 11, 1970 (carbon), Anthony MSS, SRC; "Mrs. Dorothy Tilly" (editorial), Atlanta *Journal*, March 18, 1970.

36. Tilly to Sarah Cunningham, September 26, 1966 (carbon), Tilly MSS, SRC; Long, "Tilly," p. 35.

37. Sosna, *Silent South*, p. 207.

19

JAMES McBRIDE DABBS: SPOKESMAN FOR RACIAL LIBERALISM

Robert M. Randolph

On a hot evening near the end of August 1954, nearly a thousand people gathered in Sumter, South Carolina, to discuss the possibility that their schools would be desegregated in the fall. Across the South, similar meetings were taking place as white citizens sought to respond to the *Brown* decision. In Sumter, the public reaction had been moderate. In early June, the school board had adopted a wait and see attitude, and *The Sumter Daily Item* generally ignored the issue. Beneath the surface, however, reaction was growing. Black citizens began to exert pressure for changes. Modest requests were made to the Sumter City Council. Nothing was said about the schools. Initial council reaction was negative, but the efforts by the black community clearly indicated that the days of supposed satisfaction with the status quo were over.

As the weather warmed during the summer, so did the reaction across the South. No politician in the former Confederacy dared urge compliance with the *Brown* decision, and the number urging defiance grew daily. White Citizens' Councils were organized and spread through the South. Sumter would eventually have the strongest council in the state. Those who supported the *Brown* decision and dared to speak were few.[1]

But in Sumter, one man did dare to speak out, and he continued to speak out for the remaining sixteen years of his life. Emotions at the meeting were high as Hugh Agnew, president of the South Carolina Farm Bureau Federation, addressed the crowd. Like an evangelist, he exhorted the people to prevent the South Carolina Legislature from doing anything that would comply with the Court's decision. As a first measure, Agnew advocated a mail campaign that would flood the legislators' offices in Columbia with mail opposing any breech in the wall of segregation. The audience was responsive and apparently of one opinion until, as John Mitchell of *The Sumter Daily Item* reported, "one dissenting voice caused a brief furor." James McBride Dabbs, responding to Agnew's plea that the people of Sumter stand up and be counted, stood up and began to speak to the audience. He told them they were not acting as Christians. The people quieted as he told them he was disappointed in them. They remained silent as he said that he agreed with Agnew that the people of the South faced a serious problem, but "I do not agree with him about what we should do or can do about it. We must shake off the past and face the future." As the tone of his remarks became clear, the cat-calls and boos from the crowd drowned him out. The chairman of the State's Rights League of Sumter County calmed the crowd, and a vote was called for on Agnew's plan for the mail campaign. It was endorsed without noted dissent. Later, in a poignant moment near the close of the meeting, McBride Dabbs, the brother of James, spoke to the crowd and talked of those who have beautiful, but impractical, theories that can never work. He concluded: "It is a matter of difference, and all should go to school with their own kind."[2] James Dabbs summed up his own feelings about the evening later in a letter to his good friend Marion Wright:

I am glad you didn't refer to my "courage" as others have because *courage* doesn't seem the word for it . . . you have a conviction about something, and you are going to say so come hell or high water. In fact I believe my chief feeling in Sumter was one of exasperation: the speaker's talk was mainly a tissue of illogicalities; and after I hear a certain amount of publicly spoken nonsense, I feel it's time for somebody to point it out.[3]

Among white South Carolinians, James Dabbs was almost alone in his willingness to point out publicly spoken nonsense in the fall of 1954. This essay will explore the origins of James Dabbs's views on race. It will examine the influence that his views had on the racial climate of his day, the limitations of his influence, and it will conclude with an evaluation of the role of the racial liberal in the post-1945 South.

From colonial days, all branches of James McBride Dabbs's family had been South Carolinian. His earliest paternal ancestor had been killed by Tories, and members from both sides of his family had served in the Civil War. The McBrides had come to the Maysville region in 1806. At one time, they owned more than 10,000 acres, but by the beginning of the twentieth century, hard times had cut severely into the size of the family holdings. Dabbs's home, Rip Raps, had been built in 1858 by eighteen-year-old James McBride. He died in 1863, leaving his wife and two children to witness the death of the Confederacy. His assessed wealth was modest, but he died owning about 130 slaves. His wife never remarried, and their two children never wandered far. She and her son, Guy McBride, fought a holding action to keep the maximum amount of their landholdings. Their success was ensured by the daughter's marriage to Eugene W. Dabbs.

Dabbs was an assertive newcomer who had been the overseer of the Witherspoon plantation, Coldstream. He was a prohibitionist long before it was a popular cause. The McBrides were skeptical of reforms and reformers, and this skepticism applied to prohibitionists. It was in this context that Guy McBride told Aunt Alice, "Ideals are a sin, Alice. We should love God."⁴ Of more importance was Eugene Dabbs's notion that the way the region farmed had to change. He was an early and prominent member of the Farmer's Union in South Carolina. He eventually became president of the union, traveled widely throughout South Carolina, and wrote regularly for *The Progressive Farmer and Southern Farm Gazette*.

Eugene Dabbs's influence on his sons meant that they would be known as among the most innovative farmers in the state. James Dabbs began his romance with the printed word by having an article written when he was sixteen published in the *Progressive Farmer*.⁵ It was a hymn to the virtues of crop diversification. From youth, therefore, Dabbs knew what it was like to endorse views divergent from majority opinion.

But how did Dabbs get from diversified farming to endorsing the desegregation of South Carolina's institutions? The Dabbs family held racial attitudes common among the "best families" in the South. Racial slurs were never used because it was felt that such terms would be demeaning to the family. Segregation was accepted, and the racial status quo was never questioned. But at sixteen, in September 1912, Dabbs left his tight community to attend the University of South Carolina, and it was there that he first confronted unorthodox views on race.

In 1957, Dabbs wrote, "I remember nothing about race during my four years at college."⁶ But his memory was selective. At the university, he became close friends with Marion Wright, a student from Johnston, South Carolina, who had entered the university in 1911. Their careers would intertwine over the following half century. Wright remembers that Dabbs was first prodded into thinking about race relations by Professor Josiah Morse. Morse was a Jew who had come to the University of South Carolina in 1911 at the invitation of President Samuel Childs Mitchell. He had studied under G. Stanley Hall at Clark University in Worcester, Massachusetts. He changed his name from Moses to Morse upon graduation "so that it shall not look so flagrantly Jewish."⁷ Acquainted with racism as he was, it is not surprising that Morse made the study of prejudice a professional focus. It was, believes Wright, Dabbs's relationship with Morse that first opened Dabbs's eyes to racism. Morse organized interracial student discussion groups that drew students from the black colleges in and near Columbia.⁸ In his class, Dabbs read Charles Gardener Murphy's *The Basis of Ascendance*. Wright argues that "that book opened a lot of our eyes because Murphy placed emphasis upon the distinctive and equal natures of the races."⁹

Not only did Morse open Dabbs's eyes to the issues of race relations, but he broadened his educational horizons. As he neared the end of his years as a student at the university, Dabbs concluded that he wanted to be a missionary. He had been much influenced by the Student Volunteer Movement. Morse rightly saw that this decision was an immature one and encouraged Dabbs to pursue broader educational goals. He encouraged Dabbs to study with G. Stanley Hall at Clark, and he went so far as to write Hall directly:

If it is not too late . . . I want to beg a Junior Fellowship for Mr. James McBride Dabbs. Mr. Dabbs is the best man we have this year, and one of the best men we have ever had. An "A" student, a fine mind, splendid character. . . . He wishes to prepare himself for Foreign Mission work, and I have told him that the best place for that is Clark.[10]

Hall gave Dabbs a fellowship based on Morse's recommendation. When news of the award reached Dabbs, Morse arranged a personal loan for Dabbs so that nothing would stand in the way of his attending Clark. A year later, in June 1917, having completed his M.A. at Clark, Dabbs prepared to use his passable French in the service of his country.

He returned from World War I unscarred, well-traveled, and married to a South Carolinian whom he had met shortly before entering the service. A year of farming proved a disaster, and so he served for a year as principal of a high school in North Carolina. In 1921, he returned to the University of South Carolina and took a position in the English Department. Again, the university setting provided an opportunity for Dabbs to confront racial issues in an atmosphere more open to divergent views than we might expect. Two specific areas of involvement are noteworthy.

Although a Presbyterian by heritage, Dabbs was now a Baptist by marriage. He and his wife, Jessie, were active in the Shandon Avenue Baptist Church. The minister was F. Clyde Helms, a man who had been involved in efforts to unionize the mines of eastern Kentucky before coming to South Carolina and who was known as a union supporter in the mills of South Carolina. He belonged to the Commission on Interracial Cooperation and later served as vice-president of the Southern Conference for Human Welfare. His friendship with Dabbs continued long after Dabbs left his church. While by the standards of a later generation of social activists Helms was found wanting, his involvement in the social issues of this period touched Dabbs. He also encouraged and worked with Dabbs on projects related to the YMCA.[11]

During this period, Dabbs looked again at his commitment to the missionary enterprise. He and Jessie still talked of the idea, but her health meant that they could never go beyond the talk stage. Instead, Dabbs's missionary zeal went into the "Y," and as a result, he took a group from the university to the Student Volunteer Convention for 1923.

Held in Indianapolis, the convention was called "critical and at times almost radical" in tone.[12] Those attending were told that ". . . the joyous Negro is learning to hate. The dark world will remain in submission just as long as necessary—no longer."[13] The program was impressive, the ideas controversial. The concern of the meeting emerged as the desire for justice for all men. A student who attended reflected later:

In many quarters there was felt the need for a more continuous emphasis on the place of the individual in the fight for a finer world, with consecration brought down out of the clouds and incarnated in practical suggestions and clean cut delineations.[14]

Dabbs was far from clear-cut in his summation of the conference:

The questions of Race Relations and the War received by far the most attention. Though the Convention took no definite action on the race question, the delegates came away resolved that the spirit of Christ must rule in all personal and social relationships.[15]

James Dabbs did not make "race relations" his concern for another quarter century, but the genesis of his ideas and convictions is to be found in his years at the University of South Carolina. The South could always defend its institutions and folkways from frontal assault, but the subtle impact of ideas and ideals that grow and change as young men grow up in a changing world could not be ignored.

Dabbs taught at the university until 1924, when he left for New York City and graduate study at Columbia University. Despite his wife's strong encouragement, he never completed his doctorate, and he eventually came to regret the effort he had made to obtain the degree. He returned in 1925 to Coker College in Hartsville, South Carolina, and a successful teaching career. A women's college, with Baptist connections, Coker was the sort of community in which Dabbs was quite at home. He later recalled his first days there:

My first days in class were dazzling—I mean for me. I had never seen so many girls together before. It was like . . . talking to flowers who occasionally replied.[16]

His family now included two children, but the birth of the second daughter had further weakened Jessie. Her health continued to deteriorate, and in November 1933, Jessie Armstrong Dabbs died. For Dabbs, the death of his wife was a major turning point:

Turning from her grave, I was turning I knew, from my youth. It may seem strange to speak of youth at thirty-seven. Indeed, during the several preceding years I had often felt that youth was gone, though I had not been resigned to its going, and had attempted by thought to bring it back. Now I knew how much I had fooled myself. If she had lived I should never have grown old.[17]

Dabbs made two important decisions after his wife's death. First, he determined to continue writing. His articles had been appearing in national magazines since 1933, when *Scribner's* published "I'm Going Home" between selections by Ernest Hemingway and Eleanor Roosevelt. Delighted by his success, he had continued to write, and he would not stop because of Jessie's death. His work touched primarily on three themes. First, he was concerned with the impact of industrialization on the South. He saw what had been done to the North by uncontrolled industrial development, and he called on his region to learn from the mistakes that had been made. Second, he was concerned with the quality of life in an industrial era. If one found no pleasure in what he did for a living, where could pleasure be found? Third, he was concerned with the quality of human relationships in the world he saw emerging. Concern with matters of race followed logically.

His concerns were heightened and given shape by the second major decision made after Jessie's death. He returned home to his family lands and to Rip Raps. He had remarried by this time, and his new family took its place in the community where he had grown up. They filled a pew in the church of his youth. Trying to make sense of what had happened to him, he turned to his religion. Considering the symbols of Christianity, he concluded that there was a social dimension to Christianity that he had ignored, or at least had not acted on. "A symbolic religious service expresses the truth that only as we are socially one can we be saved individually."[18] Later, reflecting on Jessie's death, he wrote:

The death of a loved one is, for most of us . . . the end of meaning. The intricate pattern of our lives collapses. . . . The first lesson, and perhaps the greatest . . . is the realization of our oneness with mankind. Having failed with them we can endure with them and perhaps conquer.[19]

His growing recognition of the interconnectedness of mankind caused Dabbs to publicly address himself for the first time to race relations. He did so in 1940 in an article in *The Christian Century*. The article asked whether it was possible for a Christian community to exist in the South; his answer was no. The relationships between the races would not change without a revolution, and without change, a Christian community was impossible. Unhappy with what he saw to be true, he concluded:

But I am in favor, always, of recognizing as clearly as we can what we have, what we want and what we may have. We may then become humble and ask God to be merciful to us.[20]

He took his own advice, and recognizing what he had, he determined to find out what he wanted. The World War II years were years of discovery and introspection:

Except indirectly, I am not a student of American life. It is true that during the '30's and '40's I wrote some articles for *The Christian Century* dealing with the problems of industrialism and urbanism, but even as I wrote them, I was aware of the paradox: from the heart of a conservative, country community, I was criticizing urban and industrial life. Therefore, I really didn't know what I was talking about. The tragic affair at Hiroshima made me effectively aware of this. . . . So following Voltaire's advice, I cultivated my garden. I ran my tractor. But then came the 1950's and trouble . . . broke out in my front yard: the Negroes began to march. . . . When modern life broke out around me, then I did begin to have something to say. I have spent most of my life since thinking about the racial situation in the South.[21]

Dabbs's memory again tended to simplify the process. He had not been uninvolved in public affairs during the 1940s. His was one of the few voices to oppose the White Primary in 1944. Alice Spearman, a long-time advocate of human rights in South Carolina, recognized Dabbs's potential and enlisted Marion Wright to draw him into the South Carolina chapter of the Southern Regional Council. By 1950, he was president of the organization, and he was writing again. He wrote now of the South and the future, and he had concluded that the issues of industrialization and the quality of life could not be dealt with until the South dealt with the problem it had inherited:

But to solve this problem of the future, it must forget the problem of its past, the worn out problem of a fixed status, the so-called Negro problem, and lifting into the clear light of reason the essential virtues of status, it must discover some ways of incorporating these virtues in a free and fluid society. As it does this, it will show both the industrial West and the industrializing East how to be both free and secure at the same time; and it will have solved the problem of racial equality by having let it alone.[22]

Knowing that the church was an influential institution in the South, Dabbs directed many of his written words to the church. His articles appeared regularly in denominational publications. His call was clear: "Now, if ever, is the time for the church in the South to be the Christian church. . . ." But he recognized that his words were not being heard: "Regardless of what we say, or what we affirm, the general attitude of the white South today proves that we do not really believe in the God and Father of our Lord and savior Jesus Christ."[23] His own presbytery passed a resolution in September 1954 condemning the *Brown* decision. "I belong to a presbytery the chief concern of which is the protection of the past," he lamented.[24]

In 1957, Dabbs became president of the Southern Regional Council, an organization dedicated to dealing with the economic and social problems of the South. After an agonizing period of indecision, the council had determined in 1951 that the racial issue had to be dealt with before the region could confront the other pressing problems of the day.[25] Dabbs followed Marion Wright as president of the Southern Regional Council and served until 1963. While the council continued to keep a low profile, Dabbs was an extremely visible president. He traveled widely and enjoyed the role of traditional Southerner. To the non-Southerner, during this period of tension and anguish, it was refreshing to find a Southerner who looked like a Southerner should look and who argued for racial equality. He argued the case well in person and in print. His most widely read book, *The Southern Heritage*, took the materials of Southern history and reworked them, arguing that the present state of affairs was an aberration. The words he spoke were familiar, but his conclusions shocked. Those who were standing squarely in the Southern tradition, he argued, were the blacks who were demanding recognition. Those in the North who cared were reassured.

But Dabbs was more than a reassuring figure. He was a prophet who believed that the South would lead the nation in improving race relations:

It is the lack of indifference in the South about the racial problem that gives the South the edge in solving this problem. Because we have lived together for a long time, Southern whites and Negroes have had to pay attention and be concerned about each other. . . . It is the grace of God that we have been given difficult neighbors; neighbors of a different class, or of different economic positions, of a different history. All these differences are the voice of God jarring us into the recognition that these are men . . . and that we should see them truly and have compassion on them.[26]

When the Black Power movement swept through the organizations he was devoted to, the Penn Community, the Southern Regional Council, the Presbyterian Church in the United States, he never hesitated. When some pulled away out of anger at the lack of gratitude for what had been done, Dabbs hung on and sought to interpret, to understand, and eventually to endorse the concept of Black Power.

Dabbs had evolved into a racial liberal. He had taken from his family a strong sense of identity that gave him a willingness to act independently of those about him. His educational and travel experiences had broadened his perspective, and his intellectual capabilities had allowed him to use and reflect on what he had learned from both book and kin. But the key ingredient in his development had been the experience of Jessie's death. He saw then clearly that he was a "man among men," and that insight set him on the path that led him to confront racism. He had nothing to prove. He was recognized by his peers as an able farmer, a man of books, something of a dreamer. Secure in his place, he was able to speak his mind. His life confirms the insight of Amos Elon, who has written in another context: "The liberal conscience is often a function of success and not failure. It does not grow of insecurity and weakness, which are more likely to produce a callous fanaticism, but of self-assurance and strength."[27]

But was anyone listening? It is hard to measure the influence of a man like Dabbs. Paul Anthony argues that as president of the Southern Regional Council he was the most influential leader the organization had had at that time. His leadership was subtle but real. As the organization faced the beginnings of the Black Power movement, Dabbs emphasized the purpose of the organization as an interracial body and reaffirmed again and again the truth he saw in the commonalities that unite Southern blacks and whites. By the strength of his leadership, he helped hold the council together.[28]

At home in Sumter, Dabbs was dismissed as a "damn fool," and his influence was primarily of a personal nature. He "converted" members of his own family and touched others who lived around him. In the black community, Dabbs was recognized as the one white man in the region who would speak out in support of black aspirations. The pattern was a consistent one. From the way he dealt with blacks living on his land or working for him, to raising bail for blacks arrested for civil rights disturbances, the black community knew him as a friend and co-worker.[29]

I believe, however, that it was at a wider level that Dabbs had his greatest influence, and here I must speak partly from personal experience. To be of the white South in the 1950s and 1960s, to care about the people, and to hope for change was exceedingly lonely. There were no models, no statesmen, no churchmen, no educators pointing the way. But suddenly, there was James McBride Dabbs. "He was not so much a 'liberalizing' force," wrote a young history professor, "but he was the means of reconciling the alienation from the South which I then felt as a result of my hostility to racism. Earlier I had drawn a circle leaving the black folks out, later replacing it with a circle replacing the blacks with the red-necks. Dabbs opened the circle."[30] Others have voiced similar feelings.

Over the years, a steady stream of visitors made their pilgrimage to Rip Raps. Uncounted young and old Southerners drove up the dusty, rutted drive to Rip Raps and to the piazza hospitality he wrote so often about. Dabbs placed his confidence in the young, both black and white. He told young blacks: "Don't think you have it made because there have been changes. You have a long road ahead. The court says this, but what are you going to do about it? What are you going to do to break it down?"[31] To whites marching at Selma, he wired his encouragement: "It is right that your group of white professional and religious leaders should make their witness at Selma. For it is the good white people of the South who are primarily responsible for the situation there."[32] He spoke as one who has everything Southern youth had been taught to revere: his hands had been calloused by honest work; he was a scholar; he was a man of God. Therefore, knowing Dabbs, reading Dabbs, or simply hearing about Dabbs gave support and inspiration to nearly three generations of Southerners who thought of themselves as liberals in matters of race.

What of those who found Dabbs too slow moving, too deferential to the mores of the culture, too Southern? I think the key to understanding Dabbs and his approach is to acknowledge readily that he saw change coming slowly. After all, the situation had been created by three hundred years of history. But that history was the history of black and white together, and as whites were led to see the common ties that bound them to blacks as equal products of the "Southern heritage," then the new age would come. As did the Southern Regional Council, Dabbs spoke to the leaders of his day. Those who read his books and articles and heard his speeches and were moved to act did not seem to be many at the time, but they were the ones he was aiming at because he believed they would eventually tilt the balance. "I am an activist, but most indirectly," he wrote with not uncommon contradiction. "I find myself continuously asking of a proposed idea, will it work? But I am willing to take a long time understanding the roots and relationships of an idea in the belief that the better we understand these the better chance we have of making it work."[33]

Finally, what can we learn from James McBride Dabbs about racial liberalism in the postwar South? First, Dabbs reminds us that there was a fragile network of white men and women who supported racial equality in the 1940s and 1950s. Names like Lillian Smith and J. Waties Waring are well known, but there were many others who knew each other, supported each other, and on occasion mourned for each other.

Second, Dabbs illustrates clearly the truth of Leslie Dunbar's observation of fifteen years ago:

What, in this context, is worth remarking is the long sustained refusal of southern liberals to repudiate the South, and this is one side of the tolerance which they have elevated above all other social virtues. Few liberals have acted out their beliefs. . . . This is not well described as either hypocrisy or timidity. It is something a good bit more basic. The general conformity of the liberal to social practices which he opposes is a mark of his dogged refusal to alienate himself from southern society.[34]

Southern liberalism has always been much more relativistic than liberalism at the national level. Harold Fleming, president of the Potomac Institute, told me of the pain he felt when Dabbs told of the difference between the greetings he gave the white banker and the black workman. Dabbs justified the difference on the grounds that he was buying time, the time needed to bring about fundamental change. So, too, with Southern liberals who held their concern for the communities of which they were a part in tension with their commitment to change.

Finally, the institutional expressions of liberal sentiment in the South were crippled in the postwar years by the institutions' inability to reach a decision to oppose racial discrimination. This inability fragmented the liberal community when it needed all the strength it could muster. The Southern Regional Council committed itself to end discrimination only three years before the *Brown* decision. One can only wonder what the organization might have been able to do in shaping public opinion if it had been financially viable and clear as to its strategies and goals in its early years. Dabbs's evolution as a liberal personifies the struggle that went on within the council. His final recognition of the merits of the Black Power movement reminds us that there came a time when the true liberal could no longer presume to do for blacks what blacks could do for themselves. Paternalism had to be put aside, and Dabbs did so with grace.

James McBride Dabbs was a "damn fool" not only to many of his neighbors but also to others, both black and white, whose timetable for change was shorter than his. In 1970, when he died, the critics seemed to be carrying the day. Now, however, given the balm of hindsight, the reality of change, and a Georgian recently in the White House, I am not so sure. He always chuckled when he told of being called a fool. He enjoyed it, and maybe it was because he believed that anyone who tried to bind, heal, and understand in an age of sundering, wounding, and ignoring was a fool. Or maybe he remembered, as we do, that the fool in drama is often the bearer of truth, and because he comes as a fool, he is able to speak more freely than those the world counts wise.

Notes

1. Benjamin Muse, *Ten Years of Prelude: The Story of Integration Since the Supreme Court's 1954 Decision* (New York: Viking Press, 1964), p. 20; Richard Kluger, *Simple Justice* (New York: Knopf, 1976) pp. 709–14.

2. News item in *The Sumter Daily Item*, August 25, 1954.

3. James M. Dabbs to Marion Wright, September 5, 1954, Marion Wright Papers in the Southern Historical Collection, University of North Carolina.

4. James M. Dabbs, *The Road Home* (Philadelphia: Christian Education Press, 1960), p. 16.

5. James M. Dabbs, "What Diversification and Rotation Mean to the Farmer and How They Help Make Him Independent," *The Progressive Farmer and Southern Farm Gazette* XXVII (July 26, 1912), p. 743.

6. James M. Dabbs, *The Southern Heritage* (New York: Knopf, 1959), p. 11.

7. G. Stanley Hall to Professor Allen S. Whitney, June 4, 1907. Archives of Clark University, Worcester, Massachusetts.

8. Marion Wright, personal interview, Linville Falls, North Carolina, February 25, 1973. Harry C. Brearly to Marion Wright, no date. Marion Wright Papers.

9. Marion Wright interview.

10. Josiah Morse to G. Stanley Hall, May 15, 1916. Josiah Morse file in the archives of Clark University, Worcester, Massachusetts.

11. Clyde Helms, personal interview, Charlottesville, Virginia, February 3, 1973.

12. "The Students Volunteer," *The Survey*, February 15, 1924, pp. 529-31.

13. James McBride Dabbs, undated notebook containing notes on the Ninth International Student Volunteer Convention, Indianapolis, Indiana, in the James McBride Dabbs Papers in the Southern Historical Collection, University of North Carolina.

14. "Student Views of the Indianapolis Convention," *The Missionary Review of the World*, February 1924, p. 173.

15. Dabbs, undated notebook in the Southern Historical Collection.

16. Dabbs, *The Road Home*, p. 87.

17. Ibid., p. 159.

18. James McBride Dabbs, "Worship and Our Common Life," *Christendom* II, no. 2 (Spring 1937), p. 182.

19. James McBride Dabbs, *Give Sorrow Words*, p. 3. Published originally in *The Christian Century*, the article was reprinted privately in 1943 as a pamphlet by J. Russell Carpenter of Newark, New York.

20. James McBride Dabbs, "Is Christian Community Possible in the South?" *The Christian Century* LVII, no. 28 (July 10, 1940), p. 876.

21. James McBride Dabbs, "Structures of Grace and Evil in the Racial Problem." Speech delivered at Valparaiso University, Valparaiso, Indiana, July 1, 1963.

22. James McBride Dabbs, "The South's Opportunity," *The South Atlantic Quarterly* III, no. 2 (April 1953), p. 206.

23. James McBride Dabbs, "Our Faithless Generation," *The Presbyterian Outlook* 137, no. 42 (November 7, 1955), p. 7.

24. James McBride Dabbs, "Spiritual Lag in Today's World," *The Christian Century* LXXII, no. 3 (January 19, 1955), p. 77.

25. Marion Wright to Judge J. Waties Waring, December 4, 1951. Marion Wright Papers in the Southern Historical Collection, University of North Carolina. Waring and his wife joined the council in December 1951.

26. James McBride Dabbs, "The Burden of the Neighbor," Southern Churchmen Speak, no date, Vol. II, no. 20, p. 1. This is a script for a radio spot produced by the Committee of Southern Churchmen. Dabbs served for a time as president of the organization.

27. Amos Elon, *The Israelis Founders and Sons* (New York: Holt, Rinehart and Winston, 1971), p. 261.

28. Paul Anthony, personal interview, Atlanta, Georgia, August 27, 1973.

29. The Reverend James Herbert Nelson, personal interview, Orangeburg, South Carolina, August 21, 1973. The Reverend Nelson grew up in the Salem community where his father was minister for the Goodwill Presbyterian Church.

30. Charles W. Joyner to Robert M. Randolph, June 13, 1971. For another expression of appreciation of Dabbs by a then young Southerner, see Donald W. Shriver, Jr., "He Made You Feel Like Somebody," *The Christian Century* (July 15, 1970), pp. 866-68.

31. James Herbert Nelson interview.

32. James McBride Dabbs to the Reverend Joseph Ellwanger, March 14, 1965.

33. James McBride Dabbs to Ed Hamlett of the Southern Student Organizing Committee, December 22, 1966.

34. Leslie Dunbar, "The Changing Mind of the South," in Avery Leiserson, ed., *The American South in the 1960's* (New York: Praeger, 1964), p. 7.

SUGGESTIONS FOR FURTHER READING

Introduction

The volume of historical literature on the South since 1850 is large, rich in its diversity, and growing at a geometric rate. In this brief bibliographical essay, it is the editors' goal to call the reader's attention to only a few of the more important works that have relevance to the essays in this volume. A good starting point for the study of Southern history is Idus A. Newby's *The South: A History* (New York, 1978), which surveys the Southern experience in America and is perhaps most valuable for its synthesis of different interpretations. Another standard text is Francis B. Simkins and Charles P. Roland, *A History of the South*, 4th ed. (New York, 1972). Somewhat narrower but also valuable for their general treatments of the Old and New South, respectively, are Clement Eaton, *A History of the Old South*, 3rd ed. (New York, 1975); Thomas D. Clark, *The Emerging South*, 2nd ed. (New York, 1968); Monroe L. Billington, *The Political South in the Twentieth Century* (New York, 1975); and John S. Ezell, *The South Since 1865*, 2nd ed. (Norman, 1975). The best reference work on the South is David C. Roller and Robert W. Twyman, eds., *The Encyclopedia of Southern History* (Baton Rouge, 1979).

In addition to these general histories, there are several chronological treatments of major eras in Southern history. On the coming of the Civil War, the most recent work is William J. Cooper's *The South and the Politics of Slavery, 1828-1856* (Baton Rouge, 1978). Two older but still standard works on the subject are David Potter, *The South and the Sectional Crisis* (Baton Rouge, 1968), and Kenneth Stampp, *The Southern Road to Appomattox* (El Paso, 1969). By far the best work on the Confederacy is Emory Thomas, *The Confederate Nation, 1861-1865* (New York, 1979), which incorporates the most recent research on the topic with fresh insights provided by the author. Somewhat dated but still useful on selected themes are Clement Eaton, *A History of the Southern Confederacy* (New York, 1954); E. M. Coulter, *The Confederate States of America, 1861-1865* (Baton Rouge, 1950); and Charles P. Roland, *The Confederacy* (Chicago, 1960). Reconstruction continues to be one of the most fertile areas of scholarship in Southern history. The classic, "traditional" view on this subject is William A. Dunning's *Reconstruction, Political and Economic, 1865-1877* (New York, 1907). The standard "revisionist" works on Reconstruction are W. E. B. Du Bois, *Black Reconstruction in America, 1860-1880* (New York, 1935); John Hope Franklin, *Reconstruction After the Civil War* (Chicago, 1962); and Kenneth Stampp, *The Era of Reconstruction* (New York, 1965). Over the last fifteen years, much new information and insights have been developed (see works cited in subsequent sections of this essay), but as yet, there has been no synthesis of this new material in one volume. Eric Foner's projected volume on Reconstruction in the *New American Nation Series* promises to fill this need.

Any study of the post-Reconstruction South must still begin with C. Vann Woodward's classic, *Origins of the New South, 1877-1913* (Baton Rouge, 1951), which, although challenged on certain points (see below), continues to dominate historical debate on that period of Southern history. For the South between the two world wars, the best treatment is a lengthy and highly influential work by George Tindall, *The Emergence of the New South, 1913-1945* (Baton Rouge, 1967). As an introduction to "recent" trends, see Charles P. Roland, *The Improbable Era: The South Since World War II* (Lexington, 1976).

In addition to these narrative histories, many volumes are devoted almost exclusively to interpretation. The reader should begin with Wilbur J. Cash's landmark study, *The Mind of the South* (New York, 1941), and the various works of C. Vann Woodward, including *The Burden of Southern History* (Baton Rouge, 1968) and *American Counterpoint* (Boston, 1971). Other important works on this subject are George B. Tindall, *The Ethnic Southerners* (Baton Rouge, 1976) and *The Persistent Tradition in New South Politics* (Baton Rouge, 1975); Jack Temple Kirby, *Media-Made Dixie: The South in the American Imagination* (Baton Rouge, 1978); Michael O'Brien, *The Idea of the American South, 1920-1941* (Baltimore, 1979); and Carl Degler, *Place over Time: The Continuity of Southern Distinctiveness* (Baton Rouge, 1977). Also valuable are such older works as Monroe L. Billington, *The South: A Central Theme* (New York, 1969); Dewey W. Grantham, Jr., ed., *The South and the Sectional Image: The Sectional Theme Since Reconstruction* (New York, 1968); Frank E. Vandiver, ed., *The Idea of the South* (Chicago, 1964); T. Harry Williams, *Romance and Realism in Southern Politics* (Athens, 1961); Charles G. Sellers, ed., *The Southerner as American* (Chapel Hill, 1960); and Howard Zinn, *The Southern Mystique* (New York, 1959). For more detailed analyses of many of the issues raised in these books, see the following sections of this essay.

The Origins of Jim Crow Laws Revised

For nearly three decades, any discussion of the factors leading to statutory disfranchisement and segregation of blacks in the South has been shaped by the writings of C. Vann Woodward; most notably in *Origins of the New South* (Baton Rouge, 1951), *American Counterpoint* (Boston, 1971), and *The Strange Career of Jim Crow*, 3rd ed. (New York, 1974). Woodward argues that the years 1877-90, while not a "golden era" in race relations, were, nevertheless, a period of relative flux in which alternatives to the virulent racism, disfranchisement, and segregation of the 1890s were available. Thus, he contends that the racial policies of the 1890s were not predestined but rather were the result of specific forces that emerged during that decade.

The first major challenge to the Woodward thesis came in Joel Williamson's *After Slavery: The Negro in South Carolina During Reconstruction, 1865-1877* (Chapel Hill, 1965). Williamson argues that de facto disfranchisement and segregation developed immediately after the war and that the white South never seriously considered any other "alternatives." Howard Rabinowitz lends much support to this view in *Race Relations in the Urban South, 1865-1890* (New York, 1978). A summary of the controversy between these two interpretations is available in Joel Williamson, ed., *The Origins of Segregation* (Boston, 1968). At least one attempt had been made to reconcile this dispute. "A Strange Chapter in the Career of 'Jim Crow,' " in August Meier and Elliott Rudwick, eds., *The Making of Black America* (New York, 1971), suggests that the views of Woodward and his critics are not necessarily incompatible in that white attitudes toward blacks rigidified shortly after the war but that specific events of the 1890s did cause the racial climate to become worse. For the most part, however, scholarly treatment of this issue has polarized into support for either the Woodward or the Williamson interpretation, and no significantly different interpretation has emerged until the article by David Herbert Donald in this volume. A good survey of the period is provided in Robert Hawes, ed., *The Age of Segregation* (Jackson, 1978).

To explore this phenomenon in greater depth, one should examine some of the many volumes on race relations. Among these are August Meier, *Negro Thought in America, 1880-1915* (Ann Arbor, 1963); Rayford W. Logan, *The Negro in American Life and Thought* (New York, 1954); George M. Fredrickson, *The Black Image in the White Mind* (New York, 1971); Laurence J. Friedman, *The White Savage: Racial Fantasies in the Postbellum South* (Englewood Cliffs, 1970); Raymond Gavins, *The Perils and Prospects of Southern Black Leadership* (Durham, 1978); and William F. Holmes, "The Demise of the Colored Farmers Alliance," *Journal of Southern History* XLI (May 1975). For the manner in which the racial ideas affected white politics, see J. Morgan Kousser, *The Shaping of Southern Politics* (New

Haven, 1974); Jack T. Kirby, *Darkness at the Dawning: Race and Reform in the Progressive South* (Philadelphia, 1972); Paul M. Gaston, *The New South Creed* (New York, 1970); George B. Tindall, *The Persistent Tradition in New South Politics* (Baton Rouge, 1975); Lawrence Goodwyn, *Democratic Promise: The Populist Movement in America* (New York, 1976); and James T. Moore, "Redeemers Reconsidered: Change and Continuity in the Democratic South, 1870-1900," *Journal of Southern History* XLIV (August 1978).

Those readers desiring a more specialized treatment of the subject on the state level should consult William J. Cooper, *The Conservative Regime: South Carolina, 1877-1890* (Baltimore, 1968); Thomas Holt, *Black over White: Negro Political Leadership in South Carolina During Reconstruction* (Urbana, 1977); George B. Tindall, *South Carolina Negroes, 1877-1900* (Columbia, 1952); Sheldon Hackney, *Populism to Progressivism in Alabama* (Princeton, 1969); Vernon L. Wharton, *The Negro in Mississippi, 1865-1900* (Chapel Hill, 1947); Roger L. Hart, *Redeemers, Bourbons, and Populists: Tennessee, 1870-1896* (Baton Rouge, 1975); Joseph H. Cartwright, *The Triumph of Jim Crow: Tennessee Race Relations in the 1880's* (Knoxville, 1976); Charles E. Wynes, *Race Relations in Virginia, 1870-1902* (Charlottesville, 1971); Frenise A. Logan, *The Negro in North Carolina, 1876-1894* (Chapel Hill, 1964); Helen G. Edmonds, *The Negro and Fusion Politics in North Carolina, 1894-1901* (Chapel Hill, 1951); Jeffrey J. Crow and Robert F. Durden, *Maverick Republican in the Old North State: A Political Biography of Daniel L. Russell* (Baton Rouge, 1977); Dewey W. Grantham, Jr., *Hoke Smith and the Politics of the New South* (Baton Rouge, 1958); Gordon B. McKinney, "Southern Mountain Republicans and the Negro, 1865-1900," *Journal of Southern History* XLI (November 1975); William Ivy Hair, *Bourbonism and Agrarian Protest: Louisiana Politics, 1877-1900* (Baton Rouge, 1971); and Roger A. Fischer, *The Segregation Struggle in Louisiana, 1862-1877* (Urbana, 1974).

Southern Leadership: Change or Continuity?

For an understanding of the notion of "planter hegemony" in the antebellum South—the concept that the planter elite dominated the economic, political, and cultural affairs of the region—see Eugene Genovese, *The Political Economy of Slavery: Studies in the Economy and Society of the Slave South* (New York, 1965); Gavin Wright, " 'Economic Democracy' and the Concentration of Agricultural Wealth in the Cotton South, 1850-1860," *Agricultural History* XLIV (January 1970); and Randolph B. Campbell, "Planters and Plain Folk: Harrison County, Texas, as a Test Case, 1850-1860," *Journal of Southern History* XL (August 1974).

Studies published during the early twentieth century that lionized the planter elite and argued that they and their progeny perpetuated their control in the years following the Civil War include Philip A. Bruce, *The Rise of the New South* (Philadelphia, 1905); Holland Thompson, *The New South: A Chronicle of Social and Industrial Evolution* (New Haven, 1920); and Walter L. Fleming, *The Sequel of Appomattox: A Chronicle of the Reunion of the States* (New Haven, 1921). Wilbur J. Cash in *The Mind of the South* (New York, 1941) argued that the planters' offspring who served as officers in the Confederacy became captains of industry following the war and that therefore there was "scarcely a ripple in the social structure" from the Old South to the New.

But even before the publication of Cash's work, historians of the South were revising the image of the leaders of the New South. These revisionists asserted that a "new class of money-hungry townsmen . . . upstart capitalists" became the leaders of the postwar South. Among these historians and their works were Alex M. Arnett, *The Populist Movement in Georgia: A View of the "Agrarian Crusade" in the Light of Solid-South Politics* (New York, 1922); Benjamin B. Kendrick and Alex M. Arnett, *The South Looks at Its Past* (Chapel Hill, 1935); and Albert D. Kirwan, *Revolt of the Rednecks: Mississippi Politics, 1876-1925* (Lexington, Ky., 1951). For an historiographical account of this revisionist work, see Dewey W. Grantham, Jr., "The Southern Bourbons Revisited," *South Atlantic Quarterly* LX (Summer 1961), and Paul M. Gaston, "The 'New South,' " in Arthur S. Link and Rembert W. Patrick, eds., *Writing Southern History: Essays in Historiography in Honor of Fletcher M. Green* (Baton Rouge, 1965). The culmination of the revisionist writing came with the publication of C. Vann Woodward's *Origins of the New South, 1877-1913* (Baton Rouge, 1951). Professor Woodward argued that in the postwar South power passed "from the hands of the landowners to manufacturers and merchants" and brought "changes of a profound and subtle character in the Southern ethos—in outlook, institutions, and particularly in leadership."

For an assessment of the profound and pervasive influence of Woodward's thesis on historians of the New South, see Sheldon Hackney, "*Origins of the New South* in Retrospect," *Journal of Southern History* XXXVIII (May 1972). Hackney declared that Woodward's thesis "has survived relatively untarnished through twenty years of productive scholarship."

Yet when Hackney's article was published in 1972, counterrevisionist studies of Woodward's thesis of the discontinuity and nature of leadership in the postbellum South were underway. Among the traditional eclectic approaches, recent studies that have returned to the theme of a persisting planter hegemony from the Old South to the New are James Tice Moore, *Two Paths to the New South: The Virginia Debt Controversy, 1870-1883* (Lexington, Ky., 1974); Carl N. Degler, *Place over Time: The Continuity of Southern Distinctiveness* (Baton Rouge, 1977); and James L. Roark, *Masters Without Slaves: Southern Planters in the Civil War and Reconstruction*

(New York, 1977). Sharp challenges to Woodward's thesis have come also from Marxist social historians, Jonathan M. Wiener, Jay R. Mandle, and Dwight Billings, who have been inspired by Genovese's studies of the antebellum period and influenced by W. E. B. Du Bois and Barrington Moore, Jr. In Wiener, *Social Origins of the New South: Alabama, 1860-1885* (Baton Rouge, 1978); Mandle, *The Roots of Black Poverty: The Southern Plantation Economy After the Civil War* (Durham, 1979); and Billings, *Planters and the Making of a "New South": Class, Politics and Development in North Carolina, 1865-1900* (Chapel Hill, 1979), is the thesis that the planter elite of the Old South retained its domination of the economic, political, and cultural affairs into the New.

For a historiographical account and assessment of the recent new methods and approaches to the study of the social and economic history of the New South, see Harold D. Woodman, "Sequel to Slavery: The New History Views the Postbellum South," *Journal of Southern History* XLIII (November 1977), and James Tice Moore, "Redeemers Reconsidered: Change and Continuity in the Democratic South, 1870-1900," *Journal of Southern History* XLIV (August 1978), who concludes after a survey of the most recent literature that there is much to support "the notion of continuity between the Old and New Souths. Professor Woodward's revisionist interpretation of Redeemer origins is itself in need of revision."

The City Elite: The Case of Charleston, South Carolina

Until quite recently, historians of the South have neglected to investigate the role of the elite in the cities as well as other aspects of the Southern urbanization experience. This neglect has been due largely to the traditional view that the Old South and much of the New was a region of "planters, plantations, staple crops, Negroes all set in a backward agrarian scene." See David L. Smiley, "The Quest for a Central Theme in Southern History," *South Atlantic Quarterly* LXII (Summer 1972), and James M. Russell, "Urbanization," in David C. Roller and Robert W. Twyman, eds., *The Encyclopedia of Southern History* (Baton Rouge, 1979). But during the 1970s a handful of scholars began to explore this neglected area of Southern history and to compare the Southern and non-Southern urbanization process. See Lyle W. Dorsett and Arthur H. Shaffer, "Was the Antebellum South Anti-urban?: A Suggestion," *The Journal of Southern History* XXXVIII (February 1972); Blaine A. Brownell, "Urbanization in the South: A Unique Experience?" *Mississippi Quarterly* XXVI (Spring 1973); Leonard P. Curry, "Urbanization and Urbanism in the Old South: A Comparative View," *The Journal of Southern History* XL (February 1974); and Blaine A. Brownell and David R. Goldfield, eds., *The City in Southern History: The Growth of Urban Civilization in the South* (Port Washington, N.Y., 1977), which includes a series of original scholarly essays covering the course of urban development in the South from the earliest times to the present. The "Notes" for each essay offer an excellent bibliographical introduction to both the primary and the secondary sources on Southern urban history. See also David R. Goldfield, *Urban Growth in the Age of Sectionalism: Virginia* (Baton Rouge, 1977), who like Wilbur J. Cash sees more continuity than change in Southern history.

For the role of the elites in the Southern urbanization process, see Blaine A. Brownell, "Birmingham, Alabama: New South City in the 1920's," *The Journal of Southern History* XXXVIII (February 1972) and *The Urban Ethos in the South, 1920-1930* (Baton Rouge, 1975), who views the "commercial-civic elite" as holding "a chiefly positive attitude towards urbanization." See also Brownell, "The Urban South Comes of Age, 1900-1940," in Brownell and Goldfield, *The City in Southern History*, which argues that a "mono-lithic commercial-civic elite" dominated city politics, and Brownell, "The Commercial-Civic Elite and City Planning in Atlanta, Memphis, and New Orleans in the 1920's," *The Journal of Southern History* XLI (August 1975). Charles Paul Garofalo's "The Sons of Henry Grady: Atlanta Boosters in the 1920's," *The Journal of Southern History* XLII (May 1976), concludes that "like businessmen elsewhere, Atlanta's businessmen delineated many of their city's goals and provided much of the power needed to reach them." See also Samuel M. Kipp, III, "Old Notables and Newcomers: The Economic and Political Elite of Greensboro, North Carolina, 1880-1920," *The Journal of Southern History* XLIII (August 1977); Kenneth W. Wheeler, *To Wear a City's Crown: The Beginnings of Urban Growth in Texas, 1836-1865* (Cambridge, 1968); Carl V. Harris, *Political Power in Birmingham, 1871-1921* (Knoxville, 1977); and Eugene J. Watts, *The Social Bases of City Politics: Atlanta, 1865-1903* (Westport, Conn., 1978).

For much information on the formation and role of the elite in Charleston, see the brief history of the city by George C. Rogers, Jr., *Charleston in the Age of the Pinckneys* (Norman, 1969). However, like most works on Charleston, it concludes with the Civil War. A brief summary of the postwar period may be found in Robert Goodwyn Rhett, *Charleston: An Epic of Carolina* (Richmond, 1940). For the most recent work and bibliography on the postbellum period and a comparison of the economic elites of Charleston and other Southern urban centers, see Don Harrison Doyle, "Urbanization and Southern Culture: Economic Elites in Four New South Cities (Atlanta, Nashville, Charleston, Mobile), 1865-1910," in Vernon Burton and Robert McMath, eds., *Toward a New South?: Studies in Post-Civil War Southern Communities* (Westport, Conn., forthcoming).

Law and Disorder: Case Studies in Georgia

Few historians of the antebellum South have investigated the region's process of criminal justice for whites. This is surprising since such studies, as David Bodenhamer points out, could reveal much about the nature of the society. For a recent, brief essay and bibliography that touches on the subject, see Joseph Balogh, "Crime," *Encyclopedia of Southern History* (Baton Rouge, 1979). See also Robert M. Saunders, "Crime and Punishment in Early National America: Richmond, Virginia, 1784-1820," *Virginia Magazine of History and Biography* (January 1977), and for a comparison of criminality and the criminal process in South Carolina and Massachusetts, consult Michael S. Hindus, "The Contours of Crime and Justice in Massachusetts and South Carolina, 1767-1878," *American Journal of Legal History* XXI (July 1977). For an older, but good, study, see Jack K. Williams, *Rogues in Villainy: Crime and Retribution in Antebellum South Carolina* (Columbia, 1959).

Due to the neglect of research on the court systems of the antebellum South, the few recent works on the topic have been touted highly. Reviewers of Robert M. Ireland, *The County Courts in Antebellum Kentucky* (Lexington, Ky., 1972), and Mary K. Bonstell Tachau, *Federal Courts in the Early Republic: Kentucky, 1789-1816* (Princeton, 1978), noted that the studies were unique and "testimony to the fact that gold is waiting to be mined in legal records."

Violence and vigilantism in the postbellum South, long recognized as pervasive themes throughout the region's history, have received considerable attention from historians of the South. See Wilbur J. Cash, *The Mind of the South* (New York, 1941). John Shelton Reed, *The Enduring South: Subcultural Persistence in Mass Society* (Lexington, Mass., 1972), accounts for the persistence of Southern violence. Sheldon Hackney's, "Southern Violence," *American Historical Review* LXXIV (February 1969), provides an excellent treatment of the subject and extensive notes. See also the bibliography of Jerry L. Butcher, "Violence," *Encyclopedia of Southern History* (Baton Rouge, 1979).

Although William Holmes has investigated other aspects of whitecapping (see "Whitecapping: Agrarian Violence in Mississippi, 1902-1906," *Journal of Southern History* XXXV [May 1969]), his study of whitecapping relative to moonshining is unique. Richard Maxwell Brown probably would agree with Holmes that whitecapping, like other vigilante violence, was a socially conservative movement. See Richard Maxwell Brown, *Strain of Violence: Historical Studies of American Violence and Vigilantism* (New York, 1975).

Southern Mythology: Fiction and Film

Scholars have long recognized that history is not so much what happened as what people believed happened. Or put another way by Ernest Cassirer: "the central myth of a society is less a product than a producer of its history." One of the first historians of the South to approach the region's past from this perspective was Francis Pendleton Gaines, *The Southern Plantation: A Study in the Development and Accuracy of a Tradition* (New York, 1925), in which he traced the rise and progress of the plantation myth. However, not until nearly forty years later, when George Tindall suggested that the central theme of Southern history may be found by studying the region's mythology, did scholars in significant numbers begin to focus on myth in their attempts to explain Southernism. See George B. Tindall, "Mythology: A New Frontier in Southern History," in Frank E. Vandiver, ed., *The Idea of the South: Pursuit of a Central Theme* (Chicago, 1964). Historians have offered new insights into such varied topics as the New South creed, the Southern lady, the Lost Cause, and the role of both fiction and film in perpetuating the South's mythology. See Paul M. Gaston, *The New South Creed: A Study in Southern Mythmaking* (New York, 1970); Anne Firor Scott, *The Southern Lady: From Pedestal to Politics, 1830-1930* (Chicago, 1970); Rollin G. Osterweis, *The Myth of the Lost Cause, 1865-1900* (Hamden, Conn., 1973); F. Garvin Davenport, Jr., *The Myth of Southern History: Historical Consciousness in Twentieth-Century Literature* (Nashville, 1970); and Jack Temple Kirby, *Media-Made Dixie: The South in the American Imagination* (Baton Rouge, 1978).

An excellent sampling of what historians of the South both before and since Tindall's seminal essay have uncovered by focusing on the South's mythology may be found in Patrick Gerster and Nicholas Cords, eds., *Myth and Southern History: The New South* (Chicago, 1974). See also Patrick Gerster and Nicholas Cords, "The Northern Origins of Southern Mythology," *Journal of Southern History* XLIII (November 1977), for an intriguing investigation into why the North sustained and perpetuated the legends of the Old South and the New.

In sum, although much has been done since Tindall's call for historians to focus on the region's mythology, it remains still a fruitful frontier for exploration.

Following the Color Line: Questions of Race Relations

The best surveys of Afro-American history are John Hope Franklin's narrative treatment, *From Slavery to Freedom*, 5th ed. (New York, 1979), and August Meier and Elliott Rudwick's interpretative volume, *From Plantation to Ghetto*, 3rd ed. (New York, 1976). Within that broader framework, one issue of particular concern is the economic status of blacks after the Civil War.

The main outlines of historical debate on this question are sketched in two excellent articles by Harold D. Woodman, "Sequel to Slavery: The New History Views the Postbellum South," *Journal of Southern History* XLIII (November 1977), and Jonathan Wiener, "Class Structure and

Economic Development in the American South, 1865-1955," *American Historical Review* LXXXIV (October 1979). Several scholars have attempted to modify the portrait that C. Vann Woodward and others have painted of a postwar South beset by extreme poverty and economic stagnation caused by a system of sharecropping and peonage. Robert Higgs, *Competition and Coercion: Blacks in the American Economy, 1865-1914* (Cambridge, 1977); Stephen J. De Canio, *Agriculture in the Postbellum South: The Economics of Production and Supply* (Cambridge, 1974); and Joseph D. Reid, Jr., "Sharecropping as an Understandable Market Response: The Postbellum South," *Journal of Economic History* XXXIII (March 1973), all present a more benign view of Southern economic trends. Relying on a competitive model, they portray the postbellum economy as an efficient, rationally organized one in which blacks, and the South as a whole, were able to make more solid economic gains than previously thought.

The conclusions of these historians are challenged by Roger Ransom and Richard Sutch in *One Kind of Freedom: The Economic Consequences of Emancipation* (Cambridge, 1977). Their cliometric approach agrees that emancipation had an immediate and short-term economic benefit for blacks. In the long term, however, the South's "free market" system produced a matrix of landlord and storekeeper monopolies, sharecropping, tenant farming, and peonage that led to economic deterioration, stagnation, and dependency for all Southern farmers, especially blacks. Approaching the question from a neo-Marxist perspective, Jay Mandle's *The Roots of Black Poverty: The Southern Plantation Economy after the Civil War* (Durham, 1978), and Jonathan Wiener's *Social Origins of the New South: Alabama, 1860-1885* (Baton Rouge, 1978), both tend to reinforce Ransom and Sutch's conclusions. Other books on this topic that should be consulted are Claude Oubre, *Forty Acres and a Mule: The Freedmen's Bureau and Black Land Ownership* (Baton Rouge, 1978); Louis Gerteis, *From Contraband to Freedman: Federal Policy Toward Southern Blacks, 1861-1865* (Westport, Conn., 1973); James L. Roark, *Masters Without Slaves* (New York, 1977); Peter Kolchin, *First Freedom: The Response of Alabama's Blacks to Emancipation and Reconstruction* (Westport, Conn., 1972); Theodore Rosengarten, *All Gods Dangers* (New York, 1974); Willie Lee Rose, *Rehearsal for Reconstruction* (New York, 1964); Donald Spivey, *Schooling for the New Slavery: Black Industrial Education, 1868-1895* (Westport, Conn., 1978); and David Sansing, ed., *What Was Freedom's Price?* (Jackson, 1978). For the cases of extreme deprivation that this system produced, see Pete Daniel, *The Shadow of Slavery: Peonage in the South, 1901-1969* (Urbana, 1972) and "The Metamorphosis of Slavery, 1865-1900," *Journal of American History* LXVI (June 1979); Daniel A. Novak, *The Wheel of Servitude: Black Forced Labor After Slavery* (Lexington, 1978); and William Cohen, "Negro Involuntary Servitude in the South, 1864-1940: A

Preliminary Analysis," *Journal of Southern History* XLII (February 1976). Several other studies enrich the debate on the newly freed men by emphasizing the social aspects of their lives. Among these are Hortense Powdermaker, *After Freedom: A Cultural Study in the Deep South* (New York, 1968); Herbert Gutman, *The Black Family in Slavery and Freedom* (New York, 1976); Lawrence W. Levine, *Black Culture and Black Consciousness: Afro-American Folk Thought from Slavery to Freedom* (New York, 1977); and particularly Leon Litwack's *Been in the Storm So Long: The Aftermath of Slavery* (New York, 1979), which emphasizes the resourcefulness of the black community in preserving its dignity amidst new and difficult relationships with whites.

Throughout American history, the most extreme manifestation of racial tension has been violence. The best introductions to this problem are Arthur L. Waskow, *From Race Riot to Sit In: 1919 and the 1960's* (Garden City, 1966), and Allen D. Grimshaw, ed., *Racial Violence in the United States* (Chicago, 1969). See also the general works on Southern violence cited in the above section on Law and Disorder. Several studies provide important background on the problems that sometimes produced violence during the World War II era. Among these are: John B. Kirby, *Black Americans in the Roosevelt Era* (Knoxville, 1979); Harvard Sitkoff, *A New Deal for Blacks* (New York, 1978); Bernard Sternsher, ed., *The Negro in Depression and War: Prelude to Revolution* (Chicago, 1969); Raymond A. Walters, *Negroes and the Great Depression* (Westport, Conn., 1970); A. Russell Buchanan, *Black Americans in World War II* (Santa Barbara, 1977); Richard M. Dalfiume, *Desegregation of the U.S. Armed Forces: Fighting on Two Fronts* (Columbia, 1969); Lee Finkle, *Forum for Protest: The Black Press During World War II* (Rutherford Heights, 1975); Herbert Garfinkel, *When Negroes March* (Glencoe, 1959); Louis Ruchames, *Race, Jobs, and Politics: The Story of the F.E.P.C.* (New York, 1953); and Richard M. Dalfiume, "The 'Forgotten' Years of the Negro Revolution," *Journal of American History* LV (June 1968).

There is no monographic study of racial violence during World War II, but a helpful overview is provided in Harvard Sitkoff, "Racial Militancy and Interracial Violence During the Second World War," *Journal of American History* LVIII (December 1971). To test Burran's thesis on the different causes of urban racial violence in the North and South, one should consult case studies such as Dominic J. Capeci, Jr., *The Harlem Riot of 1943* (Philadelphia, 1977); Merl A. Reed, "The F.E.P.C., the Black Worker, and the Southern Shipyards," *South Atlantic Quarterly* LXXXIV (Autumn 1975); and Harvard Sitkoff, "The Detroit Race Riot of 1943," *Michigan History* LIII (Fall 1969). The reader may also wish to compare these episodes to the race riots of the World War I era. Among the most recent literature on this subject are Robert V. Haynes, *A Night of Violence: The*

Houston Race Riot of 1917 (Baton Rouge, 1976); David A. Levine, *Internal Combustion: The Races in Detroit, 1915–1926* (Westport, Conn., 1976); William M. Tuttle, *Race Riot: Chicago in the Red Summer of 1919* (New York, 1970); and Constance M. Green, *The Secret City: A History of Race Relations in the Nation's Capital* (Princeton, 1967).

Cash's Book: *The Mind of the South* Revisited

Forty years after its original publication, W. J. Cash's *The Mind of the South* (New York, 1941) still exerts a major influence on the historical literature of the region. Joseph L. Morrison's biography, *W. J. Cash: Southern Prophet* (New York, 1967), provides a good background on the author and the forces that shaped his thinking. Many articles, most of them critical, have analyzed Cash's book over the last four decades. Among the best are Donald Davidson, "Mr. Cash and the Proto-Dorian South," *Southern Review* VII (Summer 1941); Dewey W. Grantham, Jr., "Mr. Cash Writes a Book," *Progressive* XXV (December 1961); C. Vann Woodward, "The Elusive Mind of the South," in *American Counterpoint* (Boston, 1971); Richard King, "The Mind of the South: Narcissus Grown Analytical," *New South* XXVII (Winter 1972); Sheldon Hackney, "Origins of the New South in Retrospect," *Journal of Southern History* XXXVIII (May 1972); Joseph L. Morrison, "W. J. Cash: The Summing Up," *South Atlantic Quarterly* LXXVI (Autumn 1977); and Michael O'Brien, "W. J. Cash, Hegel, and the South," *Journal of Southern History* XLIV (August 1978). Given the sweeping nature of *The Mind of the South*, nearly every work on Southern history either attacks or defends the ideas raised by Cash. Especially helpful, however, for putting Cash in the context of subsequent literature are the interpretative volumes cited in the first section of this essay and the books discussed in the text of Wyatt-Brown's article.

One of Cash's most enduring concepts, as recognized by Mark Bauman, has been that of a "savage ideal," which stifled freedom of thought and debate in the South. For closer analysis of this phenomenon, see Morton Sosna, *In Search of the Silent South: Southern Liberals and the Race Issue* (New York, 1977); Carl Degler, *The Other South: Southern Dissenters in the Nineteenth Century* (New York, 1974); Charles E. Wynes, ed., *Forgotten Voices: Dissenting Southerners in an Age of Conformity* (Baton Rouge, 1967); Bruce Clayton, *The Savage Ideal: Intolerance and Intellectual Leadership in the South* (Baltimore, 1972); Idus A. Newby, *Jim Crow's Defense: Anti-Negro Thought in America, 1900-1930* (Baton Rouge, 1965); and George Fredrickson, *The Black Image in the White Mind* (New York, 1971).

For more detailed background on the "Debate of 1903," the reader should examine Henry Warmock, "Andrew Sledd, Southern Methodists, and the

Negro: A Case History," *Journal of Southern History* XXXI (August 1965); John Talmadge, *Rebecca Latimer Felton: Nine Stormy Decades* (Athens, 1960); Paul N. Garber, *John Carlisle Kilgo: President of Trinity College, 1894-1910* (Durham, 1937); Earl W. Porter, *Trinity and Duke, 1892-1924* (Durham, 1964) and "The Bassett Affair: Something to Remember," *South Atlantic Quarterly* LXXII (Autumn 1973); John Dittmer, *Black Georgia in the Progressive Era* (Urbana, 1977); and two articles by Charles Crowe, "Racial Violence and Social Reform—Origins of the Atlanta Race Riot of 1906," *Journal of Negro History* LII (July 1968), and "Racial Massacre in Atlanta, September 22, 1906," *Journal of Negro History* LIV (April 1969).

Mind or Mindlessness, Persistence or Paradox?: Currents of Southern Thought

One much-debated aspect of Southern thought is the degree to which a sense of Southern nationalism existed prior to 1861. Good surveys of the issues involved are available in David Potter, *The Impending Crisis* (New York, 1976), and Emory Thomas, *The Confederate Nation* (New York, 1979). Many historians contend that no significant sense of Confederate nationalism had developed before 1861. Earlier works that present this viewpoint are Frank L. Owsley, *States Rights in the Confederacy* (Chicago, 1925); Avery Craven, *The Coming of the Civil War* (New York, 1942); and James Z. Rabun, "Alexander Stephens and Jefferson Davis," *American Historical Review* LVIII (1953). The argument is developed more fully in Kenneth Stampp's, *The Southern Road to Appomattox* (El Paso, 1969), and David Potter, *The South and the Sectional Conflict* (Baton Rouge, 1968). The most recent study of the deficiencies of Confederate nationalism is Paul D. Escott's excellent volume, *After Secession: Jefferson Davis and Confederate Nationalism* (Baton Rouge, 1979).

Of those who argue that a widespread Southern nationalism had developed by 1861, Raimondo Luraghi is perhaps the most influential in works such as "The Civil War and the Modernization of American Society," *Civil War History* XVIII (September 1972), and *The Rise and Fall of the Plantation South* (New York, 1978). Supporting Luraghi's Marxian concept of Confederate nationalism is Eugene Genovese's *Roll, Jordan, Roll* (New York, 1974). Other authors who tend to emphasize Southern nationalism are Frank Vandiver, *Jefferson Davis and the Confederate State* (Oxford, 1964), and Louise B. Hill, *State Socialism in the Confederate States of America* (Charlottesville, 1936). An excellent book that explores the ways in which slavery and Confederate nationalism interacted is Robert F. Durden's *The Gray and the Black: The Confederate Debate on Emancipation* (Baton Rouge, 1972).

The challenging questions raised in Goodwyn's essay on "Hierarchy and

Democracy" can be pursued further in W. E. B. Du Bois' "Reconstruction and Its Benefits," *American Historical Review* XV (1910), *The Souls of Black Folk* (Chicago, 1903), and *Black Reconstruction in America* (New York, 1935); and in C. Vann Woodward's *Tom Watson: Agrarian Rebel* (New York, 1938), *Origins of the New South* (Baton Rouge, 1951), and *The Burden of Southern History* (New York, 1968). For contrasting ideas on the nature of American democracy, see Richard Hofstadter, *The Age of Reform* (New York, 1955), and Louis Hartz, *The Liberal Tradition in America* (New York, 1955). The manner in which Southern historians have dealt with their region is surveyed in Wendell Holmes Stephenson, *The South Lives in History: Southern Historians and Their Legacy* (Baton Rouge, 1955), and *Southern History in the Making: Pioneer Historians of the South* (Baton Rouge, 1967). As an introduction to literary analysis of the region, see Louis D. Rubin, Jr., and Robert D. Jacobs, eds., *Southern Renascence: The Literature of the Modern South* (Baltimore, 1953), and Rubin, ed., *A Bibliographical Guide to the Study of Southern Literature* (Baton Rouge, 1969). On the limitations of a specific reform movement, consult C. Eric Lincoln, *Sounds of the Struggle: Persons and Perspectives in Civil Rights* (New York, 1968), and Debbie Lewis, *And We Are Not Saved: A History of the Movement as a People* (New York, 1970).

Goodwyn's thesis of Southern reform can be tested further in several monographs on the topic. Surveying respectively nineteenth- and twentieth-century reformers are Carl Degler, *The Other South* (Baton Rouge, 1974), and Morton Sosna, *In Search of the Silent South* (New York, 1977). On Southern reform during the progressive era, see Jack T. Kirby, *Darkness at the Dawning* (Philadelphia, 1972). Although some specialized works on the New Deal's impact in the South have appeared, the best general treatment is still found in Tindall's *The Emergence of the New South* (Baton Rouge, 1967). Older works that still contain useful insights are Virginius Dabney, *Liberalism in the South* (Chapel Hill, 1932); Hodding Carter, *Southern Legacy* (Baton Rouge, 1950); and Ralph McGill, *The South and the Southerner* (Boston, 1957).

To date, no major studies of either Dorothy Tilly or James M. Dabbs have appeared. Other than a dissertation by Ann Ellis, "The Commission on Interracial Cooperation" (University of Georgia, 1975), information on Tilly must be gleaned from contemporary periodicals. Among the best of these articles are Helena Smith, "Mrs. Tilly's Crusade," *Colliers* (December 30, 1950); Jesse Arndt, "Women's Crusade," *Christian Science Monitor* (January 9, 1953); Florence Robin, "Honeychile at the Barricades," *Harpers* (October 1962); and Beulah McKay, "Dorothy Tilly, Pioneer," *The Church Woman* (March 1964). On Dabbs, the best available works are those written by him, including *The Southern Heritage* (New York, 1958), *Who Speaks for the South* (New York, 1964), *The Road Home* (Philadelphia, 1960), and *Haunted by God* (Richmond, 1972).

Despite the lack of scholarly research on Tilly and Dabbs, biographies of other Southern reformers contain information about them and the problems of their era. Among these are Hugh C. Bailey, *Edgar Gardner Murphy* (Coral Gables, 1968); Wilma Dykeman and James Stokley, *Seeds of Southern Change: The Life of Will Alexander* (Chicago, 1962); John M. Cooper, *Walter Hines Page: The Southerner as American* (Chapel Hill, 1979); Louise Blackwell and Francis Clay, *Lillian Smith* (New York, 1971); and Jacqueline Dowd Hall, *Revolt Against Chivalry: Jesse Daniel Ames and the Women's Campaign Against Lynching* (New York, 1979), which is the best analysis of women reformers in the South. On that subject, see also Anne Firor Scott's *The Southern Lady: From Pedestal to Politics* (Chicago, 1970).

INDEX

Agnew, Hugh, 252-53
Alabama, 26, 27, 29, 44; race riot in Mobile in 1943, 169-71; socioeconomic patterns in Dallas County, 33-39
Alabama Dry Dock and Shipbuilding Company, 169-70
Ames, Jesse Daniel, 242-43
Arnall, Ellis, 243
Association of Southern Women for the Prevention of Lynching, 216, 242, 243

Barney, William L., 21, 22, 33
Bassett, John Spencer, 181, 190, 197
Bauman, Mark K., 179, 181
Billings, Dwight, 21, 22, 26, 27, 28, 29, 44
Bishop, Joel P., 109
Black Belt, 6, 33-39
Black Power Movement, 260-61
Blacks: aspirations of, 236-37; conduct after emancipation of, 10-11, 153, 155-65; disfranchisement of, 3, 5-7; and Fellowship of the Concerned, 244-49; labor of, 13-15, 27, 28, 29, 153, 155-65; proposed colonization of, 183, 186-87, 193n; as sharecroppers, 153, 155-65; in South during World War II, 167-77; wealth of in antebellum Charleston, 70-73; white attitudes toward, 11-18, 157, 181-93, 236-37, 241-64 passim
Bodenhamer, David J., 107, 109
Bourbon Restoration, 24-25, 200
Brown v. Board of Education decision, 247, 253-54, 259, 263
Burran, James A., 154, 167

Cable, George Washington, 137
Cameron, Paul, 13-15
Campbell, Edward D. C., Jr., 133, 143
Carlton, David, 22, 30, 43
Carter, Dan T., 21, 23
Cash, Wilbur J., 25, 50, 179-80, 181, 190 195-214; "savage ideal" of, 179, 181, 189, 190, 196, 197-98, 204, 205
Caste system, 153, 155, 158, 232
Channing, Steven A., 214, 219
Charleston, S.C., 48, 65-106; building patterns in, 84-87; capitalists in, 52, 101-3; class divisions in, 72-74; commercial organizations of, 98-101; compared with other cities, 67-70, 95; distribution of wealth in, 65-74; economic decline in after the Civil War, 93-104; economic leadership in after the Civil War, 95-104; geographic patterns of, 81-89; Interstate and West Indian expositions in, 102-3; phosphate mining in, 100-101; racial divisions in, 71-74; railroads, 100; social organizations of, 96-97; tourist industry in, 101-3
Chesnut, Mary Boykin, 225
Churches in the South, 242-43; role of, 256-63 passim
Civil War, 7-11, 24, 27, 43, 127; battle of Gettysburg, 232-35, 237; Confederate nationalism in, 219-26; first battle at Manassas, 219-20
Cleghorn, Bill, 246
Collins, George and Anne, 13-15
Colored Alliance, 5, 161

Commission on Interracial Cooperation, 216, 242, 243, 256
Confederate nationalism, 219-26
Confederate soldiers, as a generation, 7-18; at Gettysburg, 233-34; homage to, 39; literary images of 135-41
Congress of Industrial Organization (CIO), 170
Converse, D. E., 50, 53
Cooke, John Esten, 137
Cooper, William J., 4
Corrington, John William, 140
Credit lien system, 159, 160-61
Crime, 109-19, 122, 125-27; and criminal justice system in the South, 109-10, 182. *See also* Violence
Crop lien system, 155, 161

Dabbs, James McBride, 217, 253-64
Dabbs, Jessie Armstrong, 256, 257, 258, 260
Davidson, Donald, 138-39, 196, 199
Davis, Jefferson, 9
Davis, Ronald L. F., 153, 155
Davis, Stephen, 133, 135
Dawson, Francis W., 101-3
Degler, Carl, 25, 30, 195
Democratic party, 5-6, 16, 17, 22, 35-36, 38, 129-30, 182, 190, 200, 235; Breckinridge Democrats, 35, 38; Douglas Democrats, 36
Detroit Race Riot of 1943, 172-73
Disfranchisement, 3, 5-7, 17; codified into law, 3-4, 5-9
Donald, David H., 2, 3
Dos Passos, John, 169
Dowdey, Clifford, 138
Doyle, Don H., 64, 93
Du Bois, W. E. B., 173, 228-31; influence of, 229-31, 237, 238

Elites, 21, 22, 44, 52, 55, 57, 73-74, 84-89, 95-104, 156, 158
Elkins, Stanley, 201, 203
Emancipation, 10, 24, 43, 54-55, 232
Engerman, Stanley, 156, 203
Erikson, Erik, 16
Evans, Jane Augusta, 139

Fair Employment Practices Commission, 169, 170
Farmers, 121, 123, 128

Faulkner, William, 139-40, 205, 207, 208, 209, 210, 228, 232
Federal Bureau of Investigation (FBI), 172, 247
Fellowship of the Concerned, 216, 244-49
Felton, Rebecca Latimer, 126, 181, 190, 192n
Fleming, C. E., 55, 56
Fogel, Robert, 156, 203
Franklin, John Hope, 197
Fredrickson, George M., 209
Freedmen's Bureau, 157
Fundamentalism. *See* Protestantism, fundamentalist

Garvey, Marcus, 173
Genovese, Eugene, 26, 30, 43, 109, 155, 180, 195, 196, 201, 203, 205, 206, 207, 208, 209, 215, 221, 222
Georgia, 109-32; attitude toward outsiders, 128-30; criminal process in, 109-19, 122, 125-27; moonshining in, 121-22; newspaper debate in, 181-93; whitecapping violence in, 121-32
Glasgow, Ellen, 138
Gone With the Wind, 133; as motion picture, 143-51; popular reception of, 147-50
Goodwyn, Lawrence, 215, 216, 227
Graham, Frank, 243
Gramsci, Antonio, 26, 30, 221
Gutman, Herbert, 156, 203

Hackney, Sheldon, 24, 195
Hall, G. Stanley, 255, 256
Harlem Race Riot of 1943, 173
Harris, Joel Chandler, 137
Hayne, Paul Hamilton, 136
Heyward, DuBose, 96-97
Holmes, William F., 107, 121

Jefferson, Thomas, 209, 235, 236
Jim Crow Laws, 3-18, 154, 169, 171; interpretations of, 4-7
Johnson, Michael P., 63, 65
Jordan, Winthrop, 224

Kirby, Jack Temple, 135
Kousser, J. Morgan, 5-6
Ku Klux Klan, 123, 127, 128, 130, 246-47
Kurtz, Wilbur J., 144

Lee, General Robert E., 9, 135, 181, 233, 234, 235, 237, 238

Levinson, Daniel J., 16
Lewinson, Paul, 5-6
Lincoln, Abraham, 9, 10, 135, 138, 223, 225; Emancipation Proclamation of, 10, 232
Lodge Bill, 4-5
Logan, Rayford W., 3
Longstreet, General James, 233, 235, 237, 238
Los Angeles Race Riot of 1943, 172
Lost Cause, 18, 39, 201, 235, 236, 237. *See also* Myth; Confederate soldiers
Louisiana: merchants of, 159-61; Natchez district of, 156, 162
Luraghi, Raimondo, 206, 215, 221, 222, 225

McWhiney, Grady, 199
Mandle, Jay, 16, 21, 22, 26, 27, 28, 29, 44, 161
March on Washington Movement, 167, 169
Marxist theories, 26-29, 201, 221-22; and "Prussian Road" to economic development, 26-29, 44
Meier, August, 172
Mencken, H. L., 138
Merchants, role of, 159-61
Miller, Perry, 190, 198, 200
Mind of the South, The, 179-80, 181, 195-214
Mississippi: disfranchisement in, 6-7; merchants of, 159-61; Natchez district of, 156, 162; planters of, 155-59, 162
Mitchell, Broadus, 50, 56
Mitchell, Margaret, 133, 144, 145, 147
Montgomery, John H., 55, 56
Moonshiners, 121, 122, 123, 125, 128, 129
Moore, Barrington, 26, 30, 43, 44
Moore, James Tice, 24, 25
Morse, Josiah, 255, 256
Murphy, Charles Gardener, 255
Myrick, Susan, 144, 145
Myth, 135; in literary images of Johnny Reb, 135-41; in motion pictures on the South, 143-51

Natchez district of Mississippi and Louisiana, 156, 162
National Association for the Advancement of Colored People (NAACP), 170
National Cotton Exchange, 99
Newspaper debate in Georgia, 183-89
North Carolina, 27, 28, 29. 44

O'Connor, Flannery, 140
Odum, Howard W., 197, 198, 206
Ortega y Gasset, José, 16

Pelzer, Francis J., 52, 102-3
Pennsylvania Shipyards, 171
Phillips, Ulrich B., 161, 182, 203
Pickett's charge, 234-35
Planters, 21, 22, 26, 27, 28, 29, 34, 38, 43, 44, 48-50, 155-59, 162, 200, 205-7, 223-25; class hegemony of, 26-29, 44, 205-8, 222-25
Pollard, Edward, 219, 220
Populism, 5, 24-25, 129-30, 231, 236, 238-39n. *See also* Colored Alliance
Potter, David, 220
Protestantism, fundamentalist, 4, 25

Race Riots of 1943-44, 168, 172-74; in Beaumont, Texas, 171-72; in Detroit, 172-73; in Harlem, 173; in Mobile, Alabama, 169-71
Radford, John P., 63, 81
Randolph, Robert M., 217, 253
Ransom, Roger L., 11, 15, 43, 55, 160
Rape: black attitudes toward, 188; fear of, 171-72, 182-83, 185-86, 187
Reconstruction, 4, 24, 27, 83, 86-87, 127-30, 199, 235-36; interpretations of, 228-29
Republican party, 4-5, 34, 39, 199, 235
Revenue agents, 122-25
Roosevelt, Franklin D., 169
Roosevelt, Theodore, 182
Rudwick, Elliott, 172
Russell, William Howard, 224

Saint Cecelia Society, 96-97
Scott, Anne F., 12
Second Reconstruction, 154, 230-31, 239n, 253-55
Sellers, Charles G., Jr., 200-201
Selznick, David D., 133, 144, 145
Shankman, Arnold, 216, 241
Simms, William Gilmore, 136, 204
Slavery, 67-68; in Charleston, 84, 156, 162; and Confederate nationalism, 219-26
Sledd, Andrew, 181, 190
Smyth, Ellison A., 51, 52
Socioeconomic patterns: in Charleston, S. C., 68-74; in Dallas County, Alabama, 33-39; in the Natchez district, 156-63; and "Social Geography" of Charleston, S.C., 81-89; in the South, 68-69

South: attitude toward outsiders of, 179; economic problems of, 11-12, 54-55; effects of emancipation on, 10-11, 54-55; motion pictures portraying, 143-45 (see also *Gone With the Wind*); psychological problems of after Civil War, 10-18; theme of defeat in, 7-11; urbanization and industrialization of, 57

South Carolina, 22; "Eight-Box" law in, 6; industrialization of upcountry, 43-62; textile industry, 44-47; textile mill directors, 47-52, 54-57; textile mill presidents, 52-53, 55-57; upcountry town development and leaders, 54-57

Southern Farmer's Alliance, 5

Southern liberals, 29, 236-37, 241-64

Southern Regional Council, 216, 217, 243, 244, 245, 246, 248, 249, 259, 260, 261, 262, 263

Stampp, Kenneth, 215, 221, 222

Sumter, S.C., desegregation in, 253-55

Sutch, Richard P., 11, 15, 43, 55, 160

Talmadge, Eugene, 242-43

Tate, Allen, 138-39, 203

Texas, race riot in Beaumont, 171-72

Textile industry, 44-47

Thomas, Emory, 8, 33

Thompson, John R., 136

Tillman, Benjamin, 182, 187, 188, 190

Tilly, Dorothy, 216, 241-52

Tilly, Eben, 242, 249

Tilly, Milton Eben, 241-42, 248

Timrod, Henry, 136

Tindall, George Brown, 24, 25, 30, 135

"To Secure These Rights," 243

Turner, Frederick Jackson, 202, 204

United States Commissioners, 122-25

"Unity of Mankind" debate. *See* Newspaper debate in Georgia

Violence, 3, 4, 5, 112-15, 127-28, 130, 161, 162; lynching, 3, 168, 181-93, 244-45; racial, 153-55; sectional differences and, 173-74; urban racial, during World War II, 167-77; whitecappping, 121-32. *See also* Crime; Ku Klux Klan

Wade, Richard C., 84

Wagener, Frederick W., 102-3

Walker, Joseph, 55, 56

War Manpower Commission, 170

Washington, Booker T., 181, 182; "Atlanta Compromise" speech, 5

Whigs, 35-36, 200

White sharecroppers, 159

White supremacy concept, 151, 201, 202. *See also* Newspaper debate in Georgia

Wiener, Jonathan, 13, 21, 22, 26, 27, 28, 29, 33, 44

Williams, George W., 95, 102-3

Williamson, Joel, 88

Wohl, Robert, 7

Wolfe, Thomas, 8, 205

Woodman, Harold D., 43

Woodward, C. Vann, 3, 21, 23, 24, 25, 26, 27, 30, 43, 88, 195, 196, 198, 199, 200, 201, 202, 205, 228-34; influence of, 230-31, 237, 238

Wright, Marion, 253, 254, 255, 259, 260

Wyatt-Brown, Bertram, 179, 180-81, 195

Yeoman farmers, 26, 27, 205-7

NOTES ON THE CONTRIBUTORS

DAVID HERBERT DONALD is Charles Warren Professor of American History at Harvard University. A specialist in late nineteenth-century America, he has won a Pulitzer prize for biography and written numerous books, including *Charles Sumner and the Rights of Man, The Nation in Crisis,* and *Liberty and Union*.

DAN T. CARTER is Andrew Mellon Professor of History at Emory University. He has written several articles on Southern history and won the Bancroft prize for his book *Scottsboro: A Tragedy of the American South*.

WILLIAM L. BARNEY is an Associate Professor of History at the University of North Carolina, Chapel Hill. His studies have focused on the sociopolitical behavior of the American South during the Civil War, and he is currently at work on his fourth book, a study of the impact of the Civil War in the Alabama Black Belt.

DAVID CARLTON was recently a Visiting Assistant Professor of History at Texas Tech University. His research is concerned with the impact of industrialization on society in post-Civil War South Carolina.

MICHAEL P. JOHNSON is Associate Professor of History at the University of California, Irvine. His publications include *Toward a Patriarchal Republic: The Secession of Georgia* and articles on the social history of slaves and planters.

JOHN P. RADFORD is an Associate Professor of Geography at York University, Toronto. He is the author of several papers on the social geography of nineteenth-century North American cities.

DON H. DOYLE is an Associate Professor of History at Vanderbilt University. He is the author of several articles on American social and urban history.

DAVID J. BODENHAMER is an Assistant Professor of History at the University of Southern Mississippi. He is the author of several articles and papers on crime and criminal justice in the antebellum United States.

WILLIAM F. HOLMES is an Associate Professor of History at the University of Georgia. He is a specialist in the late nineteenth-century South, and among his published works is *The White Chief: James Kimble Vardaman*.

STEPHEN DAVIS is Assistant Director of the Graduate Institute of the Liberal Arts at Emory University. He has published several articles on Civil War history and Southern literature and is the author of the forthcoming book, *Johnny Reb in Perspective*.

EDWARD D. C. CAMPBELL, JR. is Director of the Museum of the Confederacy in Richmond and an adjunct faculty member of Virginia Commonwealth University. He is the author of a forthcoming work on varying film images of the South since 1900.

RONALD L. F. DAVIS is a Professor of History at California State University, Northridge. He is the author of several articles in scholarly journals and several essays in edited books. He recently has completed a book-length manuscript entitled *Good and Faithful Labor*, and is presently interested in the colonial economy of the Chesapeake.

JAMES A. BURRAN is Assistant Professor of History and Assistant to the Academic Dean at Abraham Baldwin Agricultural College. He is the author of several articles on twentieth-century Southern history and is at work on a manuscript dealing with racial violence in the South during World War II.

MARK K. BAUMAN is an Assistant Professor of History at Atlanta Junior College. He is the author of several articles on minorities and religion in American culture and a prize-winning study of Bishop Warren A. Candler and is collaborating in the writing of a textbook on American and Georgia government.

BERTRAM WYATT-BROWN is Professor of History at Case Western Reserve University. He is the author of *Lewis Tappan and the Evangelical War against Slavery* and editor of *The American People in the Antebellum South*, and his articles and book reviews have appeared in various scholarly publications. His current project is the completion of a book entitled *Bondage of Honor: The Southern Ethic in the Old Republic*.

STEVEN A. CHANNING is Associate Professor of History at the University of Kentucky. He is the author of the award-winning *Crisis of Fear: Secession in South Carolina* and *Kentucky: A History*. His principal current interest is the production of historical programming for public television.

LAWRENCE GOODWYN is an Associate Professor of History at Duke University. He is the author of *Democratic Promise* and *The Populist Moment*.

ARNOLD SHANKMAN is Associate Professor of History at Winthrop College. He has published numerous articles on ethnic history, the Civil War, and recent Southern history, and was editor of Marion Wright's *Human Rights Odyssey*, which won the Lillian Smith prize in 1979.

ROBERT M. RANDOLPH is Assistant Dean for Student Affairs at Massachusetts Institute of Technology. He has written a number of articles on religion in the South, and is completing a study of the life of James McBride Dabbs.

About the Editors

WALTER J. FRASER, JR., is a Professor of History at The Citadel. He is the author of a book on Charleston during the Revolutionary era, and he has published articles on Southern history in various journals.

WINFRED B. MOORE, JR., is an Assistant Professor of History at The Citadel. He is the author of an article on James F. Byrnes and is currently working on a biography of Byrnes.